BOB DYLAN

THE RECORDING SESSIONS 1960–1994

BOB DYLAN

THE RECORDING SESSIONS 1960–1994

CLINTON HEYLIN

ST. MARTIN'S GRIFFIN ✠ NEW YORK

Design by Sara Stemen

All lyrics quoted are for review, study, or critical purposes.

Photographs appearing after page 106 by Joe Alper

Library of Congress Cataloging-in-Publication Data

Heylin, Clinton.
   Bob Dylan : the recording sessions, 1960–1994 / Clinton Heylin.
      p.   cm.
   ISBN 0-312-15067-9
   1. Dylan, Bob, 1941—Discography.   I. Title.
ML156.7.D97H49   1995
789.42162'0092—dc20   95-23265
                                                              CIP
                                                              MN

First St. Martin's Griffin Edition: March 1996

10   9   8   7   6   5   4   3   2   1

This book is dedicated to Joel Bernstein and Glen Korman.

It is NOT dedicated to Jeff Rosen.

ACKNOWLEDGMENTS

Quoted or not, this book would not have been possible without the following: Ivan Augenblink, Bob Bettendorf, Mitch Blank, Ken Buttrey, Jay Craven at the Local 802 of the AF of M, the Country Music Foundation, Peter Doggett, Glen Dundas, Michelle Egbert, Erik Flannigan, Raymond Foye, Rob Fraboni, Geoff Gans, Ellen Gilbert, Allen Ginsberg, John Green, Nick Hill, Pete Howard, Robby King (those basement ditties—oh wow), Reid Kopel, Russ Kunkel, Rod McBeath, Greil Marcus, Mark and Matt at Sony, Elliott Mazer, Blair Miller, Andy Muir, Bill Pagel, Freddie Patterson, Arthur Rosato, Rani Singh, Wes Stace, Rob Stoner, Bob Strano, Pete Vincent, and Roy Whitaker. Take a bow one and all.

CONTENTS

INTRODUCTION

Don't talk to me about perfection
I ain't never seen none.
　　　　—Bob Dylan (1979)

In this book, I endeavor to examine Dylan the recording artist, something I feel I only touched upon in my biography, *Dylan Behind the Shades,* a self-conscious attempt to link the life to the work, the vision to Dylan's worldview at any given point in time. This time around I have focused exclusively on the man's art. I intend to look at the process by which he has attempted to transfer that vision to tape. For the recording artist, composing a great song is not enough. Dylan, of all artists, has been wont to transubstantiate the merely leaden with a twenty-four-carat performance. Yet he has only imperfectly realized some of his finest works in the studio—the essential contradiction. Hence this book.

There have been several attempts to analyze the entire body of studio recordings (not just the official corpus) of major rock artists (it may even qualify as a new form of criticism). I myself have often referred to the commendable efforts of Ernst Jorgensen, Erik Rasmussen, and Johnny Mikkelsen on Elvis Presley when considering how best a reader might digest such an overload of information. Likewise, two pioneers in the analysis of Dylan's recordings, Paul Cable and Paul Williams, have regularly been consulted when my thoughts needed provoking.

But perhaps the best-known "sessionography" remains Mark Lewisohn's *The Complete Beatles Recording Sessions,* a lavish production, entered into with the full cooperation of EMI. Lewisohn was allowed the fullest kind of access—the opportunity to hear every Beatle recording then residing at Abbey Road (though "complete" is certainly a misnomer; no Decca audition tape, no Twickenham Film Studios sessions).

Of course, Lewisohn was already a celebrated authority on the Beatles and there was no real danger of him expressing serious doubts about the "creative" decisions that George Martin and the Beatles made in the studio. After all, this was the man who informed all those who purchased the CD version of *Sgt. Pepper's Lonely Hearts Club Band*—courtesy of some liner notes already ODing on hyperbole—that the sessions for *Sgt. Pepper* were "perhaps the most creative 129 days in the history of rock music."

I could have called this book "129 Days of Studio-Time" but it is most certainly not about the fey indulgences of the Fab Four in the winter of 1966–67. If part of my raison d'etre for *Bob Dylan: The Recording Sessions 1960–1994* is to question the creative decisions Dylan has made in the studio, it also celebrates his refreshing attitude to making records ("Go in, cut it, and get the fuck out!"). To put Lewisohn's (staggeringly ignorant) "most creative 129 days in the history of rock music" in context, Dylan managed to record his *entire* studio output up to and including 1976's *Desire* in just ninety days!

Perhaps Mr. Lewisohn may feel a collection of albums that includes *Freewheelin', Bringing It All Back Home, Highway 61 Revisited, Blonde on Blonde, John Wesley Harding,* and *Blood on the Tracks* fails to suggest a genius equal to the powerful forces (cough!) at work in the Abbey Road studios that winter. I, on the other hand, firmly believe that the Beatles, and any of the many bands who have taken *Sgt. Pepper* as a benchmark in the use of studio technology, are missing the point.

Dylan's work in the studio is of a different caliber than the Beatles. It was achieved in a fraction of the studio time and generally with musicians who did not know his working methods or the songs he intended to record. There is a story, which I have often wanted to embroider, that at the beginning of May 1966 Paul McCartney visited Dylan in his suite at the Mayfair Hotel in London bearing with him the acetates of the Beatles' new album, *Revolver*. He plays the acetates to Dylan, who reciprocates by playing McCartney the acetates he is carrying of *Blonde on Blonde*. My embellished version of this meeting has McCartney tossing himself out of the bay windows of Dylan's suite, shouting, "I give up!"—only to discover that the Mayfair has a balcony.

Revolver is, I believe, the closest the Beatles came to painting their masterpiece, their finest amalgam of catchy hooks, studio wizardry, and enviable harmonics. But it pales alongside the scale of Dylan's achievements on *Blonde on Blonde*. (I don't think anyone seriously versed in rock music would consider this a particularly contentious point of view.)

Of all the leaders of the pack in 1966—the Beatles, the Stones, the Beach Boys, the Velvets (albeit unheralded), Hendrix, Dylan—it was only Dylan who was not increasingly beguiled by the flashing lights of a studio console. And yet at the crucial midpoint of the decade (1965–67), none of the others would come close to Dylan's studio output—*Bringing It All Back Home* in three days, *Highway 61 Revisited* in six days, *Blonde on Blonde* also in six days (six pre-Nashville sessions had resulted in just one usable cut—proof that

Dylan's laissez-faire approach in the studio didn't always work), and *John Wesley Harding* in three days.

Even the seminal, fourteen-song Dwarf Music acetate, recorded in the basement of his backing band's house in West Saugerties, on a domestic tape recorder, came from a few informal sessions in the summer of 1967—a season when Dylan shut himself off from the madness that had threatened to engulf him the previous year (the songs that actually make up the acetate appear to come from just five afternoon sessions). As part of the healing process he began to make music on a daily basis with the recently relocated Hawks (minus Levon Helm). In the Big Pink basement, Dylan found the perfect environment in which to make music, willingly turning his back on the gimmickry presaged by the dreaded *Sgt*.

Bob Dylan: *"I didn't know how to record the way other people were recording and didn't want to. The Beatles had just released Sgt. Pepper, which . . . I thought it was a very indulgent album . . . I didn't think all that production was necessary."*

Since those glory days, Dylan has continued to strive to get albums over and done with in a matter of days, but after *John Wesley Harding* he has not always found it easy to translate his vision onto vinyl. It is as if the process itself has somehow slipped from his grasp. The irony is that the genius driving his songwriting, at least in periods of inspiration (1974–83 and 1988–90), has remained largely intact.

Beginning with the true advent of the "multitrack" recording (sixteen tracks or more) in the early '70s, studio technology has grown increasingly sophisticated (hence the advent of a new breed of producers, technicians first and foremost). Part of Dylan's failure to come to terms with new demands has been the result of his notoriously short attention span or, to put it bluntly, his chronic lack of discipline when it comes to the art of recording. One rule that seems constant in Dylan's career is that the longer an album's sessions progress, the less willing he is to refer back to something recorded early on in the exercise. In at least two cases (*Infidels* and *Knocked Out Loaded*) the sheer length of the recording process caused him to reevaluate his entire approach midpoint and abandon a lot of good work.

With his most recent trio of albums (*Under the Red Sky, Good as I Been to You,* and *World Gone Wrong*)—and the two Wilburys albums that "previewed" them—Dylan has returned to cutting his albums in a handful of sessions with a minimum of fuss (an approach which, to quote Paul Nelson, "has wed the most avant-garde styles to the corniest of archetypes—and deliberately ignored the public's penchant for pasteurized product by rampantly (im)perfecting . . . [a] crude but spontaneous recording technique.") For a while there he seemed to have reached the point where he had come to terms with his gloriously imperfect working methods, preferring to just go with the flow.

Of course, the speed with which Dylan has completed most of his albums is directly related to his distaste for the studio and his desire to get the hell out of it (and back on the road?). Most of his studio work has been an attempt to get back to some imagined point where it was just a question of going into a room and cutting a song live in one, maybe two, takes à la Robert Johnson (hence his delight with the basement tape setup). As one of Dylan's producers recently informed me, "It's whatever it is when it comes out of him. There is no philosophy of recording to him. It just comes out or it doesn't."

Yet Dylan's studio work contains more truly great music than any of his contemporaries, much of it unreleased or released only in bastardized form. His haste to get in and out of the studio

has occasionally proved disastrous. More often than not, it has simply resulted in Dylan presenting a less-than-perfect reflection of songs/performances cut.

In this sense Dylan's official output is a long way short of the Beatles'—as a reflection of the possibilities for a song in the cold isolation of a studio. The Beatles, virtually without exception, picked the best cut and the best take for their records (hence the lack of danger to their reputation in letting Lewisohn loose on their tapes). Their unreleased recordings may illustrate exactly how they got from *A* to *B* but there is very little genius hidden from view.

With Dylan the situation could not be more different. It has been said before, notably by the two Pauls (Cable—*Dylan: The Unreleased Recordings*—and Williams—*Performing Artist Vols. 1+2*), but I reiterate: Despite *Biograph*, despite *The Bootleg Series*, it is impossible to fully appreciate the scope of Dylan's work in the studio (or his songwriting genius) without hearing his many unreleased recordings. These include "I'm Not There," "Sign on the Cross," 1980's "Caribbean Wind," the electric "Blind Willie McTell" and "New Danville Girl," and might as well include "Dignity," so bastardized is its 1994 incarnation. To my mind, here are six cuts with no obvious peers on *The Bootleg Series* (okay, maybe "She's Your Lover Now" and "Farewell Angelina").

Dylan as a recording artist certainly represents a fascinating mass of contradictions: a man who can record albums of the stature of *Bringing It All Back Home, Highway 61 Revisited, John Wesley Harding,* and (the original) *Blood on the Tracks* in less than a week apiece, yet drive producers to distraction with his seeming inability to grasp basic studio techniques; an artist constantly rewriting his material in the studio, usually to great effect, yet losing the emotional connection that tied him to the song in the first place (I am thinking here of "Jokerman" and "Idiot Wind," of which more later); someone who hates the studio and all it stands for, and yet becomes increasingly involved in "conceptualizing" an album as the sessions progress; and, finally, someone who abhors the permanence of the recording process yet has often reserved his best performances for the studio's icy confines.

Here, above all, is a man who could write, less than three years after his first recording session: "Do not create anything. It will be misinterpreted. It will not change. It will follow you the rest of your life." It is this idea, above all others, that terrifies Dylan and that he rails against: that however great a performance of, say, "Simple Twist of Fate" he delivers in concert (and it has remained rather fine) the one he recorded in September 1974 in A&R Studios is the one that will be remembered, cited, and analyzed. However much he has altered a song to his enduring vision in later performances, the artifact remains. And it does not change, it does indeed follow him. (How many reviewers bemoan the fact that his live versions don't sound like the record?—God preserve us!)

The making of any new record, these days at least, also involves adding one more piece of baggage to the legend (or, to take the cynical line, chips another chunk off the edifice of genius others have mounted). Even though Dylan, of all rock artists, has been most resistant to the notion of giving audiences what they expect, each album becomes another notch on the belt. In a fascinating conversation between Dylan and Larry Sloman on the 1975 Rolling Thunder Revue, Sloman attempted to convince Dylan to rerecord the *Desire* album because the performances of the songs on tour had become so much more intense (I can't argue with Sloman's assessment here). Dylan is dismissive of Sloman and retorts, "It's just another album." (Ironi-

cally, the one time Dylan took the notion to heart—the *Saved* album, recorded after three months of touring with the songs—the result was catastrophic.)

Dylan has never believed in the definitive in his art and implicit in the manic tinkerings in the studio of bands like the Beatles is the idea that they are working toward the perfect representation of a song (whither thou then?). When Dylan has attempted another take of a song—and he has always studiously resisted multiple takes throughout a thirty-five-year recording career—it is usually because he wishes to try the song in a different way, or the take may simply lack connection to an original feeling he seeks to resurrect (which presumably also explains why he sometimes comes back to songs at a subsequent session), not because the seventh note of the middle-eight's crescendo is a semitone out.

For Dylan, indeed any great artist, the feeling at the heart of a performance—and Dylan tends to evaluate his recordings as performances—remains the overriding criterion for selecting cuts for release. (There is a telling moment at a session for the *Pat Garret & Billy the Kid* soundtrack in Mexico City when, after Dylan has delivered a fine take of "Billy," the engineer informs him that there were a couple of clunks on the microphone. Dylan, unimpressed, snorts, "Mmmm. Too bad.") Yet there have also been times when Dylan has felt he has laid a little too much of himself on the line in the studio—the original "Idiot Wind" and "Caribbean Wind" spring to mind. In both instances, the "authorized" versions attempt to mask the nakedness of the originals.

Whatever the drawbacks of his cut-it-and-run approach in the studio, it remains preferable to the working methods of a Springsteen, constantly rewriting and reworking the same motifs until the very breath of the song has faded. When reevaluating work already completed, the temptation "to disguise what he's got left behind his eyes" always has a tendency to take over.

Several Dylan albums have been subject to change after getting to the test-pressing stage (though nowhere near as many as Neil Young, the king of lost albums). These include some of his most important artifacts: *Freewheelin', Highway 61 Revisited, Blood on the Tracks, Shot of Love, Infidels,* as well as *New Morning, Dylan* (okay—nothing to do with the man, I know), and *Down in the Groove.*

If there really is no success like failure (and, remember, Dylan penned those words shortly before insisting, "I have given up at making any attempt at perfection"), then this book is at least as much about why Dylan has failed as why he may have succeeded. This is not

because I believe Dylan's recording career to be a grand failure. You cannot extract the perversity, the restlessness, the fear of his own nakedness—the traits that have sometimes neutered better instincts in the studio—from who Dylan is: a perverse, restless, fearful individual, just like the rest of us. That Dylan has chronicled his fearful restlessness with such humanity and compassion is what sets him apart.

The work will survive, the work will endure. But the work does not begin and end with Dylan's twenty-nine studio albums, two boxed sets and two Wilbury collections. It is found in every grain of ferrochrome ever recorded of the man at work, before an audience or behind closed doors.

Clinton Heylin
January 1995

NOTES ON THE SESSIONOGRAPHY

Each chapter in this book is prefaced by a sessionography, which details all the sessions for a particular album/project. Though Dylan's "studio" excursions almost always coincide with making an official album, the few extant "home sessions" that predate his first Columbia session have also been included, as they were quite self-conscious, albeit informal, attempts at recording his repertoire at the time (the Minneapolis Hotel Tape, though it post-dates the *Bob Dylan* sessions, could hardly be omitted here, particularly given the inclusion of one song on *The Bootleg Series*. The three main collections of early publishing demos—for Leeds Music, *Broadside* magazine, and Witmark—are included for much the same reasons. They include some essential early Dylan originals not attempted at any Columbia session ("Ballad for a Friend," "Tomorrow Is a Long Time," "Long Time Gone," and "Guess I'm Doing Fine" spring to mind).

Dylan's appearances in a studio as a guest musician I have largely omitted on the grounds that they reveal little about his methods, are almost uniformly uninteresting, and only in rare circumstances have given him scope to show his vocal dexterity or lyrical turn of phrase. The exceptions—if they feature Dylan as a vocalist, singing words of his own making—I have not neglected. Thus Dylan's attempt to cut an album with Allen Ginsberg (the tapes of which revealed two previously undocumented jams with Dylan vocals) and his duets with the likes of Eric Clapton, Bette Midler, and Willie Nelson have not eluded my grasp.

It is inevitable that, as a study of Dylan's working methods and creative decisions in the studio, the emphasis in my text has been on his unreleased recordings (I have necessarily had to assume a good knowledge of the man's released works from the reader). This is not meant to imply some diminution of the official works. Because of the emphasis on what Dylan has chosen to omit from his albums, I have included an appendix detailing all the bootleg CDs currently available featuring studio recordings unavailable on official Sony product. Hopefully this will help the reader fill in some of the holes—at least till the next tape hits the mat!

All officially released cuts, which are listed at the beginning of the relevant section, are also highlighted in bold type in the session listings. All other takes/songs recorded at the relevant session appear in normal type or in italics. Those that appear in normal type are performances that, though unreleased as yet by Dylan's record label, circulate freely among Dylan tape collectors (and on bootleg albums/CDs). Takes that appear in italics do not currently reside in collectors' hands, though in some instances I have been fortunate enough to hear these recordings and have made comments accordingly.

Some songs listed in the sessionography, all highlighted in bold, also bear an asterisk. This indicates that, though the released version derives from this take, there has been some significant kind of tampering with the original "live" take prior to release: i.e., a verse may have been edited out; a new vocal may have been overdubbed; instruments may have been tacked on; in certain rare instances, a released version may be an edit of two separate takes (e.g., "Hurricane"). In most instances an explanation of what the unadulterated take reveals will be found in the accompanying text.

Thanks to the helpfulness of those at Sony's archives in New York, *Bob Dylan: The Recording Sessions, 1960–1994,* is by far the most complete and accurate record of Dylan's Columbia recordings to date, highlighting a wealth of material that has so far eluded the tentacles of collectors. Fans might assume that these days it is simply a matter of clicking up a computer screen to establish what took place at any given Columbia session. I'm afraid not. An enormous amount of cross-referencing between Sony's infant computer system, their anachronistic cardex system (still the most reliable guide, studio sheets excepted), and—where possible—the tape boxes themselves was necessary to get the information herein utilized.

If my knowledge of recording session dates and Dylan's penchant for witty working titles (see Appendix II) saved me from a fair few wild-goose chases, I was still sometimes led astray by information gleaned from Sony. In particular, song titles were sometimes more than a little inaccurate. The long-rumored *Blonde on Blonde* outtake "What Can I Do for Your Wigwam" was indeed listed on Sony's cardex. On cross-referencing the CO number, though, it became apparent that it was simply a working title for "Pledging My Time" (damn). Likewise there are no *Self Portrait* outtakes called "All for the Sake of Thee," "Sing Tattle O'Day," or "This Evening So Soon," whatever the studio sheet for March 4, 1970, might say (try "House Carpenter," "Little Brown Dog," and "Tell Old Bill" instead). As a general guide, readers should assume that a take listed in italics has been derived from Sony's records or aural evidence (a handful of "missing" songs have been mentioned in print by eyewitnesses, but only those corroborated by some kind of written record have been included in the main discography; otherwise they are noted separately, under "Rumored").

For most of Dylan's Columbia sessions up to 1975's *Desire* I was able to ascertain the CO and NCO numbers assigned to each cut at any given session (CO numbers apply to sessions in New York, NCO to sessions in Nashville, HCO to sessions in Los Angeles). These numbers were often assigned at both original studio sessions *and* mixing sessions, so a New York session may end up with an NCO number if the mix was completed in Nashville—as happened with much of *Self Portrait*. Though sessions themselves are filed initially under Job Number and eventually under Project Number, the advantage of the CO numbering system is that it indicates the actual songs cut, the order the songs were recorded in, and—where there may be gaps—how many songs may be missing. Indeed these CO numbers, far more than documented recording dates, were the starting point for my investigations. With just a couple of dozen CO numbers and access to Sony's overfull cardex system, I could at last begin to reconstruct session after session. As the CO numbers multiplied, so the gaps began to be plugged.

Where it has been possible to examine tape boxes (and/or the studio sheets within), I have been able to establish how many takes of a song were recorded (or, at the very least, which take the released performance version is). However, in the old Columbia system—unlike just about every record company of note—false starts, both long and short, would be counted as takes on their studio sheets (and marked with a "b" or an "a" in the F. S. column). So CO 78975–4 does not necessarily mean four complete takes of CO

78975 (actually none of the four takes of "Farewell" recorded that day is complete). Also, it was common practice in the sixties to reuse a CO number already assigned to a song when cutting it again at a subsequent session (though take numbers often reverted back to –1. Confused? And you wonder how all those wrong takes got issued in the sixties? Now you know). Unfortunately, even this bizarre practice was not always adhered to (each of the four attempts at "Leopard Skin Pillbox Hat"—21/1, 27/1, 14/2, 9/3/66—were assigned CO numbers). Save for unfinished takes already in general circulation (marked [inc.]), I have only listed complete takes. If I have listed more than one take—for example, the four takes of "Mary Ann" recorded on June 2, 1970, CO 106779–1, –5, –6, and –7 respectively—it is because I have been able to establish that this many complete takes were recorded. If I have been unable to ascertain how many takes were recorded, I have simply omitted the take numbers.

Unfortunately for the researcher, after *Desire* Dylan largely abandoned working in Columbia's studios. From 1975 on, Dylan fans have had to rely on copyright records for the most accurate information about Dylan's unreleased studio recordings. Hard and fast recording information becomes progressively scarcer after this date, although I was fortunate enough to locate studio records (albeit incomplete) for Dylan's crucial Christian trilogy: *Slow Train Coming, Saved,* and *Shot of Love.* Evidently I have my own saving grace o'er me.

Dylan himself seems to have developed a profound distaste for those who attempt to document his work. However, such distaste has failed to dissuade me from getting as much down before the man fades from view. Having spent some time examining the records of Dylan's work held by his record label, and seen the state some of their tapes are in, I am more than ever convinced that a meticulous archiving (as in state-of-the-art digital transfers) of Dylan's work is urgently required before the tapes deteriorate beyond the point of no return (already the vast majority of Dylan's post–*Blonde on Blonde* studio tapes will need to be baked before they can even be dubbed), or are so misfiled, misplaced, and mislaid that they will eventually be missing altogether (Sony recently attempted to instigate a gold CD Master Sound release of *Blood on the Tracks,* perhaps the greatest collection of love songs ever recorded—spare me your contenders—only to discover that they could not locate the two-track masters of the Minneapolis sessions).

My own work seems to have so incensed the ostensible overseer of Dylan's archive, Jeff Rosen, that he has finally put one lesser Dylan authority to work on his behalf, rummaging through the very same vaults. Such archiving should really have taken place before the release of either of the two scattershot collections to date—*Biograph* and *The Bootleg Series.* But then, it seems that Dylan fans, like the man himself, must learn to accept chaos.

Note: Though a full notation of my sources for each session and areas of dispute is beyond the scope of this book, I may yet produce a mimeograph along these lines, and I do welcome any correspondence via the publishers on the more academic aspects of my research.

BOB DYLAN

THE RECORDING SESSIONS 1960–1994

BEFORE COLUMBIA

Official cuts:
The Bootleg Series: Hard Times in New York Town
Highway 61 Interactive CD-ROM: Dink's Song. Baby, Please Don't Go.

Musician:
1–2 Bob Dylan (guitar/vocals) 3–5 Bob Dylan (guitar/vocals/harmonica)

1. KAREN WALLACE'S APARTMENT
   ST. PAUL, MINNESOTA
   MAY 1960
Gotta Travel On
Doney Gal
I'm a Rovin' Gambler
Go Down You Murderers
Bay of Mexico
The Two Sisters
Go Way from My Window
This Land Is Your Land
Go Tell It on the Mountain
Fare Thee Well
Pastures of Plenty
Rock A Bye My Saro Jane
Take This Hammer
Nobody Loves You (When You're Down and
   Out)
The Great Historical Bum
Mary Ann
Every Night When the Sun Goes In
Sinner Man
Delia
Wop Da Alano
Who's Gonna Shoe Your Pretty Little Feet?
Abner Young
Nine Hundred Miles
Mule Skinner Blues
One Eyed Jacks
Columbus Stockade Blues
Payday at Coal Creek

Recorded by Karen Moynihan née Wallace

2. HUGH BROWN'S APARTMENT
   MINNEAPOLIS, MINNESOTA
   SEPTEMBER 1960
Red Rosey Bush
Johnny I Hardly Knew You
Jesus Christ
Streets of Glory
K.C. Moan
Mule Skinner Blues

I'm a Gambler
Talkin' Columbia
Talkin' Merchant Marine
Talkin' Hugh Brown
Talkin' Inflation Blues

Recorded by Bonnie Beecher

3. THE GLEASONS'
   EAST ORANGE, NEW JERSEY
   FEBRUARY 1961
San Francisco Bay Blues
Jesus Met a Woman at the Well
Gypsy Davey
Pastures of Plenty
Trail of the Buffalo
Jesse James
Southern Cannonball
Remember Me (When the Candle Lights Are
   Gleaming)

Recorded by Bob Gleason

4. BONNIE BEECHER'S APARTMENT
   MINNEAPOLIS, MINNESOTA
   MAY 1961
Ramblin' Round
Death Don't Have No Mercy
It's Hard to Be Blind
This Train
Harmonica instrumental
Talkin' Fish Blues
Pastures of Plenty
This Land Is Your Land
Still a Fool
Wild Mountain Thyme
Howdido
Car, Car
Don't You Push Me Down
Come See
I Want It Now
San Francisco Bay Blues
Young But Daily Growin'

Devilish Mary
Railroad Bill
Will the Circle Be Unbroken?
Man of Constant Sorrow
Pretty Polly
Railroad Boy
James Alley Blues
Bonnie, Why'd You Cut My Hair?

Recorded by Tony Glover

5. BONNIE BEECHER'S APARTMENT
   MINNEAPOLIS, MINNESOTA
   DECEMBER 22, 1961
Candy Man
Baby, Please Don't Go*
Hard Times in New York Town
Stealin'
Po' Lazarus
I Ain't Got No Home
It's Hard to Be Blind

Dink's Song*
Man of Constant Sorrow
East Orange, New Jersey
Deep Water
Wade in the Water
I Was Young When I Left Home
In the Evening
Baby, Let Me Follow You Down
Sally Gal
Gospel Plow
Long John
Cocaine Blues
VD Blues
VD Waltz
VD City
VD Gunner's Blues
See That My Grave Is Kept Clean
Ramblin' Blues
Black Cross

Recorded by Tony Glover

Although Dylan has stated "I got nothing more to live up to!" his fans—ever avaricious for more of the man's work—rarely appreciate just how fortunate we are that such a major artist was so meticulously documented at the very outset of his career. No contemporary has had as much early studio or "home" material leak through the cracks, nor have the embryonic recordings of the Beatles, the Stones, or the Who—perhaps Dylan's most important mainstream contemporaries—forced any major reevaluation of their art. In Dylan's case there exist a half-dozen "home tapes" recorded well before his first album hit the racks, clearly charting his development as an interpreter and his passage into original songwriter.

The most obvious reason why Dylan is so well-documented in these crucial months has to be his folk background. The folk process has always been concerned with such documentation. Two of Dylan's earliest heroes were Alan Lomax and Carl Sandburg, who between them (and Alan's father, John) collected an impressive smattering of the best folk songs to survive in America into the twentieth century. Initially at least, Dylan saw himself as part of this process—as an interpreter of a hoary ol' tradition of self-expression, not as an originator of new forms of song.

When Bonnie Beecher, the real "Girl from the North Country," made what may well be the first tape of Dylan-as-Dylan (there were several home tapes made by John Bucklen of a young, pre-Minneapolis Robert Zimmerman, parts of which were broadcast on BBC documentary, *Highway 61 Revisited,* but they sound like what they are: two teenagers mucking about with a tape recorder), Dylan told her, "I don't want you to let anyone make a copy of these tapes, so that when someone from the Library of Congress asks you for them, [you can] sell them for two hundred dollars." Sadly Beecher's tape—which probably included the likes of "1913 Massacre," "San Francisco Bay Blues," "Columbus Stockade Blues," "Omie Wise," "Car, Car," "I'm Gonna Sit at the Welcome Table," "I Thought I Heard That Casey When She Roll," and "Man of Constant Sorrow," songs Bonnie recalls from those days—was "mislaid" some time back.

As such, the first extant tape of the

young Bob Dylan and the starting point of his recording career, for now at least, is the so-called St. Paul Tape. Though only a home recording, made on a cheap reel-to-reel at 3¾ ips, the St. Paul Tape contains twenty-seven songs sung by a nineteen-year-old Dylan in May 1960, just six months after he adopted his new identity and barely a few months after he dropped out of Minneapolis University for good.

The St. Paul Tape unfortunately remains almost as inaccessible as the first Beecher tape. The original tape remains in the hands of Karen Moynihan née Wallace, the sister of Terri Wallace, perhaps Dylan's first serious devotee and the person who cajoled Dylan into sitting down and making a tape in the first place. Three fragmentary versions of the tape were made at various points when the tape was up for sale in the late seventies, though no one stumped up the $10,000 asking price. Mrs. Moynihan disappeared from view in the early eighties around about the time a respected Dylan collector dismissed the tape as a fake (the tape was eventually authenticated by both Ms. Beecher herself and Tony Glover; see my own article on the subject, "What's Real and What Is Not" in *The Telegraph*, no. 40).

The only really listenable (partial) version, obtained from Mrs. Moynihan by a British collector, contains just four songs, "The Two Sisters," "Pastures of Plenty," "Mule Skinner Blues," and "Payday at Coal Creek." However even these four songs provide a fascinating glimpse at Dylan pre-Guthrie, pre-Denver, pre-Jesse Fuller. The guitar-playing is predictably perfunctory and the harmonica non-existent, so it is the voice that must carry the songs. Though it rarely soars, the St. Paul voice certainly fits contemporaries' descriptions of Dylan's pre-Guthrie voice as "sweet [and] pretty." The closest comparison one can make with his released work is *Nashville Skyline* (Beecher, talking about that early

voice, later commented, "I was startled when I heard [it] again on *Nashville Skyline* . . . I thought he had lost that sweet voice altogether"). What Dylan had not as yet learned to do was hold his breath three times as long as Caruso.

Though collectors cannot yet enjoy the St. Paul Tape in its entirety (let us hope that Mrs. Moynihan has the tape safely locked away), details of the songs that are on the tape provide some kind of insight into Dylan's nascent repertoire. Of the twenty-seven songs, just "Sinner Man," "Columbus Stockade Blues," and "Go Down You Murderers" were definitely part of his then-standard set. Only "The Two Sisters," "Who's Gonna Shoe Your Pretty Little Feet?," "Mule Skinner Blues," "Doney Gal," and "Rock A Bye My Saro Jane" appear in John and Alan Lomax's authoritative collection *Folk Songs of North America*, first published that year.

Even if one discounts the Woody Guthrie songs a fledgling folkie was obliged to include—"This Land Is Your Land," "The Great Historical Bum," and "Columbus Stockade Blues" in this instance—that leaves more than a dozen songs that do not come from the obvious folk sources most coffeehouse crooners referred to. Of these, three or four have reappeared in later Dylan incarnations: Paul Clayton's "Gotta Travel On" (*Self Portrait*, 1976 RTR); "I'm a Rovin' Gambler" (1991); "Mary Ann" (*Dylan*) and probably "Delia" (we do not know if this is Blind Willie McTell's "Delia"—it may well be Blind Blake's "Delia's Gone"). Clearly when contemporaries like Harvey Abrams called Dylan "the purest of the pure" sourcewise, they were not jesting.

The St. Paul Tape also contains what Robert Shelton has called Dylan's first composition, "One Eyed Jacks," which showed the kid working on a world-weary persona eighteen months before he debuted it for Columbia: "Twenty years old . . . I'll never reach twenty-one."

A second Twin Cities tape postdates both Dylan's trip to Denver and his discovery of Guthrie. Yet the so-called first Minneapolis Tape contains no harmonica-work either. Given that it was recorded at Dylan's part-time apartment it seems unlikely that he did not have one at hand unless this tape predates him taking up the harmonica. Although his attempts at a Scottish brogue on "Johnny I Hardly Knew You" are mildly amusing, and there is a stab at an original talkin' blues about his indolent roommate Hugh Brown, the first Minneapolis Tape consists largely of Dylan's attempts to replicate some of Guthrie's more obscure (not to say turgid) originals. That said, a recognizable Dylan twang is now well in place, and though his fascination with Guthrie (in evidence on all tapes made in this period) gets to be a little wearisome, the September 1960 Dylan sounds a helluva lot more like a folksinger than the honey-drippin' country cousin recorded by the Wallace sisters four months earlier.

There appear to be no tapes from the final couple of months in Minneapolis although, according to contemporaries, Dylan was now advancing at a terrifying pace. If many felt his obsession with Guthrie was holding him back, he was developing a harmonica style, under the occasional tutelage of local hip cat Tony Glover, that helped him finally abandon these Minnesotan backwoods and take on New York.

Indeed the next home tape, probably recorded in the first two weeks of February 1961 (just days before Dylan wrote "Song to Woody"), was made at the home of Sid and Bob Gleason in East Orange, New Jersey. As fastidious folk collectors, the Gleasons were bound to have a goodish reel-to-reel lying around the place (though apparently this is Dylan's only Gleason tape because the recorder broke shortly afterward and

was never repaired). The Bob Dylan singing at the Gleasons is almost unrecognizable from the SAMmy recorded in Karen Wallace's apartment. For the first time, the fidelity of a Dylan home recording allows for an enjoyable listening experience, while a couple of the performances are very Dylanesque indeed. Though the way he holds a note still sounds incredibly forced, his guitar-playing has passed beyond the merely competent and the few harmonica bursts that embellish the guitar work add an appropriate dimension. The least Guthriesque, and therefore the most satisfying, performance on the Gleason tape is its concluding song, the first "fare thee well" in a long line of Dylan "bid ye adieus." The words to "Remember Me (When the Candle Lights Are Gleaming)" draw on country music's hoariest clichés, salvaged in part by Dylan's authentic hick delivery (at times he seems on the verge of slipping into his St. Paul voice, as he was to do later on "Young But Daily Growin'" at Carnegie Recital Hall in November 1961).

The Gleasons' tape offers just a glimmer of the newly Yorked Dylan. Thankfully, the last home tape Dylan made before signing to Columbia provides the most complete document of the second stage of his development. Just five months after heading for New York, Dylan returned to Minneapolis, where he recorded what is generally known as the Minneapolis Party Tape, defining his May 1961 repertoire as exhaustively as the St. Paul Tape had an earlier era. A new, confident Dylan certainly surprised a couple of the locals he'd left behind.

The repertoire he had acquired in New York had yet to transcend the Guthrie influence (now transposed via Ramblin' Jack Elliott)—there are nine Guthrie songs on the tape—though the highlights once again lie elsewhere. Possibly Dylan felt obliged to cater to his friends' expectations in what was, after all, an informal homecoming session.

He may even have believed that the Guthrie covers continued to be his strongest songs. It is curious that he plays none of the originals he had begun writing ("Talkin' New York" predates this tape, as do "California Blue-Eyed Baby" and "Song to Woody"). He does, however, play a couple of songs that date from his Minneapolis days, "Bonnie, Why'd You Cut My Hair?" an early joke song that Beecher presumably requested, and "Man of Constant Sorrow," performed in a happy-go-lucky manner that belies its lyrical content. But it is the likes of "James Alley Blues" (often called "Times Ain't What They Used To Be") and a tentative but tender "Young But Daily Growin'" (aka "Lang a-Growing") that most strongly suggest a Dylan about to pass beyond his former friends' command.

Indeed the time between this visit to Minneapolis and the next at Christmas (ever the dutiful son?), demarcates his true leap into originality. The last of the early home tapes, the Minneapolis Hotel Tape remains perhaps the most legendary of non-Columbia Dylan recordings, the basements excepted. Though Dylan would continue to make the occasional home tape over the next couple of years—at Tony Glover's, at the McKenzies', at Cynthia Gooding's apartment, at Eric Von Schmidt's—they became vehicles for him to display his prowess as a songwriter—"look at what I just writ"—rather than self-conscious documents of a growing awareness of the folk process.

The Hotel Tape, although it derives from a bare month after Dylan's first Columbia sessions, is far more of a tour de force than its official precursor. Dylan had carried over just five songs from those first album sessions—"See That My Grave Is Kept Clean" (radically reworked), "Gospel Plow," "Man of Constant Sorrow," "Baby, Let Me Follow You Down," and "Ramblin' Blues" (which had not made the album).

Dylan's guitar-playing on these and the other twenty-one songs on the Hotel Tape must have convinced those attending that this was someone with the potential to develop into the kind of white blues guitarist the world had yet to see. The playing on "Wade in the Water" has a pentecostal fury rarely evident in Dylan's later work, while the bottleneck on "Baby, Please Don't Go" carries the song in a way that would have made even Leadbelly proud. Dylan has by this point all but overcome his Guthrie fixation. Aside from an amusing "VD medley," only a couple of Guthrie songs are meat for his muse.

The laconic charm Dylan turns on as he moves through the songs on the Hotel Tape suggests someone entirely at ease with his environment. These were his friends, he knew the setting (the Hotel is actually a little insider's joke—Bonnie's apartment being "The Beecher Hotel," presumably a reference to how many people crashed there), and, according to Tony Glover, who did such a fine job taping the session, Dylan managed to polish off an entire bottle of Jim Beam in the two and a half hours it took to lay down twenty-six songs. Possibly these factors explain why the choice of material is so much more ambitious than at the *Bob Dylan* sessions. Certainly "Black Cross," an inspired monologue about the hanging of a well-read black farmer because "the son o' a bitch never had no religion," would never have got passed Columbia's lawyers (as Dylan was soon to find out with the notorious "Talkin' John Birch"). "Dink's Song," on the other hand, a song John Lomax really did collect from a lady called Dink, is one of Dylan's most convincing vocals. Though the guitar sometimes lags a little, it sets up a rhythm that only triggers his increasingly desperate vocal.

The Hotel Tape also serves to illustrate Dylan's newest guise—songwriter.

Two songs with original words set to traditional tunes, "Hard Times in New York Town" (taken from "Down on Penney's Farm") and "I Was Young When I Left Home" (from "Nine Hundred Miles") are both rather fine (the former largely retreads "Talkin' New York," which presumably explains its thirty-year omission from the official corpus). By the time of the Minneapolis Hotel Tape, Dylan was a recording artist—and for the prestigious Columbia label, no less—yet the Hotel Tape has a half-dozen moments I would trade for anything on *Bob Dylan*. Which may well suggest that Dylan's problems with recording in a studio began the minute he walked through the doors of Columbia's Studio A. Peter McKenzie, talking about the home tapes made at his parents' home in New York, the first of which was made the day after Dylan completed his debut album, feels that these home tapes present a very different Dylan to the one that can be heard on his studio recordings. Thankfully, awareness of the folk process in the circles he traveled has ensured that these early home tapes have been dutifully preserved.

BOB DYLAN

Recorded: November 20 and 22, 1961
Released: March 19, 1962

Side 1: You're No Good. Talkin' New York. In My Time of Dyin'. Man of Constant Sorrow. Fixin' to Die. Pretty Peggy-O. Highway 51 Blues. Side 2: Gospel Plow. Baby, Let Me Follow You Down. House of the Rising Sun. Freight Train Blues. Song to Woody. See That My Grave Is Kept Clean.

Other official cuts:

The Bootleg Series: He Was a Friend of Mine. Man on the Street. House Carpenter.

Producer:
John Hammond

Musician:
Bob Dylan (guitar/harmonica/vocals)

1. COLUMBIA STUDIO A
   NEW YORK
   NOVEMBER 20, 1961

CO 68726–1	*You're No Good [I]*
CO 68726–2	*You're No Good [II]*
CO 68726–5	**You're No Good [III]**
CO 68726–8	"Connecticut Cowboy"
CO 68727–1	*Fixin' to Die [I]*
CO 68727–2	*Fixin' to Die [II]*
CO 68727–3	**Fixin' to Die [III]**
CO 68728–2	**He Was a Friend of Mine**
CO 68729–2	*House of the Rising Sun [I]*
CO 68729–3	*House of the Rising Sun [II]*
CO 68730–1	*Talkin' New York [I]*
CO 68730–2	**Talkin' New York [II]**
CO 68731–2	**Song to Woody**
CO 68732–1	**Baby, Let Me Follow You Down**
CO n/a	*Man of Constant Sorrow [incomplete]*
CO 68733–1	**In My Time of Dyin'**

2. COLUMBIA STUDIO A
   NEW YORK
   NOVEMBER 22, 1961

CO 68743–2	**Man on the Street**
CO 68744–1	*Ramblin' Blues [I]*
CO 68744–2	*Ramblin' Blues [II]*
CO 68745–1	*Man of Constant Sorrow [I]*
CO 68745–3	**Man of Constant Sorrow [II]**
CO 68746–1	*Pretty Peggy-O [I]*
CO 68746–2	**Pretty Peggy-O [II]**
CO 68747–2	*See That My Grave Is Kept Clean [I]*
CO 68747–3	*See That My Grave Is Kept Clean [II]*
CO 68747–4	**See That My Grave Is Kept Clean [III]**
CO 68748–1	**Gospel Plow**
CO 68749–1	**Highway 51 Blues**
CO 68750–1	**Freight Train Blues**
CO 68751–1	**House Carpenter**

The two sessions required to produce Dylan's debut, *Bob Dylan* (at a cost of $402, legend says), suggest that one, he had yet to fully conceive of an identity he wished to project and, two, that, undisciplined as he undoubtedly was, he could be a very quick learner (even if the studio would always remain an alien environment). His coffeehouse apprenticeship done, this twenty-year-old, in the space of two afternoon sessions (Columbia records indicate both sessions ran from two to five P.M.), recorded his entire debut album. He also went from requiring five takes (including two false starts) to secure an acceptable "You're No Good" at the outset of the first session (intriguing that the album's opening volley should be recorded first), to recording the last four songs of these sessions in four consecutive takes, wrapping it all up with the devastating rendition of "House Carpenter" finally released on *The Bootleg Series*.

Though Hammond would later bemoan Dylan's studio technique ("I [initially] wanted to get something down on tape and hear what Bobby was capable of. In a word, he was terrible. Bobby popped every *p*, hissed every *s*, and habitually wandered off mike. Even more frustrating, he refused to learn from his mistakes. It occurred to me at the time that I'd never worked with anyone so undisciplined before"), both first album sessions seem to have progressed very smoothly.

After a frustrating recording session as a harmonica-player with Harry Belafonte—Belafonte insisting on take after take of "Midnight Special"—Dylan had already developed a finely tuned aversion to multiple takes. Indeed he would later say of his first sessions, "I just played the guitar and harmonica and sang those songs and that was it. Mr. Hammond asked me if I wanted to sing any of them over again and I said no. I can't see myself singing the same song twice in a row." Allowing for a little Dylanesque exaggeration, that's a pretty fair summary of the sessions. Five of the album tracks really were cut in just one take ("Baby, Let Me Follow You Down," "In My Time of Dyin'," "Gospel Plow," "Highway 51 Blues,"

and "Freight Train Blues"), while "Song to Woody" made the grade after just one false start.

Yet Dylan was quick to grow dissatisfied with the results achieved over the two November afternoons. As early as December 1961, he told journalist Robert Shelton (who was writing the album's liner notes under a pseudonym) that the notes were better than the record (not true).

The real problem was the material Dylan had chosen to record. He could never hope to provide an accurate cross-section of the vast repertoire he had acquired in the previous two years. But then *Bob Dylan* is about as unrepresentative as Dylan could reasonably have managed. At the shows given in the preceding three months only "See That My Grave Is Kept Clean," "Gospel Plow," "Pretty Peggy-O," "Fixin' to Die," and the three originals "Song to Woody," "Talkin' New York," and "Man on the Street" were definitely in the repertoire. Though Dylan wisely steered clear of any Guthrie covers or Jack Elliott favorites—suggesting some awareness of the need to assert his own identity—the songs on *Bob Dylan* (much like those on his two '90s acoustic excursions) do not sound like songs he has really lived with. When Dylan described the songs to Hammond as "some stuff I've written, some stuff I've discovered, some stuff I stole," there is an implied casualness to the choices made. Clearly Dylan had yet to understand the importance of delivering on record.

That said, there are still some exhilarating moments here. "Baby, Let Me Follow You Down" is a fitting start to the long line of pleas for forgiveness on Dylan albums. "Song to Woody" (with a tune copped from Guthrie's "1913 Massacre") is a most appropriate way of expressing a debt. "House of the Rising Sun" is a refreshing reinterpretation of an evergreen folk standard, albeit Dave Van Ronk's refreshing reinterpretation (which Dylan shamelessly pur-loined, despite Van Ronk asking him to not use the cut). That said, Dylan's performance leaves Van Ronk's own released version at the railroad gate.

Dylan also probably took his arrangement of "House Carpenter" from Van Ronk. Though a less radical reworking, it is certainly the most notable omission from *Bob Dylan*. "House Carpenter" would have rooted the album in the most ancient of folk traditions, something even his highly Americanized "Pretty Peggy-O" fails to do. (Dylan has recently returned to a more authentic version of this Scottish ballad in concert, replete with images of guineas clinking.)

"House Carpenter" itself dates at least as far back in time as the seventeenth century, when it was collected by Samuel Pepys under the heading: "A Warning for Married Women, being an example of Mrs. Jane Reynolds (a West Country woman) born near Plymouth who, having plighted her troth to a sea-man, was afterward married to a Carpenter and at last carried away by a Spirit, the manner of which shall presently be recited." In this original form, the returned lover is actually a demon from hell. As Alan Lomax relates

in *Folk Songs of North America,* "The Devil disappeared from most American versions, but the man stands out, as all the more demonic, as Death himself." Dylan himself decides to preface the song by announcing, "Here's a story about a ghost come back from out in the sea, come to take his bride away from the house carpenter."

Dylan's performance—even though it is once again a song he has seemingly picked out of thin air (there are no other documented performances from this era)—is certainly as demonic as the "daemon lover" who takes the lady down to hell. As the final song cut at the sessions it strikes me as achieving a level of intensity Dylan was searching for all along in the assorted tales of death and misfortune. Perhaps this is not simply because it is a genuinely great performance but also an equally fine song. Although there are exceptions ("Man of Constant Sorrow," "Rising Sun"), there are precious few great songs herein.

Thankfully, by the time he returned to Columbia Studio A in April 1962 Dylan had started to write his own songs. As the man himself later observed, "There came a point where . . . I had to write what I wanted to say."

BROADSIDE REUNION

Recorded: January 1962 to May 1962
The Ballad of Donald White. The Death of Emmett Till.

Musicians:

1–2 Bob Dylan (guitar/harmonica/vocals)
2 Gil Turner (backing vocals)

2 Pete Seeger (backing vocals)
2 Sis Cunningham (backing vocals)

1. LEEDS MUSIC OFFICES
    NEW YORK
    JANUARY 1962
Man on the Street (incomplete)
Hard Times in New York Town
Poor Boy Blues
Ballad for a Friend
Ramblin' Gamblin' Willie
Man on the Street
Talkin' Bear Mountain Picnic Massacre Blues
Standing on the Highway

2. "BROADSIDE SHOW"
    RECORDED FOR WBAI-FM
    NEW YORK
    MAY 1962
The Ballad of Donald White
The Death of Emmett Till
Blowin' in the Wind

Although Dylan was writing his own material as early as February 1961, it was only in the new year that stories of his prolific nature began to develop apace (helped along by some suitably modest pronouncements from Bobby D. as regards writing five songs before breakfast). In the crucial years of 1962–63, when he assumed and denied the mantle of Prince of Protest as the mood took him, the Columbia sessions for *Freewheelin'* and *Times* provide only a very partial picture of the man's development.

Even though Dylan hurried back into Columbia's Studios when the first album failed to shoot lightning through the entertainment world, the five-month hiatus still allowed him the chance to write, rewrite, and discard enough songs to make up an entire post–*Bob Dylan,* pre-*Freewheelin'* collection. Among the songs "lost" in these months were "I Was Young When I Left Home," "Hard Times in New York Town," "Poor Boy Blues," "Ballad for a Friend" (originally called "Reminiscence Blues"), "Standing on the Highway," and "The Ballad of Donald White."

Thankfully, John Hammond had arranged a deal with a music publishing house to copyright and publish Dylan's songs, hoping to financially tide him over until his album took the world by storm (or not). The seven originals Dylan cut for Leeds Music (presumably shortly before he composed "The Death of Emmett Till" in late January) were a democratic half and half of favorites from his fall 1961 club repertoire— "Man on the Street," "Talkin' Bear Mountain," and "Hard Times in New York"—and brand-new ink-not-dry efforts, a couple of which are, frankly, pretty bloody awful ("Poor Boy Blues" and "Standing on the Highway"). Amid such debris, though, lies one exquisite gem, "Ballad for a Friend," a song any Dylan fan should hear. Where the idea for this song came from I know not. In the gospel according to Paul Williams it is dismissed as just another "pedestrian reworking of familiar folk and blues themes." In fact, the song has a very unusual structure for Dylan (six unrepeated three-line verses). Combining, as it does, elements of "Bob Dylan's Dream," "Percy's Song," and "North Country Blues," it is a remarkably mature view of lost youth (set against the backdrop of the death of a friend, it reflects Dylan's abiding obsession with early death and unfulfilled promise at this point in his career). The economy of phrasing and the cascading guitar runs suggest a new songwriter already looking beyond the norms of folk platitudes. Yet, much like "I Was Young When I Left Home," recorded in Minneapolis a fortnight earlier, "Ballad for a Friend" was passed over when Dylan discovered the delights of topical song.

The following month, he made his first contribution to a mimeographed "topical song" magazine, produced by "Sis" Cunningham and Gorden Friesen. *Broadside* quickly became a useful vehicle for new Dylan songs. The immediacy with which *Broadside* was published meant that certain songs— notably "Blowin' in the Wind"—passed into common currency (at least in the Village) months before Columbia could release an authentic Dylan version. Inevitably Dylan also dispensed songs to *Broadside* that he considered unsuitable for Columbia's purposes. *Broadside* songs like "Ain't Gonna Grieve," published in the August 1962 *Broadside* (and based on an old spiritual, "Ain't Gonna Grieve My Lord No More"), "John Brown" (perhaps surprisingly, given its longevity in live performance), and "Train a-Travelin'" were never attempted at Studio A.

Although it would be November 1962 before Dylan began demoing songs specifically for coeditors Cunningham and Friesen, his first recording for *Broadside* was three songs cut in May 1962, during a three-month respite from Columbia, for a folk program *Broadside* was making for the WBAI radio station. They provide us with the earliest known versions of "The Ballad of Donald White" and the full three-verse "Blowin' in the Wind," two of Dylan's most eloquent broadsides.

THE FREEWHEELIN' BOB DYLAN

Recorded: April 24, 1962, to April 24, 1963
Released: May 27, 1963

Side 1: Blowin' in the Wind. Girl from the North Country. Masters of War. Down the Highway. Bob Dylan's Blues. A Hard Rain's a-Gonna Fall. Side 2: Don't Think Twice, It's All Right. Bob Dylan's Dream. Oxford Town. Talkin' World War III Blues. Corrina, Corrina [II]. Honey, Just Allow Me One More Chance. I Shall Be Free.

Other official cuts:

The Bootleg Series: Ramblin' Gamblin' Willie. Let Me Die in My Footsteps. Talkin' Hava Negeilah Blues. Talkin' Bear Mountain Picnic Massacre Blues. Quit Your Lowdown Ways. Worried Blues. Walls of Redwing.
Biograph: Babe, I'm in the Mood for You. Mixed Up Confusion [III].
45: Mixed Up Confusion [IV]/Corrina, Corrina [III]
Freewheelin' MK.1: Talkin' John Birch Paranoid Blues. Rocks and Gravel.

Producers:

1–7 John Hammond
8   Tom Wilson

Musicians:

1–8 Bob Dylan (guitar/harmonica/vocals)
4–6 Richard Wellstood (piano)
4   Howie Collins (guitar)
4–6 Bruce Langhorne (guitar)
4   Leonard Gaskin (bass)
4–6 Herb Lovelle (drums)
5   Art Davis (bass)
5–6 George Barnes (guitar)
6   Gene Ramey (bass)
2   Bill Lee (bass)

1. COLUMBIA STUDIO A
   NEW YORK
   APRIL 24, 1962

CO 70085–2	I'm Going to New Orleans
CO 70086–4	Sally Gal
CO 70087–4	**Ramblin' Gamblin' Willie**
CO 70088–2	Corrina, Corrina
CO 70089–1	The Death of Emmett Till
CO 70090–3	Talkin' John Birch Paranoid Blues
CO 70091–2	(I Heard That) Lonesome Whistle

2. COLUMBIA STUDIO A
   NEW YORK
   APRIL 25, 1962

CO 70096–3	Rocks and Gravel [Solid Road]
CO 70097–1	**Let Me Die in My Footsteps***
CO 70098–1	**Talkin' Hava Negeilah Blues**
CO 70086–1	Sally Gal (remake)
CO 70099–3	Baby, Please Don't Go
CO 70100–3	Milk Cow Blues [I]
CO 70100–4	Milk Cow Blues [II]
CO 70101–1	Wichita Blues [I]

CO 70101–2 Wichita Blues [II]
CO 70102–3 **Talkin' Bear Mountain Picnic Massacre Blues**

3. COLUMBIA STUDIO A
   NEW YORK
   JULY 9, 1962
CO 75717–3 **Babe, I'm in the Mood for You [I]**
CO 75717–4 **Babe, I'm in the Mood for You [II]**
CO 75718–3 **Bob Dylan's Blues**
CO 75719–3 **Blowin' in the Wind**
CO 75720–1 **Quit Your Lowdown Ways**
CO 75721–1 **Honey, Just Allow Me One More Chance**
CO 75722–1 **Down the Highway**
CO 75723–2 **Worried Blues**

4. COLUMBIA STUDIO A
   NEW YORK
   OCTOBER 26, 1962
CO 76981–4 **Corrina, Corrina [II]**
CO 76982–5 Mixed Up Confusion
CO 76983–1 That's All Right, Mama

5. COLUMBIA STUDIO A
   NEW YORK
   NOVEMBER 1, 1962
CO 76982–10 Mixed Up Confusion [II]
CO 76983–3 That's All Right, Mama [II]
CO 76984–1 **Rocks and Gravel**

6. COLUMBIA STUDIO A
   NEW YORK
   NOVEMBER 14, 1962

CO 76981   Corrina, Corrina [III]
CO 76982–11 Mixed Up Confusion [III]
CO 76982–14 Mixed Up Confusion [IV]
CO 77002–1 **Don't Think Twice, It's All Right**
CO 77003–2 The Ballad of Hollis Brown
CO 77004   **Kingsport Town**
CO 77005   Whatcha Gonna Do?
Rumored: *Mixed Up Confusion [Dixieland]*
            Don't Think Twice, It's All Right [electric]

7. COLUMBIA STUDIO A
   NEW YORK
   DECEMBER 6, 1962
CO 77020–1 Hero Blues [I]
CO 77021–1 Whatcha Gonna Do?
CO 77022–1 **Oxford Town**
CO 77023–1 **I Shall Be Free [I]**
CO 77023–3 I Shall Be Free [II]
CO 77023–5 I Shall Be Free [III]
CO 77020–2 Hero Blues [II]
CO 77020–4 Hero Blues [III]
CO 77024–1 **A Hard Rain's a-Gonna Fall**

8. COLUMBIA STUDIO A
   NEW YORK
   APRIL 24, 1963
CO 78487   **Girl from the North Country**
CO 78488   **Masters of War**
CO 78489–3 Walls of Redwing
CO 78490   **Talkin' World War III Blues**
CO 78491   **Bob Dylan's Dream**

The recording of *Freewheelin'*, Dylan's second Columbia effort and his first collection of original songs (okay, "Honey, Just Allow Me One More Chance" is only semi-original), began (in late April 1962) against a backdrop of corporate machinations aimed at dumping Bobby D., branded "Hammond's Folly" by those who sought to question Hammond's "ear" for talent. Even if Dylan was unaware of these internal divisions, he clearly knew he needed to make this album count.

Ironically, within nine months—with *Freewheelin'* not even in the can— Dylan's manager, Albert Grossman, tried to extricate Dylan from his Columbia contract (on the tenuous grounds that he had signed his original contract when not yet twenty-one). By December 1962, though, people at Columbia were determined to hang on to Dylan with all their might, even though this was an artist with one album and one single ("Mixed Up Confusion") to his name, the former of which had sold 5,000 copies and the latter, less.

Clearly, between the first *Freewheelin'* session (April 24) and Hammond's last session with Dylan (December 6), much changed—and Columbia's new interest in the career of the young Minnesotan was based largely on what was coming out of Columbia Studio A. Of course, by December 1962 Dylan had written (and recorded) "Blowin' in the Wind" and "A Hard Rain's a-Gonna Fall," the two songs most responsible for his ascending reputation in folk circles ("Blowin' in the Wind" was published in folk's most prestigious magazine, *Sing Out,* in October 1962, two months before "A Hard Rain's a-Gonna Fall" was accorded the same honor).

One of the curious things about the *Freewheelin'* sessions is the freedom afforded Dylan to record as and when the feeling took him. Six months separate the first *Freewheelin'* sessions from the first band session, during which time Dylan entered a Columbia studio just once (perhaps Dylan was reluctant to record new songs until his future at Columbia was more certain).

Freewheelin' in its released form is essentially a "best of" from one of the most creative years in Dylan's life. The lag between sessions resulted in an album whose sound metamorphosed at least twice. As indicated earlier, Dylan does not seem to have initially realized the importance of giving each album its own identity. If so, he learned the error of his ways real quick! The original working title for *Freewheelin'* was *Bob Dylan's Blues* and the songs recorded in April and July 1962 certainly suggest that—despite recording the likes of "The Death of Emmett Till," "Let Me Die in My Footsteps," and "Blowin' in the Wind"—he initially envisaged an album with its roots in the blues. Dylan's increasing infatuation with figures like Robert Johnson was certainly given full expression at the April 1962 sessions.

"Milk Cow Blues" as cut on the twenty-fourth is a fascinating melting pot of the form, distilled by a Dylan vocal that owes as much to Elvis Presley as Kokomo Arnold ("Milk Cow Blues'" ostensible author). The two extant takes

(which came after two false starts) both have much to recommend them, though it is only on the second take that Dylan decides to add a verse from Leadbelly's "Good Morning Blues," hoping to achieve the requisite blend (a lovely example of how he can "adapt" a song between takes). When Dylan sings "I believe I need a suck!" he betrays a lasciviousness that may not have been in keeping with his then image, but directly presages the bawdiness of *The Basement Tapes.*

The April sessions contained two further stabs at the blues—"Corrina, Corrina" and "Rocks and Gravel"—both later attempted with a makeshift band (apparently at Hammond's suggestion) at sessions in the fall. The acoustic versions have perhaps more to recommend them (they certainly have a lot more to recommend them than the two halfhearted "talkin' blues" cut at these sessions—"Talkin' Hava Negeilah" and "Talkin' Bear Mountain"—both later included on *The Bootleg Series*). "Corrina, Corrina," in particular, takes the folk process to its limits, turning a simple folk ballad into a tortured blues, transposing lines (indeed one entire verse) from Robert Johnson's "Stones in My Passway" to achieve Dylan's purpose. (In a live rendition at Gerdes a few days before this session he had interpolated lines from three further Johnson gems— "32.20 Blues," "Me and the Devil Blues," and "Hellbound on My Trail.")

Presumably Dylan's intention was always to straddle the traditional/topical divide—integrating the topical songs he cut in April and July with these examples of the blues. As it is, of the various blues tunes recorded in April and July, only "Down the Highway," an original blues that owes an enormous debt to Robert Johnson's "Crossroads Blues," and Dylan's adaptation of Henry Thomas's "Honey, Just Allow Me One More Chance," survived the transition from *Bob Dylan's Blues* to *Freewheelin'.*

Among those songs lost in the flood is perhaps the best vocal performance given at the *Freewheelin'* sessions. "Worried Blues" convinces you that this man was always one of the finest of blues singers.

Freewheelin' only became more black and white, and consequently less blue, after the failure of the three band sessions (October 26, November 1, and November 14). Though Dylan certainly didn't stint from recording topical songs at the April and July sessions, it was really the likes of "Oxford Town," "A Hard Rain's a-Gonna Fall" (quickly, and erroneously, seized on as dealing with the Cuban Missile Crisis), "Talkin' World War III Blues," and "Masters of War"—all recorded at the final two *Freewheelin'* sessions in December 1962 and April 1963—that first defined Dylan as a spokesman for his generation.

The electric *Freewheelin'* sessions were one of the first points in Dylan's career when he seemed on the verge of losing his sense of purpose. The fact that he spent three sessions trying to cut (and, in the case of "Mixed Up Confusion," recut twice) four songs with electric backing—"Corrina, Corrina," "That's All Right, Mama," "Rocks and Gravel," and "Mixed Up Confusion"—hardly suggests an impromptu idea that came up one afternoon. Clearly there was some reasoning behind the author of "Blowin' in the Wind" recording—and even releasing—the most rockabilly representation of a yesterimage Robert Zimmerman (or was it Elston Gunn?) could muster.

What might have added to the sense of confusion (sic) would have been a single which included "That's All Right, Mama," attempted at both the October 26 and November 1 sessions and presumably originally envisaged as a B side to "Mixed Up Confusion." The song's unmistakable association with Presley, and its unimaginative rearrangement here (Dylan still impertinently copy-

righted his arrangement), hardly suggested a great new talent (although it is worth hearing the October 26, 1962, version just to hear Dylan say at the end, after the most ridiculously frantic version imaginable, "Let's do it again—fast!"). Despite expressing his admiration for early Presley to both Rachel Price of *FM Stereo Guide* and Robert Shelton, Dylan's rock and roll affiliations were largely unknown in the Village at this time. (When Cynthia Gooding, on her "Folksinger's Choice" radio show in March 1962, talks about meeting him three years earlier in Minneapolis, when he "wanted to be a rock and roll singer," Dylan quickly changes the subject.)

That Dylan himself, and presumably Albert Grossman (who was in attendance at these sessions), always intended "Mixed Up Confusion" to be an A-sided single seems self-evident. Their reasons remain harder to fathom. Three sessions, fourteen takes, a couple of new arrangements (the accentuated acoustic guitar of takes five and ten eventually losing out to the honky-tonk piano) all suggest real effort being expended on "Mixed Up Confusion." Yet, according to Dylan himself, he stormed out of the third electric session (November 14) in disgust. If so, it may well have been after Grossman convinced him to attempt a Dixieland version of the song with Dick Mosman on piano and Panama Francis on drums (no substantive evidence of this Dixieland take—long rumored—now resides in Columbia's records though possibly they never got as far as a finished take). All of which may well suggest a certain exasperation on Dylan's part at his first experience of recording with a band (though he did store guitarist Langhorne's name in the ol' memory bank, making the call two years later that resulted in his sterling work on *Bringing It All Back Home*).

It is presumably also Langhorne who contributes the tasteful guitar fills that embellish the last three songs recorded at the November 14, 1962, session. If Dylan did leave in a huff after the Dixieland "Mixed Up Confusion," he evidently returned in a minute and a huff. Four songs—all acoustic—were recorded after the *Freewheelin'* band packed up their instruments and left Studio A. I say four but, if Nat Hentoff's liner notes to *Freewheelin'* are to be believed, "Don't Think Twice, It's All Right" was actually recorded with the November 14 band and an electric version was assigned to the album. Even more mysteriously, according to Columbia's files, the released version of "Don't Think Twice" was a first take (again, a remarkable performance for a first take—perhaps Dylan put all his own mixed-up confusion into this one song). Could it be that the released version was recorded with the session musicians, who were then subsequently removed from the mix? It seems inconceivable—a band rip-roaring through the same rendition as on the album? I think not. Yet, as of 1995, the mystery (and the liner notes) remains.

Whatever the case, "Don't Think Twice" sees Dylan getting back on track. Also cut in quick succession at the end of this November 14 session were three songs that, although not destined to make the album, or match the exhilaration of "Don't Think Twice," all have some worth. The version of "Hollis Brown," with some tasteful embellishment from Langhorne, I believe, has the extra verse (the happy-go-lucky one about the gangrene in his side cutting like a knife) that the Witmark version contains but the *Times* take does not. It is a more enjoyable performance than the unrelenting one on *Times* (yes, I know that's the idea but it still feels a bit like banging your head against a wall— nice when it stops). "Kingsport Town" is a curiosity—nothing more, nothing less—simply because it is such an obvious rewrite of "Who's Gonna Shoe Your Horse?" while "Whatcha Gonna Do"

could have fit very nicely into the fast-fadin' *Bob Dylan's Blues* concept. Dylan was to recut this song at the final session of the year (December 6), along with an early stab (actually three early stabs) at the deeply misogynistic "Hero Blues," sentiments better expressed on "It Ain't Me Babe."

The December 6, 1962, session was presumably intended to complete Dylan's second album. It was certainly another inspirational session. Thankfully a complete record of this session has passed to collectors, presumably as a result of Columbia mislaying the session after marking it "Audition—Folk Singer" (see the accompanying studio sheet). Dylan again manages to stamp definitive performances on songs in a single take. The recording of "Oxford Town" even elicits Hammond's astonished response at song's end—"Don't tell me that's all?" If "Oxford Town" is just the sort of riposte one might expect Dylan to dispatch in one go, managing "A Hard Rain's a-Gonna Fall" in a single take suggests a remarkable level of determination and concentration on his part. He had been playing the song for a couple of months, and that month it appeared in *Sing Out,* but the version on *Freewheelin'* still sounds as fresh (and relevant) as the night he wrote it in the Gaslight Café.

The other song from this session to make (indeed close) *Freewheelin'* was also a first take. "I Shall Be Free," though, is one of those rare instances where—after cutting a perfectly good first take—Dylan attempts to cut a superior version, before deciding he preferred the original take all along. Dylan's gift for vocal improvisation is beautifully illustrated by the very next take of "I Shall Be Free," Dylan taking Leadbelly's "We Shall Be Free" and then introducing a totally new off-the-cuff introduction in the same talking blues style, complete with rhyming lines and complaints about his current situation, but updated and modern references such as telephone books being burnt to keep warm and even a casual reference to his own trademark, his Huckleberry Finn hat.

The December session was not in fact to be the final *Freewheelin'* session. At the end of April 1963, Dylan was to cut five further tracks, four of which would make the album. There is something rather curious about the fact that Dylan returned to Columbia's studios in April 1963, nineteen days *before* the rehearsal for the "Ed Sullivan Show" that supposedly led to the removal of "Talkin' John Birch" from *Freewheelin'*. There seem several possibilities, none entirely satisfactory: (1) that the April 24 session was originally intended to be the first session for Dylan's next album. This seems unlikely given that *Freewheelin'* was not even in the shops; (2) that the decision by the powers-that-be to cut "John Birch" had already been taken before the "Ed Sullivan Show," in which case why would Dylan attempt to rehearse the song unless he was being deliberately confrontational (it has been known); or (3) that Dylan had already decided he wanted to resequence the album, thus always intending to replace the four offending items with the songs cut at the April 24 session.

The last of the three possibilities seems the most plausible, though it still does not explain Columbia's willingness to recall an already sequenced, pressed, cut-and-dried album by one of their minor artists (a couple of hundred copies on the West Coast eluded Columbia's attempts to recall them and now command five figure sums). That said, the removal of "Talkin' John Birch" (to its wittier cousin "Talkin' World War III Blues"), the hokey "Ramblin' Gamblin' Willie," and the anomalous "Rocks and Gravel" hardly qualify as great losses—particularly as they allowed Dylan to show how much his time in England had improved his awareness of the folk

process and the need to span all themes of folk music convincingly: whether it be remembrances of a lost love ("Girl from the North Country"), longing for a yesteryear ("Bob Dylan's Dream"), or the taunting of the powers-that-be ("Masters of War").

These last-minute changes also meant that no songs on this new *Freewheelin'* were recorded before July 1962—the beginning of a soon-to-be-familiar pattern (Dylan has always tended to discard the results of early sessions). Though the exclusion of "Let Me Die in My Footsteps," perhaps the finest of Dylan's pre-"Blowin'" efforts, was a sad loss (the song as scheduled for *Freewheelin'*, and as it appears on *The Bootleg Series*, has verse five edited from the full take), the new *Freewheelin'* did not suffer the fate of *Bob Dylan*, disowned by its author before it had even made the shops. *The Freewheelin' Bob Dylan* was a collection Dylan felt he could be proud of and clearly still is. He has continually pulled songs from it on all his post-accident tours. The April 1963 session and a Town Hall show twelve days earlier (which Columbia wisely recorded for a possible live album) gave Dylan a little breathing space to consider his next move.

He barely needed it. At this stage in his writing, the songs really did pour out of him. In the rock field, many artists stockpile their songs for years before making their recording debut—and much fine flotsam can be lost along the way. In Dylan's case he was already a Columbia artist when the words he sang became his own. Perhaps the scale of his writing in the early months of 1963 can best be illustrated by his Town Hall set. Of the fifteen original songs he performed on April 12, 1963, just three were already Columbia recordings, and only one of these was destined to appear on *Freewheelin'*—"A Hard Rain's a-Gonna Fall."

THE WITMARK AND
BROADSIDE DEMOS

Recorded: July 1962 to Summer 1964

The Bootleg Series: Walkin' Down the Line. When the Ship Comes In. The Times They Are a-Changin'. *Broadside Reunion:* I'd Hate to Be You on That Dreadful Day. Train a-Travelin'. *Broadside Ballads Vol. 1:* Only a Hobo. Talkin' Devil. John Brown. Let Me Die in My Footsteps.

Other official cuts:

"XTV 221567" (PROMO): John Brown. Long Ago, Far Away. Only a Hobo. Long Time Gone. Ain't Gonna Grieve. The Death of Emmett Till. I'd Hate to Be You on That Dreadful Day. I Shall Be Free.

Musicians:
1–17 Bob Dylan (guitar/harmonica/vocals)
6 Gil Turner (backing vocals)
7 Happy Traum (vocals)

1. THE WITMARK STUDIO
   NEW YORK
   JULY 1962
EU 731107 Blowin' in the Wind

2. THE WITMARK STUDIO
   NEW YORK
   NOVEMBER 1962
EU 747454 **Long Ago, Far Away**

3. BROADSIDE OFFICES
   NEW YORK
   NOVEMBER 1962
I'd Hate to Be You on That Dreadful Day
Oxford Town
Paths of Victory
Walkin' Down the Line
I Shall Be Free
Train a-Travelin'
Cuban Missile Crisis

4. BROADSIDE OFFICES
   NEW YORK
   NOVEMBER 1962
Ye Playboys and Playgirls

5. THE WITMARK STUDIO
   NEW YORK
   DECEMBER 1962
EU 757677 A Hard Rain's a-Gonna Fall
EU ??   Tomorrow Is a Long Time
EU 757679 **The Death of Emmett Till**
EU 757680 Let Me Die in My Footsteps
EU 757681 The Ballad of Hollis Brown
EU 757683 Quit Your Lowdown Ways
EU 757684 Babe, I'm in the Mood for You

6. BROADSIDE OFFICES
   NEW YORK
   JANUARY 19, 1963
Talkin' Devil
Farewell

7. BROADSIDE OFFICES
   NEW YORK
   JANUARY 24, 1963
Masters of War
Let Me Die in My Footsteps [Traum vocal]

8. BROADSIDE OFFICES
   NEW YORK
   FEBRUARY 1963
John Brown
Only a Hobo

9. THE WITMARK STUDIO
   NEW YORK
   WINTER 1963
EU ??   Bound to Lose
EU ??   All Over You
EU ??   **I'd Hate to Be You on That Dreadful Day**
EU ??   Talkin' John Birch Paranoid Blues

10. THE WITMARK STUDIO
    NEW YORK
    MARCH 1963
EU 766003   Don't Think Twice, It's All Right

11. THE WITMARK STUDIO
    NEW YORK
    MARCH 1963
EU 765994   **Long Time Gone**
EU 765995   Masters of War
EU 765996   Farewell
EU 765997   Oxford Town

12. THE WITMARK STUDIO
    NEW YORK
    MARCH 1963
EU ??   **Walkin' Down the Line**

13. THE WITMARK STUDIO
    NEW YORK
    APRIL 1963

EU 773440   **I Shall Be Free**
EU ??   Bob Dylan's Blues
EU 773442   Bob Dylan's Dream
EU 773443   Boots of Spanish Leather

14. THE WITMARK STUDIO
    NEW YORK
    MAY 1963
EU 775845   Girl from the North Country
EU ??   Seven Curses

15. THE WITMARK STUDIO
    NEW YORK
    MAY 1963
EU 775851   Hero Blues

16. THE WITMARK STUDIO
    NEW YORK
    AUGUST 1963
EU 790675   Whatcha Gonna Do?
EU 790676   Gypsy Lou

17. THE WITMARK STUDIO
    NEW YORK
    AUGUST 1963
EU 793656   **Ain't Gonna Grieve**
EU 793657   **John Brown**
EU 793658   **Only a Hobo**

In the crucial months either side of Dylan's first trip to London in December 1962, it was not Columbia Studios that best documented Dylan's personal and professional traumas in song. Rather he began to call on Broadside's humble abode on a regular basis, where he would play Sis Cunningham and Gordon Freisen his new songs. At a time when he chose to spend just one afternoon in a Columbia studio (December 6, 1962), Dylan recorded a half dozen "sessions" at Sis Cunningham's, who dutifully transcribed the best of the bunch for the magazine. This period coincided with an equal willingness on Dylan's part to "call in" on Witmark Music, his music publishers, and demo a few more hot-off-the-press ditties. It is these Broadside and Witmark demos that truly document Dylan's writing between November 1962 and late April 1963, when

he returned to Columbia's Studios to flesh out the recalled *Freewheelin'*.

Having cut just one publishers' demo for Witmark between July—when Grossman skillfully extricated Dylan from his Leeds Music contract—and November 1962, Dylan was to demo some twenty-two songs for his new publishers between November 14, 1962 (the final "Mixed Up Confusion" session) and April 24, 1963 (the last *Freewheelin'* session)—as well as the thirteen songs he recorded for *Broadside*.

The Witmark demos were recorded by a young engineer, Ivan Augenblink, in full-track mono on quarter-inch tape at 7½ ips (the engineer was expected to reuse tape, such was the parsimonious nature of the operation) in a small room on the fifth floor of 488 Madison Avenue, almost directly across the street from Columbia's main building. Acetates would be cut on a lathe at the time of the sessions to be forwarded to interested parties, though Dylan himself never asked for an acetate or tape (Augenblink's boss, Artie Mogull, would direct him to discard demos after they came out on a record. Though this advice was evidently not always heeded, some Dylan demos were almost certainly discarded before copies could be made.) According to Augenblink, the music arrangers on the same floor would ask him to shut the studio door (as well as closing their own) when Dylan came in, lest his idiosyncratic vocals disturb their delicate sensibilities.

Among the songs recorded by Witmark in these months are seven for which no Columbia studio take is known. Once again, aesthetic quality was not necessarily a key factor in these omissions.

Certainly "Tomorrow Is a Long Time," "Long Time Gone," and "Walkin' Down the Line" (one of the more pleasant oddities on *The Bootleg Series*) might all have warranted reexamination at Studio A. "Long Time Gone" is a typical Dylan "gotta travel on" song, crossing the fatalism of a "Moonshine Blues" with the sense of yearning for something better that occurs in "Restless Farewell" ("just give to me a tombstone/ with it clearly marked upon . . .") while "Walkin' Down the Line," is a less cynical "Guess I'm Doing Fine."

Then there is "Tomorrow Is a Long Time," which, even with a lapse like "sunrise in the sky" (where else, pray tell, would it be), is one of Dylan's most poetic love songs. That Dylan never recorded this song for *Freewheelin'* (or *Times* or *Another Side*) is one of the greater mysteries the man has thrown up in the last thirty-something years. It is certainly not because he quickly discarded the song. The first known recording was made back in August 1962—just two months after Suze Rotolo took his heart in a suitcase all the way to Italy—at Tony Glover's Minneapolis apartment (this tape remains in the sole possession of Glover).

The last known version (at least from this era) can also be found on a Glover home tape, made in July 1963. In April he played the song at New York's Town Hall (just twelve days before cutting five new songs for *Freewheelin'*). Betwixt these three recordings, and shortly before leaving for Europe and a hoped-for rendezvous with Suze in December '62, Dylan recorded his demo version for Witmark.

Of all the many versions of "Tomorrow"—and it is a song Dylan has returned to in 1970, 1978, and even the occasional Never-Ending Tour surprise (notably a shouted request at Toronto in 1990, to which he replied, "It sure is. Awfully long," before delivering the goods)—the Witmark version transcends them all (and that includes the many fine covers of the song by the likes of Elvis Presley, Rod Stewart, Sandy Denny, and Nick Drake). I can express it no better than Mr. Cable, back in 1978, "This song has been recorded by many people but nothing comes close to this magnetically emotive rendering." The only reason I can think of for not cutting this song at the final *Freewheelin'* session was that Dylan and Suze had, by this point, become reconciled and he no longer felt at one with the song's sentiments (the Town Hall performance came after, and was possibly as a result of, a furious row between the pair that very afternoon).

The "Broadside" sessions contain no such gems, but they certainly illustrate Dylan's (and Cunningham's) burgeoning conception of him as "the voice of a generation." After his return from England, Dylan did not debut his new ballads for the magazine ("Girl from the North Country" or "Boots of Spanish Leather," both based heavily on Martin Carthy's arrangement of "Scarborough Fair"), nor his rewrite of "Lord Franklin," "Bob Dylan's Dream." Instead, he pulled out "Masters of War" just days after grafting these antiwar sentiments onto the traditional Child ballad, "Nottamun Town." A couple of weeks later, he returned to Cunningham's apartment with another antiwar anthem, the turgid "John Brown," and a reworking of an earlier effort, "Man on the Street." Based loosely on "Only a Miner," "Only a Hobo" once again illustrated Dylan's enduring fascination with those on the outer rim of society.

Though March would mark the end of Dylan's Broadside sessions, he would continue to demo material for Witmark (including another "Only a Hobo") while cutting his third album. He also began the practice of lodging Columbia outtakes as "demo" recordings with Witmark, perhaps indicative of a move away from others presenting songs on his behalf (versions of "Walls of Redwing" and "Eternal Circle" from the August Columbia sessions appear on the Witmark reels, raising serious doubts about the attribution of "Walls of Redwing" to the final *Freewheelin'* session in *The Bootleg Series* notes).

THE TIMES THEY ARE A-CHANGIN'

Recorded: August 6 to October 31, 1963
Released: January 13, 1964

Side 1: The Times They Are a-Changin'. The Ballad of Hollis Brown. With God on Our Side. One Too Many Mornings. North Country Blues. Side 2: Only a Pawn in Their Game. Boots of Spanish Leather. When the Ship Comes In. The Lonesome Death of Hattie Carroll. Restless Farewell.

Other official cuts:

The Bootleg Series: Seven Curses. Paths of Victory. Moonshine Blues. Only a Hobo. Eternal Circle. Suzy (The Cough Song).
Biograph: Percy's Song. Lay Down Your Weary Tune.

Producer:
1–3, 6–8 Tom Wilson

Musicians:
1–2, 8 Bob Dylan (guitar/harmonica/vocals)
3–7 Bob Dylan (guitar/harmonica/piano/
    vocals)

1. COLUMBIA STUDIO A
   NEW YORK
   AUGUST 6, 1963
CO 78969   *Boots of Spanish Leather*
CO 78970   *Only a Pawn in Their Game*
CO 78971   **North Country Blues**
CO 78972   *The Ballad of Hollis Brown*
CO 78973   **Seven Curses**
CO 78974   *With God on Our Side*
CO 78975–4 Farewell
CO 78976   *New Orleans Rag*

2. COLUMBIA STUDIO A
   NEW YORK
   AUGUST 7, 1963
CO 78972–3 **The Ballad of Hollis Brown**
CO 78974–4 **With God on Our Side**
CO 78970–6 **Only a Pawn in Their Game**
CO 78969   **Boots of Spanish Leather**

CO 78977   **Walls of Redwing**
CO 78978   Eternal Circle
CO 78976   *New Orleans Rag*

3. COLUMBIA STUDIO A
   NEW YORK
   AUGUST 12, 1963
CO 78979   **Paths of Victory**
CO 78976   New Orleans Rag
CO 78980   Hero Blues
CO 78981   **Moonshine Blues**
CO 78978   Eternal Circle
CO 78982   **Only a Hobo**

4. THE WITMARK STUDIO
   NEW YORK
   SEPTEMBER 1963
EU ??   **When the Ship Comes In**

5. THE WITMARK STUDIO
   NEW YORK
   EARLY OCTOBER 1963
   EU 798069 **The Times They Are a-Changin'**

6. COLUMBIA STUDIO A
   NEW YORK
   OCTOBER 23, 1963
   CO 79679   **The Lonesome Death of Hattie Carroll**
   CO 79680   **When the Ship Comes In**
   CO 79681   *The Times They Are a-Changin'*
   CO 79682–1   Percy's Song
   CO 79683–1   East Laredo Blues
   CO 79684–1   *Key to the Highway*
   CO 79685–1   That's All Right, Mama

7. COLUMBIA STUDIO A
   NEW YORK
   OCTOBER 24, 1963
   CO 79689–1   **Eternal Circle**
   CO 79690   **One Too Many Mornings**
   CO 79681–7   **The Times They Are a-Changin'**
   CO 79682–3   **Percy's Song**
   CO 79691–1   **Lay Down Your Weary Tune**
   CO 79692–1   **Suzy (The Cough Song)**
   CO 79693–1   New Orleans Rag

8. COLUMBIA STUDIO A
   NEW YORK
   OCTOBER 31, 1963
   CO 79788   **Restless Farewell**

The gap between the first and last sessions of *Times* and *Freewheelin'*, barely three months, remains by far the shortest between Dylan albums. As such, it should not be unduly surprising that his third album incorporates large elements of the style, tone, and content of its predecessor. Indeed, five of the songs debuted at April's Town Hall showpiece—"New Orleans Rag," "Hollis Brown," "Walls of Redwing," "Hero Blues," and "With God on Our Side"—were attempted at the first round of *Times* sessions in August 1963. Also composed before the final *Freewheelin'* session but held over for the next project were "Boots of Spanish Leather," "Farewell" (first recorded back in January), "Paths of Victory," "Only a Hobo," and probably "Seven Curses" (all of which were demoed for Broadside and and/or Witmark between November 1962 and May 1963).

"Only a Pawn in Their Game," the harrowing "North Country Blues," and "Eternal Circle," on the other hand, all date from the weeks leading up to the August sessions (6, 7, 12). Not surprisingly, these songs receive three of Dylan's most arresting performances. "Eternal Circle," in particular, bears little relation to anything recorded by Dylan up to this point. Indeed it is

Dylan's first song-within-a-song. He was to make two attempts at the song in August, the second of which has only come down to collectors as a "long false start" (this first attempt contains a far more distinctive melody and inventive guitar work in general than either of the complete takes). Though the October version now released on *The Bootleg Series* has much to recommend it, one can't help feeling that Dylan lost the thread of the song somewhere (though he persevered with the song in concert, performing it as late as May 1964 at the Royal Festival Hall). Alternately, Dylan may have come to feel that, as songs-within-songs, "Lay Down Your Weary Tune" and "Mr. Tambourine Man" fulfilled his intentions far better (although, as it happens, neither of these songs would be released in their original incarnations either).

In fact *Times* stands as the first "great lost album" of Mr. Dylan's checkered career. The truth to tell, at least five songs of a caliber only matched by a couple of the cuts on *Times* were discarded back in October 1963: "Seven Curses," "Eternal Circle," "Moonshine Blues," "Percy's Song," and "Lay Down Your Weary Tune." The omission of "Moonshine Blues" and "Seven Curses" was almost certainly a reflection of their "traditionality" (the former is a traditional arrangement, the latter a clever adaptation of the traditional "Anathea"—which has thirteen, not seven, curses but fails to name them).

Indeed, Dylan came to discard all but one of the songs cut at the first *Times* session and everything recorded at the third (and final) August session, suggesting that he was once again failing to hang on to good things from his past when reviewing songs prior to sequencing. "Moonshine Blues," cut on August 12, certainly has a pathos that the man had been hunting for since *Bob Dylan* (and, frankly, fails to find on several, more sanctimonious cuts on *Times*).

Thankfully, the August 7 session was one of those inspirational days, Dylan recording four album tracks in the first two hours, then cutting "Eternal Circle" and "Walls of Redwing," both of which were lodged with Witmark for copyright purposes. However . . . the August 12 session found Dylan unsure about what to record and resorting to a little metaphoric rummaging through the drawers. The results are certainly interesting, even if—of the six songs cut— "Eternal Circle" was the only "new work" and D. had already recorded a complete version on the seventh.

This third session began with Dylan at the piano, experimenting with three uptempo throwbacks, the sardonic "Hero Blues" coming last. After his first real piano work in a Columbia studio, Dylan reverted to guitar for the next two songs, "Moonshine Blues" and "Only a Hobo," both depicting a life without mercy and a death without honor. The sense one gets from all the songs Dylan attempted on the twelfth— "Eternal Circle" excepted—is that this was a session booked in advance, that Dylan had already attempted all the top-drawer songs he had at hand on the seventh, and that this was more a session for trying out ideas than making progress on album number three. The

songs needed to fill out this album were not destined to be leftovers from the *Freewheelin'* era. Dylan recognized the need for another batch of songs to match the likes of "North Country Blues" and "Boots of Spanish Leather."

The remaining songs came fast. A couple of weeks on the road, followed by a week in Carmel, and voilà! *Times* was not going to be another *Freewheelin'*—a year of hard labor and false starts. Dylan was learning how to say what he wanted to say—the heavy concentration on message songs was no accident (even the outtakes are mostly "message" songs, albeit ones relying on subtle social observation). Just two months after the initial trio of sessions, Dylan was back at Studio A, with Tom Wilson at the helm, nodding where necessary and rolling tape. In just two more afternoons, Dylan cut the requisite songs to craft a full album, while still finding time to tinker at the piano at both sessions.

Though a public debut for his piano-playing would have to wait until the next album ("Black Crow Blues"), a few songs long attributed to the *Another Side* session actually date from these final *Times* sessions. While "East Laredo Blues" and "Suzy" (aka "The Cough Song") are innocuous enough, the highlight of these piano workouts is undoubtedly his (third Columbia) rendition of "That's All Right, Mama" on the 24th (at least until one gets to hear the version of Big Bill Broonzy's "Key to the Highway" he recorded in a single take at the same session). This "That's All Right, Mama" puts both *Freewheelin'* outtakes to shame, Dylan maintaining a rhythm all his own while retaining the song's lyrical grit with a highly individual vocal interpretation. Even when the song begins to drag at the end, it sounds for a split second like Dylan is about to start up his very own penny-ante piano roll. A fascinating performance, a lovely example of the man's sense of spontaneity and, one suspects, a great tension reliever at the end of a fraught session.

If the first October session started promisingly enough, after cutting usable versions of "Hattie Carroll" and "When the Ship Comes In," Dylan had become bogged down while working on what he probably already envisaged as the album's title track, "The Times They Are a-Changin'." Much has been made of this song (note recent howls of outrage at Dylan permitting its use in a TV ad for an accountancy firm) but there seems little doubt that—as opposed to "Blowin' in the Wind," the impact of which was largely fortuitous—with this song Dylan set out to write an anthem. When Tony Glover asked why he had written such an obvious rallying call, Dylan apparently told him, "It seems to be what the people like to hear." Before entering Studio A, Dylan had already played the song to Cunningham in her apartment and demoed it at the piano for Witmark. Yet he couldn't seem to get the song in a releasable form. Eventually he gave up, moving onto another anti-judge song, "Percy's Song." "Percy's Song," though, proved equally unsatisfactory and Dylan abandoned himself in a little honky-tonkin'.

The following day, things could not have been more different. "Eternal Circle" may have been intended as just a loosener, but he still got it in one take. "One Too Many Mornings," perhaps the best "performance" on the released album, came next, followed by the "Times" he'd been looking for on the twenty-third, recorded with a minimum of fuss. "Percy's Song" had also been mysteriously transformed overnight, embellished by a cascading refrain that turned what was already a good tune into something truly fine. If "Percy's Song" was a beautiful performance, the last genuine take of the day, "Lay Down Your Weary Tune," is simply one of Dylan's most sublime works (and yet again, Dylan cut this hymn in one take).

Which begs the question, why were "Percy's Song" and "Lay Down Your Weary Tune" absent from *Times*? Both songs were played at Carnegie Hall two days later (and were scheduled for inclusion on the nixed *Bob Dylan in Concert* album), and "Percy's Song" would certainly not have been out of place alongside the likes of "Hattie Carroll." Cable speculates that it may have been just one long song too many (it clocks in at eight minutes), given that "With God on Our Side" and "The Ballad of Hollis Brown" were already planned for the album.

"Lay Down Your Weary Tune" is, I suspect, another matter. I would think there is really only one suitable slot for this song on *Times*—and that is as the album's finale. Whereas "Restless Farewell" is nothing more than a (very self-conscious) apologia for a misspent youth, "Lay Down Your Weary Tune" marked a new phase in Dylan's songwriting. This is the link between the highly symbolic "Hard Rain" and the soon-to-come "Chimes of Freedom" and "Mr. Tambourine Man." The song, based on a traditional Scottish tune (though you'd hardly know it), is one of Dylan's most inventive arrangements. The anthemic quality Dylan had been searching for on "Paths of Victory" and "When the Ship Comes In," to name but two, is fully realized in this paean to the beauty of nature and song.

That "Restless Farewell" ended up on *Times* instead was clearly a last-minute decision based not on the song's relative merits—enjoyable as "Restless Farewell" is—but on the closing message Dylan wished to deliver: a final few digs on an album of message songs. Recorded at a session organized with the express purpose of cutting this song, "Restless Farewell" was Dylan's immediate reaction to the "dust of rumors" a *Newsweek* reporter had attempted to bury him in the previous week and was probably written at the same time as the eighth and ninth outlined epitaphs. Details of this final *Times* session were impossible to find in Sony's records under the song's published title. When finally located, its working title turned out to be "Bob Dylan's Restless Epitaph"—evidently Dylan was already looking to write his farewell to song. "Restless Farewell" does not just confront Dylan's past but expresses a wish that he could just walk away from it all.

In this sense alone, "Restless Farewell" is very much a departure from the rest of *Times*. Prior to October 31, *Times* had been an album with a one-dimensional sound, a one-dimensional message in a one-dimensional world. Even as great a song as "Hattie Carroll" is a gross misrepresentation of the facts of the case it was based upon. "Restless Farewell" at least suggested that Dylan was becoming aware of the need to step into the three-dimensional world of confused motives and misguided conceits.

ANOTHER SIDE OF BOB DYLAN

Recorded: June 9, 1964
Released: August 8, 1964

Side 1: All I Really Want to Do. Black Crow Blues. Spanish Harlem Incident. Chimes of Freedom. I Shall Be Free No. 10. To Ramona. Side 2: Motorpsycho Nitemare. My Back Pages. I Don't Believe You. Ballad in Plain D. It Ain't Me Babe.

Other official cuts:

The Bootleg Series: Mama, You Bin on My Mind.
XTV 221567 (PROMO): I'll Keep It with Mine.
Highway 61 Interactive CD-ROM: Mr. Tambourine Man. I Shall Be Free.

Producer:
5 Tom Wilson

Musician:
Bob Dylan (guitar/harmonica/piano/vocals)

1. THE WITMARK STUDIO
   NEW YORK
   DECEMBER 1963
EU ?? Paths of Victory

2. THE WITMARK STUDIO
   NEW YORK
   JANUARY 1964
EU 810147 Guess I'm Doing Fine
EU ??   Baby, Let Me Follow You Down

3. THE WITMARK STUDIO
   NEW YORK
   JUNE 1964
EU 848210 Mr. Tambourine Man
EU 848211 Mama, You Bin on My Mind

4. DEMO LODGED WITH WITMARK
   NEW YORK OR WOODSTOCK, N.Y.
   SUMMER 1964
EU 903122 **I'll Keep It with Mine**

5. COLUMBIA STUDIO A
   NEW YORK
   JUNE 9, 1964
CO 82213 Denise, Denise
CO 82214 **It Ain't Me Babe**
CO 82215 **To Ramona**
CO 82216 **Spanish Harlem Incident**
CO 82217 **Ballad in Plain D**
CO 82218 **I Don't Believe You**
CO 82219 **Chimes of Freedom**
CO 82220 **Motorpsycho Nitemare***
CO 82221 **Mr. Tambourine Man**
CO 82222 **All I Really Want To Do**
CO 82223 **Black Crow Blues**
CO 82224 **I Shall Be Free No. 10***
CO 82225 **Mama, You Bin on My Mind**
CO 82226 **My Back Pages**

The one song Dylan recorded in the two and a half months between the completion of *Times* and its release—at one of his last sessions for Witmark—suggested that the troubles of the world were beginning to rest rather firmly on this twenty-two-year-old's shoulders. The way Dylan delivers "Guess I'm Doing Fine"—shortlisted for the original four-CD version of *The Bootleg Series*—belies the seeming optimism in the song title. He self-evidently was not doing fine. Recorded at the onset of a new year, "Guess I'm Doing Fine" did not bode well for Dylan's psychological well-being.

Unfortunately, save for three extremely crude piano demos he made for Witmark, the only other studio recordings made by Dylan in 1964, the year when he advanced from restless farewells to the gates of Eden, resulted from a single night in June. While polishing off a couple of bottles of Beaujolais, Dylan cut his fourth Columbia album in one all-night session.

A single day in the studio in fourteen months might not cause undue alarm today, when every album must be hyped into existence, but back in 1964 it must have caused a fair few jitters in corporateland, especially as *Times* had just cracked the Top Twenty. Hence, one presumes, Columbia's seeming determination to keep recording Dylan shows for a possible stopgap live album (the May Royal Festival Hall show, the July Newport Festival set, and his triumphant return to the New York stage in October were all recorded by Dylan's label).

Rather than providing evidence of an increasing distaste for the studio, though, Dylan's single-session album was the result of a six-month search for some new direction (as in *Another Side*). That this search is not documented by any known Dylan studio recordings save "Guess I'm Doing Fine" and what are presumably early June piano demos of "Tam-

bourine Man" and "Mama, You Bin on My Mind" (the master tapes of which have been lost. They come down to us only from acetates cut at the time) is a real shame. Dylan's discovery of "chains of flashing images" (with "Chimes of Freedom" and "Mr. Tambourine Man," both begun on his February "on the road" jaunt) seemed to presage a whole new approach to lyric writing. Unfortunately the traumas of his irrevocable breakup with Suze Rotolo in March led Dylan (temporarily) into a period of self-recrimination and personal doubt that reached its nadir in a Greek village and "Ballad in Plain D," one of a half-dozen songs completed in a single week in Vernilya at the end of May.

Another Side is an album that has survived the ravages of critical opinion remarkably well. According to Paul Cable, the *Another Side* session "illustrates that the use of the word 'genius' in referring to Dylan is not just something that has arisen out of the semantic excesses of pop journalism," while Paul Williams calls *Another Side* "a rich, complex album." Even Shelton believed it successfully captures "weariness, cynicism, and road ennui," all the while enunciating "new self-reliant directions." All three, I believe, view the album with the benefit of hindsight. Dylan's playful rearrangement of language, first evidenced on *Another Side*, culminated in *Bringing It All Back Home* and *Highway 61 Revisited*. It is this that transforms Dylan's fourth album in their eyes from a series of half-formed "abstract threats" into an audacious refutation of the "Protesty people."

In reality, the *Another Side* session was a typical Dylan session—flashes of sheer brilliance, improvisational flair, songs coming together and falling apart (in fairly equal measures)—in the studio. The difference this time is that Dylan decided to construct an album entirely from one session rather than going back and working on some of the songs

again, or writing the couple of songs required to knock "I Shall Be Free No.
10" and "Motorpsycho Nitemare"—
two not-very-funny humorous songs—
into the trash can. There is no doubt
that Dylan (and Wilson) intended all
along to record the album in one go.
Wilson told journalist Nat Hentoff as
much before the session began.

And yet the most important song of
the session was seemingly abandoned
with nary a thought. Dylan recorded just
one take of "Mr. Tambourine Man,"
with Jack Elliott on harmonies. Elliott's
description of the take suggests that
Dylan was already unwilling to hone his
material:

*"I knew he was going to try to record
'Tambourine Man' and he invited me to
sing on it with him but I didn't know the
words 'cept for the chorus, so I just har-
monized with him on the chorus. The
first time I heard that song was when I
was visiting my ex-wife, who was staying at an uptown apartment which belonged to Sally Buhler, who later
married Albert Grossman. Patty sang
me this new song that Dylan had written, which she'd already memorized. So
Bob said, 'Let's do this song . . . "Tambourine Man."' I said, 'Patty sang it to
me, but I don't know the words.' So I
asked him for the words 'cause he'd
been reading most of those songs from
freshly typed sheets of paper 'cause he'd
just written them. He said 'No' . . .
[even though] it was one of the only
ones he actually knew. So I just sang the
choruses. Maybe because I didn't sing
with him on the verses, they found it uninteresting or unworthy of being included on the album."*

Dylan's explanation for the song's
omission from *Another Side* (to Martin
Bronstein in March 1966) was more
cryptic: "I felt too close to it to put it
on." As it is, the legendary Dylan/Elliott
version does not really cut it. The guitar
merely trundles through the song, while
Dylan's vocals are uncharacteristically

hesitant (at one point he throws himself
by adding an extra line after "ragged
clown behind"—"and if to you he looks
blind"—losing the rhythm in the process).
What is quite different from the *Bringing It All Back Home* version is Dylan's
use of the harmonica. Anticipating the
mesmerizing tonal breath control of the
'66 performances, the harmonica break
before the penultimate verse is a soaring
tour de force (as with early live performances, Dylan also prefaces the first
verse with a harmonica burst).

"Tambourine Man" was one of just
three leftovers from the *Another Side*
session (even though for years collectors
assigned everything from "I'll Keep It
with Mine" to "Lay Down Your Weary
Tune" to this single night). Of the other
outtakes, "Denise, Denise" qualifies as
little more than a warm-up at the piano
to limber Dylan up vocally for the night
ahead. "Mama, You Bin on My Mind,"
on the other hand, is a most baffling
omission from the official work. Lyrically it is certainly one of the stronger
songs he wrote about the end of his rela-
tionship with Suze and the *Another Side*
version is really quite touching. Perhaps
he already intended to donate the song
to Baez, who adopted it as her own in
the ensuing months. Dylan had already
donated the superb "I'll Keep It with
Mine" to Austrian chanteuse Nico while
in Paris, not even cutting an official version himself until January 1965. (A
godawful-sounding home demo from
the summer of 1964, belatedly lodged
with Witmark at the end of 1965, suggests that Dylan might have been looking for the other half of the tune.)

Much has also been made of "Black
Crow Blues" signifying a move toward
Bringing It All Back Home—namely
that it's rock and roll minus the ensemble (the track was even rumored to have
been recorded with a band). But then
the *Times* version of "That's All Right,
Mama" could just as easily be seen as
some statement of intent, save that

Dylan chose not to release it, and did not go on to record with a band six months later. The fact is that Dylan never abandoned his love of rhythm and blues—that was part of what made him different from the "traditional for tradition's sake" brigade. According to Pete Stampfel, "He was doing all traditional songs, but his singing style and phrasing were stone rhythm and blues"—and he had been looking for a way to fuse the two sensibilities from the very outset of his association with Columbia. The time was at hand.

BRINGING IT ALL BACK HOME

Recorded: January 13 to 15, 1965
Released: March 22, 1965

Side 1: Subterranean Homesick Blues. She Belongs to Me. Maggie's Farm. Love Minus Zero/No Limit. Outlaw Blues. On the Road Again. Bob Dylan's 115th Dream. Side 2: Mr. Tambourine Man. Gates of Eden. It's Alright, Ma (I'm Only Bleeding). It's All Over Now, Baby Blue.

Other official cuts:

The Bootleg Series: Subterranean Homesick Blues. Farewell Angelina. If You Gotta Go, Go Now [I].
Biograph: I'll Keep It with Mine.
45: If You Gotta Go, Go Now [II].
Highway 61 Interactive CD-ROM: House of the Rising Sun.

Producer:
Tom Wilson

Musicians:
1 unknown
2–4 Bob Dylan (guitar/harmonica/piano/vo-
cals)
2 John Sebastian (bass)

3–4 Bruce Langhorne (guitar)
3–4 Bobby Gregg (drums)
3 John Hammond, Jr. (guitar)
3 William E. Lee (bass)
4 Al Gorgoni (guitar)
4 Kenny Rankin (guitar)
4 Paul Griffin (piano)
4 Joseph Macho, Jr. (bass)

1. 30TH STREET STUDIO
   NEW YORK
   DECEMBER 8, 1964
CO 84438–11 *Mixed Up Confusion*
CO 84439–10 *Rocks and Gravel*
CO 84440-7 **House of the Rising Sun**

2. COLUMBIA STUDIO A
   NEW YORK
   JANUARY 13, 1965
CO 85270 Love Minus Zero/No Limit
CO 85271 **I'll Keep It with Mine**
CO 85272 It's All Over Now, Baby Blue
CO 85273 *Bob Dylan's 115th Dream*
CO 85274 She Belongs to Me
CO 85275 **Subterranean Homesick Blues**

CO 85276 California
CO 85277 *On the Road Again*
CO 85278 **Farewell Angelina**
CO 85279–1 *If You Gotta Go, Go Now [I]*
CO 85279–2 *If You Gotta Go, Go Now [II]*
CO 85280 You Don't Have to Do That
CO 85281 *unknown*

3. COLUMBIA STUDIO A
   NEW YORK
   JANUARY 14, 1965
CO 85270–1 **Love Minus Zero/No Limit**
CO 85275–1 **Subterranean Homesick
             Blues**
CO 85282–3 **Outlaw Blues**
CO 85283–1 **She Belongs to Me**

CO 85284–1   Bob Dylan's 115th Dream
             (intro.)
CO 85284–2   Bob Dylan's 115th Dream
CO 85285–2   *On the Road Again [I]*
CO 85285–4   *On the Road Again [II]*
Rumored: *Mr. Tambourine Man*

4. COLUMBIA STUDIO A
   NEW YORK
   JANUARY 15, 1965

CO 85286   Maggie's Farm
CO 85285–13 On the Road Again
CO 85287–2   It's All Right, Ma (I'm Only
             Bleeding)
CO 85288   Gates of Eden
CO 85289–6   Mr. Tambourine Man
CO 85290   It's All Over Now, Baby Blue
CO 85291–3   If You Gotta Go, Go Now [I]
CO 85291–4   If You Gotta Go, Go Now [II]

Although Dylan did not return to Columbia's Studio A until 1965, something mysterious went on at Columbia's 30th Street Studio before he could make his long-delayed return to rhythm 'n' blues. Six months after *Another Side,* Dylan's producer, Tom Wilson, spent a December afternoon overdubbing instruments on three songs cut by Dylan in 1961 and 1962, two of which had already been recorded with electric backing at the *Freewheelin'* sessions.

The "House of the Rising Sun" from this session, whose inclusion on the recent CD-ROM was accompanied by much (highly misleading) fanfare, self-evidently attempts to copy the Animals' electric arrangement (forget the studio sheets, forget the CO numbers, one listen should be all it takes to date this take *after* the Animals').

Wilson would do something similar, apparently without Simon and Garfunkel's knowledge, grafting the *Bringing It All Back Home* musicians onto the duo's acoustic rendition of "I Am a Rock." In Dylan's case, though, Wilson was hardly in a position to ignore his artist's wishes. Dylan was not Tom and Jerry. If the most plausible explanation is that Wilson was trying out musicians, to see if he could create an electric Dylan sound before beginning work on *Bringing It All Back Home,* he also hoped to show Dylan just what sort of results were possible.

Tom Wilson: *"So we tried by editing and by overdubbing to put like a Fats Domino early rock and roll thing on top of what Dylan had done [with 'House of the Rising Sun'], but it never quite worked to our satisfaction. We flirted with putting this record out as a cover of the Animals record, which had just come on the charts . . . but we never put that version out. That's where I first consciously at Columbia started to try to put these two different elements [folk and rock] together."*

Evidently Dylan was not impressed. As it happens, when Dylan did begin recording *Bringing It All Back Home* in earnest, there was no electric band there to lend a hand. For the first of three sessions Dylan was accompanied by just John Sebastian on bass, who played on just a couple of songs. For a long time, it was believed that *Bringing It All Back Home* was the result of just two days of recording, January 14 and 15, 1965 (despite photographer Daniel Kramer referring at one point in his account of the sessions to a "next to last" session)—but that has been definitively disproved by Jeff Rosen, who included (most of) the studio data sheet for a January 13 session in the booklet accompanying *The Bootleg Series.*

All the cuts that eventually appeared on *Bringing It All Back Home* do originate from the latter two sessions. Because of this, at least one Dylan scholar has sought to dismiss the first session as one "at which Dylan laid down guide demos that he would use at the two later sessions to introduce the studio musicians to the songs he was going to record." Yet there are performances on this first session on the thirteenth that sound remarkably intense for guide demos. Indeed the two songs most stamped with genius, "I'll Keep It with Mine" and "Farewell Angelina," were never attempted with electric backing, suggesting (to me at least) that *Bringing It All Back Home* was always going to be a halfway house, part acoustic, part electric. Both songs were presumably omitted from the album because of their thematic similarities to "Baby Blue" (although "I'll Keep It with Mine" might have snuck by most people). Though this version of "Farewell Angelina" is not perfectly executed, it might still seem surprising that Dylan did not return to the song at one of the later sessions unless, of course, he was already convinced that he had the song as he wanted it. I personally do not subscribe to the "just guide demos" theory.

Of the seven songs attempted at this acoustic session, only to end up in electric incarnations one or two days later, three remain unheard by collectors in their acoustic guise ("115th Dream," "On the Road Again," and "If You Gotta Go, Go Now") though it seems unlikely—on the evidence of "California" (the prototype for "Outlaw Blues") and the "Subterranean Homesick Blues No. 10" included on *The Bootleg Series*—that all three did not benefit from electric embellishment. The acoustic "She Belongs to Me" and "Love Minus Zero/No Limit," on the other hand, both have much to recommend them.

On "Love Minus Zero," for example, Dylan seems a little more at one with the song than on its electric counterpart. The "Baby Blue" from the thirteenth is also on a par with the released version. Less accusatory in tone, Dylan manages to retain some sense of having the other person's best interests at heart. The released version sounds like the man who, when asked at a December 1965 press confer-

ence whether he wrote such songs because he wanted to change people's lives, duly retorted, "I just want to needle them."

Whatever Dylan's intentions in beginning the sessions solo, the following day (the fourteenth) must have been daunting even for someone as self-confident as Dylan circa 1965. He was not used to working with other musicians and he was no longer the young apprentice, attempting something a little different, who had cut "Mixed Up Confusion." The presence of John Sebastian and Bruce Langhorne, both individuals known to him, presumably helped to settle his nerves. Nevertheless the studio sheet for the fourteenth notes at the beginning of reel number one, "Producer talks to musicians"!!! I presume Wilson was briefing the musicians as to Dylan's idiosyncratic working methods. As it is, for much of the session Dylan did not allow himself to get bogged down by any one song, cutting everything in one or two takes. The first two songs, "Love Minus Zero" and "Subterranean Homesick Blues" were both cut in single takes. "Outlaw Blues," barely recognizable from the previous day's "California," was a third take.

As Daniel Kramer, who witnessed the session, noted in his book, "If he tried something that didn't go well, he would put it off for another session." Of the songs attempted on the fourteenth only two were put off: "Mr. Tambourine Man" and "On the Road Again." Why "On the Road Again," little more than a twelve-bar electric blues, should require four attempts on the fourteenth and another nine on the fifteenth to get the version we know and, in my case, love, I cannot imagine. A "Mr. Tambourine Man" from the fourteenth sounds potentially quite intriguing since there were no (other) songs tried acoustically at this second session. "Tambourine Man" on the fourteenth (Kramer insists it was attempted) would surely be an attempt at a band arrangement. If so, it evidently proved a bad idea since it was never even assigned a CO number at this session (implying that no take was ever completed). All in all, though, Dylan once again displayed a remarkable ability to record quickly—even when weighed down by electric instruments clattering around him. (I agree with Paul Williams that "at Dylan's moments of greatest power he plays the musicians with his voice; they are helpless but happy instruments.")

The final *Bringing It All Back Home* session was less of a test. Four of the seven songs had been regulars in Dylan's repertoire since October 1964 and three of them were presumably already set aside for an all-acoustic side two. According to Daniel Kramer, Dylan announced to Wilson and the other attendees that he was going to record "It's Alright, Ma," "Gates of Eden," and "Mr. Tambourine Man" in one go. If the story is true, Dylan's bravado for once let him down. Though "It's Alright, Ma" (after one false start) and "Gates of Eden" came easily enough, "Mr. Tambourine Man" proved no eas-

ier to record than at the previous day's session (or, indeed, the previous June). According to Columbia's files, the *Bringing It All Back Home* version of "Mr. Tambourine Man" was actually take number six.

Dylan still managed to wrap up the sessions on the same day, going out in style with two full band versions of "If You Gotta Go, Go Now," which could easily have been a teen hit for Dylan if it had been released as a single after "Subterranean Homesick Blues." But then Dylan's fans might have considered it a little frivolous—an accusation made on behalf of all the electric cuts on *Bringing It All Back Home*. As Dylan was later informed by that poor Scouse teenager in *Don't Look Back* who looked in desperate need of an afternoon 'round the back of the bicycle shed, "You sound like you're just having a good laugh!" Evidently the near-hysterical laughter of Tom Wilson at the start of "115th Dream" proved contagious (in one famous shot, Dylan was photographed by Kramer punching the air with the glee of it all). He would never sound quite so young again.

DON'T LOOK BACK

Recorded: May 3 to 8, 1965
Released: May 17, 1967

Musicians:
1–2 Bob Dylan (guitar/vocals)
1 Joan Baez (guitar/backing vocals)

1. HOTEL ROOM, SAVOY HOTEL
   LONDON
   MAY 3 OR 4, 1965
What a Friend I Have in Jesus [instrumental]
I Forgot More Than You'll Ever Know
Remember Me (When the Candle Lights Are
  Gleaming)
More and More
Blues Stay Away from Me
Weary Blues from Waitin'

Lost Highway
I'm So Lonesome I Could Cry

2. HOTEL ROOM, SAVOY HOTEL
   LONDON
   MAY 8, 1965
It's All Over Now, Baby Blue
Love Minus Zero/No Limit
She Belongs to Me

Don't Look Back is a rare document of a man caught in a time warp. At the time of his spring '65 English tour, Dylan was just about to hit number one with *The Freewheelin' Bob Dylan,* an album made by another Bob Dylan, the Dylan his fans expected to see on tour. *Don't Look Back* captured a Dylan interrogating a band who had their own electric versions of his songs, meeting the first English Dylan, Donovan, and— above all—doing numbers on the press.

What Dylan was not doing throughout the tour was writing songs (the piece he is working on at the typewriter in one scene is "Alternatives to College," a typically *Tarantula*esque scree he intended for *Esquire*). Indeed, between January and the beginning of June, when he composed "Like a Rolling Stone," his only known composition was "Love Is Just a Four Letter Word," composed in Carmel (apparently for Baez) but never finished to Dylan's satisfaction. Perhaps he felt he had gone as far as he could with song. Perhaps he believed that the novel he was working on would create a new medium for him to conquer (it quickly deteriorated into a stream of muddled self-consciousness).

That Dylan lacked any direction home seems born out by a particularly disastrous session at Levy's Recording Studio in London shortly after the final show of his brief English tour. With John Mayall's Bluesbreakers providing makeshift support, Dylan could not even manage a complete take of "If You

Gotta Go, Go Now" during five hours of recording, despite the presence of his own producer, Tom Wilson (flown in especially for this session). The highlight of the resultant tape is Hughie Flint saying to Dylan, "You haven't worked much with bands, have you?" Eventually Dylan and Wilson, having consumed even more Beaujolais than at the *Another Side* all-nighter, staggered out into the streets of Soho.

Then one day, when Dylan was about to leave England, some twenty pages of "vomit" (his word) began to sing to him, "How does it feel?" The result, condensed down to something a little less vomitific, was "Like a Rolling Stone." Just as "A Hard Rain's a-Gonna Fall" and "Mr. Tambourine Man" had shown Dylan new ways of putting his words in song, "Rolling Stone" now tipped him headlong into a maelstrom of electricity and a one-year roller-coaster ride that would leave him lying in a midtown hospital saying, "I can't believe it, I can't believe I'm alive."

HIGHWAY 61 REVISITED

Recorded: May 12 to August 4, 1965
Released: August 30, 1965

Side 1: Like a Rolling Stone [II]. Tombstone Blues. It Takes a Lot to Laugh, It Takes a Train to Cry. From a Buick 6 [II]. Ballad of a Thin Man. Side 2: Queen Jane Approximately. Highway 61 Revisited. Just Like Tom Thumb's Blues. Desolation Row.

Other official cuts:

The Bootleg Series: Sitting on a Barbed Wire Fence. Phantom Engineer. Like a Rolling Stone [I].
Biograph: Positively 4th Street.
Highway 61 Revisited (mispress): From a Buick 6 [I].
45 (mispress): Can You Please Crawl Out Your Window?
Highway 61 Interactive CD-ROM: Like a Rolling Stone [various excerpted takes].

Producers:
1–3 Tom Wilson
4–7 Bob Johnston

Musicians:
1–7 Bob Dylan (guitar/harmonica/piano/ vocals)
1 Hughie Flint (drums)
2–7 Mike Bloomfield (guitar)

2–6 Paul Griffin (organ/piano)
2–6 Al Kooper (organ)
2–4 Russ Savakus (bass)
2–6 Bobby Gregg (drums)
4–6 Harvey Brooks (bass)
4–6 Sam Lay (drums)
5 Frank Owens (piano/maraccas)
6 Charlie McCoy (guitar/vibes)

1. LEVY'S RECORDING STUDIO
   LONDON
   MAY 12, 1965
   CO ??   If You Gotta Go, Go Now

2. COLUMBIA STUDIO A
   NEW YORK
   JUNE 15, 1965
   CO 86443   *It Takes a Lot to Laugh*
   CO 86444   Sitting on a Barbed Wire Fence [I]
   CO 86444–6 **Sitting on a Barbed Wire Fence [II]**
   CO 86445-1 **It Takes a Lot to Laugh**
   CO 86446-1 **Like a Rolling Stone**

CO 86446–2 **Like a Rolling Stone**
CO 86446–5 **Like a Rolling Stone**

3. COLUMBIA STUDIO A
   NEW YORK
   JUNE 16, 1965
   CO 86446–1 **Like a Rolling Stone** *
   CO 86446–2 **Like a Rolling Stone** (inc.)
   CO 86446–4 **Like a Rolling Stone**
   CO 86446–6 **Like a Rolling Stone** (inc.)
   CO 86446–8 **Like a Rolling Stone** *
   CO 86446–10 **Like a Rolling Stone** (inc.)
   CO 86446–11 *Like a Rolling Stone*
   CO 86446–13 *Like a Rolling Stone*
   CO 86446–15 **Like a Rolling Stone** *
   CO 86449   *title unknown*

4. COLUMBIA STUDIO A
   NEW YORK
   JULY 29, 1965
   CO 86838   *Tombstone Blues [I]*
   CO 86838   **Tombstone Blues [II]**
   CO 86839   **It Takes a Lot to Laugh, It
               Takes a Train to Cry**
   CO 86840   *Positively 4th Street [I]*
   CO 86840   **Positively 4th Street [II]**
   Rumored: Desolation Row

5. COLUMBIA STUDIO A
   NEW YORK
   JULY 30, 1965
   CO 86843   **From a Buick 6 [I]**
   CO 86843   **From a Buick 6 [II]**
   CO 86844   Can You Please Crawl Out
               Your Window? [I]
   CO 86844   **Can You Please Crawl Out
               Your Window? [II]**

6. COLUMBIA STUDIO A
   NEW YORK
   AUGUST 2, 1965
   CO 86845-1   Desolation Row
   CO 86846-3   *Highway 61 Revisited [I]*
   CO 86846-5   **Highway 61 Revisited [II]**
   CO 86846-6   *Highway 61 Revisited [III]*
   CO 86846-9   *Highway 61 Revisited [IV]*
   CO 86847-3   *Just Like Tom Thumb's Blues
                 [I]*
   CO 86847-5   **Just Like Tom Thumb's Blues
                 [II]**
   CO 86848-7   **Queen Jane Approximately**
   CO 86849-2   *Ballad of a Thin Man [I]*
   CO 86849-3   **Ballad of a Thin Man [II]**

7. COLUMBIA STUDIO A
   NEW YORK
   AUGUST 4, 1965
   CO 86937   **Desolation Row**

The evidence that Dylan had very little in reserve songwise in June 1965 can be found at the two sessions that resulted in his first major hit single, "Like a Rolling Stone." "Like a Rolling Stone" excepted, Dylan and the guys passed the hours jamming and riffing (to the extent that Dylan dares his listeners to recognize "Sitting on a Barbed Wire Fence" as "just a riff"). Dylan's initial intention at these sessions may have been to record songs for his next album—cutting just a single had not previously been Dylan's style—but he soon focused exclusively on his vomitific masterpiece.

"Like a Rolling Stone" was actually the third and last song cut at the June 15 session. First up was a fast blues number listed on the studio sheet as "Phantom Engineer Number Cloudy," later to become "It Takes a Lot to Laugh." Perhaps Dylan just wanted to see how his new band dealt with a double shot of rhythm and blues. The words are a hodgepodge of allusions from blues songs, easy enough to improvise over a band like this. Next up was "Sitting on a Barbed Wire Fence," slightly more ambitious, with Bloomfield cutting loose

a couple of times over an organ vamp, presumably played by Paul Griffin (forget the musician credits in *The Bootleg Series* booklet—that's Dylan on piano, and according to Kooper, he didn't play on anything at this session before "Like a Rolling Stone"). The lyrics are what will come to be recognized as a typically Dylanesque strange brew of women killing him alive, the odd Arabian doctor, and amateur numerology. Though there is already an unmistakable musical alchemy unfolding in Studio A, nothing too ambitious is going on here.

"Like a Rolling Stone" works on a whole other level. Switching Griffin to piano and putting Kooper on organ definitely qualifies as inspired (all credit to Dylan for hearing something in Kooper's tentative fills—Kooper later described it as "like a little kid fumbling in the dark for a light switch"). On the single the whole band play as if they are all connected to the same dynamo—Mr. D.

The one useful service that the *Highway 61 Interactive* CD-ROM performed was to shatter the myth of "Like a Rolling Stone" being cut in a single full take, first propagated by Al Kooper in his autobiography, *Backstage Passes,* and willingly reaffirmed on *The Bootleg Series*, with its studio sheet for the June 15th session (but not the 16th), as well as a wonderfully misleading quote from Dylan:

"I recorded it last on a session after recording a bunch of other songs. We took an acetate of it down to my manager's house on Gramercy Park and different people kept coming and going and we played it on the record player all night. My music publisher just kept listening to it, shaking his head saying, 'Wow, man, I just don't believe this.' An A&R man from Columbia Records was also there. He kept saying, 'This is gonna be a hit single.'"

In fact, though the fifth and final take on the fifteenth was the first complete run-through of the song (a section of this take appears on the CD-ROM, suggesting that Kooper wasn't the only one fumbling for the light switch), the musicians had to resume work the following day. As it happens, the sublime single, released four weeks later, was the second complete take of the day, a culmination of three sessions—May 12, June 15, and June 16—which often seemed without direction home. Yet Dylan persevered with the song, seemingly unaware of the perfection he had fleetingly achieved. A further nine takes, four of them complete, were attempted before an exhausted crew listened back to the playbacks and realized they had been there all along.

According to Kooper, in *Backstage Passes,* they also cut versions of "Tombstone Blues" and "Queen Jane Approximately" at this session. However, there is no Columbia record of June 16th takes of these songs and they probably originate in the same fantasy world as the "single take" "Like a Rolling Stone." The only other known song recorded on the sixteenth, listed in the records as "title unknown (CO 86449)," is an-

other improvisation à la "Sitting on a Barbed Wire Fence" that fails to get airborne. The song is once again peopled with extras from *Freaks,* another half-idea Dylan was hoping to flesh out into a song.

June 16 would prove to be Tom Wilson's last session with Dylan. When recording resumed at the end of July, Bob Johnston—another in-house Columbia producer, with roots in Nashville—was behind the console. Wilson soon moved to Verve, where he had a hand in Zappa's first vinyl excursions as well as unleashing the Velvet Underground on an unsuspecting world. Meanwhile Dylan needed to write some songs that wouldn't feel amiss in the company of a "Rolling Stone."

If it weren't for "Like a Rolling Stone," the June sessions would be viewed as little more than a dry run for *Bringing It All Back Home*'s successor. It was in the six weeks between sessions that Dylan figured out how to use his increasingly kaleidoscopic imagination to conjure up a "Desolation Row"; how to best target his bile for the world's neophytes ("Positively 4th Street"); and how to fully reproduce that "Rolling Stone" sound: stately yet hard, precise yet free-flowing—mathematical music.

By the time Dylan began working on *Highway 61* for real, "Like a Rolling Stone" was already climbing the charts and his new sound had been given a less-than-generous reception at the Newport Folk Festival. Indeed, the Newport experience probably fueled him through the first two July sessions, when he cut both "Positively 4th Street" (the most obvious reaction to Newport) and "Can You Please Crawl Out Your Window?" (aka "The Continuing Saga of Baby Blue"). He also returned to "Phantom Engineer," the fast blues romp tried at the "Rolling Stone" session and subsequently performed (intact) at Newport. According to Tony Glover, who was in attendance at these sessions:

"After finishing [another] rollicking, hard-driving, rock and roll version [of the song], and while the group took a lunch break, Dylan reworked the tune alone at the piano and came back with [the] sweeter, bluesy version which appeared on Highway 61 Revisited. *The juxtaposition of these extremely variant versions made a lasting impression."*

The Columbia files bear out Glover's recollection. "Phantom Engineer" was indeed recorded the morning of the July 29 session—a session which apparently ran from ten in the morning until six in the evening—along with the album version of "Tombstone Blues." After "Tombstone Blues," bassist Russ Savakus, who apparently "freaked out a bit during the ending of [the song]," was replaced (after one quick phone call) by one of Kooper's friends, Harvey Brooks.

Though the sessions on the twenty-ninth and thirtieth progressed smoothly enough, Dylan seemed to be saving his more ambitious material for after the weekend break. According to Glover a full-band version of "Desolation Row" was attempted on the Friday afternoon [the thirtieth], but Dylan remained badly out of tune throughout the take. This might tie in with the painfully out-of-tune guitar-playing on the first take of "Can You Please Crawl Out Your Window?," also recorded that afternoon. However, this time, there is no corroboration for Glover's recollections in Columbia's records, though an acetate of "an alternate" "Desolation Row" was recently put up for auction. Dylan spent much of the weekend working further on his new songs. Having initially intended to spend it in Woodstock, he ended up returning to New York alone on the bus around suppertime on Saturday.

The August 2, 1965, session certainly suggests a concerted effort on Dylan's part to finish the album (a test pressing cut at the end of this session suggests that he thought the album *was* finished).

At Johnston's suggestion, Dylan had flown guitarist Charlie McCoy in from Nashville to play on a couple of songs. The first song they attempted was in fact a version of "Desolation Row" with Dylan on acoustic guitar, McCoy on electric, and Harvey Brooks on bass. This "Desolation Row," though inferior to the released version, lyrically is almost identical (except that they are spoon-feeding Casanova "the boiled guts of birds"). The semi-electric backing, on the other hand, gives it a quite different feel. Dylan's vocal delivery is more precise—he clearly wanted everyone to hear the words—without a trace of the hoarseness that mars the official version (probably the result of cutting such a long song without warming up the vocal chords first). It certainly must have been a relief to McCoy that he managed to get through the song without any major fuckups. According to McCoy, they ran through the song twice but Columbia records indicate that this version was cut in a single take. (It's possible that Dylan ran through the song once without tape running just to give McCoy an idea of what lay in store—a most unDylanlike gesture, but then he was paying the guy's airfare!)

The remainder of the August 2 session was dedicated to less lyrically ambitious but more musically inventive new works. McCoy, after contributing uni-vibes to a first attempt at the album's title track, scurried out of the studio, leaving Dylan and his regular crew to their sea of madness. Of the four songs cut on August 2 to later appear on the finished album—"Highway 61 Revisited," "Just Like Tom Thumb's Blues," "Queen Jane Approximately," and "Ballad of a Thin Man"—"Queen Jane Approximately" proved the most arduous, requiring seven takes. "Thin Man," which features a far more ghostly organ on the rough mix than its official guise, wrapped up an album which still bears the authentic brand of genius, and—save for the 45-rpm advance warning—warranted just three days of studio time.

An acetate of rough mixes of all the songs shortlisted for the album seems to have been cut for Dylan's benefit at the end of this session. This acetate (or, more accurately, a tape thereof, though acetate noise makes it clear what the original source was) eventually passed into collectors' hands (as such artifacts tend to do), being bootlegged first as "I Never Talked to Bruce Springsteen" (on vinyl) and then "Highway 61 Revisited Again" (on CD). The acetate contains eleven tracks, eight of which made the final album (including the "correct" "From a Buick 6," suggesting that the alternate "Buick 6," included on early Columbia mispressings, was never under consideration for the album), plus the electric "Desolation Row" (the acoustic version not having as yet been recorded), "Positively Fourth Street," and, curiously, the first take of "Can You Please Crawl Out Your Window?" (the out-of-tune one).

The acetate was presumably cut to enable Dylan to make some final decisions about which songs to pull (otherwise *Highway 61 Revisited* would have clocked in at more than fifty-five minutes—unheard of in 1965). Hearing the songs in this form seems to have convinced Dylan to go back and recut the one song he felt didn't work in its quasi-electric form, "Desolation Row" (making it one of at least four instances where Dylan has cut an acoustic finale to an album at the last minute, after the album was thought to be in the can:

"Restless Farewell" on *Times,* "Wedding Song" on *Planet Waves,* and "Dark Eyes" on *Empire Burlesque* all corresponding to the same pattern). The new, all-acoustic version, with Bloomfield providing some appropriate flamenco flourishes, was recorded on August 4, at what was presumably scheduled as a mixing session.

The acetate itself seems to contain what may be a genuine attempt at a sequence, since the tracks (as pulled from the master reels) would not have come up in this order. The sequence on the acetate runs: "Like a Rolling Stone," "Ballad of a Thin Man," "Just Like Tom Thumb's Blues," "Highway 61 Revisited," "Positively 4th Street," "It Takes a Lot to Laugh," "Tombstone Blues," "Can You Please Crawl Out Your Window?," "Desolation Row," "Queen Jane Approximately," "From a Buick 6." Dylan completely revised this sequence for the released album, which, according to Columbia's records, was out less than four weeks later. Of course, looking back it seems inconceivable that the album would not end with "Desolation Row."

Even with the problems involved in arranging songs for full electric accompaniment, and two early sessions that failed to generate a single fully realized cut (May 12 and June 15), Dylan's transition to rock and roll in the first eight months of 1965 had been nothing short of remarkable. Having cut *Bringing It All Back Home* in three days and *Highway 61 Revisited* in six, though, Dylan was to find his next project altogether more arduous.

BLONDE ON BLONDE

Recorded: October 5, 1965, to March 10, 1966
Released: May 16, 1966

Side 1: Rainy Day Women #s 12 & 35. Pledging My Time. Visions of Johanna. One of Us Must Know (Sooner or Later). Side 2: I Want You. Stuck Inside of Mobile with the Memphis Blues Again. Leopard Skin Pillbox Hat. Just Like a Woman. Side 3: Most Likely You Go Your Way and I'll Go Mine. Temporary Like Achilles. Absolutely Sweet Marie. 4th Time Around. Obviously 5 Believers. Side 4: Sad Eyed Lady of the Lowlands.

Eat the Document

Recorded: May 11 to 19, 1966
Released: February 8, 1971

I Still Miss Someone. On a Rainy Afternoon. I Can't Leave Her Behind. What Kind of Friend Is This?

Other official cuts:

The Bootleg Series: She's Your Lover Now. I'll Keep It with Mine.
Biograph: Can You Please Crawl Out Your Window? I Wanna Be Your Lover.
Highway 61 Interactive CD-ROM: Medicine Sunday.

Producer:
1–12 Bob Johnston

Engineers:
13   Robert Shelton
14–15 Robert Van Dyke

Musicians:
1–15 Bob Dylan (guitar/harmonica/piano/
        vocals)
1–13, 15 Robbie Robertson (guitar)
1–4 Garth Hudson (organ)

1–6 Rick Danko (bass)
1–6 Richard Manuel (piano)
1–2 Levon Helm (drums)
3–6 Bobby Gregg (drums)
5–12 Al Kooper (organ)
7–12 Wayne Moss (guitar)
7–12 Jerry Kennedy (guitar)
7–12 Charlie McCoy (guitar)
7–12 Joe South (bass)
7–12 Hargus "Pig" Robinson (piano)
7–12 Kenneth Buttrey (drums)
10–12 Henry Strzelecki (bass)
14   Johnny Cash (backing vocals)

1. COLUMBIA STUDIOS
    NEW YORK
    OCTOBER 5, 1965
CO 87183–1   Medicine Sunday [I]
CO 87183–2   Medicine Sunday [II]

CO 87184–2   Can You Please Crawl Out
             Your Window? [I]
CO 87184   **Can You Please Crawl Out**
             Your Window? [II]

CO 87185   *I Don't Want to Be Your*
              Partner
CO 87186   **Jet Pilot**

2. COLUMBIA STUDIOS
   NEW YORK
   OCTOBER 20, 1965
CO 87185   I Wanna Be Your Lover [I]
CO 87185–6   **I Wanna Be Your Lover [II]**

3. COLUMBIA STUDIOS
   NEW YORK
   NOVEMBER 30, 1965
CO 88581–7   Visions of Johanna
CO 88582   **Can You Please Crawl Out**
              Your Window? (stereo mix)

4. COLUMBIA STUDIOS
   NEW YORK
   JANUARY 21, 1966
CO 89210   She's Your Lover Now [I]
CO 89210   **She's Your Lover Now [II]**
CO ??   Visions of Johanna

5. COLUMBIA STUDIOS
   NEW YORK
   JANUARY 25, 1966
CO 89215   *Leopard Skin Pillbox Hat*
CO 89216   **One of Us Must Know**
              (Sooner or Later)

6. COLUMBIA STUDIOS
   NEW YORK
   JANUARY 27, 1966
CO 89218   instrumental track [Number
              One]
CO 89219   *Leopard Skin Pillbox Hat*
CO ??   **I'll Keep It with Mine**

7. COLUMBIA MUSIC ROW STUDIOS
   NASHVILLE, TENNESSEE
   FEBRUARY 14, 1966
NCO 83182   **4th Time Around**
NCO 83183   **Visions of Johanna**
NCO 83184   **Leopard Skin Pillbox Hat**

8. COLUMBIA MUSIC ROW STUDIOS
   NASHVILLE, TENNESSEE
   FEBRUARY 15, 1966
NCO 83185   Keep it with Mine (instru-
              mental)
NCO 83186   **Sad Eyed Lady of the Low-**
              lands

9. COLUMBIA MUSIC ROW STUDIOS
   NASHVILLE, TENNESSEE
   FEBRUARY 16, 1966
NCO 83187   **Stuck Inside of Mobile with**
              the Memphis Blues Again

10. COLUMBIA MUSIC ROW STUDIOS
    NASHVILLE, TENNESSEE
    MARCH 8, 1966
NCO 83259   **Absolutely Sweet Marie**
NCO 83264   **Just Like a Woman**
NCO 83265   **Pledging My Time**

11. COLUMBIA MUSIC ROW STUDIOS
    NASHVILLE, TENNESSEE
    MARCH 9, 1966
NCO 83274   **Most Likely You Go Your**
              Way and I'll Go Mine
NCO 83275   **Temporary Like Achilles**

12. COLUMBIA MUSIC ROW STUDIOS
    NASHVILLE, TENNESSEE
    MARCH 10, 1966
NCO 83276   **Rainy Day Women #s 12 &**
              35
NCO 83277   **Obviously 5 Believers**
NCO 83278   *Leopard Skin Pillbox Hat*
NCO 83279   **I Want You**

13. HOTEL ROOM
    DENVER, COLORADO
    MARCH 13, 1966
Positively Van Gogh
Don't Tell Him
If You Want My Love
Just Like a Woman
Sad Eyed Lady of the Lowlands

14. BACKSTAGE AT CAPITOL THEATRE
    CARDIFF, WALES
    MAY 11, 1966
I Still Miss Someone

15. HOTEL ROOM
    GLASGOW, SCOTLAND
    MAY 19, 1966
What Kind of Friend Is This?
I Can't Leave Her Behind [I]
I Can't Leave Her Behind [II]
On a Rainy Afternoon

Blonde on Blonde, begun on October 5, 1965, and completed on March 10, 1966, was to be both the culmination of Dylan's search for "that wild mercury sound" and the writing on the wall for all subsequent terrors in the studio. Dylan may have completed *Highway 61 Revisited* in six days, but after two sessions in October 1965, one in November, and three in January 1966, he had exactly two singles—a rerecorded "Can You Please Crawl Out Your Window?" and "One of Us Must Know"—to show for all his endeavors.

Even more curiously, the musicians at these sessions had been drawn from his touring band, the Hawks, a flexible Canadian combo of no fixed style (Al Kooper, the one addition, had his own Dylan pedigree by now). It is one of the great mysteries why Dylan and the Hawks—who would blaze such a trail across the world in the spring of 1966, before making hours of mysteriously timeless recordings in a basement "studio" in the summer of 1967—should fail to spark in the studio when at the very peak of their seemingly telepathic powers.

Part of the problem seems to have been Dylan's abiding assumption that he could come to a session with barely more than fragments of a lyric, half a melody and somehow bring it into focus in the studio. This was certainly the case with his first post–*Highway 61* session, on October 5, 1965. For only the third time in his career ("Mixed Up Confusion" and "Like a Rolling Stone"), the ostensible reason for this session was to cut a single, not to begin work on *Highway 61*'s successor. "Positively 4th Street" was already climbing the charts and Dylan was keen to keep the momentum going. Reluctant to use the *Highway 61* version of "Can You Please Crawl Out Your Window?" as a follow-up to "4th Street," Dylan took Levon and the Hawks into his beloved Studio A to recut the song (the Hawks had held

their first rehearsal with Dylan less than three weeks earlier and made their Carnegie Hall debut just four days before). As such, the Hawks could hardly have had an opportunity to fully assimilate Dylan's working methods.

The 45 version of "Can You Please Crawl Out Your Window?" should be considered something of a triumph for the Hawks—they certainly give the song, another Dylan tirade against some (probably quite real) Miss Lonely, a very different sound from Dylan's two previous hits. In fact, the session largely followed the pattern Dylan set with "Like a Rolling Stone": a series of false starts (one of which has been widely bootlegged), before the song miraculously emerged, fully formed, just as the musicians and producer seemed on the verge of despair.

Dylan also insisted on attempting to see if a couple of ideas might take on a life of their own from his usual ragbag of surrealist allusions. Dylan told Allen Ginsberg in 1965 that he would sometimes "go into a studio and chat up the musicians and babble into the microphone then rush into the control room and listen to what he said, and write it down, and then maybe arrange it a little bit, and then maybe rush back out in front and sing it [again]!" Well, that's exactly what the likes of "Medicine Sunday" and "Jet Pilot" (both cut on October 5) sound like. Dylan was about to discover this approach didn't go down too well in Nashville.

Just as "Phantom Engineer" had emerged into the light of day as "It Takes a Lot to Laugh," two of the three prototypes Dylan attempted at this session later developed into recognizable songs. He retained just one line from the one-verse "Medicine Sunday" (aka "Midnight Train") for "Temporary Like Achilles," though it was an important one—"Mama, why are you so hard?"—while "I Don't Want to Be Your Partner" contains far more of its eventual form in "I Wanna Be Your Lover," even if it still does not constitute more than a fragment. Ditto "Jet Pilot" (or "Pilot Eyes," as it was originally called). With "Jet Pilot," though, nothing more came of the fragment, probably because it shares just about everything—structure, riff, words, delivery—with half a dozen tracks on *Highway 61.*

One suspects that this was also the reason why "I Wanna Be Your Lover," even in finished form, never graced a Dylan album until Jeff Rosen started rummaging through the vaults (no criticism intended). Again it contains the prototypical retinue of characters— "Phaedra with her looking glass," "the undertaker in his midnight suit"—and the jokey "Beatle" reference in the song title is strictly a onetime gag. Nevertheless, Dylan and the boys spent one whole session (October 20) working on the song, awaiting the next cascade of inspiration that would take Dylan away from *Highway 61,* down past Grand Street, to where the neon madmen climbed.

They did not have to wait long. On November 30, 1965, Dylan made the first of three concerted efforts to get an acceptable studio version of his most perfectly realized song to date, "Freeze Out" (it was later renamed "Visions of Johanna," though only after Dylan abandoned a reference to examining the "nightingale's code" in the last verse— or perhaps "he examines the night and gets cold"?). Dylan refers to recording the song "the other night" at the San Francisco Press Conference on December 3.

For some reason lost in the mists of rhyme, this November 30/December 1 session has always been credited as "The L.A. Band Session," though a Los Angeles session between gigs in Washington, D.C., on the twenty-eighth and San Francisco on the third always struck me as a shade illogical—particularly as Dylan managed to get married and

switch drummers in the process (from Levon Helm to Bobby Gregg—I'd say it's Gregg on "Freeze Out"). The legendary "L.A. Band Tape"—the one Cable described as "essential, classic, superlative stuff"—is in fact a composite of outtakes from five of the six pre-*Blonde on Blonde* sessions (yes, it really is the *Blonde on Blonde* outtakes tape, if there is such a thing). The only session not represented on this tape is November 30 (the "Freeze Out" included on the famous "L.A. Band Tape" comes from January 1966). Collectors had to wait until 1980 and the auctioning of a set of Columbia reference recordings—the famous "Goldmine" acetates— to hear this earlier "Freeze Out."

A comparison of all three, radically different studio versions of "Freeze Out," aka "Visions of Johanna" (recorded in November 1965, January 1966, and February 1966 respectively), is an exercise I recommend to any serious Dylan fan. Dylan has always refused to embrace the idea of a "definitive" version of any of his songs, always believing that there will be some level of meaning permanently hidden within the "mathematics" of a song. Even after as seemingly definitive a performance as, say, "Idiot Wind" on the *Hard Rain* album and TV special (*definitive* in the sense that it expresses the song's raging glory best), Dylan found a new level of understanding when rediscovering the song in concert in the spring of 1992. Few fans, I suspect, on hearing the alternate Johannas, will prefer them to the exquisite performance on *Blonde on Blonde.* Yet despite only the most marginal lyrical differences ("nightingale's code" notwithstanding), each recorded performance needs to be heard on its own terms. What Dylan was searching for with the fast and slow "Freeze Outs" (to use Paul Williams's parlance) was only partially revealed in Nashville. Indeed, in his own discussion of these three performances, Mr. Williams manages to neatly summarize what it is that separates Dylan from so many of his contemporaries when it comes to working in the studio:

In jazz it is common to see alternate takes released from a recording session, particularly after the passage of time . . . This is accepted practice because jazz is implicitly understood to be an art form the units of which are improvised (i.e., at least partially spontaneous) performances. In rock music, however, musicians are working in a historical context in which finished music is created by striving to arrive at the best (most attractive, most commercial) possible representation of the song in question. Studio recording is seldom done in one take, and so there often are no "alternate takes," because each take is a building block that is either added to at the next stage of the process, or else put aside, incomplete.

Even at this stage in his career, Dylan did not fit conveniently into this model of the rock artiste. The first "Freeze Out" Williams describes as "the rock version" and it's easy to see why. Though Dylan and the Hawks never played the song live (as far as I know), the November 30 version would not have sounded out of place on the recently emerged Berkeley 1965 electric set. Driven initially by some impromptu harmonica whoops from Dylan himself, before Danko and Robertson take up the challenge, this "Freeze Out" features the sort of defiant vocal more in keeping with "She's Your Lover Now." Though it sounds like a very close cousin of "Tombstone Blues," "Freeze Out" is only a very distant relative of "Stuck Inside of Mobile with the Memphis Blues Again." For this reason alone, it would not have fit easily onto *Blonde on Blonde*, exhilarating as this initial performance/recording is. (Sadly, the tape of the acoustic set from Berkeley, where

Dylan premiered the song acoustically appears to have been mislaid, so no comparison is possible.)

The November 30 session seems to have been set up with the specific purpose of cutting "Freeze Out." Much like the composition of "Rolling Stone," "Freeze Out" seems to have excited Dylan so much that he insisted on transferring it to tape pronto. Writing "Freeze Out" opened another new door for Dyian-the-songwriter and he wanted to see where it led in the studio. Slotting in this session the night before flying to the West Coast certainly suggests a resolve on Dylan's part to record while the initial vision remained. However, even after seven attempts, Dylan had yet to divine what kind of "Freeze Out" he was looking for.

The fall 1965 sessions had been slotted into a sporadic tour schedule that whisked Dylan and the Hawks away for long weekends and deposited them back in New York to while away their weekdays. As such, Dylan had no real hiatus allowing him to concentrate on the studio process—at least not until January 1966. With six weeks off the road over Christmas and New Year, Dylan made a last attempt to cut songs for an album with his touring band. The sessions, over three days in late January—though responsible for such oft-bootlegged goodies as the slow "Freeze Out," the electric *and solo* "She's Your Lover Now," and the instrumental "Number One"—yielded Columbia just one single, "One of Us Must Know," after Al Kooper was drafted in at short notice to apply some of his designer organ fills.

Among the many mysteries thrown up by these sessions is why Dylan and the guys never completed versions of "I'll Keep It with Mine" and "She's Your Lover Now." On both songs they are so close to securing fully realized versions that it seems like one more take will get them there. "She's Your Lover Now," in particular, with Gregg's glorious ratatat drumming and Hudson's ethereal organ (the *Bootleg Series* notes are a disaster—it couldn't be Konikoff on drums and that *must* be Dylan on piano), only breaks down on the last verse because (choose your own theory): Dylan inverts an image ("now your mouth cries wolf" should be "now your eyes cries wolf") and/or somebody in the band breaks something. "I'll Keep It with Mine" is somewhat more tentative. Indeed, it comes across as wholly impromptu (presumably a suggestion of Dylan's). Yet by the fade everyone seems to have figured their parts out (in particular Kooper, who sounds more than ever like a ghost train rattling across the track). Which begs the question: what happened next?

Kooper's belated involvement in these sessions—he was brought in during the (protracted) recording of "One of Us Must Know" on the twenty-fifth and stayed for the final session on the twenty-seventh (according to Columbia, there was a session on January 31, between 11:30 P.M. and 2:30 A.M., though this was probably only a mixing session)—suggests that Dylan was still not latching on to "that wild mercury sound" with the versions of "She's Your Lover Now," "Visions of Johanna," and "Leopard Skin Pillbox Hat," attempted before Kooper was drafted in.

The "Freeze Out" cut on the twenty-first is the most realized of all the January recordings, "One of Us Must Know" excepted. Built around the interplay between Dylan's barroom piano and some of Robertson's most tasteful fills, this is a far more ambitious arrangement than its November counterpart. Each instrument contributes to the heady brew, while the sublime lyrics benefit from a less aggressive vocal. Yet even this remarkable recording was consigned to the scrapheap of vaultdom when Dylan reevaluated the nightingale's code.

Equally remarkable but deemed "un-

releasable" at the time is the solo piano version of "She's Your Lover Now," recorded the same day as "Freeze Out." Unlike the electric take, Dylan completes this slow, brooding performance, perhaps his most naked studio recording. The purpose of a solo piano take we can only guess—I can't really see how hearing this rendition would prepare the musicians for cutting a band version and there is no concession to what might be termed an arrangement in the performance, unless you can call Dylan exercising a little tonal breath control an arrangement! Possibly Dylan conceived of it as an album closer à la "Desolation Row."

Of course, this was all before Dylan had the whizzo idea of taking up an entire side with one song, something he could only get away with if *Blonde on Blonde* was a double album. The question is, when did he conceive of *Blonde on Blonde* as a double album? It always seemed to me unlikely that the "real" *Blonde on Blonde* sessions—the Nashville ones—would yield more treasures than the thirteen album cuts simply because of the album's not overly generous playing time (seventy-two minutes). So proved to be the case. According to Columbia's files, exactly one genuine outtake was recorded in Nashville, one of Dylan's circular instrumentals curiously entitled "Keep It with Mine" (though it sure doesn't sound like "I'll Keep It with Mine" to me), long misattributed by collectors to the *Bringing It All Back Home* sessions. Which still means sixty-eight minutes' worth of new songs resulted from two sets of Nashville sessions, four days in February and three days in March 1966. Nothing went to waste.

I doubt that the notion of a double album occurred to Dylan before recording "Sad Eyed Lady of the Lowlands," which was cut at the second session (he had gotten all of the songs written in advance—"Visions of Johanna,"

"Leopard Skin Pillbox Hat," and "4th Time Around"—out of the way at the first session). I also doubt that Dylan felt he had a worthy successor to *Highway 61* at the end of the February sessions, despite having recorded thirty-two minutes' worth of new songs, including all three *Blonde on Blonde* epics—"Sad Eyed Lady of the Lowlands," "Visions of Johanna," and "Stuck Inside of Mobile."

That both sets of sessions were slotted into Dylan's irksome touring schedule suggests how anxiously Columbia awaited new product. The March sessions may even have been booked only when Dylan realized he didn't have enough for an album after three days spent working on "Sad Eyed Lady" and "Stuck Inside of Mobile" in the studio. The musicians insist that they cut "Sad Eyed Lady" in one take. According to Ken Buttrey:

He ran down a verse and a chorus and he just quit and said, "We'll do a verse and a chorus then I'll play my harmonica thing. Then we'll do another verse and chorus and I'll play some more harmonica and we'll see how it goes from there." That was his explanation of what was getting ready to happen. It was a first take. Not knowing how long this thing was going to be, we were preparing ourselves dynamically for a basic two- to three-minute record because records just didn't go over three minutes. . . . If you notice that record, that thing after like the second chorus starts building and building like crazy and everybody's just peaking it up 'cause we thought, Man, this is it. This feels like a normal song. This is gonna be the last chorus and we've gotta put everything into it we can and he played another harmonica solo and went back down to another verse and the dynamics had to drop back down to a verse kind of feel, bang. We [then] had to do a big, huge buildup into the [next] chorus, and the thing would just drop again to an-

other verse. After about five, six minutes of this stuff we start looking at the clock, everyone starts looking at each other, we'd built to the peak of our limit and, bang, [there] goes another harmonica solo and [we'd] drop down to another verse. After about ten minutes of this thing we're cracking up at each other, at what we were doing. I mean, we peaked five minutes ago. Where do we go from here? How does this thing peak some more?

The story about Dylan writing the songs for *Blonde on Blonde* while the musicians sat around playing cards has long had common currency. Certainly on the evidence of the recording session data for the February sessions there seems little doubt that Dylan was not doing all that much recording at Columbia Music Row Studios after the first day. The "Sad Eyed" session took from six in the evening till one in the morning, while the recording of "Stuck Inside of Mobile" actually spilled over into the following day. Considering the pedigree of musicians like Joe South, Charlie McCoy, and Ken Buttrey, Dylan could hardly attempt his "babble into the microphone, then rush into the control room and listen to what I said" technique. Thankfully he was shrewd enough to bring along Al Kooper and Robbie Robertson to act as intermediaries between his intuitive demon-child genius and Nashville's highest echelon of session men. Kooper would go up to Dylan's hotel room during the day (most of the sessions took place in the evening) and Dylan would teach him the basic structure of whatever song he was working on. Kooper was thus able to run through the basic changes with the other musicians while Dylan continued to hone the song in the studio, the idea being that when Dylan *was* ready, things could proceed smoothly.

Despite Kooper's and Robertson's input, and the undoubted "chops" these

Tennessee dudes could bring to a session, Dylan's working techniques were unlike anything they had ever encountered. "Stuck Inside of Mobile" proved especially difficult. Despite using eleven and a half hours of studio time on the sixteenth, it was seven A.M. on the seventeenth before they had finished recording the song. Yet as an example of what makes *Blonde on Blonde* such a unique fusion of "that wild mercury sound" and a surrealism seven degrees beyond the beats, "Stuck Inside of Mobile" reigns supreme. If it is Dylan's light acoustic strum and a brief harmonica rasp that kicks the song off, it is Buttrey's "omnipresent metronomic drumming" that everyone is hanging on to when Dylan finally rattles off his waterfall of images. As one eyewitness at the sessions commented, "Everyone would fall in with the drums."

I suspect that when Dylan returned to Nashville in March he was still not sure how his seventh album would pan out. However, with an album's worth of songs already cut, the more epic songs all in usable form, and with the musicians at least halfway conversant with their eccentric paymaster's ways, the March sessions were bound to be less fraught than the January or February sessions. Indeed, nine songs were cut in three days (including a version of "Leopard Skin Pillbox Hat"—complete with doorbell noises, although Dylan eventually decided to go for the more rough-and-ready version cut at the first Nashville session). At last Dylan had enough tracks for one of rock's few double albums bereft of filler (though the single-sided "Sad Eyed Lady" is all of one second longer than *Highway 61*'s "Desolation Row").

Mixing *Blonde on Blonde* (cut on three-track, it is best heard on one-track—mono vinyl—though the Master Sound CD is fine; it's a shame that Sony doesn't think all of Dylan's sixties albums deserve such attention to detail),

apparently took place under Dylan's direct supervision over a couple of days in Los Angeles. The work was concluded on April 7, just two days before he embarked on his first world tour. It would be more than eighteen months before Dylan would be willing to reenter a Columbia studio.

In the interim, he would produce his wildest ever music (on various stages around the world), as well as his most therapeutic (in a basement in Woodstock). Between these particular doors he would tumble from his motorcycle one bright summer day in late July 1966. So did Dylan attempt to record anything in the five months that separated the finished *Blonde on Blonde* from a motorcycle's rear axle? In the couple of months after Dylan's second Royal Albert Hall show brought the curtain down on an increasingly fraught world tour, there is no evidence he arranged any Columbia sessions. With another major American tour penciled in to begin in late August, and a book and a film to deliver before then, not to mention a newborn son, Jesse, Dylan's attentions lay elsewhere.

The only evidence we have of a possible direction, post–*Blonde on Blonde*, pre-accident, derives from two hotel room sessions with Robbie Robertson. That Dylan and Robertson were at this point blowtorching the candle at both ends— staying up late into the night, smoking a little (okay, a lot of) hash, and working on songs with a couple of acoustic guitars—is well-documented. Melbourne's answer to Allen Ginsberg, Adrian Rawlins, wrote at the time of Dylan playing him "Sad Eyed Lady of the Lowlands" at six-thirty in the morning after a night of smoking hash, while actress Rosemary Garrette witnessed an even more extensive all-nighter just five days later:

I was able to listen to a composing session. Countless cups of tea . . . Things happened, and six new songs were born.

The poetry seemed already to have been written. Dylan says "Picture one of these cats with a horn, coming over the hill at daybreak. Very Elizabethan, you dig? Wearing garters." And out of the imagery, he and [Robbie] work on a tune and Dylan's leg beats time with the rhythm, continuously, even when the rhythm is in his own mind.

Robert Shelton had already taped such a session in a Denver hotel room, three days after Dylan completed *Blonde on Blonde* (though he lacked the foresight to have enough blank tape, and ended up having to record all but one song of the thirty-five-minute session at 1⅞ ips— hence the poor quality). Though Dylan was anxious to play Shelton a couple of the songs he had just recorded—"Just Like a Woman" and "Sad Eyed Lady of the Lowlands," the latter of which he seemed particularly proud of—Shelton also witnessed Dylan and Robertson working on some newer ideas.

The opening song, the lyrics of which revolve around a painting by Van Gogh, is the most listenable track because Shelton has not as yet knocked the speed of his reel-to-reel down to 1⅞ ips (from 3¾). It shows Dylan returning to "babbling into the microphone." The words are largely nonsensical, suggesting only a marginal affiliation with narrative structure. This sets the pattern for the other two songs (which Dundas, in his Dylan discography, provisionally titles "Don't Tell Him" and "If You Want My Love"). Dylan's primary concern (and presumably Robertson's) appears to have been building a melody and rhythm around a possible "line of thinking," expressed in a catchphrase or "feeling." However, the exact purpose of these nightly sessions remains difficult to discern since there is no evidence that Dylan made any attempt to tape the results or return to previous ideas or riffs.

The one time that tapes were rolling for any quasi-official purpose was on a rainy afternoon in Glasgow when Don Pennebaker's camera was rolling for a documentary Dylan had been commissioned to make of his European tour by the ABC television network. Three songs recorded in a Glaswegian hotel room appear in partial form in *Eat the Document*: "What Kind of Friend Is This?", virtually a solo Dylan performance of what is a radically reworked arrangement of Koko Taylor's "What Kind of Man Is This?"; "I Can't Leave Her Behind," which lasts barely a minute in the movie but already sounds like a classic Dylan heartbreaker; and "On a Rainy Afternoon" (obviously a whimsical reference to the circumstances of the recording rather than anything to do with the song itself, usually listed as "Does She Need Me" before being copyrighted in 1978). In this last instance, aside from the one minute and forty-two seconds included in "ETD" (the closing sequence), there is also a running tape of the duo working on the song.

Clearly Dylan wanted this performance preserved. At the beginning he even says, "Let's get this one." At crucial points he can be heard tutoring Robertson on what exactly he wants: "Play the bridge again. . . . That's not the bridge. . . . Nah, something's wrong with the ending . . . [Well,] we're going to play it all anyway." Evidence that he is trying to concentrate on the tune more than the words is borne out by one comment to the camera: "I'm into melody now." Doubtless Robertson would like to take credit for this switch, given latter-day comments about talking Dylan into "making records" not "bashing away in the studio." I'm not convinced. I tend to think, after *Highway 61* and *Blonde on Blonde*, that this was pretty much a preordained direction. Even if Dylan told Ginsberg shortly after the accident that "he was writing shorter lines, with every line meaning something."

1. MILLION DOLLAR BASH
2. BOTTLE OF BREAD
3. BUT ITS NOT HERE
4. PLEASE MRS. HENRY
5. MAMA AIN'T YOU GONNA MISS YOUR BEST FRIEND NOW
6. LO & BEHOLD
7. WHEEL'S ON FIRE
8. YOU AIN'T GOIN' NOWHERE
9. I SHALL BE RELEASED

TAILS OUT

10. TOO MUCH OF NOTHING
11. NOTHING WAS DELIVERED [SHORT VERSION]
12. LOST TIME IS NOT FOUND AGAIN
13. GET YOUR ROCKS OFF
14. ANSWER TO ODE [Is silly so]
15. APPLE SYCKUN TREE
      2 TAKES
16. OPEN THE DOOR RICHARD
     1
     2
     3
17. NOTHING WAS DELIVERED TK1

18. NOTHING WAS DELIVERED TK 2
19. TEARS OF RAGE ①
20. TEARS OF RAGE ②
21. QUINN...

THE BASEMENT TAPES

Recorded: June to November 1967
Released: June 26, 1975

Side 1: Odds and Ends. Million Dollar Bash. Goin' to Acapulco. Side 2: Lo and Behold! Clothes Line Saga. Apple Suckling Tree. Please, Mrs. Henry. Tears of Rage. Side 3: Too Much of Nothing. Yea! Heavy and a Bottle of Bread. Crash on the Levee (Down in the Flood). Tiny Montgomery. Side 4: You Ain't Going Nowhere. Nothing Was Delivered. Open the Door, Homer. This Wheel's on Fire.

Other released cuts:

Biograph: The Mighty Quinn (Quinn the Eskimo)
The Bootleg Series: I Shall Be Released. Santa Fe.

Engineer:

1–4 Garth Hudson

Musicians:

1–4 Bob Dylan (guitar/piano)
1–4 Robbie Robertson (guitar/drums)
1–4 Richard Manuel (piano/drums/
   backing vocals)

1–4 Rick Danko (bass/mandolin/vocals)
1–4 Garth Hudson (organ/clavinette/accor-
   dion/piano)
4 Levon Helm (drums)

Note: The line breaks between batches of songs on the basement tapes represent my guestimate as to which songs were recorded together.

1. "THE RED ROOM,"
   DYLAN'S HOUSE, WOODSTOCK
   JUNE 1967
Lock Your Door
Baby, Won't You Be My Baby
Try Me Little Girl
I Can't Make It Alone
Don't You Try Me Now

Young But Daily Growin'
Bonnie Ship the Diamond
The Hills of Mexico

Down on Me
One for the Road
I'm Alright

One Single River
People Get Ready
I Don't Hurt Anymore
Stones That You Throw
One Man's Loss

Instrumental with Dylan [with D.]
Baby, Ain't That Fine
Rock, Salt and Nails
A Fool Such as I

2. "BIG PINK,"
   WEST SAUGERTIES
   "THE RED ROOM" (AND POSSIBLY
   DYLAN'S HOUSE, WOODSTOCK)
   JUNE TO AUGUST 1967

Silouette
Bring It on Home
King of France
. . . . [details of this reel incomplete]

Even If It's a Pig Part 1 [the Hawks]
Ruben Remus [the Hawks]
900 Miles
No Shoes on My Feet
Spanish Is the Loving Tongue
"lot of piano"
On a Rainy Afternoon

I Can't Come in with a Broken Heart
Come All Ye Fair and Tender Ladies
Under Control

Ol' Roison the Beau
I'm Guilty of Loving You
Johnny Todd
Cool Water
Banks of the Royal Canal
Po' Lazarus

Belchezaar
I Forgot to Remember to Forget Her
You Win Again
Still in Town, Still Around
Waltzin' with Sin
Big River [I]
Big River [II]
Folsom Prison Blues
Bells of Rhymney

It's Just Another Tomato in the Glass
. . . [details of this reel incomplete]

I'm a Fool for You [I]
I'm a Fool for You [II]

Next Time on the Highway
The Big Flood
You Gotta Quit Kickin' My Dog Aroun'
See You Later, Allen Ginsberg

Tiny Montgomery

The Spanish Song [I]
The Spanish Song [II]
I'm Your Teenage Prayer

Four Strong Winds
The French Girl [I]
The French Girl [II]
Joshua Gone Barbados

I'm in the Mood for Love
All American Boy
Sign on the Cross

Don't Ya Tell Henry

Bourbon Street
. . . [details of this reel incomplete]

Silent Weekend
Santa Fe
Wild Wolf
. . . [details of this reel incomplete]

Million Dollar Bash [I]
Yea! Heavy and a Bottle of Bread [I]
Million Dollar Bash [II]
Yea! Heavy and a Bottle of Bread [II]

I'm Not There (1956)
Please Mrs. Henry
Down in the Flood (Crash on the Levee) [I]
Down in the Flood (Crash on the Levee) [II]
Lo and Behold [I]
Lo and Behold [II]

You Ain't Going Nowhere [I]
This Wheel's on Fire
You Ain't Going Nowhere [II]
I Shall Be Released
Too Much of Nothing [I]
Too Much of Nothing [II]
. . . [details of this reel possibly incomplete]

3. "BIG PINK,"
   WEST SAUGERTIES
   SEPTEMBER/OCTOBER 1967
Tears of Rage [I]
Tears of Rage [II]
Tears of Rage [III]
The Mighty Quinn [I]
The Mighty Quinn [II]

Open the Door Homer [I]
Open the Door Homer [II]
Open the Door Homer [III]
Nothing Was Delivered [I]
Nothing Was Delivered [II]
Odds and Ends [I]
Nothing Was Delivered [III]

Odds and Ends [II]

Get Your Rocks Off
Clothes Line Saga
Apple Suckling Tree [I]
Apple Suckling Tree [II]

4. "BIG PINK,"
   WEST SAUGERTIES
   OCTOBER/NOVEMBER 1967
Goin' to Acapulco
Gonna Get You Now

Wild Wood Flower

How much Robbie Robertson con-tributed to the songs composed in hotel rooms on the 1966 tour is open to debate (he does get a cocredit on both "I Can't Leave Her Behind" and "On a Rainy Afternoon"). Clearly Dylan needed a sounding board to bounce ideas off and Robertson was the most suitable Hawk. Possibly Dylan was also trying to ease Robert-son into writing songs himself. If so, it was a spectacular success, at least as and when Robertson's songs started flowing, the following year. By then Robertson was no longer writing songs with Dylan (indeed he quickly tired of writing songs with anybody, erstwhile Band leader Richard Manuel in-cluded).

Dylan himself seems to have had no obvious interest in recording the (pre-sumably dozens of) half-songs he and Robertson had conjured up in these twilight hours. When he lost his back wheel down a country road, the only thing he seemed bent on was keeping keeping on. If, before the accident, Dylan was waiting for the next wave of ideas to hit, after his spell in the hos-pital he quite self-consciously turned off the tap. For nine months the faucet remained closed. When asked by a journalist in May 1967 what he had been doing, he replied: "What I've been doing mostly is . . . poring over books by people you never heard of, thinking about where I'm going, and why I'm running, and am I mixed up too much."

When he decided the time had come to let his muse do the plumbing again, it was a very different Dylan that greeted her. A quarter of a century on, Dylan's motorcycle accident is still viewed as the central pivot of his ca-reer. As a sudden, abrupt moment when the wheel on which he was bound really did explode, it has become a convenient demarcation, allowing one to shut out what comes after—as if beyond this point the shuddering of his genius is somehow too erratic, too hard to put one's finger on. The greatest irony of this is that 1967, the year *after* the acci-dent, is by far the most prolific year of his life (sure, the man wrote dozens of songs in the winter of 1961–62, but a fair few of 'em were terrible. I'm talking real quality here).

Aside from *John Wesley Harding*—which appears to have been conceived, written, and recorded in one six-week period—Dylan and the Hawks recorded at least thirty Dylan originals in the basement of the Hawks' rented house in West Saugerties, daubed by some twisted soul in garish pink, in the sum-mer of 1967. Considering that these included songs like "Yea! Heavy and a Bottle of Bread," "Million Dollar Bash," and "Tiny Montgomery," this legendary—and much misunderstood—material could hardly be said to have been stripped of those surrealist phrases that hold so many critics in thrall.

The Basement Tapes may well be Dylan's greatest collection of songs. They certainly represent the most com-fortable, informal recording setup he would ever enjoy. In a sense, all of his best post-basement recordings have at-tempted such informality. Dylan himself would later tell Jann Wenner, "You know, that's really the way to do a recording—in a peaceful, relaxed setting, in some-body's basement, with the windows open and a dog lying on the floor." Never again would he be able to call on the camaraderie evident in the knock-about spontaneity of a throwaway ditty like "I'm Your Teenage Prayer." In the wake of *Music from Big Pink,* even his work with the Band never fully recaptured the spirit that flits from basement song to song.

That these songs were released in such a bastardized form in 1975, deformed in part by the ego of one Jamie Robertson, is an even greater artistic loss than what Dylan himself would do to *Blood on the Tracks, Infidels,* or *Oh Mercy* (the three corrupted masterpieces of the last twenty years). Something approximating an understanding of these remarkable sessions has only really been possible with the gradual passage into collectors' hands—since 1986—of the bulk of "original" basement tape reels. (These reels have been considerably collected together as one five-volume bootleg CD set, *The Genuine Basement Tapes.*) With these reels collectors and fans can at last hear around a hundred of the hundred and fifty or so basement recordings that are believed to exist. What they represent is a bounty of American song unparalleled in modern music (methinks I can smell the knotted pine of Americana, Greil). What these tapes display, aside from the sheer wealth of traditional music these guys were conversant with, is a process, an unfolding of not merely Dylan's muse but also a sensibility Robbie Robertson and the Band could really latch on to. The sessions, which offer a stark contrast to what came before and after, were the key (no, it wasn't Frank) that unlocked both *John Wesley Harding* and *Music from Big Pink.* For the Band, in particular, Dylan's rediscovery of the wellspring of his music set an example that would finally transform their music into something genuinely unique. The Band's music, more than Dylan's, would be permanently imbued with the spirit they found collectively in the basement of Big Pink.

Robertson has talked a lot of stuff and nonsense about his tutoring of Dylan (cough). According to Mr. Robertson,

"We would talk about early rockabilly records and stuff like that and I [would try] to get him to see that there was a vibe, a sound quality, to certain records, whether it was a Motown thing or a Sun Records thing or a Phil Spector thing." The idea that Dylan would need to be tutored on the Sun sound is truly laughable. Indeed one of the early "basement" sessions consists of a Johnny Cash Sun medley, Dylan and the Hawks beginning with a super-obscure Sun chestnut, "Belchezaar," eventually wrapping the session up with the evergreen "Big River" and "Folsom Prison Blues."

On the early basement sessions Dylan is largely content to run through old folk, country, and blues standards, clearly suggesting that it was he who was doing the tutoring and that it was Robertson—as the figure in the Band least steeped in rural American music—who was being shown "a vibe, a sound quality." This was, after all, very different material from what they had hawked around the world the previous year. The diversity of traditional or quasi-traditional material they recorded is quite remarkable: everything from Johnny Cash to the Stanley Brothers, from Ian Tyson to Ric Von Schmidt, from sea shanties to country tearjerkers, from pure gospel to simple morality tales, from the English and Irish dales to the Appalachian Mountains.

So what is it about the circumstances surrounding this material that makes it so special? Well, the first myth to explode is that there are hours and hours of basement tapes yet to come, filled with unimagined wild calypso songs wrung from a collective Woodstockian consciousness. The reality is that the basement tapes we have—and those we do not—are snapshots from the end of the day. Dylan and the Hawks spared collectors the world over their fumbling through the genesis of songs (unlike, say, the Beatles at Twickenham film studios, a self-conscious attempt to replicate the informality of Big Pink). No, Mr. Hudson only ran the tapes when they felt they wanted to get something down (yes, they really did want to record "Flight of the Bumble Bee" in C). With the original Dylan compositions (and virtually no Band originals were attempted at these summer 1967 sessions), what has been preserved are largely finished versions (sometimes after a few informal run-throughs off tape, sometimes not). The largest number of extant takes for any basement song is three ("Nothing Was Delivered," "Tears of Rage," and "Open the Door, Homer," though in all three cases only two takes are complete). In most instances complete disasters or fluffed takes ("false starts") were actually erased as the sessions progressed. At one point on the tapes Dylan tells Garth Hudson, "You don't have to record this. You're just wasting tape." (Cue much gnashing of teeth from all collectors.)

Yet for all the informality and spontaneity, the basement tapes were hardly your average 1967 home recordings. The honed nature of the songs and the rich sound on the original (stereo) tapes does not suggest an entirely casual approach to these sessions. There was a purpose to this documentation, and a desire to set things up so that "the real stuff" came out sounding good.

There has been much misinformation written about the recording of the basements over the ensuing years: from the misleading "It was cut live on a home tape recorder, with from one to three mikes" of Greil Marcus's CBS sleeve-notes to Paul Cable's "It seems very unlikely, in view of the full stereo [sic] of the tracks on the official album, that they were recorded, as is also claimed, on a domestic tape recorder." Of course, the official *Basement Tapes* album is not full stereo (would that it was) but "collapsed" mono (meaning that the stereo tapes have actually been compressed into mono)—even the cuts on *Biograph*

and *The Bootleg Series* being collapsed mono. Certain songs were also tampered with before their release, notably "You Ain't Going Nowhere," "This Wheel's on Fire," "Clothes Line Saga," and "Odds and Ends," all of which unfortunately have had piano and/or guitar/drums dubbed over the original recordings.

The original reels are all stereo, save for one (horribly distorted) session that consists of "Gloria/Station" (aka "Even If It's a Pig"), an instrumental "Ruben Remus," a fragment of a cacophonous "Nine Hundred Miles," something called "No Shoes on My Feet," an incongruously beautiful "Spanish Is the Loving Tongue," and one seriously overloaded blastout, listed on the reel as "On a Rainy Afternoon" (no, not the 1966 one). This session is in very primitive mono, and may well be the first Dylan/Hawks Big Pink session (not an auspicious start).

The remainder of the basement recordings are all in a "panned" stereo similar to the Beatles' debut album, with absolute separation of instruments between channels (if not quite as absolute as the Beatles achieved). This is because these are—whatever Cable may think—home recordings, and so there is some leakage between channels on particularly loud instruments (drums bleeding into electric guitar, and even occasionally the vocals). Thankfully the setup at Big Pink was the responsibility of Garth Hudson, the most technically minded of the Hawks. He was able to use some "leftovers" from the PA equipment used on the 1965–66 world tour. These included a couple of Altech PA tube (as opposed to transistor) "mixers" that allowed up to three microphone inputs per channel, and four or five studio-quality Neumann microphones. The use of something as state of the art as Neumann mikes plus the two tube mixer units explains why the sound of the basements has that deliciously rich warmth (indeed what sounds suspiciously like reverb on Dylan's vocals is actually the result of this Neumann/Altech combination). Sadly the official CBS album conveys little of this richness.

Rob Fraboni remembers from his discussions with Garth:

Garth had the tape recorder next to him and he had a little [Altech] mixer and there weren't a lot of mikes, [but] there were the vocal mikes, and the mikes that picked up other things in the room. I don't think they really miked the drums. It was done with loose miking. One of the reasons it has such a cool atmosphere is because the vocalist was in the room with everybody. It's not a very big room, and [with] the leakage from the instruments getting into the vocal mike and then the room pickup you sort of feel the room—and that's because there wasn't [sic] a lot of mikes used.

The "soundstage" Garth Hudson achieved with this Altech/Neumann setup obviously varied from reel to reel, sometimes from song to song, depending on whether Manuel or Robertson was playing drums (most basement cuts have no drums), Dylan was on acoustic, Danko and/or Manuel were providing harmonies. Indeed the ever-changing soundstage allows those so inclined (and with too much time on their hands) to surmise which songs might have been recorded together, and speculate as to what order the tapes might have been recorded in (the basement reels themselves have no notation as to recording dates, though they are mostly numbered and track listed, even if the numbering was probably done at a later date [by Garth] from memory). Certainly once the guys got into their daily ritual there was a standard setup that was generally adhered to—which went something like:

[LEFT CHANNEL] *bass—organ— [drums]—[electric guitar]—[2nd harmony vocal]*

[RIGHT CHANNEL] *Dylan vocal— acoustic guitar—[piano]—[harmony vocal]*

Again, there is one exception among the reels, one session when the bass and Dylan's vocals are both located in the left channel (not a good idea since the bass tends to drown out the vocals). Unfortunately this is one of the more interesting tapes, a folk medley session: "Ol' Roison the Beau," "I'm Guilty of Loving You" (which cuts abruptly), "Johnny Todd," "Cool Water," "The Banks of the Royal Canal," and "Po' Lazarus." This session (which closely follows the mono "Gloria/Station" session on its respective reel) probably dates from early in the summer, just as Dylan and the Hawks were easing themselves back into the process of music-making (and before Dylan began churning out a song a day). It also cogently defines some of Dylan's more obscure folk roots. "Banks of the Royal Canal" (often entitled "The Ol' Triangle") is a particularly affecting performance (one that engineer Rob Fraboni pulled to his own compilation reels at the time the CBS album was being compiled).

A close examination of the various basement reels had long suggested to me that at least two separate rooms were used for the recordings (though I'm doing my best to avoid technical gobbledegook, I based this on the amount of leakage between channels, particularly on Dylan's vocals). On certain of the basement songs—notably "One Single River," "People Get Ready," "I Don't Hurt Anymore," "Stones That You Throw," "Baby Ain't That Fine," "Rock Salt and Nails," "A Fool Such as I," "Young But Daily Growin'," "Bonnie Ship the Diamond," and "The Hills of Mexico" (all of which come from the three reels accessed in 1986)—it almost sounds like Dylan's vocals have been double-tracked such is the leakage into the nonvocal channel. This suggests that these songs were recorded in a smaller room (or that the guys were more closely miked) than the bulk of basement material, where the leakage (at least on Dylan's vocals) is only minimal. In fact, Garth Hudson recently confirmed that the sessions did not begin at Big Pink but at Dylan's own house, in what was known appropriately as "The Red Room." However, the daily distractions of family life were such that the boys soon decided a relocation was in order.

The poorer quality basement recordings—the bass/vocal session, the sessions with the vocal leakage, probably both recorded at 3¾ ips (as were a handful of Big Pink sessions)—almost exclusively comprise cover songs and experimental jams. This may well suggest that some or all of them derive from The Red Room rather than Big Pink and, irrespective of location, that they were recorded either in late spring or early summer 1967. Should these sessions turn out to be the first batch of Woodstock recordings—Hudson has suggested that most of the copyrighted Dylan originals were recorded at a midpoint in the Woodstock workouts—then there is a certain symmetry to the basement material as it has come down to us. What the reels seem to document is the passage from drought to flood (and maybe even back to drought). Evidently what started out as a bit of fun only slowly evolved into a body of songs.

Robbie Robertson: *"There was no particular reason for it. We weren't making a record. We were just fooling around. The purpose was whatever comes into anybody's mind, we'll put it down on this little tape recorder. Shitty little tape recorder . . . we had that freedom of thinking, Well, no one's ever gonna hear this anyway, so what's the difference? And then we thought, Well, maybe some of these songs would be good for other people to record."*

It certainly appears that Dylan and the Hawks only began recording *any* of the sessions some weeks—possibly even a couple of months—after they began their daily routine of sessions. According to Danko, sessions began back in March (certain sources have dated the earliest basement tapes to April). Al Aronowitz, a New York journalist, visited Dylan in Woodstock in the spring of 1967 and found him working on ideas for songs. Yet there is no evidence that any of the material Aronowitz heard was recorded. All available information suggests that the actual basement tapes were recorded over a three- to four-month period (with one hiatus, of which more later). The last "regular" Dylan/Hawks basement session probably took place in early to mid September 1967, just before Dylan started work on *John Wesley Harding* and Levon Helm rejoined the Hawks (though not in time for their first demo session in a New York studio). It seems unlikely that any Red Room recordings date to before late May/early June.

According to Robertson, the original idea behind the sessions had been simply to pass the time or, more accurately, to stop time. Certainly the sense of isolation that Woodstock still enjoyed in the mid-sixties would have convinced these guys that they had all the time in the world—ABC, MacMillan, Albert Grossman, and Columbia could all wait their turn!

So the sessions began as an excuse to play some songs. Then, at some point, the guys felt the urge to lay down some of the songs on tape and—as a direct result of these early basement tape sessions—Dylan felt inspired enough to begin writing songs again. Only at this point did things become serious (possibly it was the first flutterings of Dylan's muse that persuaded Dylan and company to move out of the Red Room and mike up Big Pink).

But even as the sessions were resuming at Big Pink, Dylan was already looking for a way to move on. The songs he began writing at this point may be peopled with the usual extras from *Freaks*—"Gorgeous George," "Mrs. Henry," "Tiny Montgomery"—but now Dylan's dry, laconic delivery sought to highlight an absurdity in the human condition that led not to the existential despair of a song like "Desolation Row" but to an almost fatalistic hedonism— take me down to California, baby, and bring that bottle of bread!

That these sessions were informal to its square root is reflected in the routine these guys devised. In the morning Dylan would drop off his stepdaughter at pre-school, head on up to Big Pink, put a large pot of painfully strong, high-octane coffee on the stove and sit at a typewriter tapping out words, ideas, lines, thoughts. Around noon, he would begin to rouse the comatosed Band members with the promise of flagons of 90-proof caffeine. They would then sit around and smoke some weed before the music-making would begin. Hence the somewhat exuberant spirits evident on so many of the basement recordings. These boys were flying low over the Rockies by the time music commenced. In the light of their likely state of mind, I think Dylan's wild exhortations in the middle of songs like "Sign on the Cross" might best be taken with the odd truck-load of salt.

"Sign on the Cross" itself might well have been one of the first songs recorded at Big Pink itself. It is certainly one of the greatest performances of Dylan *and* the Band's careers. Its continued omission from Dylan's official oeuvre is one of the greater mysteries for Jeff Rosen (compiler of *Biograph* and *The Bootleg Series*) to explain. It comes at the end of what may be the second Big Pink reel, a reel that also includes "Tiny Montgomery" and the scathing "All American Boy" (a more sarcastic "Dear Landlord" if you like!, which was copyrighted in 1973).

One curious aspect to this reel is the subsequent omission of both "Sign on the Cross" and "Tiny Montgomery" from the "safeties" that were made of the important basement tape songs. Shortly after *Music from Big Pink,* Garth Hudson arranged for John Simon to make a safety of nineteen songs, all Dylan originals, in stereo, under studio conditions onto 10-inch reels at 15 ips. The songs selected were the obvious ones—thirteen of the fourteen acetate tracks plus the likes of "Clothes Line Saga" and "Apple Suckling Tree." However, there are two major anomalies: one, "Tears of Rage" and "The Mighty Quinn" are in mono, suggesting that the engineer did not have access to the original reel (both cuts were certainly recorded in stereo); two, the total absence of "Tiny Montgomery"—the only one of the fourteen "acetate" songs to be omitted—and "Sign on the Cross" suggests that the reel with these songs had also been mislaid. "I'm Not There (1956)," the other lost basement masterpiece, *is* on the safety. This safety, which ended up residing in Neil Young's archive, was not referred to for any of the archival digs that have led to basement material being officially released.

This (second) Big Pink reel contains every magical element that makes the basements such a unique odyssey through American music. It is certainly my favorite basement reel. Aside from the three copyrighted Dylan "originals"— "Tiny Montgomery," "All American Boy," and "Sign on the Cross"—there are three songs that appear to be almost entirely improvised, "See You Later, Allen Ginsberg," a pastiche of "See You Later Alligator"; "I'm in the Mood for Love," which seems to be largely an exercise in how much innuendo Dylan and Manuel can put into the phrase itself; and "I'm Your Teenage Prayer," an homage to doo-wop that leaves *Reuben and the Jets* back in the bus shelter, Dylan and presumably

Richard doing some of their best verbal jousting (there was a mike set up in the middle of the room called "the voice of conscience," plugged direct into the Al-tech; often someone would lean into it mid-song and intone something, hence the strange ad-libs that often pepper these songs):

Dylan: *Take a look at me babe.*
Richard: *No, take a look at me babe.*

"Teenage Prayer" was not the only song cut at these first few sessions to display such exuberance. After opening the reel with a couple of furtive attempts at a Dylan original called "I'm a Fool for You" (a musical cross between "Like a Rolling Stone" and the later basement tape original, "All You Have to Do Is Dream"), a consignment of particularly mean Moroccan Black must have been delivered ("I tell this truth to you . . . "). Digging deep into the obscurest roots of American popular music, Dylan comes up with "First Time on the Highway," a raucous blues that is on the point of collapsing when he lights into Manuel for "playing that piano shit-faced," before suggesting that he "piss[es] on that piano," then a quick cut. Dylan, now in best country hick mode, is intoning "Down in Bearsville . . . ," before telling the down-home story of a big flood, which becomes progressively more absurd, "I was just a little boy . . . twenty-two years old."

Before the next cut, Dylan can be heard laying down instructions as to what harmonies are warranted on Gid Tanner and his Skillet-Lickers' 1926 opus "You Gotta Quit Kickin' My Dog Aroun'." His instructions are barely adhered to by his tanked-up ensemble. Sandwiched between "See You Later, Allen Ginsberg," and a ridiculously over-the-top stab (actually two over-the-top stabs) at some traditional Spanish ballad (a tragic tale of lost love treated with the sort of contempt Dylan usually

reserves for Paul Simon songs) comes "Tiny Montgomery," a sudden island of sanity (albeit surreal sanity) on this reel of madness.

Just when the listener is starting to suspect these sessions to be nothing more than a series of drunken revelries, Dylan comes up with the most beautiful trio of covers to grace this (indeed any Dylan) session. In one gorgeously inspirational burst, he gives a couple of Ian Tyson (of Ian and Sylvia fame) originals the sort of caressingly tender vocals they always required. "Four Strong Winds" in particular should put splinters in any listener's heart. "The French Girl" (which Dylan was to attempt twenty years later with the Grateful Dead) he seems less happy with, changing first the key, then the tempo, but it's still a knock-'em-dead performance. Finally Dylan manages 75 percent of Eric Von Schmidt's "Joshua Gone Barbados." The vocal style he uncovers here—an abrasive, tugging delivery that lacks his usual nasal quality—he carries over to the last two songs on the reel: "All American Boy" and "Sign on the Cross."

"All American Boy," a monologue (or should that be a tirade) on how to become a star, with assorted asides from Garth and company and a simple strummed accompaniment, reveals a lot about Dylan's feelings of bitterness at those who led him astray. Though copyrighted by Dylan's people in 1973, this is in fact a reworking of a 1958 Bobby Bare single. Nothing, though, prepares the listener for the ethereal beauty of "Sign on the Cross." The interplay between Hudson and Robertson on this cut is extrasensory, while Dylan's uncanny ability to veer between the transcendent and the hokey (and back again) tells anyone who is paying attention just what he assimilated from those "race records" savored during a misspent youth.

In many ways "Sign on the Cross" marks the passage into the Basements proper. From here on the sessions largely become the unleashing of a "new" Dylan, albeit one destined to be discarded before his next public unveiling. In the months of July and August, Dylan and the Hawks recorded ten of the fourteen songs on the famous Dwarf Music acetate. (These songs were copyrighted at the beginning of October 1967. Given that it takes about a month for songs to be registered after submission, this implies that these ten songs, and therefore the bulk of the basement sessions, were over by the end of August.)

This mono acetate of fourteen publishers' demos comprises both the best-known and the most commercial tracks from Big Pink. The order of the acetate is interesting (it may even be chronological, though I personally doubt it):

"Million Dollar Bash"
"Yea! Heavy and a Bottle of Bread"—
    same session
"Please, Mrs. Henry"
"Crash on the Levee (Down in the
    Flood)"
"Lo and Behold!"—same session
"Tiny Montgomery"—isolated session
"This Wheel's on Fire"
"You Ain't Going Nowhere"
"I Shall Be Released"
"Too Much of Nothing"—same ses-
    sion(s?)
"Tears of Rage"
"The Mighty Quinn"—same session
"Open the Door, Homer"
"Nothing Was Delivered"—same ses-
    sion

When the official album was released, not only were there extraneous overdubs on "This Wheel's on Fire" and "You Ain't Going Nowhere," but "The Mighty Quinn" and "I Shall Be Released" had both been omitted and inferior alternates of "Tears of Rage" and "Too Much of Nothing" selected. This is particularly unfortunate because the session(s) tapes from which "This

Wheel's on Fire," "You Ain't Going Nowhere," "I Shall Be Released," and "Too Much of Nothing" derive have so far eluded collectors (there were stereo versions on the reels accessed in 1986, but they sound like a 3¾ ips dub of a 3¾ dub of a 7½ ips master and much of its clarity has gone AWOL). This means that the only really good versions of these cuts in general circulation are the mono versions taken from the original acetate. It also means that we can only hazard a guess as to what other songs (if any) may be on this particular reel.

Certainly on the reel are alternate takes of "Too Much of Nothing" and "You Ain't Going Nowhere." The first "Too Much of Nothing" lacks even a bare-bones tune. Yet Robertson decided to include this version on *The Basement Tapes,* presumably as a surprise to collectors, which smacks to me of very poor judgment. "Too Much of Nothing" was the first basement song to be covered, and though it is by no means the most commercial cut from the sessions, Peter, Paul and Mary still charted with the song in November 1967 (suggesting that they had been given a copy of the song by Dylan or Grossman in July or August). The alternate take of "You Ain't Going Nowhere" is something else. Presumably recorded the day before Dylan wrote the real lyrics, "Nowhere" take one really is talking in tongues! Dylan accuses some unspecified soul (presumably the one going nowhere) of being "a bunch of basement noise," before advising "Michael" to "pick up your nose, you canary . . . you ain't no head of lettuce." We can be grateful that they even recorded this run-through. As an insight into Dylan's writing process at this time it is invaluable, even if lyrically it is closer to Lewis Carroll than to William Burroughs.

Of the acetate songs, only "Please, Mrs. Henry," "This Wheel's on Fire," and "I Shall Be Released" lack first takes on the reels, suggesting that with these songs a run-through was deemed necessary, if just to set levels. The best take was usually selected for the acetate (if not the CBS album), though I love the viciousness of the guitar and a wild Dylan vocal on the first attempt at "Crash on the Levee." In the cases of "Open the Door, Homer" and "Nothing Was Delivered," first takes were actually preferred. The first take of "Lo and Behold!" is also a delight, though this is largely because Dylan realizes at one point that he is about to sing the same line and has to admit, midtake, that he is going back to Pittsburgh—again!! Cue much merriment.

Aside from the ten acetate songs recorded in July or August and copyrighted in October, there were at least eight other Dylan originals recorded during the same Big Pink sessions—all of which were belatedly copyrighted between 1970 and 1973, when the bootlegging of Dylan was at its height and *Writings and Drawings* was in the works. These include perhaps the two most beautiful songs recorded at these sessions, "Sign on the Cross" and a song listed on the box as "I'm Not There, I'm Gone" but copyrighted (in 1970) as "I'm Not There (1956)."

Recorded amid such hedonistic revelries as "Yea! Heavy and a Bottle of Bread" and "Please, Mrs. Henry," "I'm Not There" has probably excited more discussion than just about any other unreleased Dylan song. Part of this is the inevitable result of a set of lyrics that always seem on the verge of meaning something. The sense—half-sense might be a more accurate phrase, the lyrics slide in and out of coherence—is one of regret and remorse as the singer reflects on a girl who shone "like a rainbow yesterday." Many have sought to interpret some significance to the (1956) subtitle. A seemingly authentic typescript of a skeletal version of the song (published in *The Telegraph*) seemed to confirm what I long suspected, that Dylan had the bare

outlines to the song and free-associated the rest. That said, it is the ghostly backing and an equally haunted vocal that gives the song its enticing majesty. Of course, the real question, which can never be resolved, is why Dylan would leave such a half-formed masterpiece unfinished (certainly the nightmare of transcribing this song may explain why it took until 1970 for it to be copyrighted)?

Five other lost basement songs were not copyrighted until September 1973 (a most curious date because the songs had not been bootlegged; an official basement release was some way off and *Writings and Drawings* was already on the shelves), one of which, "Wild Wolf," has yet to make it into trading circles. Of the others, "All American Boy" is the most interesting. "Silent Weekend" and "Santa Fe" are pleasant enough throwaways (though to include "Santa Fe" on *The Bootleg Series* but not "Sign on the Cross" and "I'm Not There" is definitely a case of taking the piss and leaving the Möet), while "Bourbon Street" is a cacophonous racket that only proves that tubas and booze do not mix.

At this point, I now believe, we have passed beyond the meridian of another Woodstock summer and toward the fading light of fall, and what perhaps should be considered an entirely distinct set of basement tapes. The final four songs on the Dwarf Music acetate, which derive from these sessions, include two of Dylan's darkest songs, "Tears of Rage" and "Nothing Was Delivered." "Tears of Rage," in particular, suggests that returning from the edge had failed to imbue Dylan with an unquestioning joie de vivre. These songs derive from two reels of rhyme. Though these songs were not actually copyrighted until early January 1968 (along with "Get Your Rocks Off," "The Mighty Quinn," and "Open the Door, Homer"), they clearly date from shortly after the main collection of basement songs. Why they should not have been copyrighted as promptly as the other ten Dwarf Music demos I know not (all fourteen songs began to circulate within "music" circles shortly after *John Wesley Harding*'s post-Xmas release).

That there was a break in the Big Pink sessions is, I believe, indisputable. How long it lasted we can only guess. Most likely it was something as mundane as Dylan's parents visiting him in Woodstock that caused the hiatus (we know Abe and Beattie did visit Bob and Sara in the late summer of 1967). The five songs copyrighted in January 1968 were part of what were probably no more than half a dozen sessions in September (and possibly into October). Which may well suggest that Dylan and the Band had already begun to abandon their daily routine of sessions. By this point, they were probably both looking to begin work on their respective albums. Columbia was pushing for a pukka Dylan studio effort—his first in eighteen months—while Richard Manuel and Robbie Robertson were working on their own songs, which were starting to evolve beyond the sub-Dylanesque.

Yet the various sessions from this final basement period did not just result in the five songs copyrighted in January 1968 but also the terrific "Odds and Ends" (originally entitled "Lost Time Is Not Found Again"), the authentic frontier gibberish of "Apple Suckling Tree" and that close cousin of "Frankie Lee and Judas Priest," "Clothes Line Saga."

On the safety of the Basements "Clothes Line" is actually listed as "Answer to Ode" (meaning "Ode to Billy Jo"), and—though it never occurred to me until I saw the box—it is self-evidently a parody of that song. Assuming that "Clothes Line Saga" was composed around the time that "Ode to Billy Jo" had reached saturation point on the radio, date of composition would have to be late August or early September ("Billy Jo" reached number one on

the *Billboard* charts on August 26, having entered the charts two weeks earlier).

Sandwiched between the two takes of "Odds and Ends" (for once I much prefer the first take, it has so much more vitality, even if Robertson makes a serious hash of the guitar solo) is a fragment of an uptempo "Nothing Was Delivered." On all of these songs there is some energetic drumming, presumably from Richard Manuel. Levon Helm has suggested, in his recent autobiography *This Wheel's on Fire,* that he rejoined the Band at some point in November (he is surely a few weeks out here), returning at the end of the basement sessions and playing on a version of "Nothing Was Delivered." Though this fragment does not sound like Helm it does perhaps suggest that some basement songs were recut at a later date. It also suggests that the basement sessions did not come to a crashing halt when Dylan began work on *John Wesley Harding.*

Certainly what appear to be the two final basement reels—the one that opens with "Goin' to Acapulco" and the one that, aside from much Band material, contains two takes of a new Dylan original, "All You Have to Do Is Dream"— are quite hard to place ("All You Have to Do Is Dream" was not part of Rob Fraboni's own reels, compiled in 1975, perhaps suggesting he never managed to access this reel). Neither of these Dylan originals were copyrighted with the other basement songs—despite their patent superiority to three of the songs copyrighted in 1973. This suggests that they had probably been filed away separately, forgotten about until 1975 or 1986.

"Goin' to Acapulco" and the other song attempted at the same session, the slight "Gonna Get You Now," are certainly fully imbued with the spirit of the basements—that lovely mixture of the bawdy and the Bacchanalian. However it is the next session on this reel that features perhaps the most astonishing performance of these remarkable sessions. "See That My Grave Is Kept Clean" might seem like an unremarkable choice given its inclusion on Dylan's first album but he sure as hell never sung it like this! Here we have, intact and fully formed, Dylan's *Nashville Skyline* voice, more than a year before the sound was unveiled, and (almost certainly) before he had completed the *John Wesley Harding* album.

Several Minnesotans have commented on the similarity between Dylan's *Nashville Skyline* voice and the voice he sang with before his discovery of Guthrie— i.e., the voice that can be heard on the May 1960 St. Paul tape—but nothing prepares one for "See That My Grave Is Kept Clean." Given that, like the rendition of the Stanley Brothers' "Wild Wood Flower" it precedes, "See That My Grave Is Kept Clean" should be shrouded in some otherworldly accompaniment, complete with autoharp and harmonica (not played by Dylan), only adds to the mystery. Dylan has simply dropped this vocal in on one song and then it is gone and he is rediscovering the delights of basement balladry with "Flight of the Bumble Bee" and an almost-there nod at fifties tearjerker "Confidential to Me" (destined to reappear on the Never Ending Tour).

"All You Have to Do Is Dream," though it has fewer incongruities, also hints that it may not be part of "the basements" proper but may well date from after Dylan began *John Wesley Harding*—the period after Helm had rejoined the Band (there is slide guitar, organ, bass, piano, *and* drums on this track, which means, unless Dylan is playing piano, which is highly unlikely at Big Pink, then Helm must be playing drums). The sound on this track is also unusual for the basements because amplification was usually kept to a minimum. On "All You Have to Do Is Dream" a crashing guitar solo cuts

through the second take with a savagery akin to 1966.

Other, external evidence also suggests a later date. The reel itself features not just two takes of "All You Have to Do Is Dream" but also the falsetto doodlings of Tiny Tim (with the Band) and the tentative first stage of the Band's own songwriting (one attempt at "Yazoo Street Scandal"—very basementy—two at "You Say You Love Me," both gorgeous, and a fragment of "Ferdinand the Imposter"). The lyrics of "All You Have to Do Is Dream" also seem closer to the middle-American morality of *John Wesley Harding* than something like "Please, Mrs. Henry" (it has no chorus, a rarity among basement tape originals). That said, the song's stream of non sequiturs certainly seems like an appropriate way to wrap up the salad days of Big Pink. Meanwhile the Band's own forays on this reel clearly imply that they are beginning to find their own voice.

Whether these final recordings postdate work on *John Wesley Harding*— there is no reason why Dylan might not have "popped in" while the Band were cutting some of their own material— they sound like a movement away from the basements, with its ragtime melody or two, a little wine in the afternoon, and tutorials in American roots for Canada's best bar band, looking for a way to ground their music in something a little more real than "Money Honey"—to wit, a marriage made in Woodstock, consummated in bootleg heaven.

Sadly, when this material was finally released in 1975, Robbie Robertson seemed determined to present a sleight of hand as the truth. Intermingling eight songs by the Band supposedly cut in the fall of 1967, Robertson sought to imply that the alliance between Dylan and the Band was far more equal than it was: "Hey, we were writing all these songs, doing our own thing, oh and Bob would sometimes come around and we'd swap a few tunes." In fact, the so-called Band basement tapes have nothing to do with the Dylan/Band sessions (of the eight Band cuts on *The Basement Tapes,* two are Richard Manuel Big Pink piano demos from the summer of 1967, with drums and guitars overdubbed in 1975; two are demos cut in New York in September 1967; two are recordings made shortly after Helm rejoined, probably at Big Pink; and two are actually 1975 recordings made at Shangri-La. At least three Richard Manuel compositions recorded at Big Pink in 1967—"You Say You Love Me," "Beautiful Thing," and "Ferdinand the Imposter"—were omitted from the set possibly because they highlighted how Manuel, not Robertson, was the first to pen original Band material).

Though revealing in their own right, the Band tracks only pollute the official set and reduce its stature. Dylan's songs, fully sprung from his reactivated muse, are the work of an artist at the pinnacle of his powers. The Band's songs are signposts along the way, notes detailing the search for an independent voice so magically realized on *Music from Big Pink.* No more, no less.

The inspiration of those sessions in the summer of 1967 would stay with the Band a long time. For Dylan, they were merely a way of moving on, songs discarded after he passed them to Dwarf Music (Bob Dylan has said, "Well, [they were] done out in somebody's basement. They weren't demos for myself, they were [just] demos of the songs. I was being *pushed* again into coming up with some songs"). The Band took their fair share of the fifteen Dylan songs lodged with Dwarf Music between September 1967 and January 1968 (perhaps Dylan wrote them all along for the Band to cherry pick from, unaware of the songwriting they were capable of themselves). Other artists with a Dylan pedigree snapped up most of the other demos, discreetly circulated in the early months of 1968. "This Wheel's on Fire" and "The Mighty Quinn" gave Dylan his biggest royalty checks since "Rainy Day Women." Meanwhile *John Wesley Harding* suggested that Dylan was not about to tune in to the summer of love ethos.

Posterity, though, would not allow Dylan to hide his and the Band's achievements that summer for very long. In June 1968, *Rolling Stone* ran a front cover feature on the basement tapes. Its title: THE MISSING BOB DYLAN ALBUM. The bootlegging of Bob Dylan's missing link was only a step away.

JOHN WESLEY HARDING

Recorded: October 17 to November 29, 1967
Released: December 27, 1967

Side 1: John Wesley Harding. As I Went Out One Morning. I Dreamed I Saw St. Augustine. All Along the Watchtower. Ballad of Frankie Lee and Judas Priest. The Drifter's Escape. Side 2: Dear Landlord. I Am a Lonesome Hobo. I Pity the Poor Immigrant. The Wicked Messenger. Down Along the Cove. I'll Be Your Baby Tonight.

Producer:
1–3 Bob Johnston

Musicians:
1–3 Bob Dylan (guitar/harmonica)
1–3 Charlie McCoy (bass)

1–3 Kenneth Buttrey (drums)
3 Pete Drake (steel guitar)

1. COLUMBIA MUSIC ROW STUDIOS
   NASHVILLE, TENNESSEE
   OCTOBER 17 TO 18, 1967
NCO 120927 **The Drifter's Escape**
NCO 120928 **I Dreamed I Saw**
              St. Augustine
NCO 120929 **Ballad of Frankie Lee and**
              Judas Priest

2. COLUMBIA MUSIC ROW STUDIOS
   NASHVILLE, TENNESSEE
   NOVEMBER 6, 1967
NCO 120955 **All Along the Watchtower [I]**
NCO 120955 All Along the Watchtower [II]

NCO 120956 John Wesley Harding [I]
NCO 120956 John Wesley Harding [II]
NCO 120957 **As I Went Out One Morning**
NCO 120958 **I Pity the Poor Immigrant**
NCO 120959 **I Am a Lonesome Hobo**

3. COLUMBIA MUSIC ROW STUDIOS
   NASHVILLE, TENNESSEE
   NOVEMBER 21, 1967
NCO 120960 **The Wicked Messenger**
NCO 120961 **I'll Be Your Baby Tonight**
NCO 120962 **Down Along the Cove**
NCO 120963 **Dear Landlord**

By the time fans were able to connect up the dots, Dylan had already released his long-awaited followup to *Blonde on Blonde, John Wesley Harding*. If the circumstances surrounding the basement tapes have long been shrouded in myth, the central mystery surrounding *John Wesley Harding* relates not to the recordings—three straightforward single-day sessions at Columbia's Music Row Studios in October and November 1967—but where this, Dylan's most perfectly executed album, came from, perfectly constructed, fully realized, in such a short span of time.

The gap between the basements

(proper) and the first *John Wesley Harding* session—October 17—can only have been a matter of weeks. Yet the songs on *John Wesley Harding* could hardly be more different from their basement counterparts. Nor is there any evidence to suggest that Dylan made any attempt to cut any basement songs at the Nashville sessions (the studio sheets suggest not). Evidently Dylan, who considered the basements a diversionary project, had something very specific in mind with *John Wesley Harding*. *John Wesley Harding* was to be the album made the morning after a late-night drinking moonshine and shooting the breeze in some friends' basement.

On a superficial level the *John Wesley Harding* songs lack any raucous Big Pink choruses. Indeed sound itself has been stripped bare—the only lead instruments are Dylan's voice and harmonica. On a deeper level the songs operate best in context, as a series of parables in ballad form. Though there may have been a rich moral vein running through the best of the basements, it had not been so obviously mined from the King James Bible. On *John Wesley Harding* the wicked are judged while innocents walk abroad.

Dylan's return to the ballad form, though presaged by songs like "Clothes Line Saga" and "All American Boy," was certainly a surprise to the summer of love's psychedelically inclined spawn. It may well be that the emotional jolt the death of Dylan's last idol, Woody Guthrie, gave him two weeks before the first *John Wesley Harding* session, made him cast his mind back to his own songwriting roots. Of course, such a switch barely qualified as culture shock. Dylan had been immersing himself in traditional Americana all summer long and the moralistic tone, celebration of the underdog and an underlying contempt for those who set themselves up as judge and jury—all Guthriesque motifs reiterated on *John Wesley Harding*—ulti-

mately stem from the folk tradition itself.

After eighteen months of quietude Dylan deliberately devised a muted return to the public arena. The twelve songs that make up *John Wesley Harding* were written in a single rush of inspiration, over the five weeks that span the sessions. They said all that Dylan wanted to say. There were no outtakes recorded at the *John Wesley Harding* sessions (although alternates of "All Along the Watchtower" and "John Wesley Harding" were shortlisted). What was cut was choice.

According to one source, Dylan actually wrote the initial trio of songs during the two-day train ride from New York to Nashville (perhaps Dylan took the train with this in mind), and it is these three songs—"The Drifter's Escape," "I Dreamed I Saw St. Augustine," and "Frankie Lee and Judas Priest"—that set the tone for the album.

With "Frankie Lee" in particular Dylan invented a rich new form of the surreal. "Frankie Lee and Judas Priest" is perhaps the one song on *John Wesley Harding* to closely mirror that unique Big Pink irreverence. In the style of a western ballad, the song as recorded relies heavily on Dylan's matter-of-fact delivery—previously rehearsed on the basement cover of Luke the Drifter's "(Be Careful of the) Stones That You Throw"—for its dramatic power. The point of the tale, "the moral of this song," is self-evidently not the one delivered at the end of the song, "Don't go mistaking paradise for that home along the road" (a platitude), but rather the little neighbor boy's muttered aside, "Nothing is revealed." The song is really a parody of message songs, hence the failure of every Dylan critic to unravel the song's meaning.

The subject matter of "I Dreamed I Saw St. Augustine"—which is set within the frame of "The Ballad of Joe Hill," an account of martyred union leader

Hill's death popularized by (among others) Guthrie—remains just as elusive (neither of the two historical St. Augustines were "put out to death"). However, the song does hint at some kind of moral awakening on Dylan's part, perhaps the same one he talked about on stage in Birmingham in 1981, prefacing "Dead Man, Dead Man."

"Drifter's Escape," on the face of it, seems to be more conventional, but once again the words coming from the participants' tongues fail to address the issues at hand. This is Frank's key. It is not the songs that fail to reveal, but the character's own words that rarely reflect their inner turmoil. In this sense, "Clothes Line Saga" bequeathed an approach fully embraced on *John Wesley Harding*.

The pared-down sound of the first three songs Dylan recorded was maintained for both the remaining sessions, save for two songs recorded at the final session, embellished by Pete Drake's steel guitar. However it may be overly simplistic to interpret this as Dylan making some kind of gesture to his folk audience. Admittedly recording with just Ken Buttrey on drums and Charlie McCoy on bass was hardly going for a big band sound, and Dylan's dismissal of *Sgt. Pepper* as "very indulgent" suggests a self-conscious minimalist at work here. Yet, according to Robbie Robertson, Dylan originally intended for Robertson and probably Garth Hudson to augment the basic tracks, overdubbing guitar and organ. Dylan himself has said that he was trying to get the sound Gordon Lightfoot had previously achieved with

Buttrey and McCoy. Robertson alleges that the eventual decision not to embellish the album was a mutual one. Most likely Dylan just realized that the austere sound of *John Wesley Harding* complemented its lyrical content perfectly.

In describing *John Wesley Harding* earlier as Dylan's most perfectly executed album, that austerity (in sound and lyric) is, frankly, a key element. For the first time since *Another Side* Dylan was recording only songs whose ink was barely dry. If no one song can be said to unlock Frank's door, Dylan carried one aspect of the Big Pink songs to Nashville—writing the words in advance of the melodies. As such *John Wesley Harding* operates very much as one large canvas. Some songs lack the insight of "Stuck Inside of Mobile," but the sum of the parts make for a greater whole than *John Wesley Harding*'s illustrious predecessor (such heresy!). The fact that Dylan wrote *John Wesley Harding* self-consciously as "an album of songs" in a month and a day, and recorded it in just three afternoons, gives the album a unity all its own. That Dylan entered the studio with just producer Bob Johnston and his favorite two Nashville studio cats—who well remembered the madness of the *Blonde on Blonde* sessions and were astonished by Dylan's calm professionalism—made the process as smooth as a rhapsody. It would take Dylan a long time to get back to recording another "album of songs" without the process itself getting in the way.

COLUMBIA RECORDING STUDIOS

604 16TH AVE. SO.
NASHVILLE, TENNESSEE

STEREO

PROGRAM: ~~Johnny Cash~~ & Bob Dylan

CLIENT: Columbia

ADDRESS:

STUDIO: CB   MIXER: LB
RECORDER: BHL   ORIG. RECORD DATE: 2-17-69   W.O. NO: ~~~~~45

REEL NO.   OF: TAPE MCH. NO.   TAPE SPEED: 15   C.O. NO:

EDITED OR INTERCUT BY: DATE:

STRK MASTER

MASTER NO.	TITLE	TIME
NCO 98934	I STILL MISS SOMEONE	
98935	DON'T THINK TWICE, IT'S ALRIGHT	

Box 235

MASTERS BY: DATE: STUDIO: SEC:

MASTERING DATA: ROW: BIN:

CBS RECORDS RECORDING STUDIOS TAPE DATA SHEET

NOTE: Complete this form. Secure to box containing tape described hereon.

PROJECT NUMBER	STUDIO	JOB NUMBER	REEL I	SPEED 7½

DATE	SHEET NUMBER	PROGRAM Bob Dylan + Johnny Cash	☑ MONO	☐ 8 TRACK
		CLIENT Col.	☑ 2 TRACK	☐ 16 TRACK
2 Tk 7½ Copy		PRODUCER	☐ 3 TRACK	☐ DOLBY
☐ NASHVILLE	☐ OTHER	CO. ENG. RE. ENG.	☐ 4 TRACK	OTHER

TIME	MASTER NUMBER	PROGRAM TITLE	TAKE NO.	CODES	TIME MARK
	98942	MATCH BOX BLUES			
	98943	THATS ALRIGHT MOMMA			
*	98944	BIG RIVER			
	98945	GIRL FROM THE NORTH COUNTRY			
	98946	I WALK THE LINE			
	98947	YOU ARE MY SUNSHINE			
	98948	RING OF FIRE			
	98949	GUESS THINGS HAPPEN THAT WAY			
	98950	JUST A CLOSER WALK WITH THEE			
	98951	T FOR TEXAS			
	98952	BLUE YODDLE #4			
✗	98939	MOUNTAIN DEW			
	98940	I STILL MISS SOMEONE			
	98941	CARELESS LOVE			
*	98943 ~~Match~~	MYSTERY TRAIN			
*	98944	MYSTERY TRAIN + TALK	MONO		

NASHVILLE SKYLINE

Recorded: February 13 to February 18, 1969
Released: April 9, 1969
Side 1: Girl from the North Country. Nashville Skyline Rag. To Be Alone with You. I Threw It All Away. Peggy Day. Side 2: Lay Lady Lay. One More Night. Tell Me That It Isn't True. Country Pie. Tonight I'll Be Staying Here with You.

Producer:
1–4 Bob Johnston

Musicians:
1–4 Bob Dylan (guitar/harmonica)
1–4 Norman Blake (guitar)
1–3 Pete Drake (steel guitar)
1–3 Charlie Daniels (guitar)
1–3 Bob Wilson (piano)
1–3 Charlie McCoy (bass)

1–3 Kenneth Buttrey (drums)
3–4 Johnny Cash (guitar/vocals)
3–4 Marshall Grant (bass)
3–4 W. S. Holland (drums)
3–4 Carl Perkins (guitar)
3–4 Bob Wootton (guitar)

1. COLUMBIA MUSIC ROW STUDIOS
   NASHVILLE, TENNESSEE
   FEBRUARY 13, 1969
   NCO 98921   *unknown*
   NCO 98922   **To Be Alone with You**
   NCO 98923   **I Threw It All Away**
   NCO 98924   **One More Night**
   NCO 98925   *Lay Lady Lay*
   NCO 98926   *"Blues"*

2. COLUMBIA MUSIC ROW STUDIOS
   NASHVILLE, TENNESSEE
   FEBRUARY 14, 1969
   NCO 98927   **Peggy Day**
   NCO 98928   **Tell Me That It Isn't True**
   NCO 98929   **Country Pie**
   NCO 98930   **Lay Lady Lay (remake)**

3. COLUMBIA MUSIC ROW STUDIOS
   NASHVILLE, TENNESSEE
   FEBRUARY 17, 1969
   NCO 98931   **Nashville Skyline Rag**

NCO 98932   Tonight I'll Be Staying Here
             with You [I]
NCO 98932   **Tonight I'll Be Staying Here**
             with You [II]
NCO 98933   One Too Many Mornings
NCO 98934   I Still Miss Someone
NCO 98935   Don't Think Twice, It's All
             Right

4. COLUMBIA MUSIC ROW STUDIOS
   NASHVILLE, TENNESSEE
   FEBRUARY 18, 1969
   NCO 98938   One Too Many Mornings
   NCO 98939   Good Ol' Mountain Dew
   NCO 98940   I Still Miss Someone
   NCO 98941   Careless Love
   NCO 98942   Matchbox
   NCO 98943   That's All Right, Mama
   NCO 98944   Big River
   NCO 98945   **Girl from the North Country**
   NCO 98946   I Walk the Line
   NCO 98947   You Are My Sunshine

NCO 98948	Ring of Fire	NCO 98951	T for Texas
NCO 98949	Guess Things Happen That Way	NCO 98952	Blue Yodel No. 4
		NCO 98944	*"Mystery Train and talk"*
NCO 98950	Just a Closer Walk with Thee	Rumored:	*Wanted Man*
			Understand Your Man

Nashville Skyline seems to have been an attempt to repeat the *John Wesley Harding* experiment, continuing on from that album's two pedal-steeled closers (according to Dylan, the album was going to be called *John Wesley Harding Vol. 2* at one point). He had also decided to debut a "new" voice. The fifteen months that separate the respective sessions, though, were hardly the inspirational rush preceding *John Wesley Harding*. Only "Lay Lady Lay" (for the film *Midnight Cowboy*) and "I Threw It All Away" (which he played for George Harrison when Harrison was visiting Woodstock in November 1968) were definitely composed in these intervening months. Amnesia, to use Dylan's phrase, set in.

According to Dylan, "The first time I went into the studio [to record *Nashville Skyline*] I had, I think, four songs." Four *Nashville Skyline* tracks were indeed cut at the February 13, 1969, session (though "Lay Lady Lay" needed to be reworked the following day). Two of the "new" songs cut that first day—"One More Night" and "To Be Alone with You"—lacked even the most base of Dylan lyrics. Two unknown songs, one a blues tune, the other probably an instrumental (an early "Nashville Skyline Rag"?), were also cut but were never completed to Dylan's satisfaction.

The results of the following day's session only confirmed that—whatever Dylan's original intentions in coming to Nashville—he would have been best advised to return to Woodstock and apply himself to some songs befitting a successor to *John Wesley Harding*. But, as with *Another Side* five years earlier, Dylan seemed unwilling to just "pull the plug" (as he had in January 1966) and start again at a later date. He refused to reevaluate the wisdom of cutting an album in one go even though the only album where this procedure had worked was *Bringing It All Back Home* (much of which he had already been performing in concert).

The second February session resulted in two of Dylan's fluffiest fillers, "Peggy Day" and "Country Pie," and one Presleyesque big ballad, "Tell Me That It Isn't True," songs that musicians like Pete Drake, Ken Buttrey, and Charlie McCoy could sleepwalk through. The one song that stretched them was the beguiling "Lay Lady Lay," which had been abandoned the previous day:

Ken Buttrey: *"I have very vivid memories of 'Lay Lady Lay.' He was playing it down in the studio and usually I just sit down on the drums and start doodling around until something comes as far as a drum pattern, but [with] this particular one nothing came to mind instantly. Sometimes when that happens I go to the artist and say what do you hear on drums because sometimes when people write songs they can hear it completed, they hear everything they think's gonna be on it. . . . I went over to Dylan and said I'm having a little trouble thinking of something to play. Do you have any ideas on this song? He just kind of looked back, he didn't really know either, he was just trying to think of something and he said, 'Bongos.' I said, 'What??' He said, 'Bongos.' I went, 'Okay.' I immediately disregarded that, I couldn't hear bongos in this thing at all, so [I thought] I'll go and ask Bob Johnston. So I walked into the control room and said, 'Bob, What do you hear as regards drums on this thing?' And he just sort of rolled his eyes back, he didn't have any answers ready either, and he came out and said, 'Cowbells.' I said, 'What??' He said, 'Cowbells.' I went back up to the studio and Kris Kristofferson was working Columbia Studios at the time as a janitor and he had just emptied my ashtray at the drums and I said, 'Kris, do me a favor, here, hold these two things.' There was a real cheap bongo set sitting in a corner, the heads were untunable, I just put my cigarette lighter in the drum itself to make it a higher pitch, and there was a cowbell just lying in this utility room. There was one overhead mike on the drums that was for the whole kit and I swung it over to the bass tom-tom and I said, 'Kris, hold these bongos in one hand and the cowbells in the other,' and I swung this mike over to the cowbells and the bongos and about that time somebody said, 'Hey, let's cut this thing.' I had no pattern or anything worked out. I just told Kris, 'This is one of those spite deals. I'm gonna show 'em how bad their ideas're gonna sound.' I was combining Bob Johnston's idea and Bob Dylan's idea. We started playing the tune and I was just doodling around on these bongos and the cowbell and it was kinda working out pretty cool. I'm still trying to figure out something, and come chorus time I'd go to the set of drums. Next time you hear that [cut], listen how far off-mike the drums sound. There were no mikes on the drums, it was just leakage. In those days I was only afforded the luxury of one overhead mike, one bass mike. But it worked out pretty good. It was the very first take and to this day it's one of the best drum patterns I ever came up with. Every time I hear that, I keep thinkin' how accidental that thing came. It came from nowhere."*

Dylan insisted at the time that it had not been his intention to cut an entire album at these sessions—that it just happened. If this really was the case, he would surely have taken off after this second Nashville session. Seven two-and-a-half-minute songs did not, even in the 1960s, an album make. But, after what had become the second consecutive fifteen-month gap between albums, Columbia was a little perturbed by Dylan's recalcitrance to enter the studio (even though Dylan had signed a new five-year contract prior to *John Wesley Harding* that stipulated no minimum number of albums).

Dylan, though, decided to stay in town for a couple more days in the hope of hooking up with Johnny Cash. Spending his time writing a couple of songs at the Ramada Inn, he endeavored to pad out his most lightweight excursion to date.

Dylan produced just one worthy effort during the two-day respite—"Tonight I'll Be Staying Here with You" (a manuscript of which, on Ramada Inn notepaper, resides in one collector's hands)— but at least it was equal to the two songs he had brought from Woodstock. It was also in keeping with Dylan's habit of writing (and recording) an album's finale last. However, he was still a good three or four songs short of a semi-generous collection of Nashville-style country-pop ditties.

The sessions resumed on February 17, Dylan cutting "Tonight I'll Be Staying" and a solitary instrumental rag in the early afternoon, utilizing the same ultra-competent crew on autopilot. At this point, he took a break. When he resumed later the same day, it was with Johnny Cash on hand. Evidently the idea was to see if they could cut some songs together. Though this was just an exploratory session, a feasibility exercise, the two of them did duet on three songs, two Dylan oldies—"One Too Many Mornings" and "Don't Think Twice"—and one Sun standard, "I Still Miss Someone" (a previous Dylan/Cash duet on the same song appears in *Eat the Document*). At least one of the Dylan originals, "One Too Many Mornings," was also filmed for an ABC documentary on Cash called *The Man and His Music*. The film includes a shot of Dylan and Cash listening to a playback and laughing—I trust at the absurdity of their rendition.

The jarring incompatibility of this new Dylan's dulcet tones and the ol' Man in Black begs questions: When was a Dylan/Cash collaboration first mooted, did Dylan always intend to supplement his new songs with one or more "historic" duets, and why did they persevere with it? Cash had another purpose at Columbia Studios this February day, cutting two songs with his own band, though both "Southwind" and "The Devil to Pay" were just sidelines from ongoing work. The fact that Dylan took a two-day break before Cash's arrival (while Columbia's Music Row studios remained unbooked) suggests that he was awaiting Cash all along. On the damning evidence of "One Too Many Mornings" ("Don't Think Twice" and "I Still Miss Someone" remain unheard), the Dylan/Cash idea had very little to recommend it. And yet Dylan and Cash agreed to reconvene the following day.

Indeed, by the eighteenth Dylan and Cash seemed intent on making an entire album together. If Dylan had been hoping against hope that a Dylan/Cash album might operate as stopgap product while he wrote some more songs, the actual results nixed any such thoughts. According to Bob Johnston, the musicians at the session were just calling out sug- gestions and Dylan and Cash would attempt to sing them. It certainly sounds that way! On "That's All Right, Mama" Cash has to audibly prompt Dylan when it comes to his verse. A seven-minute "Careless Love" should also have most Dylan fans banging their heads in despair before the home straight. Even Cash fans might wonder how the man managed to find a singer even more determined to sing on one note than Cash himself. Though at least fifteen Dylan/ Cash duets were cut at this single session, only one performance was eventually deemed worthy of official release— the opening cut on *Nashville Skyline*, a curiously soulless rendition of "Girl from the North Country." Yet "Girl" still manages to outshine most of its kith and kin. At least Dylan shows some kind of respect for his (or Martin Carthy's) original tune, while the backing musicians do not get the opportunity to sink into the usual chung-chung accompaniment Cash had previously turned into an art form.

Nashville Skyline's twenty-eight minutes, puffed up by an instrumental rag and one Dylan/Cash duet, could hardly disguise a dearth of inspiration on Dylan's part. Though the instrumentation on most cuts was more ambitious than on *John Wesley Harding*, Dylan's newly rediscovered country twang and the predictable arrangements sufficed to drag the album into a mire of conventionality. Dylan, though, was not about to abandon his Nashville experiments.

SELF PORTRAIT

Recorded: April 24, 1969, to March 4, 1970
Released: June 8, 1970

Side 1: All the Tired Horses. Alberta #1. I Forgot More (Than You'll Ever Know). The Days of '49. Early Mornin' Rain. In Search of Little Sadie. Side 2: Let It Be Me. Little Sadie. Woogie Boogie. Belle Isle. Living the Blues. Like a Rolling Stone.* Side 3: Copper Kettle. Gotta Travel On. Blue Moon. The Boxer. The Mighty Quinn (Quinn the Eskimo).* Take Me as I Am (or Let Me Go). Side 4: Take a Message to Mary. It Hurts Me Too. Minstrel Boy.* She Belongs to Me.* Wigwam. Alberta #2.

[asterisked cuts from the Isle of Wight festival, August 31, 1969]

Other official cuts:

Dylan: Spanish Is the Loving Tongue. A Fool Such as I.

Producer:

1–13 Bob Johnston

Musicians:

1–6 Bob Dylan (guitar/piano/vocals)
1–2 Norman Blake (guitar)
1–2 Fred Carter, Jr. (guitar)
1–2 Pete Drake (steel guitar)
1–2 Bob Moore (bass)
1–2 Bill Pursell (piano)
1–2 Kenneth Buttrey (drums)
4–6 Al Kooper (guitar/keyboards)

4–6 David Bromberg (guitar/dobro)
4–6 Ron Cornelius (guitar/dobro)
4–6 Stu Woods (bass)
4–6 Alvin Roger (drums)
4–6 Hilda Harris (backing vocals)
4–6 Maeretha Stewart (backing vocals)
4–6 Albertine Robinson (backing vocals)

Overdubs in Nashville:

1–2 June Page
1–2 Dolores Edgin
1–2 Carol Montgomery
1–2 Millie Kirkham
1–2 Dottie Dillard (all backing vocals)
2 Doug Kershaw (fiddle)
7, 9, 12 Charlie McCoy (bass/marimbas)
7–9, 12 Kenneth Buttrey (drums)
7, 11 Bob Moore (bass)
8 Fred Carter, Jr. (guitar)

10, 11, 13 Charlie Daniels (guitar/dobro)
10 Bubba Fowler (trombone)
10, 11 Karl T. Himmel (drums)
10 Ron Cornelius (guitar/dobro)
10 Bill Walker (arranger)
10 Rex Eugene Peer (trombone)
10 William Pursell (keyboards)
10 Gene Mullins (trombone)
10 Dennis Good (trombone)
10 Frank C. Smith (backing vocals?)
10 Martha McCrory (cello)

10 Byron T. Bach (cello)
10 Gary Van Osdale (viola)
10 Lillian Hunt (viola)
10 Sheldon Kurland (violin)
10 Martin Katahn (violin)
10 Marvin Chantry (viola)

10 Brenton Banks (synthesizer/violin)
10 George Binkley (violin)
10 Solie I. Fott (violin)
10 Barry McDonald (arranger)
13 Albert W. Butler (saxophone)

1. COLUMBIA MUSIC ROW STUDIOS
   NASHVILLE, TENNESSEE
   APRIL 24 AND 26, 1969
NCO 99064 **Living the Blues**
NCO 99065 **Spanish Is the Loving Tongue**
NCO 99066 **Take Me as I Am (or Let Me
            Go)**
NCO 99067 **A Fool Such as I**
NCO 99068 **I Forgot More (Than You'll
            Ever Know)**
NCO 99069 **Let It Be Me**
NCO 99070 *Running*

2. COLUMBIA MUSIC ROW STUDIOS
   NASHVILLE, TENNESSEE
   MAY 3, 1969
NCO 99083 **Take a Message to Mary**
NCO 99084 **Blue Moon**
NCO 99085 Ring of Fire
NCO 99086 Folsom Prison Blues

3. COLUMBIA STUDIO A
   NEW YORK
   EARLY MARCH 1970
NCO 101488 **All the Tired Horses***
NCO 104546 **Wigwam***
NCO 101499 **The Boxer*** [vocal track]

4. COLUMBIA STUDIO A
   NEW YORK
   MARCH 3, 1970
NCO ?? *Pretty Saro*
NCO 101492 **In Search of Little Sadie***
NCO ?? *Sittin' on the Dock of the
         Bay*
NCO ?? *Went to See the Gypsy*
NCO ?? *Universal Soldier*
NCO ?? *When a Man's Out of a Job*
NCO ?? *These Working Hands*
NCO ?? *Spanish Eyes*
NCO 101494 *Woogie Boogie*

5. COLUMBIA STUDIO A
   NEW YORK
   MARCH 4, 1970
NCO ?? *Thirsty Boots [I]*

NCO ?? *Thirsty Boots [II]*
NCO ?? *Thirsty Boots [III]*
NCO ?? *Little Brown Dog*
NCO ?? *Railroad Bill*
NCO ?? *House Carpenter*
NCO ?? *Tell Ol' Bill*
NCO 101490 **Days of '49***
NCO ?? *Take [Me] Back Again*
NCO 101491 **Early Mornin' Rain***

6. COLUMBIA STUDIO A
   NEW YORK
   MARCH 5, 1970
NCO 101489 **Alberta No. 1***
NCO 104547 **Alberta No. 2***
NCO 101498 **Gotta Travel On***
NCO 101499 **The Boxer***
NCO ?? *Annie's Gonna Sing Her
         Song*
NCO 104543 **It Hurts Me Too***
NCO 101493 **Little Sadie***
NCO 101495 **Belle Isle***
NCO 101497 **Copper Kettle***
NCO 104590 *If Not for You*
Rumored: *Happy Book*

7. INSTRUMENTAL OVERDUBS
   COLUMBIA RECORDING STUDIOS
   NASHVILLE, TENNESSEE
   MARCH 11, 1970
NCO 106648 **Alberta #1**
NCO 106649 **All the Tired Horses**
NCO 106642 **The Days of '49**
NCO 106643 **Little Sadie**

8. INSTRUMENTAL OVERDUBS
   COLUMBIA RECORDING STUDIOS
   NASHVILLE, TENNESSEE
   MARCH 12, 1970
NCO 106644 **Belle Isle**
NCO 106645 **The Boxer**

9. INSTRUMENTAL OVERDUBS
   COLUMBIA RECORDING STUDIOS
   NASHVILLE, TENNESSEE
   MARCH 13, 1970

NCO 106646	Early Mornin' Rain
NCO 106647	Woogie Boogie
NCO 106640	Copper Kettle
NCO 106641	Gotta Travel On

10. INSTRUMENTAL OVERDUBS
    COLUMBIA RECORDING STUDIOS
    NASHVILLE, TENNESSEE
    MARCH 17, 1970

NCO 106646	Early Mornin' Rain
NCO 106647	Woogie Boogie
NCO 106640	Copper Kettle
NCO 106644	Belle Isle
NCO 106649	All the Tired Horses
NCO ??	Wigwam

11. INSTRUMENTAL OVERDUBS
    COLUMBIA RECORDING STUDIOS
    NASHVILLE, TENNESSEE
    MARCH 30, 1970

NCO 106640	Copper Kettle
NCO 106644	Belle Isle
NCO 106649	All the Tired Horses
NCO ??	It Hurts Me Too

12. INSTRUMENTAL OVERDUBS
    COLUMBIA RECORDING STUDIOS
    NASHVILLE, TENNESSEE
    APRIL 2, 1970

| NCO 106645 | The Boxer |
| NCO 106643 | In Search of Little Sadie |

13. INSTRUMENTAL OVERDUBS
    COLUMBIA RECORDING STUDIOS
    NASHVILLE, TENNESSEE
    APRIL 3, 1970

| NCO 106648 | Alberta #2 |

Possibly it was the Dylan/Cash sessions that first instilled in Dylan the notion of compiling an album of country-style covers to reinforce his change of direction. More likely, he just realized the need to substitute for the lack of songs from his own pen by returning to the purely interpretive elements of his art. The initial sessions for what became *Self Portrait* certainly reinforced the country sound debuted on *Nashville Skyline*. Yet by the time the album was completed, eleven months later, Dylan had reverted to his trademark nasal whine and *Self Portrait* had developed its own confusing set of textures. The *Self Portrait* recordings, which derive from two sets of sessions almost a year apart—three days of Nashville recordings in the spring of 1969, and three more days in New York in early March of 1970—really present two very different self portraits.

The first *Self Portrait* recordings certainly suggest that Dylan was running on empty, not merely in the songwriting department but as the inspirational bandleader he had been at so many sessions in the mid-1960s. At the very first Nashville session, the most obvious evidence of loss of inspiration came with an excruciating rendition of the traditional "Spanish Is the Loving Tongue" (an idiotic inclusion on 1973's *Dylan* album). This song had been beautifully preserved with the fledgling Band in Big Pink in the summer of 1967 and an equally magnetic piano rendition, from the second *New Morning* session, would later grace 1971's "Watching the River Flow" 45. But at this juncture the best Dylan could do with this heartrending lyric was introduce a ludicrous gaggle of girls la-la-laing over this Holiday Inn version of flamenco. The other song from the April 1969 sessions to pollute Columbia's 1973 "revenge" album, *Dylan*, barely has the edge. "A Fool Such as I" had also been expressively documented in Big Pink, but this version is little more than a caricature.

"Living the Blues," the one original recorded at the April sessions, was hardly original enough to suggest an advance beyond the platitudes of "Peggy Day," even if it was scheduled to be the next Dylan single, released to tie in with his appearance on "The Johnny Cash Show." Columbia wisely decided to release "Lay Lady Lay" instead. That said, "Living the Blues" is quite a fun performance and there is a playfulness in the way Dylan chooses to mimic some of Nashville's hoariest clichés on both a lyrical and a musical level.

How quickly Dylan envisaged putting together an album of country standards—which appears to have been the original concept behind *Self Portrait*—is not known. A third session two days after his May Day taping of "The Johnny Cash Show" put four more songs in the can, making eleven songs in total. *Rolling Stone* reporter Patrick Thomas had seen Dylan walking around with the sheet music for "Take a Message to Mary" after the session and, sure enough, that was one of the four songs cut, along with the Cash standards "Ring of Fire" and "Folsom Prison Blues," the only two Cash songs recorded for *Self Portrait*. Having stripped all four songs of any redeeming features, Dylan felt he had done enough damage for one trip to Nashville (where he'd spent much of his spare time looking at property) and returned to his Woodstock haven.

The first songs recorded in New York in March 1970 (the Job records for 1969–71 have been lost by Sony, leaving me at the mercy of the AF of M files) suggested a marked movement away from Dylan's year-old concept of an album of country standards and toward a melting pot of folk and country.

If it had been Dylan's intention to put together a pleasant single album of country/folk standards, a handful of the New York recordings could have been slotted in with the best of the spring '69 material. It was his decision to integrate cuts from his Isle of Wight appearance (scrapping the planned Isle of Wight album) and to persevere with the covers process that ultimately condemned *Self Portrait* to its brutal reception on release.

Not that the material recorded in early March 1970 is particularly bad—only "In Search of Little Sadie" de-

mands recourse to the skip function on my remote—Dylan's vocal experiments having been abandoned in favor of a familiar voice, albeit one with a bad cold. Unfortunately, *Self Portrait* jumps between vocal incarnations with the sort of lurches even Jeff Rosen's *Biograph* found hard to emulate. Any sense of an original concept was decisively jettisoned with the songs Dylan chose from his March cache—the traditional "Alberta" (times two), "Belle Isle," "Copper Kettle," "The Days of '49," and "Little Sadie" (also times two), Gordon Lightfoot's "Early Mornin' Rain," Dylan's own "Woogie Boogie," "Wigwam," and "All The Tired Horses," Paul Clayton's "Gotta Travel On," Big Bill Broonzy's "It Hurts Me Too," and Paul Simon's "The Boxer."

What was long suspected (and partially confirmed by a track listing for the March 3 session rescued from Dylan's trashcan by A. J. Weberman) was the number of outtakes left over from the March sessions. At least fourteen songs were discarded from the final *Self Portrait*. Of these, the majority were traditional (almost without exception they appeared previously in the pages of *Sing Out*). For once, the portals of the Dylan archives have failed to reveal any of these March outtakes, though most of the songs themselves remain well known in folk circles. Given a choice, the two songs I'd most like to hear would have to be "House Carpenter" (erroneously listed on the session reel as "All for the Sake of Thee"), which made a welcome reappearance at these sessions, and the relatively obscure "Pretty Saro"—a quite different song from "Rock A Bye My Saro Jane"—dealing with the perennial theme of a love unrequited for lack of money:

If I were a merchant and could write a
*   fine hand,*
I'd write my love a letter that she'd un-
*   derstand.*

*So I'll wander by the river, where the
 waters o'er flow,
And I'll dream of pretty Saro wherever I
 go.*

The March New York sessions also
marked the genesis of *New Morning,* as
a newly relocated Dylan seemed mo-
mentarily galvanized. Versions of "Went
to See the Gypsy" and "If Not for You"
were recorded at these sessions, though
they remain unreleased. They represent
a starting point for a project Dylan all
but completed in the three months it took
to sequence, mix, and press *Self Portrait.*
The March sessions also allowed Dylan
to sample a nucleus of musicians he
could retain for the endeavours ahead.
Not only did Al Kooper return to the
fold, but Dave Bromberg and Ron Cornelius took turns on lead guitar and
dobro. All three would play key roles on
New Morning.

The last of the March sessions (March
5) generated the largest number of
tracks short-listed for further work in
Nashville (and just one outtake that I
have been able to ascertain—"Annie's
Gonna Sing her Song"). Of the eight
songs on *Self Portrait* that appear to
date from March 5, seven would qualify
as standard folk fare, while the other
("The Boxer") might perhaps best be
considered a concept piece. The folk
standards—Clayton's "Gotta Travel
On," Big Bill Broonzy's "When Things
Go Wrong with You" (which Dylan reti-
tled "It Hurts Me Too," while taking an
arrangement credit for himself), and the
traditional "Belle Isle," "Copper Kettle," "Alberta," and "Little Sadie" ("In
Search of . . . " having been cut on the
third)—Dylan probably took from the
relevant volume of *Reprints from Sing
Out.*

The *Self Portrait* version of "The
Boxer" is one of the more intriguing of
the album's fillers. The main Dylan
vocal (the sweet, Skyliney one) seems to
imply the same session(s) as "It Hurts

Me Too" and company. This voice is
also the one heard on the exquisite
"Copper Kettle" and the equally affecting "Belle Isle," and is a marked refine-
ment on its syrupy *Nashville Skyline*
equivalent. Though it has that catch-in-
the-throat quality found on all of *Nashville Skyline,* this "new" voice conveys a
far greater emotional range. Interestingly, this voice also occasionally comes
through on the Isle of Wight tape, suggesting that Dylan was still discovering
aspects of this new vocal approach at
each turn.

The curious thing about "The Boxer"
is that what we might term the second
Dylan vocal (the nasal one) must have
already been cut a couple of days before
the so-called first vocal (a contemporary
Rolling Stone article refers to "The
Boxer" being cut at the March sessions).
Of course, "The Boxer" cannot be anything but the product of at least one
vocal overdub, making it the first such
overdub of Dylan's career. Where the
idea came to overdub a second vocal on
top of (actually behind) the original
vocal track, the Columbia files are not
about to reveal. There has, however,
been much speculation as to Dylan's intent in doing so. Greil Marcus's solitary
comment, in his *Rolling Stone* review of
the album, was a rhetorical "Jesus, is it
awful." Others, who shall remain name-
less, have sought to suggest that Dylan
sees the boxer in the song as his old self,
parrying every blow and accepting each
come-on, and that his new, "sweeter"
voice is somehow younger than that
now. Hence the two voices vying for our
attention. All very convincing, even if
the finished article still sounds pretty
damn unlistenable. "The Boxer" in its
finished form sits uneasily on the album.

In later disavowing *Self Portrait,*
Dylan was keen to note that "we were
working on *New Morning* when the *Self
Portrait* album got put together." The
implication is that Dylan was busy
working on *New Morning* in New York

while Bob Johnston was assembling the sprawling *Self Portrait* in Nashville. Yet it had been Dylan's decision to cut a whole new batch of songs—at least twenty-six of them—in New York in early March that twisted the project. The inclusion of Dylan's throaty New York tapes alongside the pedal-steel 'n' girls tunes cut with Johnston accounts for a large part of *Self Portrait*'s all-too-obvious identity crisis. In fact, Johnston's extensive overdubs were presumably an attempt to make the New York tracks blend in with the Nashville sound rather than jutting out.

According to Charlie McCoy, the fourteen songs cut in New York were "[sent] down [to Nashville] from New York with instructions that we were to just play over what he'd already recorded on it. . . . The tape was mostly other people's songs. . . . The tempos didn't really hold together real well and he wasn't real steady with the guitar." Ken Buttrey confirms McCoy's recollection:

"We did one album, Self Portrait *I think it was, where he sent a tape down of songs that he had recorded either in the studio or at home—just vocal and guitar—and we just overdubbed our parts on it. He wasn't even there. Again it was just Charlie McCoy and myself, and for some reason, scheduling problems or something, we couldn't do the overdubs at the same time, so Charlie McCoy did his overdubs and I would come in the studio as he was leaving, and he would have his chord charts on the music stand with arrows pointing up or down. That was my cue for where Dylan rushed or dragged. Charlie was just leaving [the first time] and he said, 'You're not gonna believe this.' That's all he had time to say. [When I did get to hear the tapes] I thought, How weird."*

What state the cuts subjected to over-dubs—in particular the concept pieces "Wigwam," "All the Tired Horses," and "The Boxer"—arrived in Nashville

can only be surmised from McCoy's and Buttrey's descriptions and the sound of the tracks in their released form. "All the Tired Horses" must have arrived with musical notation and/or a guide Dylan vocal (which presumably still re-sides on the sixteen-track master). "Wigwam" was presumably also ac-companied by musical notation unless Dylan's piano and vocal (and perhaps those nice little acoustic guitar fills, courtesy Dave Bromberg?) was his idea of an arrangement. Yet the idea of pro-viding musical notation seems most unDylanlike and, if he did, why were two arrangers credited on these tracks?

Certainly the musician line-ups for the New York sessions cannot be reconciled with the details of the Nashville overdubs on the AF of M contracts. According to the AF of M, on the March 3 session he utilized three musicians (Cornelius, Kooper, and Bromberg?), the three ses-sions on March 4 required between four and eight musicians, and the session on March 5 needed six musicians. Also the list of musicians on the *Self Portrait* sleeve included bassist Stu Woods and drummer Alvin Roger, neither of whom are in evidence on the album.

All of the New York cuts on *Self Por-trait* were subjected to overdubs in Nashville, principally by the Buttrey/McCoy rhythm section. Both McCoy and Buttrey are adamant that the tapes they received contained no evidence of existing rhythm tracks. Evidently John-ston's task, to assimilate these tracks into a general concept, required him to preserve only the blandishments from the New York tracks that wouldn't sound out of place in Nashville. That Dylan had no involvement in these over-dubs, which took up seven whole days of sessions, suggests his degree of disen-chantment with the whole project at this late stage. However, rather than simply scrapping the album, Dylan simply got on with writing an album of original songs.

NEW MORNING

Recorded: March to June 30, 1970
Released: October 21, 1970

Side 1: If Not for You. Day of the Locusts. Time Passes Slowly. Went to See the Gypsy. Winterlude. If Dogs Run Free. Side 2: New Morning. Sign on the Window. One More Weekend. The Man in Me. Three Angels. Father of Night.

More Greatest Hits and 45
Recorded: March 16 to October 1971
Released: November 17, 1971

Side 1: Watching the River Flow. Side 4: When I Paint My Masterpiece. You Ain't Going Nowhere. I Shall Be Released. Down in the Flood.

Other official cuts:

Dylan: Lily of the West (Flora). Can't Help Falling in Love. Sarah Jane. Ballad of Ira Hayes. Mr. Bojangles. Mary Ann. Big Yellow Taxi.
The Bootleg Series: If Not for You. Wallflower.
45: Spanish Is the Loving Tongue.
45: George Jackson [I]/George Jackson [II]
First Blues: Vomit Express. Going to San Diego. September on Jessore Road.

Producers:
2–8 Bob Johnston
1, 9 Al Kooper
11 Leon Russell
12–13 Bob Dylan

Musicians:
1–13 Bob Dylan
 (piano/guitar/harmonica/vocals)
1–10 Al Kooper (guitar/piano/vocals)
1, 10 Stu Woods (guitar/bass)
2–8 Charlie Daniels (bass)
2–8 Ron Cornelius (guitar)
2–3 George Harrison (guitar)
3–8 Russ Kunkel (drums)
4–8 Hilda Harris (backing vocals)
4–8 Albertine Robinson (backing vocals)
4–8 Maeretha Stewart (backing vocals)

2 Alvin Rogers (drums)
9 Buzzy Feiten (guitar)
9 Harvey Brooks (bass)
9 Billy Mundi (drums)
10 David Bromberg (guitars)
10 Thomas Cosgrove (backing vocals)
10 Rick Marotta (drums)
11, 13 Leon Russell (piano/bass)
11 Joey Cooper (guitar)
11 Don Preston (guitar)
11 Carl Radle (bass)
11 Chuck Blackwell (drums)
12 Happy Traum (bass/banjo/guitar/backing vocals)
13 Ben Keith (steel guitar)
13 Kenneth Buttrey (drums)
13 Joshie Armstead (backing vocals)
13 Rose Hicks (backing vocals)

1. COLUMBIA STUDIO A
   NEW YORK
   AND MUSIC ROW STUDIOS
   NASHVILLE, TENNESSEE
   EARLY MARCH AND JULY 2, 1970
   NCO ??   *Went to See the Gypsy*
   NCO 104590   *If Not for You*

2. COLUMBIA STUDIO B
   NEW YORK
   MAY 1, 1970, AFTERNOON SESSION
   CO ??   Ghost Riders In the Sky
   CO ??   Cupid
   CO ??   All I Have to Do Is Dream
   CO ??   Gates of Eden
   CO ??   I Threw It All Away
   CO ??   I Don't Believe You
   CO ??   Matchbox
   CO ??   True Love, Your Love
   CO ??   When's My Swamp Gonna
                  Catch Fire?
   CO ??   I'm a-Goin' Fishin'
   CO ??   Honey, Just Allow Me One
                  More Chance
   CO ??   Rainy Day Women #s 12 &
                  35
   CO ??   Song to Woody
   CO ??   Mama, You Bin on My
                  Mind
   CO ??   Don't Think Twice, It's All
                  Right
   CO ??   Yesterday
   CO ??   Just Like Tom Thumb's
                  Blues
   CO ??   Da Doo Ron Ron
   CO ??   One Too Many Mornings
   CO ??   *It Ain't Me Babe*

3. COLUMBIA STUDIO B
   NEW YORK
   MAY 1, 1970, EVENING SESSION
   CO 107086–1   *Sign on the Window I*
   CO 107086–2   *Sign on the Window II*
   CO 107086–4   *Sign on the Window III*
   CO 107086–5   *Sign on the Window IV*
   CO 107087–2   **If Not for You**
   CO 107088–2   *Time Passes Slowly I*
   CO 107088–3   *Time Passes Slowly II*
   CO 107088–4   *Time Passes Slowly III*
   CO 107089–1   Working on the Guru
   CO 107090–1   *Went to See the Gypsy*

4. COLUMBIA STUDIO E
   NEW YORK
   JUNE 1, 1970
   CO 106776–1   *Alligator Man I*

CO 106776–2   *Alligator Man II*
CO 106776–4   *Alligator Man III*
CO 106777–1   **Ballad of Ira Hayes**
CO 106778–2   *Lonesome Me I*
CO 106778–3   *Lonesome Me II*

5. COLUMBIA STUDIO E
   NEW YORK
   JUNE 2, 1970
   CO 106776   *Alligator Man II*
   CO 106779–1   *Mary Ann I*
   CO 106779–5   *Mary Ann II*
   CO 106779–6   *Mary Ann III*
   CO 106779–7   *Mary Ann IV*
   CO 106780–1   *Rock A Bye My Sara Jane I*
   CO 106780–4   *Rock A Bye My Sara Jane II*
   CO 106780–7   **Rock A Bye My Sara Jane III**
   CO 106779–8   **Mary Ann V**
   CO 106781   **Spanish Is the Loving Tongue**
   CO 106782   *Mr. Bojangles I*
   CO 106782   **Mr. Bojangles II**
   CO 106783   **If Not for You**
   CO 106784–14   **Time Passes Slowly**

6. COLUMBIA STUDIO E
   NEW YORK
   JUNE 3, 1970
   CO 106785   *Jamaica Farewell*
   CO 108071–1   *Can't Help Falling in Love
                   with You I*
   CO 108071–3   **Can't Help Falling in Love
                   with You II**
   CO 108072   *Long Black Veil*
   CO 108073   *Lily of the West (Flora)*
   CO 108074   **One More Weekend**

7. COLUMBIA STUDIO E
   NEW YORK
   JUNE 4, 1970
   CO 107270–1   *Bring Me Water I*
   CO 107270–2   *Bring Me Water II*
   CO 107271–1   *Three Angels I*
   CO 107271–3   **Three Angels II**
   CO 107272–1   *Tomorrow Is a Long Time I*
   CO 107272–3   *Tomorrow Is a Long Time II*
   CO 107273   *Big Yellow Taxi I*
   CO 107273   **Big Yellow Taxi II [with
                   insert]**
   CO 107274   *New Morning [I]*
   CO 107274   **New Morning [II]**

8. COLUMBIA STUDIO E
   NEW YORK
   JUNE 5, 1970
   CO 107275–1   *If Dogs Run Free I*

CO 107275–3 **If Dogs Run Free II**
CO 107276–1 *Went to See the Gypsy I*
CO 107276–2 *Went to See the Gypsy II*
CO 107276–4 **Went to See the Gypsy III**
CO 107277–5 *Sign on the Window I*
CO 107277–8 **Sign on the Window II**
CO 107278 **The Man in Me**
CO 107279 *Ah-ooh! (instrumental)*
CO 107280–2 **Father of Night**
CO 107281 **Winterlude**
CO 107282 *I Forgot to Remember to Forget Her*
CO 108073–1 *Lily of the West (Flora) I*
CO 108073–4 **Lily of the West (Flora) II**

CO ?? *You Ain't Going Nowhere* [take 1]
CO ?? *You Ain't Going Nowhere* [take 2]
CO ?? *You Ain't Going Nowhere* [take 5]
CO ?? **You Ain't Going Nowhere** [take 6]
CO ?? *Down in the Flood* [take 1]
CO ?? **Down in the Flood** [take 2]
CO ?? *I Shall Be Released* [take 1]
CO ?? *I Shall Be Released* [take 2]
CO ?? *I Shall Be Released* [take 3]
CO ?? *I Shall Be Released* [take 4]

9. (?) COLUMBIA STUDIO
NEW YORK
OR BEARSVILLE STUDIO
WOODSTOCK, NEW YORK
CO 107470 *Day of the Locusts [I]*
CO 107470 **Day of the Locusts [II]**

10. COLUMBIA STUDIO B
NEW YORK
JUNE 30, 1970
CO 107135–3 *Blowin' in the Wind*

11. "INSTRUMENTAL OVERDUBS"
MUSIC ROW STUDIOS
NASHVILLE
JULY, 2, 1970
NCO ?? *Went to See the Gypsy*
NCO 104590 *If Not for You*
NCO 106781 **Spanish Is the Loving Tongue**

12. BLUE ROCK STUDIOS
NEW YORK
MARCH 16 TO 18, 1971
CO 110814 **Watching the River Flow**
CO ?? **When I Paint My Master-piece**
CO ?? *Spanish Harlem*
CO ?? *That Lucky Ol' Sun*
CO ?? *Alabama Bound*
CO ?? *Blood Red River*
CO ?? *Rock of Ages*

13. COLUMBIA STUDIO B
NEW YORK
SEPTEMBER 24, 1971
CO ?? *Only a Hobo* [take 2]
CO ?? *Only a Hobo* [take 3]
CO ?? *Only a Hobo* [take 4]
CO ?? *Only a Hobo* [take 5]

14. BLUE ROCK STUDIOS
NEW YORK
NOVEMBER 4, 1971
CO 111696 **Wallflower**
CO 111697-9 **George Jackson (acoustic)—take 9**
CO 111697-13 **George Jackson (Big Band)—take 13**
Rumored: *Donald and Lydia*

15. RECORD PLANT
NEW YORK
NOVEMBER 9, 1971
Mantras
Merrily to Welcome in the New Year
September on Jessore Road
Nurses Song
Gimme My Money Back

16. RECORD PLANT
NEW YORK
NOVEMBER 17, 1971
A Dream [I]
A Dream [II]
A Dream [III]
Raghupati Rashava [I]
Raghupati Rashava [II]
September on Jessore Road
Many Loves
Vomit Express
Jimmy Berman Rag
Going to San Diego
(Oh Babe) For You [I]
(Oh Babe) For You [II]
Om My Soul Shalom
Walking Down the Street

Given that it was released at the midpoint of what Dylan himself came to call "the amnesia"—the period when he could no longer do consciously what he used to do unconsciously—*New Morning* is now viewed as an innocuous midterm report from a family man. At the time, though, it was seen very much as a return to form (if not the second coming). After the calamitous reception accorded *Self Portrait, New Morning* seemed on the face of it to be Dylan's knee-jerk response, an equal and opposite reaction.

Despite Dylan's own statements, and the evidence of the March 1970 recordings of "If Not for You" and "Went to See the Gypsy," it has long been assumed that the bulk of *New Morning* postdates the release of *Self Portrait.* Actually the entire album, save for one song, "Day of the Locusts"— along with more than an album's worth of covers— directly resulted from five days in Columbia's New York studios at the beginning of June, a week before the unveiling of *Self Portrait.*

Whether Dylan planned to simultaneously release two albums, one of covers and one original, or had in mind another mishmash à la *Self Portrait,* the first seven cuts of what became the 1973 *Dylan* album were a large part of this *Self Portrait Vol. II* cut during the *New Morning* sessions. There were also six other, as yet unreleased, covers laid down at these sessions: "Alligator Man" (originally scheduled for *Dylan*), "Lonesome Me," "Jamaica Farewell" (which guitarist Ron Cornelius thought so cool he got Johnston to cut him an acetate of the song), "Long Black Veil," "I Forgot to Remember to Forget," and a song listed on the studio sheets as "Bring Me Water" (presumably the Leadbelly original, "Bring Me a Little Water, Sylvie").

Any original intentions by Dylan were presumably scuppered by the sheer vilification that greeted *Self Portrait* (and Columbia's presumed reluctance to fol-

low *Self Portrait* with more of the same), much as Dylan's talk of making another film after *Renaldo and Clara* came to naught when the film was savaged on its release. However, Dylan only reluctantly abandoned the covers he had labored over. The first sequenced version of *New Morning* incorporated elements of both *New Morning* and *Dylan,* the running order being:

Side 1: 1. Mr. Bojangles 2. Ballad of Ira Hayes 3. The Man in Me 4. One More Weekend

Side 2: 1. New Morning. 2. Father of Night. 3. Sign on the Window 4. Tomorrow Is a Long Time 5. If Dogs Run Free

(Another attempt at a sequence, marked "Al's Mix," a reference to Kooper's coproduction, has an even stranger mixture of old, new, borrowed, and blue: The Man in Me/Winterlude/Mary Ann/One More Weekend/Mr. Bojangles/Tomorrow Is a Long Time/Three Angels/If Dogs Run Free/Ballad of Ira Hayes. Huh?)

Aside from "Mr. Bojangles," "Ballad of Ira Hayes" and "Mary Ann," all of which eventually appeared on *Dylan,* the rerecorded "Tomorrow Is a Long Time" was evidently under very serious consideration for the album. The previous year Dylan had told Jann Wenner that Presley's version (on *Spinout*) was his favorite rendition of one of his own songs. Though Dylan does not attempt to copy Presley's arrangement, the girls "ah-ooh" away and there is a loping feel to the whole thing that almost smacks of Vegas. Dylan's vocal, on the other hand, has an intensity that you would only find in the gambling rooms of that town.

How much the *Dylan* record resembles what Dylan himself might have put out at the time of the sessions is another mystery waiting to be unraveled (I assume that omitting half the covers cut at these sessions and including two leftovers from the first *Self Portrait* sessions was not Dylan's idea). Few Dylan fans would consider "Spanish Is the Loving Tongue" and "A Fool Such as I" good exchanges for the likes of "Long Black Veil," "I Forgot to Remember to Forget Her," or "Jamaica Farewell," whatever Dylan did to them. And yet the *Dylan* album—even in its released form—demands reevaluation as one of Dylan's abandoned projects, not just a bunch of songs he used to warm up the musicians. The impression Dylan gave in 1974, that these covers were just warm-ups for the real business at hand, cutting an album of original songs, does not in fact appear to be true. Drummer Russ Kunkel remembers it the other way round, that they spent the bulk of the sessions working on the covers, Dylan slipping in the occasional original.

Kunkel's recollections are certainly borne out by the studio sheets for these early June sessions, which show multiple takes for songs like "Mary Ann" and "Sarah Jane" while "Sign on the Window," "The Man in Me," and "Winterlude" (three of the most successful cuts on *New Morning*) were all cut in a couple of hours at the final session, almost as an afterthought. Even then Dylan couldn't resist recutting "Lily of the West (Flora)" (already attempted at the June 3 session) before calling it quits.

The recent emergence of an all-but-complete record of the first Dylan/Harrison session from May 1970 and the short-listing of versions of "It Ain't Me Babe" and "Tomorrow Is a Long Time" suggests that Dylan also intended to blend old originals with the covers, like *Self Portrait* though with the balance more firmly tilted toward new cover versions.

A Dylan/Harrison session on May Day 1970, at Columbia's Studio B, was first reported in *Rolling Stone*. When a Dylan/Harrison tape circulated in the mid-eighties (taken from Columbia acetates auctioned by one Gelston & Co.),

it comprised seven ghastly attempts at songs of yore: five Dylan originals, of which only "Song to Woody" had anything to recommend it; one sappy Beatles tune, "Yesterday," mangled into yesteryear; and a mildly amusing rewrite of "Da Doo Ron Ron." Though Harrison's guitar had been mixed well to the fore, the tape only marginally tallied with *Rolling Stone*'s description of the fabled May Day session:

The material covered [was] an amalgam of new Dylan stuff, Beatles songs, and a number of early Sixties tunes. About five of the numbers are reportedly of high enough quality to merit inclusion on a future Dylan album (sic). *Dylan and Harrison hit it off well, and spent part of the time with Dylan singing Beatles songs and George singing Dylan songs. The new Dylan material is reportedly different from his recent stuff, but is not a radical change.*

The recent emergence of a more complete version of that seven-song Gelston acetate (from a tape source), containing a further twelve acts of sacrilege in song, suggests that this was a session in and unto itself, and Dylan's throaty singing ties it to the *New Morning* period (though Dylan and Harrison did "hang out" together in November 1968, at which time Dylan played Harrison the recently composed "I Threw It All Away"—a version of which is featured here, with a passionate vocal but the sort of unsympathetic backing Dylan would have to wait another twenty-five years to get back to). Harrison had arrived in New York on April 28 and met up with Dylan at his townhouse the next evening. Derek Taylor, who accompanied Harrison on the trip, has stated that an informal jam session took place the following day (April 30). Though it has long been assumed that this jam session was at Dylan's house, the Gelston tape and this "informal jam session" could be one and the same. However, the AF of M records, which refer to two separate sessions on May 1, tend to suggest these were the results of the afternoon session, which ran from two-thirty to five-thirty and required three additional musicians. A further session that evening, from seven till ten (with four musicians now required), seems to have had a more serious purpose.

Presumably the intention with the afternoon session was to get comfortable with the studio and musicians. Though there is very little serious music-making going on, one cut, "It Ain't Me Babe," is absent from the circulating tape, having presumably been pulled to a master reel. The studio sheet for the evening May Day session shows Dylan and Harrison working exclusively on new Dylan originals, two of which had already been attempted at the March *Self Portrait* sessions ("If Not for You" and the ubiquitous "Went to See the Gypsy"). Evidently *Rolling Stone* unwittingly combined both Dylan/Harrison sessions. The one outtake from this session to have actually passed into collectors' hands, a Dylan original called "Working on the Guru," contains a very halfhearted Dylan vocal. Lyrically it reminds me of those dumb lyrics pasted inside the covers of the hardback edition of *Writings and Drawings*. The Dylan/Harrison version of "If Not for You," supposedly once due for inclusion on *New Morning*, became one of the biggest disappointments on *The Bootleg Series*. Though Harrison delivers a lovely guitar intro, Dylan's vocal is one of those exercises in stripping a song of its tune.

In delightful contrast to this "If Not for You" (and further evidence of the scattershot way *The Bootleg Series* was compiled), the March 1970 recording of this song has much to recommend it. Indeed, this "If Not for You," which contains a melody line for the title phrase that tapers up (not down) the scale, has

a most effective, half-choking Dylan vocal. Accompanied initially by just his own piano playing (and a solitary bass line), this lovely arrangement was embellished in Nashville—under Bob Johnston's direction—with some pedal steel and an electric violin. It was evidently under serious consideration for *New Morning* (the overdubs took place on July 2, tying them conclusively to the mixing of *New Morning*).

Cut for the same album, its recording date unknown, also with just piano and bass (the bass also overdubbed on July 2), was a version of "Spanish Is the Loving Tongue" belatedly released in June 1971 as the B side of "Watching the River Flow." Aside from reaffirming Dylan's interest in cutting covers, this "Loving Tongue" marks the rediscovery of his vocal chords. This living, breathing entity puts the deadwood *Dylan* version to shame.

The third song mixed at the July 2 Nashville session was another version of "Went to See the Gypsy" (one of at least four separate "attempts" to break through the mirr'r). Listed on the master reel as "Al's Gypsy," this electric piano performance has Kooper at the keys while Dylan sticks to a vocal that actually delivers the goods (the *New Morning* vocal has always left me slightly cold but this one does the deed). The electric piano was presumably one of Kooper's ideas and it works a lot better than the official "Gypsy," with its uniform *New Morning* arrangement. Indeed Kooper's role on *New Morning* warranted more than the "special thanks" he got on the rear sleeve.

How late Dylan abandoned the notion of blending covers and old originals may be indicated by a rerecording of the song that had most dogged Dylan in recent years, "Blowin' in the Wind." In Columbia's files for June 30, 1970— four weeks after the *New Morning* sessions—there is a solitary reference to Dylan recording three takes of "Blowin' in the Wind" at Studio B. This seemed so wildly improbable that I was initially convinced it was a mistake, a misattribution of another song (maybe it was the long-lost session details for "Day of the Locusts"?). However, when scanning through the (unbelievably disorganized) files of Local 802 (New York) for the American Federation of Musicians, not only did I come across the session but found full details of the musicians present (it even gave the song's timing— 2:53 if you're interested). Why would Dylan attempt to record a version of "Blowin' in the Wind" at this juncture in his career? Unless perhaps he intended to do another "The Boxer" with it.

By June 30 Dylan had already cut all of *New Morning,* plus at least fourteen covers. He certainly wasn't hard up for material to perm an album from. The five June sessions had been a great success. If the first couple of sessions had been almost exclusively devoted to covering the work of others—Dylan easing himself back into the studio process?— the final June session generated half of *New Morning* plus a "lost" instrumental, "I Forgot to Remember to Forget Her" and a good-time version of "Lily of the West (Flora)." Dylan's piano playing also came into its own. Rather than his usual pounding away, Dylan explores the limits of his points of reference, notably on the sublime "Sign on the Window," when a scratchy middle-eight almost leads into an extended piano solo (were it not for a French horn overdub, courtesy of Kooper).

"Day of the Locusts," the one song on *New Morning* not recorded during that first week in June, was presumably cut a matter of days after Dylan's June 9 attendance at Princeton University to receive an honorary doctorate in music, the ostensible inspiration for the song. Kunkel seems to think it might even have been recorded in Woodstock, possibly at Bearsville Studios, which was up and running at this point. Certainly Co-

lumbia has no record of the session that resulted in this final *New Morning* tune.

So Dylan's ninth album of originals— what became *New Morning* once he abandoned the idea of including any covers—was actually recorded with remarkable ease. Its mutation into a finished artifact was far more tortuous. As the various provisional running orders indicate, Dylan's concept of the album changed with the breeze. By the end of it, Kooper, who bore most of the brunt of Dylan's prevarications, "never wanted to speak to him again . . . [after] he just changed his mind every three seconds" (Johnston had returned to Nashville, his "engineering" duties complete). Though Johnston was involved in the initial mixes, completed in three days in June (in Nashville), it would be late July before Dylan approved a sequenced album.

Despite its title, *New Morning* signaled the end of more aspects in Dylan's life than new beginnings. It certainly represented the end of Dylan's association with Bob Johnston, his producer since *Highway 61 Revisited.* Johnston's role in producing *New Morning* was at times little more than that of a glorified engineer.

New Morning also signaled the end of Dylan's four-year-long association with Nashville. It would be another three years before Dylan returned to a Columbia studio, and he would never again record in Nashville. The three-and-a-half-year gap between *New Morning* and *Planet Waves,* the longest gap to date between authentic Dylan studio artifacts, belied a new dawn of inspiration.

Although the all-original *New Morning* was probably forced on Dylan by both critical and commercial considerations (no artist in the public arena, even one as contrary as Dylan, is entirely immune from such pressures), it provided only the most transitory solace for those awaiting the return of Dylan's muse. Half a halfway decent album was not about to assuage his famished disciples, nor convince Dylan himself that he was about to paint a masterpiece.

Between the completion of *New Morning* in late July 1970 and the start of work on the soundtrack to *Pat Garret and Billy the Kid* in January 1973, Dylan would devote just six days to the studio (his work as a backing musician excepted). Nearly nine months separate "Day of the Locusts" from the Blue Rock sessions in March 1971. Working outside the confines of Columbia for the very first time, Dylan had booked three sessions with pianist/songwriter Leon Russell, Dylan's first independent producer. If Dylan hoped that the prospect of impending sessions might inspire him to take up the pen again—as it had in his younger days—just two new songs resulted from these sessions, the remainder of the time being spent flitting from cover to cover.

That said, "Watching the River Flow" and "When I Paint My Masterpiece" have both stood the test of time far better than anything on *New Morning* (with the possible exception of "Sign on the Window") even if both songs sound like codas on a career, neither unlocking new doors of inspiration. In a remarkably self-deprecating mood, Dylan kicks off "Watching the River Flow" by confessing, "What's the matter with me? I don't have much to say," while "When I Paint My Masterpiece" chases a chimerical future when "everything's gonna be smooth like a rhapsody."

Even the kind of sustained studio work required to carve out something as lightweight as *New Morning* now seemed beyond Dylan. The March ses-

sions presaged nothing of substance. After rerecording three basement tape ditties with Happy Traun in a single September afternoon session at Columbia, Dylan's next serious attempt at something original was another single. "George Jackson," cut six weeks later, was a sincere enough way of expressing tears of rage, but came across as little more than a whim on his part.

For the remainder of 1971 and all of 1972, Dylan was content to allow friends to bask in some reflected light, contributing to projects by Allen Ginsberg, Dave Bromberg, and Doug Sahm. The Ginsberg project was the one that demanded the greatest contribution from Dylan since it was beholden on him to come up with tunes to accompany Ginsberg's improvised words (an interesting take on Dylan's own style of improvisation between 1965 and 1967). However, when Ginsberg attempts to elicit a vocal contribution from Dylan on a final jam at their first session, he seems the most reluctant of frontmen, asking, "What are we doing, Allen? What exactly is this? . . . [Is this] for your record?" Eventually Dylan does come up with the first verse to "Gimme My Money Back," a sort of improvised New Yorkie "Something Happened to Me Yesterday," albeit a little begrudgingly. By the second session, Dylan seems a whole lot more into the idea, and a bluesy jam on which he and Ginsberg both intone, probably called "(Oh Babe) for You," seems to be largely his idea. If 1971 had been a year of sporadic activity, 1972 was largely spent working on an anthology of his complete lyrics. Dylan seemed content to leave the legacy well alone.

PAT GARRETT & BILLY THE KID

Recorded: January 20 to February 1973
Released: July 13, 1973

Side 1: Main Theme (Billy). Cantina Theme (Workin' for the Law). Billy 1. Bunkhouse Theme. River Theme. Side 2: Turkey Chase. Knockin' on Heaven's Door. Final Theme. Billy 4. Billy 7.

Pat Garrett & Billy the Kid [The Original Movie]
Released: May 1973

Main Theme (Billy). Cantina Theme. Billy. Billy Surrenders. River Theme. Billy 1. Bunkhouse Theme. Knockin' on Heaven's Door. Turkey Chase. Final Theme. Knockin' on Heaven's Door (instrumental). Billy 4.

Pat Garrett & Billy the Kid [Director's Cut]
Released: 1988

Main Theme (Billy). Cantina Theme. Billy Surrenders. River Theme. Billy 1. Bunkhouse Theme. Billy. Knockin' on Heaven's Door (instrumental). Turkey Chase. Final Theme. Billy.

Producers:
1   Chuck Plotkin
2–3 Gordon Carroll

Musicians:
1–3 Bob Dylan (guitar/vocal)
1–2 Terry Paul (bass/backing vocals)
1   Mike Utley (organ)
1   Sammy Creason (drums)
1   Stephen Bruton (electric guitar)
1   unknown girl singers
1   unknown trumpeters
2–3 Roger McGuinn (guitar)
2   Jim Keltner (drums)
2   Russ Kunkel (tambourine/bongos)
2   Carol Hunter (guitar/backing vocals)

2–3 Donna Weiss (backing vocals)
2   Brenda Patterson (backing vocals)
2   Gary Foster (flute)
2   Carl Fortina (harmonium)
2   Fred Catz and Ted Michel (cellos)
3   Bruce Langhorne (guitar)
3   Booker T (bass)
3   Donna Weiss (backing vocals)
3   Priscilla Jones (backing vocals)
3   Byron Berline (fiddle/vocal)

1. CBS DISCOS STUDIOS
    MEXICO CITY, MEXICO
    JANUARY 20, 1973
Billy [instrumental]
Billy [instrumental]
Billy [instrumental]

Billy
Billy
Under Turkey [instrumental]
Under Turkey [instrumental]
Under Turkey [instrumental]
Billy

Billy Surrenders [instrumental]
Billy Surrenders [with girls]
And He's Killed Me Too [instrumental]
And He's Killed Me Too [instrumental]
And He's Killed Me Too [instrumental]
And He's Killed Me Too [instrumental]
Goodbye Holly
Pecos Blues [instrumental]
Pecos Blues [instrumental]
Billy 4

2. BURBANK STUDIOS
   BURBANK, CALIFORNIA
   FEBRUARY 1973
Knockin' on Heaven's Door
Sweet Amarillo
Knockin' on Heaven's Door
Knockin' on Heaven's Door [instrumental]
Knockin' on Heaven's Door [HCO 117333]
Knockin' on Heaven's Door
Final Theme
Final Theme
Rock Me Mama

Rock Me Mama
Billy 7
Billy 7
Billy 7
[instrumental]
[instrumental]
Final Theme [instrumental]
Ride Billy Ride
Bunkhouse Theme

3. BURBANK STUDIOS
   BURBANK, CALIFORNIA
   FEBRUARY 1973
Main Theme
Cantina Theme (Workin' for the Law)
Cantina Theme (Workin' for the Law)
Billy 1 [instrumental]
Billy
Billy
Billy
River Theme [instrumental]
River Theme [instrumental]
Turkey Chase (instrumental) [HCO 117334]

Ever the master of understatement, when Dylan finally decided to reenter a studio it was to record the soundtrack to a Sam Peckinpah film he was playing a bit part in. The sessions for *Pat Garrett & Billy the Kid* were largely variations on a theme, that theme being the ballad of Billy the Kid.

It would be easy enough to dismiss the soundtrack—with its multiple versions of one song, "Billy," and only one other vocal track, the haunting "Knockin' on Heaven's Door"—as superfluous filler between *New Morning* and *Planet Waves*. Indeed Jon Landau did just that in one particularly asinine review. In fact, as an exercise in reacquainting himself with the studio, the *Pat Garrett* sessions were ideal, with Dylan displaying real flashes of that ability to transform material in the recording process.

The sessions were split between one (largely abortive) Mexico City all-night session (during the actual filming) and two sessions in Burbank, out of which producer Gordon Carroll compiled the

bulk of the album and (the at-times-mutually-exclusive) film soundtrack. To a collector, the Mexico City recordings contain far more of interest as only one cut on the album and two in the film derive from this session, and Dylan recorded a couple of songs that never made it to either media in any form.

"Billy Surrenders" appears in both the original released film and the director's cut, though not on the album. Unlike the circulating outtake, the film version (slightly more complete on the director's cut version, where it reappears in the brothel scene) has Dylan and bassist Terry Paul la-la-laing away for a couple of minutes. The various soundtrack recordings utilized for the two versions of the film vary considerably in both length and choice of take (for a full comparison, readers should refer to my article "The True Story of Pat Garrett & Billy the Kid" in *The Telegraph* 37). According to *Rolling Stone* reporter Chet Flippo, who provided a detailed account of the Mexico City session in the March 15, 1973, issue:

[Dylan] loped into a chunky, accelerating rhythm, trading off licks with Utley. Both were laughing and weaving and daring and challenging each other. Dylan and Terry Paul started a hypnotic "la la" lyric that grew more manic as they stood head to head and urged each other on. They jammed for four minutes and then lurched to a stuttering finish.

The version of "Billy Surrenders" on the circulating studio tape (which lasts barely two minutes) is just the furtive fumblings preceding the pukka take. The relevant part of "Billy Surrenders" had presumably already been pulled to a master reel along with "Billy 4," also absent from the circulating Mexico City tape and in fact the last thing cut at the eight-hour session.

Two songs recorded in Mexico City are absent from movie and album: "Peco's Blues" and "Goodbye Holly." "Peco's Blues" might almost be considered a revamped "Wigwam" with its use of trumpets and Dylan's attempts to hum the harmony line over the trumpeteers' tentative endeavors (its main melody line is actually a direct lift from an earlier Dylan composition, the 1963 "Troubled and I Don't Know Why"). "Goodbye Holly" was a more notable omission, partially because, "Billy" excepted, it was the only other vocal track planned for the film. Rather raucous for a lament, this two-verse ballad reflects the coarse matter-of-fact way that all deaths (Billy's excepted) are dealt with in the film. However, the arranger who Peckinpah had brought in to "arrange" Dylan's material, Jerry Fielding, felt that "Goodbye Holly" was unsuitable and pushed Dylan to come up with something else to fill out the soundtrack. In his own words, "You cannot possibly hope to deal with an entire picture on the basis of one ballad." In the few days they worked together Dylan and Fielding established the most mutual of dislikes, evidenced by a comment Dylan makes at the Mexico City session, just before cutting "Billy Surrenders," "This guy Jerry Fielding's gonna go nuts when he hears this."

Nevertheless, in the couple of weeks that separate Mexico City from Burbank Dylan complied with Fielding's request for one more song. Written in Durango, the opening lines of "Knockin' on Heaven's Door"—"Mama, take this badge off of me/I can't use it anymore"—were probably as much a reflection of Dylan's own despair at the way the shoot was disintegrating as the tears he felt for Slim Picken, the narrator of the song. The understated use of this mournful requiem to a wasted life in the film barely hints of its latter-day anthemic status, courtesy of Eric Clapton, Guns 'n' Roses, as well as others.

It would appear that Peckinpah originally intended to use the song only in instrumental form within the pertinent scene (the director's cut restores this instrumental). Even when a full vocal take was preferred—presumably at some point after MGM had taken the film out of Peckinpah's hands and reedited it without his approval—the version they used in the film was not the one Columbia was now turning into Dylan's first hit single since "Lay Lady Lay." Cut at the first Burbank session, the instrumental "Knockin' on Heaven's Door" was no backing track. Indeed, Dylan says, before the instrumental take, "All right, let's do it without a vocal . . . [but] this is the last time I work for anyone in a movie on the music. I'll stick to acting [in future]." The instrumental version is actually rather lovely. Coming after a half-formed first vocal take, the instrumental steers Dylan toward that lovely gospel feel he finds on the finished song.

If "Knockin' on Heaven's Door" proved that Dylan could still cut it as a songwriter, there is another moment on the Burbank sessions that illustrates how his spontaneous approach to recording can inspire a general serendipity from those around him. After working up the complex arrangement of "Final Theme" to Gordon Carroll's satisfaction, Dylan suddenly drops into a simple riff mouthing words to what sounds like a largely improvised tune called "Rock Me Mama" (Arthur Crudup and Sonny Terry both wrote songs with the same title but they are quite different). The beauty of this off-the-cuff performance is that the musicians—led by Terry Paul's sloping bass—soon latch on to the groove and what we end up with is an actual take, with the musicians handclapping and harmonizing to a chorus seemingly drawn out of thin air.

Though the Dylan who recorded the musical soundtrack for *Pat Garrett and Billy the Kid* in Mexico and Burbank did not yet have an album full of "Heaven's Door"s in him, he was clearly getting back to some kind of starting point, doing consciously what he used to do unconsciously.

Orson Welles was once asked what happens when one loses the confidence of ignorance. His reply was that one had to ask for the impossible with the same air one did when one didn't realize it was impossible. So much of Dylan's studio work in the sixties and early seventies has that confidence of ignorance, a confidence that only began to fade after *Desire*. The results, though not always satisfactory, sought to convey the sense of immediacy and spontaneity in each and every recording. The experience of working with an arranger and a film producer, making music that was only part of a greater whole, and seeing that greater whole wrestled from its creator and overseer, Sam Peckinpah, only further convinced Dylan of the importance of retaining control of his own work. For his next recording, he would use the most tried and tested of bands, and would reserve production duties for himself and that old cohort, Robbie Robertson.

PLANET WAVES

Recorded: June and November 2 to 10, 1973
Released: January 17, 1974

Side 1: On a Night Like This. Going, Going, Gone. Tough Mama. Hazel. Something There Is About You. Forever Young [II]. Side 2: Forever Young [III]. Dirge. You Angel You. Never Say Goodbye. Wedding Song.

Other official cuts:

The Bootleg Series: Nobody 'Cept You.
Biograph: Forever Young [I]

Producers:

2–5 Bob Dylan, Robbie Robertson, and Rob Fraboni

Musicians:

1–5 Bob Dylan (guitar/piano/harmonica)
2–4 Robbie Robertson (guitar)
2–3 Garth Hudson (organ/accordion)

2–3 Richard Manuel (piano/drums)
2–3 Rick Danko (bass)
3 Levon Helm (drums)

1. BIG BEN OFFICE
   NEW YORK
   JUNE 1973
Nobody 'Cept You
Never Say Goodbye
Forever Young [I]

2. THE VILLAGE RECORDER STUDIO B
   LOS ANGELES, CALIFORNIA
   NOVEMBER 2, 1973
Never Say Goodbye
House of the Rising Sun
Nobody 'Cept You [I]
Nobody 'Cept You [II]
Nobody 'Cept You [III]
Crosswind Jamboree [I]
Crosswind Jamboree [II]

3. THE VILLAGE RECORDER STUDIO B
   LOS ANGELES, CALIFORNIA
   NOVEMBER 5 AND 6, 1973
On a Night Like This
Going, Going, Gone [I]
Going, Going, Gone [II] [vocal overdub]
Tough Mama
Hazel
Something There Is About You
Forever Young [II]
Forever Young [III]
Forever Young [IV]
Forever Young [V]
Dirge
You Angel You

4. THE VILLAGE RECORDER STUDIO B
   LOS ANGELES, CALIFORNIA
   NOVEMBER 9, 1973
Dirge

5. THE VILLAGE RECORDER STUDIO B
   LOS ANGELES, CALIFORNIA
   NOVEMBER 10, 1973
Wedding Song

As what was considered the "real" follow-up to *New Morning, Planet Waves* is an altogether richer album, both lyrically and sonically. Though it had been three years since *New Morning,* the bulk of songs recorded for *Planet Waves* were written in the month preceding the November 1973 sessions, while Dylan was back in New York arranging his affairs before permanently relocating to Malibu. Just three songs were copyrighted before the sessions— "Forever Young," "Nobody 'Cept You," and "Never Say Goodbye" were all de-moed in June 1973 at Dylan's office (the demo of "Forever Young" later appeared on *Biograph*). According to Charles Lippincott, publicity executive at MGM (quoted in a *Rolling Stone* report in July), Dylan had also cut three songs for a "new album, the label yet to be decided." However, Lippincott is almost certainly confusing information about the three acoustic demos, transforming them into full studio versions.

Dylan's choice of musicians to accompany him on his first ever non-Columbia album (having agreed to a one-album-at-a-time deal with David Geffen at Asylum) was suitably prudent. While Geffen and Bill Graham put the finishing touches to a schedule for Dylan's first tour in eight years, fellow Malibu newcomers the Band joined Dylan in Village Recorder Studios in L.A. Despite their work together in the studio in the winter of 1965–66 and the highly productive summer of 1967, Dylan and the Band had never captured their unique sound in the studio and neither Dylan nor the Band had managed an album of original songs since 1971's *Cahoots.* Nor were the Band circa '73 the single-minded unit of yore.

Once again, though, Dylan's "wing it" approach, once harnessed to musicians able to interpret his eccentricities and translate them into sound, resulted in a coherent collection of brand new songs. With recording engineer, Rob Fraboni, directing proceedings (and getting a co-production credit for his pains), they managed to cut the first ever Dylan/Band album in just five sessions, two of which were mixing sessions.

The first session (November 2) was largely intended to check out the sound and get accustomed to the studio. Levon Helm did not even attend this first session. Nevertheless, Dylan insisted on running through something like eight songs, the most laborious of which was "Nobody 'Cept You"—one of only two outtakes from the sessions. The album version of "Never Say Goodbye" (which had lost one of the verses on the June publishers' demo); a full band arrangement of "House of the Rising Sun" (Fraboni seems to think they did a complete version; the only take I am conversant with breaks down after a single verse), the "fast" "Forever Young" (at least four different versions were recorded, one acoustic and one with Garth Hudson on accordion remain unreleased); and an instrumental, copyrighted as "Crosswind Jamboree," all appear to date from this session. Throughout the session Richard Manuel filled in on drums. At the end of the session Fraboni went to lock the studio reels away, at which point Dylan's legendary paranoia almost resulted in the loss of an entire day's work:

Rob Fraboni: *"The first night, after we finished, the Band had already left and Bob was the last to leave, I was gonna put the tapes in the tape library.*

He said, 'No, no, no, I'm taking those with me. Too much bootlegging going on. Can't trust anybody. I gotta take 'em with me.' Then he says, 'Listen, I'm going to see Bobby Blue Bland at the Whisky, you wanna come?' I says 'Sure.' He was driving one of those vans that has windows at the back but no windows at the side and there were no seats in the back. We get to the Whisky and we park the van and I look in the back of the van and there are the tapes. I say to Bob, 'Are you crazy? You don't want to leave the tapes in the studio but you'll leave 'em in the back of this van on Sunset Boulevard.' After that he left them in the studio."

"Nobody 'Cept You" had been one of the most legendary of Dylan outtakes before its release on *The Bootleg Series*—due largely to some electrifying renditions on the 1974 tour. Its inclusion on *The Bootleg Series* was expected to be one of the highlights of that set. However Dylan's vocal on the preferred take lacks the passion of the live performances and Robertson's wah-wah licks are uncharacteristically inappropriate— hence, presumably, its omission from *Planet Waves*. Subsequently, though, two alternate takes from Village Recorder have passed into collectors' hands and both sound a whole lot better. The version bootlegged on *The Genuine Bootlegged Series*—somebody's idea of a wheeze at compiler Rosen's expense— has more interplay between Hudson and Robertson and, though it starts tentatively (perhaps implying a first take), becomes increasingly intense (the released take sounds sedate by comparison).

If the November 2 session had been largely exploratory, the bulk of *Planet Waves* was wrapped up by the end of the next two sessions (November 5 and 6)—seven of the performances on the album come from these two days. Indeed Dylan, Robertson, and Fraboni began mixing the album after these sessions. The song that presented the great-

est problems was "Forever Young." Dylan began to feel he was too close to the song. Even as the preferred takes of each song were pulled to the master reel, he seemed unsure which "Forever Young" best expressed its hymnal quality.

Rob Fraboni: *"There was no producer on* Planet Waves. *I got put in the middle and I found out later why 'cause Robbie actually told me, 'Listen, sometimes I'm gonna tell you what I think should be done and you tell Bob 'cause if I tell him he won't do it.' Bob would be influenced by Robbie because he was a musician and a writer and he felt if he did what Robbie said, that it was gonna be too much slanting it in another direction, it was not going to be enough his own. Coming from me it was more neutral. This happened a lot . . . I remember a particular day, it was on a Saturday, we were doing master reels, that's where you pull the takes off individual reels so that when you assemble them you don't have to keep changing reels all the time. We [had] cut like five different versions of 'Forever Young,' an acoustic one and two others with the Band . . . The thing that was astounding during the making of* Planet Waves *was the day we cut 'Forever Young.' There was this guy called Ken who was a friend of theirs visiting. We only did one take of the slow version of 'Forever Young.' This take was so riveting, it was so powerful, so immediate, I couldn't get over it. When everyone came in nobody really said anything. I rewound the tape and played it back and everybody listened to it from beginning to end and then when it was over everybody sort of just wandered out of the room. There was no outward discussion. Everybody just left. There was just Ken and I sitting there. I was so overwhelmed I said, 'Let's go for a walk.' We went for a walk and came back and I said, 'Let's go listen to that again.' We were like one minute or two into it, I was so mesmerized by it again I didn't even notice that Bob had come into the room and I felt somebody standing behind me. I turned and I said, 'Where were you?' He said, 'I went to a movie across the street.' So when we were assembling the master reel I was getting ready to put that [take] on the master reel. I didn't even ask. And Bob said, 'What're you doing with that? We're not gonna use that.' And I jumped up and said, 'What do you mean you're not gonna use that? You're crazy! Why?' Well, [it turns out] during the recording of* Planet Waves *Jackie De Shannon and Donna Weiss came by one night and on the same night Lou Kemp and this girl came by and she had made a crack to him, 'C'mon, Bob, what. Are you getting mushy in your old age?' about 'Forever Young.' It was based on her comment that he wanted to leave [that version] off the record and I argued really hard against that. He had told me the day we did the acoustic version, 'I been carrying this song around in my head for five years and I never wrote it down and now I come to record it and I just can't decide how to do it.' "*

Fraboni also attempted to get Dylan to do his first ever conventional vocal overdub, i.e., with "cans" on (the second vocal on "The Boxer" was almost certainly recorded with a playback of the basic track running in the studio). Though in future Dylan would usually have headphones pressed to a single ear, when Fraboni asked him to try a new vocal for "Going, Going, Gone" he elected to play acoustic guitar as well. Though there doesn't seem much wrong with the official "Going, Going, Gone," and Dylan tends to have real trouble holding the pitch when left to his own devices, this first vocal overdub is quite riveting. Indeed, he gets so far into the performance that halfway through the song he temporarily stops playing the acoustic. Dylan, though, was not quite ready to embrace the "cold" vocal overdub. At the end of the take, after he has pushed his voice to its razor edge, Dylan

lets out the most dissatisfied of sighs and grunts, "We could spend all day doing this and I don't even know if it's the right thing to do." Thus endeth the first real Dylan overdub.

Without any further overdubs, and with just ten vocal tracks to perm from, sequencing and selecting *Planet Waves* should have been a straightforward affair. After a two-day break, Dylan, Robertson, and Fraboni returned to Village Recorder to do the deed. However, when it came to one of the two songs already cut acoustically, a scathing son of "Positively 4th Street" called (appropriately) "Dirge," Dylan felt he could do better and returned to the studio, with Robertson in tow, to work out a superior arrangement. With Dylan reverting to piano and Robertson embellishing on acoustic guitar, they quickly ran down the new version. Then, with the tape running for the first time, they cut the album's "Dirge" in a single take. Dylan discovered his most biting post-accident vocal for this withering look at love and fame. Though the song has its fair share of lyrical lapses ("in this age of fibreglass, I'm still searching for a gem"), the vocal and Dylan's stabbing piano make this one of his finest studio performances.

That Dylan cut both "Dirge" and "Forever Young" acoustically perhaps suggests that he always intended a balance of acoustic and electric cuts (an idea he has mentioned on a few occasions through the years). Certainly an acoustic "Forever Young" would have been a most effective finale. Once the decision had been made to include both the fast and slow takes of "Forever Young," his mind turned to finding another suitable closer. Finding nothing appropriate, he ended up writing a very personal update to "Restless Farewell," entitled "The Wedding Song." This time Dylan tried to express his devotion to his wife just at the point he was planning to walk out the door. According to

Fraboni, Dylan cut this final *Planet Waves* song at the second mixing session (which would make it November 10, though the album sleeve credits just four recording dates—2, 5, 6, 9) after some final tinkering with the lyrics in the studio. Though it is hard not to interpret the lyrics on a literal level, Dylan's performance once again transcends the at times slipshod sentimentality. Which may well stand as the motif for all of *Planet Waves*. Though it is an album suffused with brilliant performances from both musicians *and* vocalist, Dylan had yet to fully excise some bad writing habits picked up during the amnesia.

BLOOD ON THE TRACKS

Recorded: September 16 to 25, December 27 and 30, 1974
Released: January 17, 1975

Side 1: Tangled Up in Blue. Simple Twist of Fate. You're a Big Girl Now. Idiot Wind. You're Gonna Make Me Lonesome When You Go. Side 2: Meet Me in the Morning. Lily, Rosemary and the Jack of Hearts. If You See Her, Say Hello. Shelter from the Storm. Buckets of Rain.

Other official cuts:

Biograph: Up to Me. You're a Big Girl Now [I].
The Bootleg Series: Call Letter Blues. Tangled Up in Blue [I]. Idiot Wind [I]. If You See Her, Say Hello [I].

Producer:

1–5 Bob Dylan

Musicians:

1–5 Bob Dylan (guitar/harmonica)
1–3 Tony Brown (bass)
1 Charles Brown III (guitar)
1 Eric Weissberg (guitar)
1 Barry Kornfeld (guitar)
1 Richard Crooks (drums)

3 Buddy Cage (steel guitar)
4–5 Ken Odegard (guitar)
4–5 Chris Weber (guitar)
4–5 Bill Peterson (bass)
4–5 Greg Imhofer (organ)
4–5 Bill Berg (drums)

1. COLUMBIA A&R STUDIOS
   NEW YORK
   SEPTEMBER 16, 1974

CO ??   *Up to Me*
CO 118935 **Tangled Up in Blue [I]**
CO 118935 Tangled Up in Blue [II]
CO 118942 **If You See Her, Say Hello [I]**
CO 118942 If You See Her, Say Hello [II]
CO ??   **Call Letter Blues**
CO 118941 *Lily, Rosemary and the Jack of*
           Hearts
CO 118936 *Simple Twist of Fate*
CO 118937 *You're a Big Girl Now*
Rumored: *There Ain't Gonna Be Any*
              Next Time
           Bell Tower Blues

Where Do You Turn (Turning
   Point)?
It's Breakin' Me Up
Don't Want No Married
Woman
Ain't It Funny
Little Bit of Rain

2. COLUMBIA A&R STUDIOS
   NEW YORK
   SEPTEMBER 17, 1974

CO 118937   **You're a Big Girl Now**

3. COLUMBIA A&R STUDIOS
   NEW YORK
   SEPTEMBER 18, 1974

CO 118939 *You're Gonna Make Me Lone-*
           some When You Go
CO 118939 You're Gonna Make Me Lone-
           some When You Go
CO 118943 Shelter from the Storm

4. COLUMBIA A&R STUDIOS
   NEW YORK
   SEPTEMBER 19, 1974
CO 118941 Lily, Rosemary and the Jack of
           Hearts
CO 118936 Simple Twist of Fate
CO 118944 Buckets of Rain
CO 118938 Idiot Wind [I]

5. COLUMBIA A&R STUDIOS
   NEW YORK
   SEPTEMBER 23 TO 25, 1974
CO 118940 Meet Me in the Morning
           [vocal/guitar overdubs]
CO 118938 Idiot Wind [II] [vocal/organ
           overdubs]

CO 118937 You're a Big Girl Now [pedal
           steel overdub]
CO ??   Up to Me

6. SOUND 80 STUDIOS
   MINNEAPOLIS, MINNESOTA
   DECEMBER 27, 1974
CO 118938 *Idiot Wind [I]*
CO 118938 *Idiot Wind [II]*
CO 118938 *Idiot Wind [III]*
CO 118938 Idiot Wind [IV]
CO 118937 You're a Big Girl Now

7. SOUND 80 STUDIOS
   MINNEAPOLIS, MINNESOTA
   DECEMBER 30, 1974
CO 118935 Tangled Up in Blue
CO 118941 Lily, Rosemary and the Jack of
           Hearts
CO 118942 If You See Her, Say Hello
Rumored: *Meet Me in the Morning*

That *Blood on the Tracks* is considered by many Dylan fans both his true masterpiece and a case of "what might have been" illustrates the danger of definitive interpretations of the man's art. That, even after *Biograph* and *The Bootleg Series*, four of the five takes pulled from the album at the eleventh hour remain unreleased is a major oversight, requiring anyone with a more than passing interest in Dylan's art to hunt down a version of the original *Blood on the Tracks* test pressing. Copies of the actual test pressing command even larger sums than an original *Freewheelin'*, although good tapes of the album as originally conceived freely percolate through collecting circles, and all five outtakes were included on TAKRL's *Joaquin Antique* bootleg album (put out barely six weeks after the Columbia version).

The arguments that abound as to the merits of the "original" *Blood on the Tracks* versus the "released" *Blood on the Tracks* are not mere semantics. Yes, the released album features the same songs as its original New York version.

Yes, five of the ten cuts are the same New York takes scheduled from day one. Yet the reason why Dylan's revision of *Blood on the Tracks* inspires such debate is that many fans—indeed, musicians like Joni Mitchell and Robbie Robertson, both of whom told Dylan that they preferred the original version—consider the released album to be something of a cop-out. Ellen Bernstein, the Columbia A&R lady whose affair with Dylan was such a key factor in wringing the album out of him, certainly believes that Dylan went back behind his mask when he rerecorded half the songs three months after the original sessions, and just three weeks before the album was due out.

Dylan managed to cut the "original" version of this unprecedented return to form in a single week in September 1974. However, the period from when he first started playing the songs to friends (in July) to the final day of the second batch of *Blood on the Tracks* sessions, in Minneapolis at the end of December, represents Dylan's most concerted effort to conceive and execute an album since *Blonde on Blonde*. Though this only translates into five days of recording, three of overdubbing and sequencing in New York and two days in Minneapolis, *Blood on the Tracks* was not an album that came together accidentally in the studio. Dylan already knew what he had in mind when entering A&R Studios for the first time on September 16. Even the actual sequencing of the album never seems to have been in very much doubt.

Ellen Bernstein: *"I think as he wrote the songs and as he played them for the people the sequencing decided itself. . . . He was really definite when he went in, he knew what he was going to do and he knew how he was going to do it."*

A test pressing made at the final New York session (September 25), presumably cut for Dylan to evaluate the results, has the exact same sequence as the album released four months later. The only serious doubt Dylan seems to have had was what mood to finish the album on. The actual closer, "Buckets of Rain," ends an album of ghosts from the past, twists of fate, and the inevitability of loss on an upbeat note (aided by the melody line he copped from Tom Paxton's "Bottle of Wine"). As Dylan sings, "Life is sad, life is a bust, all you can do is do what you must," the tone of the whole album shifts to one of *que sera sera*.

That Dylan was considering an altogether more downbeat final note seems borne out by the recording dates for "Up to Me." Originally recorded as a solo acoustic performance at the very first *Blood on the Tracks* session, Dylan only returned to the song at the last session, having finally figured out a vocal delivery that conveyed all the lexicons of remorse he might be feeling (the version cut on the sixteenth has very few vocal idiosyncracies—he even pronounces *identity* like anyone else would). The lyrics to "Up to Me" fit previous patterns of Dylan closers—"If we never

meet again, baby remember me . . . " Its musical motifs are also largely a continuation of *Blood on the Tracks*'s penultimate song, "Shelter from the Storm." However, Dylan decided to stick with "Buckets of Rain," featuring some of his most controlled picking, to conclude one of his most musical albums.

Song selection was not the only matter Dylan thought through before beginning work. He also specifically selected A&R Studios as the venue for his first album under his new contract with Columbia. This was a return to an old stomping ground: for A&R Studio on 54th Street had once been Columbia's Studio A. It was at this studio that Dylan had recorded his first six albums, and it had always seemed like the most comfortable environment Dylan found for recording.

Ellen Bernstein: *"The theme of returning ran through the sessions. The sound of the album was such a return that it made a lot of sense to do it there."*

A familiarity with A&R Studios, and the stripped-down sound Dylan and Bernstein had already discussed, convinced Dylan that he could proceed without a conventional producer. Though Phil Ramone, who engineered the sessions, was a producer in his own right, Dylan was determined to trust his own instincts.

Ellen Bernstein: *"He knew these songs. He knew his vision for these songs [which] was very pure and very unadorned, and you don't need a producer if your vision is that personal on something. I think he had a lot of belief in the integrity of the material."*

Dylan had insisted on playing the songs and gauging reactions at every opportunity. In the six weeks that had elapsed since rejoining Columbia he had run through the album, pretty much from start to finish, on at least four separate occasions: to Michael Bloomfield at his home in the Bay Area, to Shel Silverstein on his houseboat, to Dave Crosby and Graham Nash at the St. Paul Hilton, and. to a friend in New Jersey. With the exception of Bloomfield, who wanted to play along but found it difficult because of the weird open D tuning Dylan was using, the reaction to the songs veered from positive to ecstatic.

When Dylan began work at A&R one Monday afternoon in September he seemed unusually keen to get on with the recording process. The songs themselves were no more than two months old (even if Dylan introduced "Tangled Up in Blue" in 1978 as a song it took him ten years to live and two years to write), and he was still excited by the new approach to language he had uncovered.

Even behind closed studio doors he was determined to get the songs out of his system as quickly, and with as much impact, as possible. Inevitably this resulted in some less than perfect recordings.

Ellen Bernstein: *"There were certain ones where you can hear the sound of his fingernails on the guitar. That didn't matter to him. None of that stuff was important to him. What was important was the overall emotional weight of the song."*

The first "Up to Me" and the versions of "Tangled Up in Blue" and "If You See Her, Say Hello" originally scheduled for the album both have an audible clatter, that of Dylan's (cuff?) buttons against his guitar. Dylan even intended to open the album with the sound of rattling buttons. The solo acoustic "Up to Me" had been one of at least half a dozen solo performances he cut on the first afternoon at A&R. Though these initial recordings were presumably never intended to be more than guide demos, Dylan has never been one to hold back on a recorded performance, whatever its ostensible purpose and it seems likely that he would have run down many of the songs he intended to record for Phil Ramone's benefit at this first session.

Though Columbia seem to have mislaid recording information (and some of the master tapes) for this, the most important "rock" album in their entire catalogue, this is the most likely time and place for Dylan to have cut any "lost" *Blood on the Tracks* songs. There are lyrics to at least seven unknown songs in a little red notebook that accompanied Dylan to these sessions (he would refer to the notebook when lyrics eluded him, though he had pretty much memorized the songs by now). It strikes me as likely (cross fingers) that Dylan ran through at least a couple of these songs at this initial session, much as he had with similar lost songs at the first *Bringing It All Back Home* session (two of the songs—"Ain't It Funny" and "Little Bit of Rain"—are among the last songs in the *Blood on the Tracks* notebook). That said, lyrically there were no idiot winds waiting in the wings. Dylan's choice of which songs to preserve cannot really be faulted. Once the real work got under way, Dylan stuck to the ten *Blood on the Tracks* songs (until "Up to Me" made its belated return at the final session).

After an afternoon of solo indulgence on the sixteenth, that real work began the very same evening with a session between six and twelve, during which Dylan was apparently accompanied by various members of Eric Weissberg's Deliverance. I say "apparently" as, save for bassist Tony Brown, they are inaudible on any of the circulating cuts. According to AF of M records, six songs were cut that evening, perhaps the finest tally of songs at any Dylan session. Two were good enough to be earmarked for the album, "Tangled Up in Blue" and "If You See Her, Say Hello," but in both cases just guitar and bass lighten Dylan's vocal tone. The versions of "You're a Big Girl Now," "Simple Twist of Fate," and "Lily, Rosemary and the Jack of Hearts" cut on the sixteenth remain unheard, though they may well feature full band arrangements.

One curious thing about that first evening session is the way Dylan chose to build up the sound and strip it down within a single six-hour session, settling, at the end of it, for only the lightest of embellishments. The way that Eric Weissberg tells it, he asked Dylan whether he should bring his entire band to the session and Dylan had said, "Sure." Yet when they arrived, Dylan seems to have had very little use for anyone save the bass player Tony Brown. Organist Thomas McFaul and drummer Richard Crooks may have played on just one song. According to Bernstein, Dylan was just quick to recognize when something didn't sound right.

Ellen Bernstein: *"He knew as soon as he heard something whether or not it was what he was going for. It never took him more than one time to know. . . . He worked so instinctively, more so than anyone I've ever worked with. The energy level was so high at all times because it wasn't like where you went over and over and over something until all the rawness is gone . . . it was all very immediate and very emotional."*

The one song cut on the sixteenth with the sound of Deliverance was one of those prototypical blues tunes Dylan had been playing at the afternoon session. "Call Letter Blues," when released on *The Bootleg Series*, took most fans by surprise. Rather than being a previously unknown song in its own right, it was in fact "Meet Me in the Morning" with an alternate set of lyrics.

The remainder of the songs cut that first evening were all apparently cut with between one and three acoustic guitars and electric bass. As per usual there seems to have been very little discussion about a song's arrangement before a take, although Deliverance guitarist Charlie Brown III seems to have gotten the idea pretty quickly: "[Dylan's] whole concept of making an album seemed to be go ahead and play it and whichever way it comes out, well

that's the way it is. It's what happens at the moment."

Yet the sound on the test-pressing is as threadbare as the one Dylan and Terry Paul used for most of the first *Pat Garrett* session. As to why Charlie Brown and Eric Weissberg are wholly absent from even the original album, perhaps their playing simply did not gel with Dylan's. They were certainly put at a disadvantage by his reluctance to explain the open D tuning being used on most of the songs. They were required to rely on pure instinct. As Brown told Larry Sloman, "We'd just watch his hands and pray we had the right changes." Weissberg was not impressed and later said, "If it was anybody else I would have walked out."

As it happens Dylan, having had little use for Deliverance on the sixteenth, decided he had no further use for them at the end of the session, requesting only bassist Tony Brown's presence at the following day's session. Dylan had evidently decided on a sound even more pared down than *John Wesley Harding*. Over the next three days Dylan and Tony Brown would summon up nearly the whole album. Paul Griffin was drafted in on the seventeenth to add some delicate organ fills to a heartbreaking "You're a Big Girl Now," but otherwise any guests were distractions along the way. On one occasion Mick Jagger was a surprise guest (Ellen Bernstein recollects Dylan trying "Little Red Rooster" as a nod to Mick). Dylan, Ellen, and Jagger ended up drinking through the night, blasting away the blues. On the eighteenth, the evening session was curtailed when Dylan decided to catch Little Feat at the Bottom Line, but there still seems to have been time to cut "Shelter from the Storm" and "You're Gonna Make Me Lonesome When You Go."

After two abbreviated sessions on the seventeenth and eighteenth, the nineteenth generated the epic "Lily, Rosemary and the Jack of Hearts," "Buckets of Rain"—which was probably written during the sessions—and "Simple Twist of Fate." But the main business of the day was to cut *Blood on the Tracks*'s magnum opus, "Idiot Wind." Of all the songs on the album, "Idiot Wind" went through the most changes. Even in Dylan's notebook, "Idiot Wind" stands as the exception. Whereas all the other songs have been copied into the book after their original composition—with changes made between Dylan's Minnesotan farm and New York largely confined to tightening up language— "Idiot Wind" even in the notebook exists in three hugely different forms. Wholesale change after wholesale change is wrought upon the song as Dylan turns it from being "right on target, so direct" into an allusive welding of the microcosmic and macrocosmic. By the time Dylan cut the song on the nineteenth, he had achieved a fine balance, intersecting his very personal tale with a far more wide-ranging battle of the spirit, in a way that would have done Charles Williams proud.

The version of "Idiot Wind" that closes side two of *The Bootleg Series* is credited to this very session, and is clearly the same song as the take included on the original test pressing, at least lyrically (all that stuff about throwing I-Chings and thunder at the well). On both versions the material world repeatedly comes between our star-crossed lovers. But the (patently inferior) *Bootleg Series* version fails on two important levels.

Most significantly, Dylan delivers one of the most mannered vocals of these entire sessions. The "Idiot Wind" on the original *Blood on the Tracks* is truly the only one of its kind (at least until its reappearance live in 1992) to bridge the gap between bitterness and sorrow. There is a wretchedness to Dylan's vocal that is all but absent on *The Bootleg Series* (it is even possible that this version

succeeds the take on the test pressing, that Dylan was already looking for a way to tone his performance down). Also on the test-pressing is some "spooky" organ accompaniment by Paul Griffin—a mocking reminder of that all-pervasive wind—interjected between verses (it is entirely absent from the *Bootleg Series* take, despite accompanying notes rhapsodizing about said spookiness). The organ was, in fact, a later overdub, hence its absence from the "other" outtake. Indeed there is a tape of the test-pressing version sans organ, i.e., the basic track as cut on the nineteenth. The organ was not the only overdub. In what appears to be the first instance of a vocal "punch in" by Dylan, a new vocal has been added for the lines:

You didn't trust me for a minute, babe,
I'd never known the Spring to turn so
*   quickly into autumn.*

In fact, Dylan was starting to reconsider his Luddite ways in the studio. Not only did he bring in Buddy Cage (on pedal steel) and Paul Griffin (on keyboards) to embellish the likes of "You're a Big Girl Now" and "Idiot Wind," but Dylan himself dubbed "Meet Me in the Morning" over "Call Letter Blues," no mean feat. The new "Meet Me in the Morning" seems to have occupied most of the session on the twenty-third, when Cage was also adding his pedal-steel to "You're a Big Girl Now" (and Griffin was embellishing "Idiot Wind"?). Dylan presumably must have written "Meet Me in the Morning"—one of only two songs absent from his notebook (the other being "Buckets of Rain")—over the intervening weekend, dubbing a new vocal track (and some fuzzy electric slide) onto what appears to be the basic track for "Call Letter Blues." Though the basic track for "Meet Me in the Morning" does not correspond with the version of "Call Letter Blues" on *The*

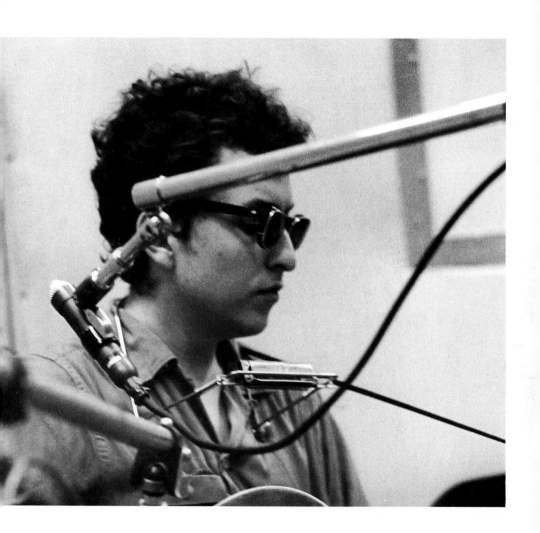

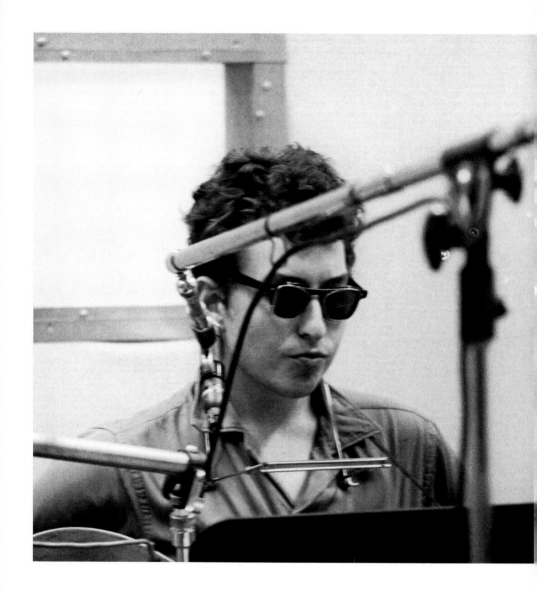

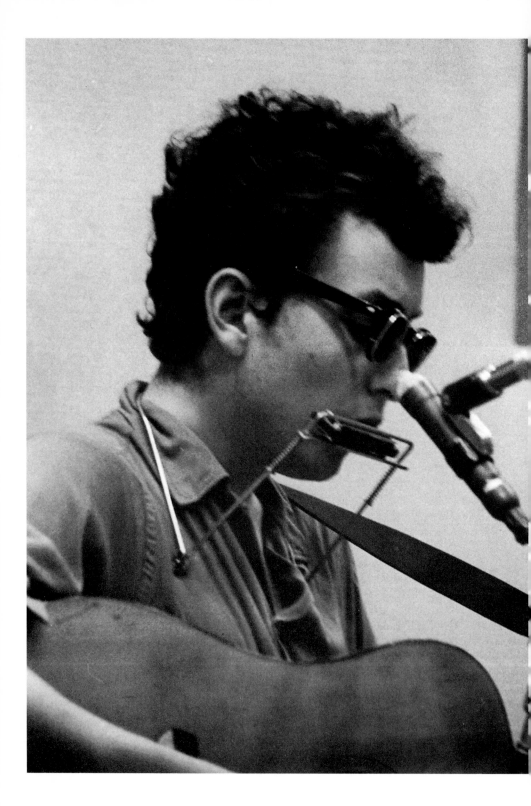

Bootleg Series, Dylan presumably found a basic track he could use. There is certainly no evidence that he recalled Deliverance to recut the only band performance at the New York sessions (there is no AF of M session sheet for any session involving Weissberg save for the sixteenth).

The final New York session (on the twenty-fifth) was given over to sequencing, save for the reappearance of "Up to Me." At the end of it Ramone cut an acetate for Dylan. This *Blood on the Tracks* was until early December scheduled to become Dylan's second studio album in less than a year.

How late Dylan decided to remake *Blood on the Tracks* can be illustrated by Columbia's mastering records which show that the original album was mastered for release, on either December sixth or sixteenth (a typo confuses the matter). By this point Dylan was in Minnesota. When he played the album to his brother, David thought that the album was a little too skeletal and suggested recutting some of the tracks with local Minneapolis musicians. By the time the Sound 80 sessions were organized Dylan had already "pulled" the original album. There was no going back, whatever the outcome of the Minneapolis sessions. In fact the first Minneapolis session, two days after Christmas, was nearly disastrous. It took four attempts to get a satisfactory "Idiot Wind" and, even with further chunks of new lyrics, it never came close to capturing the intensity of New York. "You're a Big Girl Now" was also a mere reflection of the ghost of a pale shadow of its New

York predecessor. Though the second Minneapolis session did produce a splendid "Tangled Up in Blue"—the one song that had clearly retained its emotional connection—"If You See Her, Say Hello" was another casualty of Dylan's desire to clothe his previously shorn soul. (As a further sleight of hand, Dylan seems to have actually sped up the resultant album, both Minneapolis and New York cuts, by two percent, in the mastering—presumably because he found the material dragged a little. The vinyl "half-speed master" evidently used the pre–sped up tape, making for a quite different listening experience.)

Ironically, Dylan's decision to rejig the album came so late in the day that the first pressing of the album was housed in its original cover, which not only had the original musician credits but also contained Pete Hamill's penetrating liner notes. Unfortunately these notes pertained to the New York album, Hamill having been in attendance at some of the sessions, and when he quoted from "If You See Her, Say Hello" it was the original lyrics he quoted ("If you're making love to her, kiss her for the kid"). The notes were pulled from the second pressing, just as Hamill was being nominated for a Grammy for his notes, thus requiring Columbia to reinstate them. It was inevitable that tapes of the New York version of *Blood on the Tracks* would soon pass into general circulation, making Dylan's act of self-censorship ultimately self-defeating. The studio was once again no place to hide.

DESIRE

Recorded: July 14 to October 24, 1975
Released: January 16, 1976

Side 1: Hurricane. Isis. Mozambique. One More Cup of Coffee. Oh, Sister. Side 2: Joey. Romance in Durango. Black Diamond Bay. Sara.

Other official cuts:

45: Rita Mae.
Biograph: Abandoned Love.
The Bootleg Series: Catfish. Golden Loom.

Producer:

1–6 Don Devito

Musicians:

1–6 Bob Dylan (guitar/harmonica/piano/vocals)
1 Dave Mason Band (?)
1 unknown girl backing vocalists
2–3 Mel Collins (sax/trumpet)
2–3 Neil Hubbard (guitar)
2 Eric Clapton (guitar)
2–3 Hugh McCracken (guitar)
2–3 Vinnie Bell (guitar)
2–3 Erik Frandsen (slide guitar)
2–3 Sugar Blue (harmonica)
2 Yvonne Elliman (backing vocals)

2–6 Rob Stoner (bass)
2–6 Scarlet Rivera (violin)
2–5 Emmylou Harris (backing vocals)
2–5 Sheena (tambourine)
2–3 Dom Cortese (mandolin/accordion)
2–3 Terry Stannard (drums)
2–3 unknown trumpeter
4–6 Howie Wyeth (drums)
6 Steven Soles (guitar)
6 Ronee Blakely (backing vocals)
6 Luther Rix (congas)

1. COLUMBIA STUDIOS
   NEW YORK
   JULY 14, 1975
   CO ??   *Rita Mae*
   CO ??   *Joey*

2. COLUMBIA STUDIOS
   NEW YORK
   JULY 28, 1975
   CO 121706–2   *Romance in Durango [I]*
   CO 121706–6   **Romance in Durango [II]**
   CO 121707   *Money Blues*

CO 121708   *One More Cup of Coffee*
CO 121709   *Oh, Sister*
CO 121710   **Catfish**
CO 121711   *Hurricane*
Rumored: *Wiretappin'*

3. COLUMBIA STUDIOS
   NEW YORK
   JULY 29, 1975
   CO 121712   *Black Diamond Bay*
   CO 121707   *Money Blues*

CO 121709–5   *Oh, Sister*
CO 121710   *Catfish*
CO 121713   *Mozambique*
CO 121711   *Hurricane*

4. COLUMBIA STUDIOS
   NEW YORK
   JULY 30, 1975
CO 121714–1   **Golden Loom [I]**
CO 121714–2   *Golden Loom [II]*
CO 121709–2   **Oh, Sister [I]**
CO 121709–3   *Oh, Sister [II]*
CO 121708   **One More Cup of Coffee**
CO 121715   **Isis**
CO 121713–4   **Mozambique**
CO 121716   **Joey**
CO 121712–5   **Black Diamond Bay**
CO 121711   Hurricane
CO 121717   **Rita Mae**

5. COLUMBIA STUDIOS
   NEW YORK
   JULY 31, 1975
CO 121719?–1   **Abandoned Love [I]**
CO 121719?–2   *Abandoned Love [II]*
CO 121718–5   **Sara**
CO 121715–2   **Isis**
CO 121707   *Money Blues*

6. COLUMBIA STUDIOS
   NEW YORK
   OCTOBER 24, 1975
CO n/a   *Jimmy Brown the Newsboy*
CO n/a   *Sitting on Top of the World*
CO n/a   *That's All Right, Mama*
CO n/a   *Ride 'Em, Jewboy*
CO n/a   *I Still Miss Someone*
CO n/a   *Simple Twist of Fate*
CO 121731   *Hurricane [I]*
CO 121732   **Hurricane [II]***
CO 121733   **Hurricane [III]***
CO 121734   *Hurricane [IV]*

By the time he came to record *Desire*, Dylan was back in critical favor. In the previous eighteen months not only had he secured two number one albums on the *Billboard* charts (his first, amazingly enough) but *Blood on the Tracks* had reminded fickle critics of his genius credentials. Returning to favorite haunts in the Village in June 1975, Dylan seemed on the lookout for a new starting point, though he lacked any specific plans record- or tourwise. After all, Columbia was about to put out the eight-year-old basement tapes and, though Dylan had scraps of song, only one fully formed effort, "One More Cup of Coffee," had come from his pen in the months since *Blood on the Tracks*. In the first two weeks of July all changed as Dylan encountered the two key figures in his next equation: lyricist Jacques Levy and violinist Scarlet Rivera. While Rivera was to provide him with a new, albeit slightly off-key, sound, Levy gave him a new, cinematic framework for his words.

Dylan wrote one more song solo, after a night at the Other End at the beginning of July. "Abandoned Love" continued the preoccupations of *Blood on the Tracks*. A couple of days later Dylan ran into Levy in the Village for the second time in a year. Adjourning to Levy's apartment to compare notes, they composed in a matter of days at least three songs, including the dramatic "Isis," which sought the same kind of mythological sweep as "Shelter from the Storm." The rather controversial "Joey" (aka "The Ballad of Joey Gallo"), which seemed to celebrate the life of a particularly vicious New York mafioso, also resulted from their initial collaboration.

If "Isis" was both epic in scale and visionary in intent, it was "Joey" that Dylan first attempted in the studio. Before he and Levy could retire to the Hamptons to write an album's worth of songs, Dylan snuck into a Columbia studio to cut two of the songs he had just written with Levy. This July 14 session has never been documented, though *Rolling Stone*'s "Random Notes" referred to Dylan cutting a version of "Joey" with "Dave Mason and his band." This, presumably, is that "Joey."

Even on this one-off session, certain elements of the *Desire* sound were already in place, the most significant of which was Scarlet's violin (confirmation that Dylan wanted that 'gypsy violin' tone from the very beginning). More intriguing was a lovely accordion wash only hinted at on the released "Joey." (It is interesting to note that the accordion on the *Desire* version—particularly the section after Dylan sings "the tune of an accordion"—sounds like a "punch in," although Dom Cortese did play on the fourteenth and at the first two *Desire* sessions).

Dylan clearly always envisaged adding one or more girl singer(s) to bolster his sound. Though there was no Emmylou Harris on the fourteenth, Dylan had the use of (Dave Mason's?) three girl singers, an ominous preview for his annoying over-reliance on harmony singers throughout the late 1970s and early eighties. On "Joey" the singers became a chorus of sirens, prologuing the song with its mournful refrain, "Joey, Joey, what made them want to come and blow you away?", the very question the song sought to answer.

On "Rita Mae," the other song cut at this session, the girls add the corniest of endings (singing, "Don't think twice, it's so nice" on the fade, presumably one final attempt at enticing the narrator's lesbian friend into bed). The audacious combination of instruments on this session presaged the "big band" sound Dylan was to attempt at the first two *Desire* sessions. With a mix of mandolin, accordion, violin, girl singers, and organ, Dylan was clearly looking for some sound as different from *Blood on the Tracks* as humanly possible. However, much like his attempt to utilize Weissberg's Deliverance on that album, he soon had to strip things down in order to make sense of these new songs.

On returning from East Hampton, Dylan did not hang about the Village, but went straight into the studio, where fifteen musicians awaited him. If the many eyewitnesses to these "big band" sessions are to be believed, both the July 28 and 29 sessions were absolute chaos. According to Kokomo's Neil Hubbard, "There were . . . five guitarists including me and Eric Clapton . . . and there was no one in overall control—no producer or anything." The big band experiment was a typically Dylanesque example of walking a tightrope without a safety net.

For most of the musicians it was a traumatic introduction to Dylan's working methods. Using anywhere up to six guitars (three acoustics, Dylan's included, two electrics—Eric Clapton or Hugh McCracken trading lead—and Erik Frandsen on slide), before mixing in mandolin, accordion, harmonica, trumpet, organ, tambourine, violin, and harmony vocals, in-house producer Don Devito was obliged to "stack" the organ, violin, and "percussion" on one of the sixteen recording tracks available (a disastrous decision that precluded remixing Scarlet's often off-key violin). On one particularly outrageous "nearly disco 'Hurricane'" complete with backup singers chanting "Hurricane, Hurricane," Devito was required to stack two of the three electric guitars on one track, mandolin and accordion on another, and horns, trumpet, and saxophone on yet another, just to fit all the instruments.

Dylan's choice of musicians and instrumentation seemed at times as haphazard as the recording process. Aside from assorted members of English pub-rock combo Kokomo, who chipped in on most songs, Eric Clapton contributed to six of the seven cuts attempted on the twenty-eighth. On the other hand, Clapton's regular backing singer Yvonne Elliman went largely unused, and slide guitarist Erik Frandsen's only real moment came on a subdued paean to baseball hero "Catfish" Hunter (of the four *Desire* outtakes "given air" since the album's release, "Catfish," the only one from the big band sessions, hardly represents how this band might have sounded).

When it came time to choose tracks for *Desire,* there would be big band versions (from the sessions on July 14, 28, and 29) for seven of the nine songs on the album ("Isis" and "Sara" being the exceptions), plus takes of "Money Blues," "Catfish," and "Rita Mae" (according to Larry Sloman a song called "Wiretappin'"—which contained the line "wiretapping, it can happen"—was also attempted on the twenty-eighth, although the track sheets allude to no such cut). Only "Romance in Durango" from the big band sessions would make the actual album, and even then Sugar Blue's harmonica and two acoustic guitars (presumably those played by Neil Hubbard and Hugh McCracken) were mixed out.

On the (albeit slim) evidence of "Romance in Durango," the biggest problem with this lineup was drummer Terry Stannard, whose thumping blandness was immensely frustrating to bassist "Rockin'" Rob Stoner. Stoner was, Rivera aside, Dylan's most important recruit from two weeks of talent-scouting in the Village, and soon assumed the de facto role of bandleader.

The second session on the twenty-ninth should have been less chaotic thanks to the departure of half the English contingent. Clapton and Elliman were splitting after the first session, Eric declaiming, "I had to get out in the fresh air 'cause it was madness in there." With experienced session musicians Hugh McCracken and Vinnie Bell taking turns at replacing E.C., Dylan set about recutting "Money Blues," "Oh, Sister," "Catfish," and "Hurricane." He also attempted the highly original "Black Diamond Bay," complete with harmonica, horns, piano, conga, and violin. Not surprisingly it took twelve takes to get anything usable. Clearly the musicians were still not gelling. Stoner's recollection

is that "these guys from Kokomo . . . were the main culprits . . . they kept doing takes [until] they would get their parts together. By that time Bob's bored."

Dylan needed to reconsider his grandiose notions for a big band sound. According to Stoner, producer Don Devito (on behalf of Dylan) came to him at the end of the second session and asked for suggestions to improve the sound and get the sessions moving. Never shy of expressing his thoughts, Stoner told him, "Why don't you come in with a tiny band . . . no girlfriends, no wives, no nothing! Just the smallest possible band you can get—bass player, drummer, and anybody else you wanna keep around."

In fact Dylan attempted a stripped-down "Oh, Sister" at the end of this second session. Using just bass, drums, vocal, guitar, violin, and second vocals—that is, the same setup he was to use on the two remaining sessions—Dylan cut an "Oh, Sister" good enough to warrant overdubbing a new Emmylou Harris (harmony) vocal the following day (presumably before the rest of the band trundled in). This may have been Dylan's way of taking Stoner's suggestions on board, at least on a trial basis. Satisfied that this was the way ahead, he now had the problem of finding a new drummer (the entire Kokomo outfit was due elsewhere). Though Dylan wanted ex-Domino Jim Gordon or perhaps Nashville's finest, the venerable Ken Buttrey, to replace Stannard, Devito couldn't locate Gordon or Buttrey and so Stoner suggested his old sidekick, Howie Wyeth. Dylan once again had a rhythm section that could read his mind.

The July 30 session became one of those remarkable Dylan sessions in which an album largely came about in a single night. In the words of percussionist Sheena, "Wednesday night, that was the album. I thought it was very special . . .

those who were really chosen . . . [were] there to make the candle shine. Dylan had called me that afternoon and he told me that he couldn't sleep much because the energy was so high, so intense, all this commotion, and magic, and trying to do this art form."

Both Dylan and Harris arrived early (presumably to overdub "Oh, Sister"), warming up with Little Richard numbers in Dylan's case and country standards in Emmylou's. Emmylou had at last figured out Dylan's idiosyncratic ways of singing and was now beginning to lean into the lines. With Harris, Sheena, Scarlet, Stoner, and new boy Wyeth, Dylan was keen to get down to business. Wyeth was given an insight into the man's working methods on the very first take of the evening, "Golden Loom":

"We started the song and I think they were recording it . . . and we sort of fumbled the ending. And I asked Bob, 'Are we gonna end this or is it gonna be a fade?' And he went into such a lengthy explanation . . . that everybody got so confused. . . . [And finally] he said, 'Let's not even do it.' And Stoner said [to me], 'Don't ask him anything. Just play.'"

Despite such eccentricities, Dylan was delighted by Wyeth, telling Stoner, "Your drummer sounds great, it sounds great." Wyeth's crisp dispatch, aligned to Stoner's sympatico bass lines, turned a previously cluttered sound on its head. As Stoner puts it, "We just went back into the studio and started running through tunes, bam, bam, bam, just getting every complete take, every complete tune was a take. . . . We were so hot. . . . I think we were still doing takes as late as five and six A.M. that morning." Five of the nine *Desire* songs were cut that magic night, including the eleven-minute "Joey." Even the idiosyncratic "Black Diamond Bay" failed to throw this band. Also recorded in the wake of "Golden Loom" were "Rita Mae" (at

one point scheduled to close side one of *Desire,* at the expense of the ghastly "Mozambique"), a slow "Isis" that was not destined to make the album, and the best "Hurricane."

"Hurricane" was clearly an important song to Dylan at this point. It championed a cause much like the ones he had supported before the grand disillusionment of 1964. Having attempted the song with the big band in at least two styles, the July 30 version was the one Devito pulled to the master reel (Dylan asked for an acetate to be sent to "Hurricane" Carter). To further the sense of deja vu from 1963, Columbia's lawyers eventually advised against the release of this take.

Despite the omission of this "Hurricane," the spirit of the thirtieth pervades *Desire.* Its sense of spontaneity may not appeal to all tastes (says Stoner, "We could get that first-take spontaneity because we didn't have to keep going over and over things to show them to all these musicians who were faking it"). Emmylou fades in and out of songs as Dylan's vocal idiosyncracies rise and wane, while the sharpness of Scarlet's playing occasionally cuts a little too deep. Yet, coming on the heels of anything but *Blood on the Tracks, Desire* would have been a quite masterful resumé.

As it is the most discussed song on *Desire* had not as yet been recorded. In keeping with long-standing tradition, Dylan did not record his album closer until the final session. After the euphoria of July 30, the following night's session was bound to seem anticlimactic. According to Wyeth, Dylan was "bummed out . . . we thought everything sucked at that point."

Dylan had been in court all day testifying as a character witness on behalf of ex-Columbia president Clive Davis, and when he turned up at the session, he was accompanied by the beautiful Sara, with whom he had become temporarily reconciled. The July 31 session, though, was not entirely an exercise in reconciliation. Despite Sloman's description of "a quiet session, a lot of listening to playbacks," Dylan actually reserved his two finest performances on *Desire* for this final session.

Only three songs were attempted, a stark contrast to the nine efforts completed the previous day, but as dispositions on marriage one would be hard pressed to find three better examples of the wild swings of emotion it can engender. If "Sara" was a hymn to Dylan's "Scorpio Sphinx in a calico dress," the portrait of the woman/women in the other two songs recorded, "Isis" and "Abandoned Love," was far more capricious. "Abandoned Love," in particular, paints a picture of a remarkably vain woman. The final couplet also suggests that this must be the very woman the narrator married (on the fifth day of May or the thirtieth of November, take your pick). To sing "Don't ever leave me, don't ever go" and "Won't you descend from the throne from where you sit?" in consecutive songs—at a session when your wife and subject matter (spare me your protestations, Mr. D.) sits on the other side of the mirr'r—hardly suggests an unquestioning reentry into the marriage arena.

Sadly the *Biograph* version of "Abandoned Love," potentially the most powerful piece of writing at this session, lacks some kind of necessary spark. Rewriting the last three verses since its debut at the Other End four weeks earlier had done little to dilute the song's taut, Yin-Yang quality, but this is one of the lamest Dylan vocals in many a flaming moon. The curious aspect of this performance—which is as autopilot as it gets—is that the "Sara" that follows directly after (the second take of) "Abandoned Love" is quite riveting. Of course, the way that Sloman describes the moment in *On the Road with Bob*

Dylan was bound to give it a certain mythic quality:

Dylan suddenly turned to his wife and said, "This is for you," and broke into the compelling song he had written for her that summer in the Hamptons. No one had heard it before, but Stoner and Scarlet and Wyeth picked up the tempo, Scarlet playing some exquisite fills, underlining the melancholy of the lyrics. They ran through it in one take.

One complete take, maybe, but it was actually take five. No matter. "Sara" sounds like a first take, spontaneous and fresh, with the sort of expressive, breathlike delivery absent from "Abandoned Love." Having borrowed King Midas's best set of vocal chords, Dylan takes one of his most clichéd lyrics and wrings tiers of meaning from it. The "Isis" is even better. According to the session notes, they first attempted this song with Dylan on guitar, though it is hard to imagine "Isis" without that pounding piano carrying all before it. What also sets the songs cut on the thirty-first apart from those cut on the twenty-eighth and thirtieth is the absence of Emmylou Harris (quite possibly she only had a three-day gap in her schedule at the time). Though Emmylou's vocals are part of that whole unique *Desire* sound, "Sara" and "Isis" are (to my ears) the most convincing Dylan vocals of these sessions. Perhaps he was unconsciously holding back when he and Emmylou sang together. The Dylan on "Isis" is bending notes with the best of 'em while Scarlet's bow scythes away and Stoner's bass effortlessly interweaves with Mr. D's piano, making it sound like these guys and gal had been together twenty-four years, not twenty-four hours.

The following night Dylan's modest revue reassembled to select the cuts that would make the album. Since neither

"Durango" nor "Catfish" had been cut by the Stoner/Wyeth/Scarlet ensemble, the versions cut on the twenty-eighth ended up shortlisted for the album. Nothing from the twenty-ninth even made the short list, and it remains something of a lost session. With the "Rita Mae" single, "Abandoned Love" on *Biograph* and "Golden Loom" on *The Bootleg Series* every song cut on the thirtieth and thirty-first has now been released, save for the one Dylan considered most important at the time, the tale of "Hurricane" Carter.

It seems that Dylan and Levy had managed to get certain salient parts of the events from the night of Carter's arrest wrong. In particular, they had Bradley "robbing the bodies," an accusation even a convicted felon was likely to find offensive, particularly as it was Bello, not Bradley, who was in the bar. Given that the song had been cut on sixteen-track and that Dylan had used overdubs successfully on *Blood on the Tracks,* it strikes me as curious that, rather than redoing the vocal track (or indeed "punching in" rewrites of the offensive lines), he chose to recut the entire song. Coming three months after the *Desire* sessions, and utilizing the more ostentatious lineup he was in the throes of rehearsing with, the new "Hurricane" session was one of those unfortunate sessions that oc-

curred while serendipity was on vacation. Though the October 24 session started in a light enough vein, with Dylan running through some old standards, his mood quickly turned sullen. After six takes of "Hurricane," he was getting seriously antsy, berating Devito, "Maybe you ought to decide which take by a roll of the dice . . . I mean, we can always do it better . . . I mean we can do it seventy-five times but I just want to get it out on the streets." After whimsically suggesting they cut it in mono, Dylan summoned up the energy for more takes (five of 'em) but by four-twenty in the morning he was heartily sick of the whole thing and, with four complete takes to perm from, Dylan put on his jacket and told Devito, "Hey, Don, pick a good one."

As it is the released version of "Hurricane"—the one that supplanted the July 30 take on *Desire*—is actually an edit (probably of takes six and seven). At last, *Desire* could be mastered, though for the second time in a year rerecording part of an album meant Dylan missed the important pre-Christmas release slot. *Desire* would not make its appearance until after Dylan had toured the Northeast with his Rolling Thunder Revue, playing the bulk of the album, wearing white face paint, and garnering his best live reviews in years.

RENALDO AND CLARA

Recorded: October to November 28, 1975
Released: January 25, 1978

Kaw Liga. People Get Ready. I Want You. What Will You Do When Jesus Comes? Little Moses. She Belongs to Me. If You See Her, Say Hello. One Too Many Mornings. House of the Rising Sun. Patty's Gone to Laredo. Sad Eyed Lady of the Lowlands.

Other official cuts:

Four Songs from Renaldo & Clara: People Get Ready.
Songs for the New Depression: Buckets of Rain.
No Reason to Cry: Sign Language.

Producer:
4–5 Rob Fraboni

Musicians:

1–5 Bob Dylan (piano/guitar/vocals)
1 Bette Midler (vocals)
1 Moogy Klingman (piano/harmonica)
1 Ralph Schuckett (organ)
1 Dave Webster (slide guitar)
1 John Siegler (bass)
1 John Wilcox (bass)
2–3 Rob Stoner (bass/vocals)

2 Howie Wyeth (drums)
2 Scarlet Rivera (violin)
2 Mick Ronson (guitar)
2 Stephen Soles (guitar)
2 David Mansfield (steel guitar/dobro)
4–5 Eric Clapton (guitar/vocal)
4 Robbie Robertson (guitar)
5 Ron Wood (guitar)

1. SECRET SOUND STUDIO
   NEW YORK
   OCTOBER 1975
Nuggets of Rain [I]
Nuggets of Rain [II]

2. VARIOUS LOCATIONS
   NOVEMBER 1975
Kaw Liga
People Get Ready
I Want You
What Will You Do When Jesus Comes?

Little Moses
She Belongs to Me
If You See Her, Say Hello
One Too Many Mornings
Patty's Gone to Laredo
Sad Eyed Lady of the Lowlands

3. HOTEL ROOM
   QUEBEC CITY, QUEBEC
   NOVEMBER 28, 1975
House of the Rising Sun

4. SHANGRI-LA STUDIOS
   MALIBU, CALIFORNIA
   LATE MARCH 1976
Sign Language [I]
Sign Language [II]
Sign Language [III]

5. SHANGRI-LA STUDIOS
   MALIBU, CALIFORNIA
   MARCH 30, 1976
Spanish Is the Loving Tongue
Adelita
The Water Is Wide
Idiot Wind [incomplete] [I]
Idiot Wind [incomplete] [II]
Idiot Wind [incomplete] [III]
Big River

The "Hurricane" session was not Dylan's only recording activity that month. Having rewritten "Simple Twist of Fate" and "If You See Her, Say Hello" (performing the former on a PBS special for John Hammond), he volunteered another rewritten track from *Blood on the Tracks* for Bette Midler's new album, *Songs for the New Depression.* As with the other rewrites of *Blood on the Tracks* material, the duet with Midler on this new "Buckets of Rain" was one more step away from the emotional rawness of the original.

Meanwhile, Dylan embarked on an extensive series of rehearsals at S.I.R. for a joint tour/film. According to Stoner, "[Initially] we had no idea what the purpose for these jams [at S.I.R.] was, except we were being invited to jam. . . . So we're up there jamming and it turns out what we're really doing is rehearsing." Because of the planned film, tapes were made at all these sessions. Rehearsals continued at the Seacrest Motel in North Falmouth for the couple of days preceding the Rolling Thunder Revue's Halloween assault on Plymouth Rock. It has long been presumed that these rehearsals were the source for the dozen or so nonconcert performances that Dylan intersperses on his grand celluloid experiment, *Renaldo and Clara.* Larry Johnson, who recorded the soundtrack material for *Renaldo and Clara,* says not.

In fact, though "People Get Ready" and "I Want You" sound like the sort of semi-impromptu run-throughs that tour rehearsals produce, improvised originals like "Patty's Gone to Laredo" and "What Will You Do When Jesus Comes?," played by Dylan at the piano, sound most akin to the December 1977 tape of Dylan running down new songs for *Street-Legal* at the end of a tour rehearsal after most of the musicians had gone home. The *Renaldo and Clara* soundtrack songs evidently all come from one or two sessions since the style of performance (Dylan at the piano, half-remembering words, loose as a caboose) is so uniform and so unlike anything heard onstage. Johnson recollects something like three hotel room sessions with Dylan playing the piano, all of which were recorded, one of which (possibly in Quebec) involved the likes of Stoner and Wyeth coming in to play on some of the songs (which would explain "People Get Ready"). Other sessions he remembers at Niagara Falls, on an Indian reservation at Thanksgiving, and at Gordon Lightfoot's home (though he doesn't recall Dylan playing the piano at Lightfoot's). Informal hotel jams, away from the hustle bustle of the revue, would certainly explain the potpourri of originals like "Sad Eyed Lady of the Lowlands," "One Too Many Mornings," and "She Belongs to Me"— none of which made an appearance on the 1975 tour—and folk standards like Hank's "Kaw Liga," Leadbelly's "In the Pines," and the traditional "Little Moses."

That said, the highlight of the *Renaldo and Clara* soundtrack—obligingly released on a twelve-inch promo only EP by Columbia (and quickly pirated in serious numbers)—was Curtis May-field's "People Get Ready." It has the same join-in-if-you-can spirit found on "Rock Me Mama" from the *Pat Garrett and Billy the Kid* sessions. Other songs accompanying scenes in the film vary from the barely realized ("If You See Her Say Hello," which sounds like it has the new lyrics, though who can tell?) to verging-on-greatness ("One Too Many Mornings," which not only contains some fine interplay between violin and piano but has Dylan once again experimenting with that "Hebraic cantillation" Ginsberg speaks of in his notes to *Desire*).

Compiling *Renaldo and Clara*'s soundtrack from these hotel jams would have to wait until the spring of 1977, by which time they seemed like part of a general determination on Dylan's part to create beyond the con-fines of the studio. This coincided with a determined return to the road, first on the Rolling Thunder Revue and then on a 115-date world tour, cruelly dubbed the Alimony Tour by a jaundiced media. After three studio albums in two years, Dylan avoided the studio alto-gether in 1976–77—save for a couple of days of hard drinking in March 1976 in the company of Eric Clapton and com-pany at the Band's Shangri-La Studios, the sole result of which was one (damn fine) Dylan/Clapton duet on the Dylan original, "Sign Language" (even then Clapton had to beg Dylan to do just one more take, after they were a couple of unsatisfactory takes into the session). In December 1977, Dylan inaugurated a new era for him by taking a five-year lease on a rehearsal studio in Santa Monica, the beginning of the Rundown years.

STREET-LEGAL

Recorded: April 1978
Released: June 15, 1978

Side 1: Changing of the Guards. New Pony. No Time to Think. Baby, Stop Crying. Side 2: Is Your Love in Vain? Señor (Tales of Yankee Power). True Love Tends to Forget. We'd Better Talk This Over. Where Are You Tonight? (Journey Through Dark Heat).

Producer:
4 Don Devito

Musicians:

1–5 Bob Dylan (piano/guitar/vocals)
1 Rob Stoner (bass)
1–5 Stephen Soles (guitar)
2–5 Billy Cross (guitar)
2–5 Alan Pasqua (keyboards)
2–5 Jerry Scheff (bass)

2–5 David Mansfield (violin/mandolin)
2–5 Steve Douglas (saxophone)
2–5 Ian Wallace (drums)
2–5 Helena Springs (backing vocals)
2–5 Jo Ann Harris (backing vocals)
2–5 Carolyn Dennis (backing vocals)

1. RUNDOWN STUDIOS
   SANTA MONICA, CALIFORNIA
   DECEMBER 26, 1977
   First To Say Goodbye [instrumental]
   ??
   Is Your Love in Vain?
   Señor (Tales of Yankee Power)
   No Time to Think
   True Love Tends to Forget
   We'd Better Talk This Over
   First to Say Goodbye
   Where Are You Tonight?

2. RUNDOWN STUDIOS
   SANTA MONICA, CALIFORNIA
   EARLY APRIL 1978
   We'd Better Talk This Over
   Coming from the Heart

3. RUNDOWN STUDIOS
   SANTA MONICA, CALIFORNIA
   APRIL 10 TO 15(?), 1978
   Changing of the Guards
   New Pony*
   No Time to Think
   Baby, Stop Crying
   Is Your Love in Vain?
   Señor (Tales of Yankee Power)
   True Love Tends to Forget
   We'd Better Talk This Over
   Where Are You Tonight? (Journey Through Dark Heat)

4. RUNDOWN STUDIOS
   SANTA MONICA, CALIFORNIA
   MAY 2, 1978
   Stop Now
   Coming from the Heart
   If I Don't Be There by Morning
   Walk Out in the Rain

5. RUNDOWN STUDIOS, SANTA
   MONICA, CALIFORNIA
   JUNE 8, 1978
   Stop Now

6. RUNDOWN STUDIOS
   SANTA MONICA, CALIFORNIA
   SEPTEMBER, 1978
   More than Flesh and Blood
   I Must Love You Too Much
   (You Treat Me Like a) Stepchild

Dylan's purchase of rehearsal space off Santa Monica Boulevard—known simply as 2501 Maine, it would be several months before it became Rundown Studios—gave him, for the first time in his career, an environment in which to make music whenever the feeling took him. Once a basic recording setup was installed on the ground floor of the two-story building in January 1978 (hence the excellent quality of the couple of rehearsal tapes to emerge from the winter of 1978) and he had the nucleus of a "standing" band, Dylan was finally able to work on ideas for songs without the studio clock ticking. The Rundown years—which span the fall of 1977 to the winter of 1982—would coincide with one of his most prolific bursts of songwriting.

Save for two one-week stints at Alabama's legendary Muscle Shoals and the tour of L.A. studios that preceded *Shot of Love,* Dylan steered clear of conventional studios throughout this period. The successor to *Desire,* the much misunderstood *Street-Legal,* was recorded in its entirety at Rundown (using a mobile truck), in a spare week between legs on his yearlong world tour.

Despite these imminent recording dates, the four months preceding the *Street-Legal* sessions rarely saw Dylan running down one of his new songs for his touring band, though his next album was essentially already composed. However, at one remarkable post-rehearsal session the day after Christmas 1977 he sat at the piano and played almost the entire album to a stunned Rob Stoner, Stephen Soles, and Joel Bernstein.

This December 26, 1977, run-through for most of *Street Legal* was not some-

thing Dylan intended to preserve. After warming up with a couple of half-formed tunes (the second of which has just one intelligible line: "Can you feel those lonely eyes staring across the room?"), Dylan says, presumably to Bernstein, "Don't tape this one," and pushes the microphone away. Nevertheless, the tape keeps running, bearing witness to an astonishing preview of an album he is some months away from recording.

This, in itself, raises a whole series of questions about when a session at Rundown became a tour rehearsal, was simply an excuse to jam, or when it alchemized into a recording session. Even discounting *Street-Legal* and the parts of *Shot of Love* recorded at Rundown, once a mixing console was installed, there were usually tapes running at the studio. (On a technical note, for the last two weeks of rehearsals in January 1978, Dylan had use of Yamaha's absolute-state-of-the-art PM2000 front-of-house console, which they were about to take to Japan; subsequently he got by with a Soundcraft console, with sixteen inputs.) The vast majority of songs copyrighted by Dylan in these years were lodged with ASCAP utilizing tapes made at Rundown, and, for the first time since his Witmark days, Dylan was making a regular habit of demoing songs.

Though I am not about to concern myself with Dylan's attempts to work up a reggae arrangement of "Ballad of a Thin Man" herein, the crucial years 1978–81—out of which Dylan would pull only the most flawed vinyl representations—saw all new songs (to the best of my knowledge) attempted first at

Rundown. As such, when working on new songs and not rearranging the old, I have made such recordings part of Dylan's pukka oeuvre (my two favorite words in one phrase!), that is intended to be preserved by the man himself, and part of my considerations.

With the December 26 Rundown run-through, Dylan was repeating his methodology in the lead-up to *Blood on the Tracks*, seeking to gauge the reaction before around him to his new songs prior to recording them. Even before this Boxing Day session, Dylan had popped in on Jerry Wexler as he worked on a new Etta James album at L.A.'s Cherokee Studios, where he proceeded to play Wexler some of his new songs at the piano. Dylan and Wexler had worked together on the 1973 *Barry Goldberg* album, for which Dylan had received co-production credits, and it was rumored that Wexler might produce Dylan's forthcoming album. As it is, Wexler's turn would come but not on *Street-Legal.*

Perhaps Dylan was self-consciously attempting to replicate the set of circumstances that had inspired *Blood on the Tracks.* After all, *Street-Legal* and *Blood on the Tracks* share more than a common thematic preoccupation. Like *Blood on the Tracks,* most of *Street-Legal* was written during a summer recess at Dylan's Minnesotan farm, at a time when he was estranged from his (now ex-) wife. Much as he had with Ellen Bernstein, Dylan would write songs early in the morning and then show them to the new lady in his life, Faridi McFree.

Unlike *Blood on the Tracks,* though, which had been recorded in New York with almost indecent haste, Dylan held off from recording *Street-Legal.* The fall of 1977 was spent putting finishing touches to *Renaldo and Clara,* resolving the battle for custody of his children, and assembling a band with whom he could tour the Far East. He had been made an offer he could not refuse—particularly after an expensive divorce and self-financed film had severely depleted the coffers—to play a week of shows at Tokyo's Budokan Hall and record a live album into the bargain.

As noted earlier, even after assembling the nuts and bolts of a touring band at the end of December 1977, Dylan refrained from working on his new songs with them. He was already unhappy with the new combo's lack of spontaneity. He can be heard bemoaning (to Stoner) on the December 26 sneak preview, "I can't spring anything new on this band." As such, despite the fact that what Stoner, Soles, and Bernstein heard that afternoon comprised the bulk of *Street-Legal*—only "Changing of the Guards," "New Pony," and "Baby Stop Crying" were absent, and "Guards" was certainly written by the time Dylan arrived in Australia—no new songs appear on the various extant rehearsal tapes made between December 1977 and February 1978. Indeed, only one *Street-Legal* song was previewed on the Far East tour ("Is Your Love in Vain," played just twice, both times when tapes were running for the live album).

One new song reported to have been performed at tour rehearsals *is* part of the December 26 tape but it is one tune absent from *Street-Legal.* The same melody that opens the tape in instrumental form returns near the end, complete with vocal.

The opening lyrics strongly suggest that this is "First to Say Goodbye," a song journalist Harvey Kubernik referred to in his report of the Rundown rehearsals in *Melody Maker.* The lyric soon gives way to an instrumental bridge, on which Stoner attempts to play along, only for the song to fizzle out. This is not a fate reserved solely for "First to Say Goodbye." None of the six *Street-Legal* songs here previewed is performed in its entirety. This is evidently because of the impromptu nature of the preview, not because the songs exist only as fragments. In fact, Dylan flits from song to song in a very deliberate way, as if this were more of a trailer than a preview. The only song where the lyrics seem radically unrealized is "True Love Tends to Forget." On this track Dylan is throwing in all sorts of lines he wants to rhyme with the title phrase ("I'll leave my pride on the doorstep where we met . . . "; "I'll be on top of a world that's upset . . . "; "Shall I ride into the sunset . . . "), and when he comes to the bridge of the song, the narrator is "lying on the river . . . letting the water come by . . . ". At this point, Dylan's voice trails off and he resorts to humming the remainder of the bridge.

Only after six weeks of tour rehearsals and a Far East tour did Dylan begin rehearsing his new songs with the touring band. If some of the *Street-Legal* songs were attempted at sound checks (Stoner thinks they were, though there are no details of any such sound check), it is only after Australia that we have evidence of Dylan and the band working on the songs. Within days of returning to L.A., Dylan was required to audition a new bass player. Rob Stoner wanted out and Jerry Scheff, a Presley perennial, was quickly drafted in.

What purports to be Scheff's audition tape includes an uncompromising Dylan working on two new songs, one scheduled for *Street-Legal* ("We'd Better Talk This Over"), the other not ("Coming from the Heart"). The latter was one of half a dozen songs Dylan had written with backing singer Helena Springs during the Far East tour and it has a quite different feel to the songs written alone in Minnesota. "We'd Better Talk This Over," even at this stage—days away from the *Street-Legal* sessions—was going through some final lyrical twists ("Every time we'd be alone, nothing's ever right/ Even when we're making love, it winds up in a fight"). With Scheff on board, Dylan was venturing

into unchartered seas, belatedly rehearsing an entire album with this band.

Though he knew he had very little time in which to record his first album in two and a half years (the band badly needed a break before a daunting European tour), Dylan was once again looking to cut the songs live to sixteen-track. Mirroring the *Blood on the Tracks* experience, he already knew which nine songs he intended to record and—despite the problems experienced with a big band at the *Desire* sessions—was determined to persevere with the live approach. Unfortunately the first logistical problem this created was finding a large enough studio to house his touring band.

Arthur Rosato: *"They had booked it at Record Plant and the studio they had booked was [living-room size]. The [studio people] were so used to one guy coming in and doing his parts [then] . . . and I said, 'No, we do it all at once,' and they were looking at us, like, 'Totally live?' On that album there's four overdubs on the whole thing and those were guitar parts and one sax part. I called Wally Heider's and had a truck brought in. [All] the vocalists were singing live."*

So the recording of *Street-Legal* was never originally scheduled to take place at Rundown, which was hardly set up to record a "seventies-sounding" album (certainly not with the TASCAM eight-track assembled downstairs while Dylan had been touring the Far East, the very setup responsible for all subsequent Rundown reference recordings). With no time to think, Dylan brought in a mobile truck, and recorded the album as if it was just another tour rehearsal. Astonishingly, given the lack of usable cuts from the July 1975 big band sessions, Dylan also elected to use Columbia producer Don Devito, though it was Arthur Rosato who carried out most of the engineering duties. It seems that Dylan was not about to learn his lesson from the aborted *Desire* experiment, for not only did he cut *Street-Legal* live, but he clearly felt that he could record the album in the same way Joel Bernstein had made tapes of the tour rehearsals—using floor-mounted monitors rather than conventional headphones to relay the sound to each musician.

Joel Bernstein: *"To have wedges, which are two twelve-inch speakers and a horn, aiming up at you, well, of course, when you're live you have to hear yourself. The fact that it's leaking into your vocal mike is secondary in a live situation—you really need to hear yourself above a lot of loud sound. But when you're recording, the last thing you want to have is a wedge with anything in it—including your voice. If you have your voice when you're singing into the microphone coming back into that wedge and [then] back into your microphone, first of all you've got to equalize it terribly just to make sure it's not gonna feedback. [And] no matter how you equalize it, compared with headphones, which are adding nothing to the vocal signal, you've got a lot of stuff going on there which is gonna really thin [the sound] out."*

What Dylan evidently had in mind was a naturalistic approach to recording that maintained the interplay between each musician. Uninterested in redoing vocals, and with distinct limits placed on any musician's ability to overdub, Dylan did achieve his first imperative—recording the songs quickly. According to Rosato the album was recorded in just five days and mixed—largely by Devito and Rosato, Dylan's input being a series of yeas and nays—in a further fifteen (they were, of course, hamstrung at this point by the very methods that had made recording such a breeze). Even if Dylan had been willing to indulge Devito, vocal overdubs were precluded by the amount of leakage into the vocal track from the other musicians involved.

The results were pretty much an unmitigated disaster. With hindsight, it is amazing to me that, given his recording methods, it took Dylan seventeen years to make such a badly recorded album. For *Street-Legal* is not an album unduly flawed in conception, but one dramatically flawed in execution. There would have been no way for Devito or Rosato to salvage these songs from the sixteen-track morass that is *Street-Legal*. What Greil Marcus dismissed, in his *Rolling Stone* review of the album, as Dylan "faking it" is not symptomatic of any lack of interest in the material on Dylan's part, or even a deficient vocal style, but a combination of limitations such an ill-conceived setup placed on his ability to apply his usual vocal nuances, the inevitable by-products of his failure to use headphones.

Which is all a great shame. The *Street-Legal* songs themselves are some of the most thoughtful of Dylan's career. The lyrics have clearly been worked on long and hard, while the arrangements, some of Dylan's most elaborate, generally work well. Only "No Time to Think" fails as both a lyric (too damn clever by half) and an arrangement. "Baby, Stop Crying," a fairly simplistic rewrite of Robert Johnson's "Stop Breaking Down," lacks a lyric but carries the album's best hook (a huge hit in Europe, it left cold an American public struck down with disco fever). "Is Your Love in Vain?" was a little too up-front in its depiction of Dylan's unreasonable demands on any lady companion. And yet the album remains a personal favorite of many long-standing fans prepared to work at disentangling instrument from instrument, vocal from harmony vocal, rhyming scheme from ingenious act of assonance.

Perhaps Dylan should have integrated some of the songs he had been writing with Helena Springs, which might have lightened the album's tone and provided "Baby Stop Crying" with some able-bodied companion 45s. Though Dylan excluded them from the *Street-Legal* recording process, he did record four Dylan/Springs compositions in this interim between tours. The four songs—"If I Don't Be There by Morning," "Walk Out in the Rain," "Stop Now," and "Coming from the Heart"—were given to Eric Clapton at the July 1 Nuremburg concert (they shared the bill). Clapton was clearly impressed by the demo tape, simple as it was, later admitting, "When I get down sometimes, I listen to them and it will bring me right out, because I know that no one else has got it." Clapton proceeded to record three of the songs as part of his *Backless* project ("Coming from the Heart" was recorded under its alternate title, "The Road Is Long," but omitted from the album. "Stop Now" was overlooked altogether).

What exact versions Clapton received is unknown. Rehearsal tapes from May 1978 of two of these songs differ significantly in style. "Coming from the Heart" corresponds with Clapton's description, being a scrappy tape of Dylan (at the piano) duetting with (presumably) Springs, whose histrionic second vocal threatens at times to drown out Dylan altogether, all to a basic guitar/bass/drums accompaniment. Though the lyrics to the first two verses correspond to the song as published in *Lyrics* (save for a significant slip on Dylan's part, singing "This home is filled with too much sorrow," not "This world . . . "), there is a "new" final verse that sounds like it might have been left over from "Baby Stop Crying."

As a performance this is a long way short of the terrific solitary live rendition at St. Paul in October. "Stop Now," on the other hand, exists in two forms, both Rundown rehearsal tapes, one from the beginning of May, the other from the day after the final L.A. Universal Amphitheatre show (June 8). The former take, slow and drawn out, has the same rudimentary feel as "Coming from the Heart," and is probably what Clapton received. The latter take (credited as a *Street-Legal*

outtake on *The Genuine Bootleg Series*) is considerably more spirited and features the entire 1978 ensemble. If one can overlook some very trite lyrics (a feature of most Dylan/Springs songs), the nice fat sax sound and Dylan's engaging way of pleading, "You had better stop now beeee-fore . . . it's . . . too . . . late," would have made it a fine opener to the summer shows (in place of "Love Her with a Feeling"). Hence, presumably, its inclusion at this stage of rehearsals (just a couple of days before they flew to London).

This quartet of tunes was by no means the end of Dylan's collaborations with Ms. Springs. When the touring band resumed rehearsing in September, this time for a daunting sixty-five-date tour of North America, Dylan had more new songs he wished to rehearse (and presumably record). Two new songs were subsequently played on the tour itself—"Stepchild" and "I Must Love You Too Much," the latter being another Dylan/Springs effort. It was "Stepchild," though, that became a perennial on the tour, even if it was only ever copyrighted from a live performance. Two other songs appear in Arthur Rosato's list of songs rehearsed for this leg of the Alimony Tour. One, "Angel, What'd I Do" (presumably an original composition), was never copyrighted, nor does any recording circulate. The other, "More than Flesh and Blood," was another Dylan/Springs effort—perhaps the best of the lot—and according to Rosato's listing was originally scheduled to close the first half of the U.S. 1978 shows.

This song was in fact recorded in the studio by the 1978 band, honkin' sax, girls et al., with a lead vocal by Springs for what was going to be a solo "Helena Springs" single. Dylan's old flair with words is for once well in evidence on this sorry ol' tale of unrequited lust, the best line referring to driving up in a Cadillac but leaving him with the mule, while the most telling line suggests not giving in to the spirit, for that very spirit can be adverse. Though "More than Flesh and Blood" was never performed at the shows, the frailties of flesh and blood were preying ever more on Dylan's mind. The songs he was sound-checking at the end of his mammoth fall '78 stint—just as the *Street-Legal* songs began to find their true selves in concert—included two, "Slow Train" and "Do Right to Me, Baby (Do unto Others)," which suggested a man already pressing on to a higher calling.

MUSCLE SHOALS SOUND STUDIOS

3614 JACKSON HIGHWAY
P. O. BOX 915
SHEFFIELD, ALABAMA 35660
PHONE: (205) 381-2060

INCORPORATED
PUBLISHING
AND
PRODUCTIONS

16 TRK. ☐   8 TRK. ☐
4 TRK. ☐   2 TRK. ☒   MONO ☐

MONITOR MIXES

ARTIST: BOB DYLAN
RECORD COMPANY:

SPEED
☐ 7½   ☒ 15   ☐ 30

ENGINEER/S
GREGG HAMM
DAVID YATES

PRODUCER/S WEXLER/BECKETT

DATE RECORDED
4-5/79

INSTRUCTIONS
TAILS

SELECTION TITLE	AUTHOR/S	PUBLISHER	TIME
SLOW TRAIN (☆) OLD			
AINT NO MAN RIGHTEOUS (II)			
I BELIEVE IN YOU			
TROUBLE IN MIND			
PRECIOUS ANGEL (☆) OLD			

"WHEN HE RETURNS" SONG TITLE

_____ ENGINEERS

MUSCLE SHOALS SOUND STUDIOS

ARTIST BOB DYLAN

DATE 5/4/79

REEL NUMBER	TAKE NUMBER	LOCATOR NUMBERS	COMMENTS		MI
11		~~00000~~			
	①	0-540	W/BAND		
	②	540-989	(PB) HOLD		
		~~0000000000~~			
	③	1009-1490			
	④	1490-1670	↑PARTIAL		
	5	1686-1770	↑PICK-UP		
	⑥	1770-2093	↑ "		
	⑦	2115-2300	↑PARTIAL	HOLD	
	⑧	2300-2615	PICK-UP	HOLD	

SLOW TRAIN COMING

Recorded: April 30 to May 13, 1979
Released: August 18, 1979
Side 1: Gotta Serve Somebody. Precious Angel. I Believe in You. Slow Train. Side 2: Gonna Change My Way of Thinking. Do Right to Me, Baby (Do unto Others). When You Gonna Wake Up. Man Gave Names to All the Animals. When He Returns.

Other official cuts:

45: Trouble in Mind
The Bootleg Series: Ye Shall Be Changed

Producers:

1–7 Jerry Wexler and Barry Beckett

Musicians:

1–7 Bob Dylan (guitar/vocals)
1–7 Barry Beckett (keyboards/percussion)
2–7 Mark Knopfler (guitar)
2–7 Tim Drummond (bass)
2–7 Pick Withers (drums)

2–7 Mickey Buckins (percussion)
2–7 Carolyn Dennis (backing vocals)
2–7 Helena Springs (backing vocals)
2–7 Regina Havis (backing vocals)
4–7 Muscle Shoals Horns (horns)

1. "DEMO SESSION"
   LATE APRIL 1979
When He Returns

2. MUSCLE SHOALS SOUND STUDIO
   SHEFFIELD, ALABAMA
   APRIL 30, 1979 (reels 1–2)
Trouble in Mind [I]
Trouble in Mind [II]
Trouble in Mind [III]
Trouble in Mind [IV]
Trouble in Mind [V]
Trouble in Mind [VI]

3. MUSCLE SHOALS SOUND STUDIO
   SHEFFIELD, ALABAMA
   MAY 1, 1979 (reels 4–5)
unknown song (I–VIII) Tk. 6

4. MUSCLE SHOALS SOUND STUDIO
   SHEFFIELD, ALABAMA
   MAY 2, 1979 (reel 6)
Ye Shall Be Changed [I]
Gonna Change My Way of Thinking [I]

5. MUSCLE SHOALS SOUND STUDIO
   SHEFFIELD, ALABAMA
   MAY 1 AND 2, 1979 (reels 3, 7)
Precious Angel
When You Gonna Wake Up
No Man Righteous (No Not One) [I]
No Man Righteous (No Not One) [II]

6. MUSCLE SHOALS SOUND STUDIO
   SHEFFIELD, ALABAMA
   MAY 3, 1979 (reel 8)
I Believe in You [I]
Slow Train [I]

7. MUSCLE SHOALS SOUND STUDIO
SHEFFIELD, ALABAMA
MAY 4, 1979 (reels 9–12)

Gotta Serve Somebody [I] (piano)
Gotta Serve Somebody [II]
Gotta Serve Somebody [III]
Gotta Serve Somebody [IV]
Do Right to Me, Baby (Do unto Others) [I] (acoustic and piano)
Do Right to Me, Baby (Do unto Others) [II]
Do Right to Me, Baby (Do unto Others) [III]
Do Right to Me, Baby (Do unto Others) [IV]
When He Returns [I] (with band)
When He Returns [II]
When He Returns [III]
When He Returns [VIII]
When He Returns [IX]
Man Gave Names to All the Animals [I]
Man Gave Names to All the Animals [II–IV] (last verse)
Man Gave Names to All the Animals [V]

MUSCLE SHOALS SOUND STUDIOS

SONG TITLE: SAVED
ARTIST: BOB DYLAN
ENGINEERS: GREG HAMM
DATE: 2/12/80

REEL NUMBER	TAKE NUMBER	LOCATOR NUMBERS	COMMENTS	MISC.
4	1	8 - 206	SATISFIED MIND	} PULLED TO MASTER
	2	206 - 664	SAVED PB	
		SAVING GRACE		
4	1	27	FS	2/13/80
	1	61		
	1	96 - 616	— PULLED —	
	2	623 - 1175	— PULLED — PB	
		PRESSING ON		
	1	22 -	FS	
		79 - 669	KEEP PB	1518

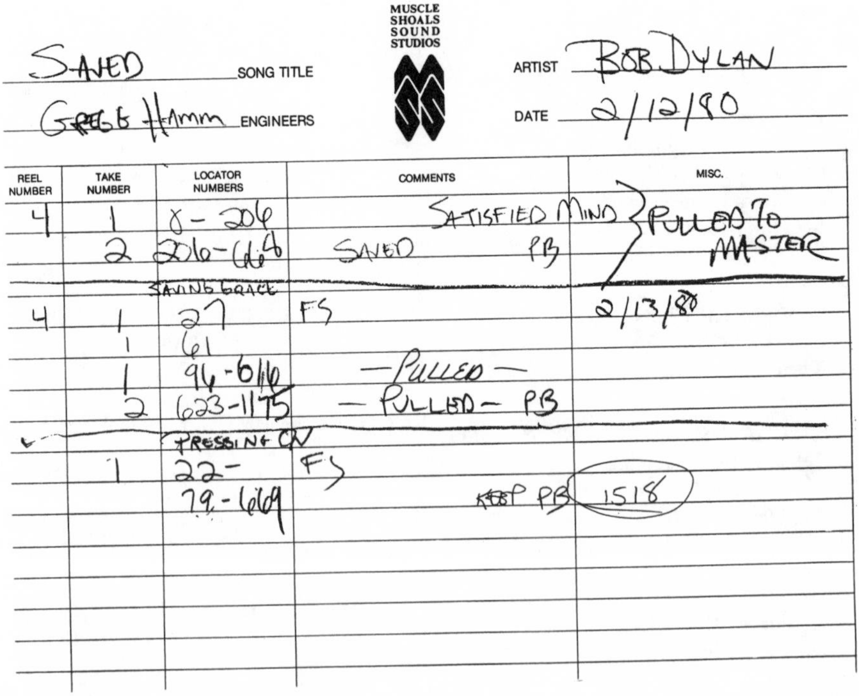

SAVED

Recorded: February 11 to 15, 1980
Released: June 20, 1980

Side 1: A Satisfied Mind. Saved. Covenant Woman. What Can I Do For You? Solid Rock. Side 2: Pressing On. In the Garden. Saving Grace. Are You Ready?

Producers:
1–5 Jerry Wexler and Barry Beckett

Musicians:

1–5 Bob Dylan (guitar/harmonica)
1–5 Fred Tackett (guitar)
1–5 Spooner Oldham (keyboards)
1–5 Terry Young (keyboards)
1–5 Tim Drummond (bass)

1–5 Jim Keltner (drums)
1–5 Clydie King (backing vocals)
1–5 Regina Havis (backing vocals)
1–5 Mona Lisa Young (backing vocals)

1. MUSCLE SHOALS SOUND STUDIO
   SHEFFIELD, ALABAMA
   FEBRUARY 11, 1980
Covenant Woman [I]
Covenant Woman [II]
Covenant Woman [III]
Covenant Woman [IV]
Covenant Woman [V]
Covenant Woman [VI]
Covenant Woman [VII] (pulled to master)
Covenant Woman [VIII]
Covenant Woman [IX]

2. MUSCLE SHOALS SOUND STUDIO
   SHEFFIELD, ALABAMA
   FEBRUARY 12, 1980
Solid Rock [I]
Solid Rock [II]
Solid Rock [III]
What Can I Do for You? [I]
A Satisfied Mind [I]
Saved [I]

3. MUSCLE SHOALS SOUND STUDIO
   SHEFFIELD, ALABAMA
   FEBRUARY 13, 1980
Saving Grace [I]
Saving Grace [II]
Pressing On [I]
Pressing On [II]
Pressing On [IV]
Pressing On [V]
In the Garden [I]

4. MUSCLE SHOALS SOUND STUDIO
   SHEFFIELD, ALABAMA
   FEBRUARY 14, 1980
In the Garden [II]
In the Garden [III]
In the Garden [IV] (piano introduction)
Are You Ready? [I]
Are You Ready? [II]

5. MUSCLE SHOALS SOUND STUDIO
   SHEFFIELD, ALABAMA
   FEBRUARY 15, 1980
Covenant Woman
Saved

Slow Train Coming and *Saved* were recorded just nine months apart, at the same studio—Muscle Shoals—with identical producers—Jerry Wexler and Barry Beckett. The two of them comprise every Dylan original in the evangelical show he took on the road between November 1979 and February 1980. As such, it is sometimes difficult to recall how different the circumstances were surrounding these two albums. The commercial and critical response to the two albums could not have been more different, nor could the musicians' approach to the material.

Slow Train Coming was a collection of songs Dylan had originally intended to donate to backing singer Carolyn Dennis. When he eventually decided to record the album himself, the session musicians he used were as unfamiliar with his working processes (and the songs he intended to record) as all but the chosen few at previous Dylan sessions. And yet the result was one of his most commercial albums.

Saved, on the other hand, was recorded after three months on the road, utilizing the same musicians who had been playing these songs night after night. Yet it was a commercial disaster from which Dylan has never fully recovered (he has not had a Top Ten album in the U.S. since) as well as being an empty vessel musically, stripped of all the evangelical fervor in evidence at the preceding shows. *Saved*—the first and last time Dylan took an album of songs on the road before recording them—is the best evidence that Dylan's previous working methods suit him best; not just recording songs in a handful of takes, but also relying on musicians forced to play "by the seat of their pants."

Of course, the songs on *Slow Train Coming* were still fresh in his recently converted mind when he adjourned to Sheffield, Alabama, to record them. More important, the session musicians were surprisingly receptive to Dylan's

(strange) mood. The choice of musicians even bore the mark of a little divine inspiration. The only remnants of the 1978 tour band were backing singers Helena Springs and Carolyn Dennis, who, along with Regina Havis, were bound to fit in well with Dylan's gospel sound. Wexler donated the famous Muscle Shoals Horns and pianist/arranger Barry Beckett, while Dylan himself came upon a guitarist and drummer after a night at the Roxy in late March. Having witnessed British new wavers Dire Straits close out a successful residency, Dylan astutely enlisted Mark Knopfler—who was in enough awe of Dylan at this point to subsume an overbearing ego—as well as original Straits drummer Pick Withers. Dylan also finally got to work with veteran session musician Tim Drummond, who could be trusted to navigate through the lower registers. All in all, Dylan had a most intriguing melting pot from which to pour a little ol' time religion onto the face of the world.

The songs Dylan intended to record were all products of his newfound faith. None of the many songs sound-checked between September and late November 1978, when Dylan experienced his change of heart, made the sessions—only brand-new testaments of a man born again. According to Knopfler, "Bob and I ran down a lot of those songs beforehand." Yet he still expressed surprise to manager Ed Bicknell when the sessions began and he realized that "all these songs are about God!"

Some thirteen songs in all were apparently recorded for *Slow Train Coming*. Aside from the nine cuts on the album, outtakes included "Trouble in Mind" (which became the B side to the first single), "Ye Shall Be Changed" and "No Man Righteous (No Not One)" (both of which were originally scheduled for *The Bootleg Series*, though only the former made the final three-CD edit), plus one unknown song (perhaps the untitled song that took up the entire second day of sessions, requiring eight takes in all).

Born again or not, the *Slow Train Coming* sessions betrayed a familiar Dylan pattern. Once again, he wrapped up the album in less than a week, despite a lack of familiarity with Wexler's methodical approach to recording, twenty-four-track studios, or Muscle Shoals itself, and even though the first couple of sessions did not proceed according to plan. According to Knopfler, "The first night was pretty awful—it just didn't happen." The solitary result of that first session was "Trouble in Mind" (the final verse of which was edited for the 45 version).

"Trouble in Mind" certainly set the tone for the sessions, Dylan slipping easily into his evangelist self for this salutary tale of a would-be believer's trials and tribulations. The vocals on "Trouble in Mind"—indeed on all of *Slow Train Coming*—drip with newfound sincerity. Dylan had never sung better, at least not behind closed doors. Knopfler also played throughout with a natural fluidity—aided no doubt by Dylan's unwillingness to recut songs when he wanted to second-guess a solo—slotting surprisingly into an authentic Muscle Shoals groove. Yet it took a couple of sessions for the telepathic connections Dylan had come to expect at his sessions to be fully soldered.

Halfway through the third session Dylan had just three songs in the can, none of which would make the album. Both "Ye Shall Be Changed" and "No Man Righteous" stuck to the theme of iniquity running amok. Only "Gonna Change My Way of Thinking" began to convey some personal sense of redemption. As with all the best Dylan studio setups, the *Slow Train Coming* sessions got better once he accepted the need to be there and embraced this alien environment.

At what was probably the penultimate day of recording—May 4, 1979—Dylan produced perhaps his greatest studio vocal in thirteen years, "When He Returns." Throughout this session—which resulted in four of the album tracks, "Gotta Serve Somebody," "Do Right to Me, Baby (Do unto Others)" "When He Returns," and "Man Gave Names to All the Animals"—Dylan continued to play around with the arrangements. "Gotta Serve Somebody" was tried at the piano; "Do Right to Me, Baby" was first attempted à la "Dirge," with just acoustic guitar and piano. But it was "When He Returns," a song Dylan had deliberately put off recording, which represented his greatest challenge.

When Dylan later commented that the songs written for *Slow Train* had initially frightened him, it was probably "When He Returns" he had most in mind. He had already laid down a guide vocal, over Barry Beckett's piano, for the girl singers to learn their parts, intending for them to sing the song on his behalf. However, only Dylan was really capable of conveying the import of his most apocalyptic song to date. The first "When He Returns" attempted at this session was a full band version, though it is not clear from the studio sheets whether Dylan left it to the girls. Whatever the case, after another seven unsuccessful takes, the musicians took a break and Dylan decided to take Beckett's original piano track and overdub a new solo vocal. Imbued with the fervor of a true disciple, Dylan delivered the most apposite representation possible of what his new faith meant to him. Stripped of all ambiguities, "When He Returns" made it plain as Judgment Day that Dylan was not about to jump off this particular holy slow train. Surprisingly enough, *Slow Train Coming*, despite its unrelenting message, reversed much of the commercial ground lost by *Street-Legal*. This was thanks in no small part to a rhapsodic two-page review by *Rolling Stone* head honcho Jann Wenner.

Unfortunately, *Slow Train Coming's* successor, *Saved,* undid the good work, not so much pointing the finger of impending damnation at all (album-buying) nonbelievers as ramming his digit down their throats. This time Dylan was unconcerned with sweetening his bitter pill.

When talking to *Rolling Stone* shortly after the *Saved* sessions, producer Jerry Wexler commented on one major difference between *Saved* and *Slow Train Coming:* "The arrangements [for *Saved*] were [already] built-in, because the band had been playing the songs live. Most of the licks are their own licks, which they perfected on the road, as opposed to the Dire Straits confections on the last album, which were all done in the studio." But an equally fundamental difference was that the band entering Muscle Shoals on February 11, 1980, two days after a show in Charleston, was fried from the rigors of the road. Aside from a brief Christmas hiatus, these guys and gals had been on the road for three months (and this after a fraught six weeks of rehearsing, during which a horn section had come and gone, the entire band had had to fly to New York to record an appearance on "Saturday Night Live" and Dylan had insisted on continually introducing new songs).

Arthur Rosato: *"We didn't go home, we went straight into the studio. [We thought] 'We're never gonna get home.' 'Cause Muscle Shoals is as far away as you could possibly be from anything. It was tiring. And Wexler really didn't have a clue how to work with Bob, either. Bob just wanted to work with him because of who he was. [Here] you have a real famous producer and a guy who's never been produced and they just don't know how to work together. So what we did was go in the studio and record everything in a studio situation but live—but we just wanted to get out of there."*

With the exception of "Are You Ready?," the songs on *Saved* had all been written in the four or five months between recording *Slow Train Coming* and debuting a brand-new show at the Warfield in San Francisco in November 1979. As such, the tone of the songs—though perhaps emphasizing personal redemption rather more than those on *Slow Train Coming*—hardly suggested a major shift in his eschatological point of view (that is, Dylan was still born again, still believed the end was *nigh,* and still bought the whole predestination ticket). The only song recorded that week in February to require a radical rearrangement was "Pressing On." The simple concert arrangement, with Dylan singing the opening section at the piano before moving to the front of the stage, mike in hand, to reaffirm his higher calling, was never going to work on album. Its stately new arrangement—which took most of the third session to resolve—and the way that Dylan berates waverers to "shake the dust off your feet, don't look back," made for one of the few successful cuts on *Saved.*

Next to "Pressing On," the most convincing cut on *Saved* is its opener. "A Satisfied Mind" sounds just like what it is, the most spontaneous moment at the sessions. It is as if Dylan has just slipped into this old gospel standard between takes and the girls, recognizing a familiar refrain, quickly pick up on it. Even the tentative piano runs lend credence to this theory of impromptuness. Well, the studio sheets confirm that "Satisfied Mind" was (the only song at these sessions) cut in a single take. "Saved" had almost been a single take, but when Wexler and Dylan came to review the studio reels on the fifth day, they decided that "Saved" and "Covenant Woman" (the latter having taken up the entire first session) were in need of reevaluation.

I find it hard to believe that all nine outtakes of "Covenant Woman" from the eleventh are as lacking in passion as the released take—presumably from the fifteenth—even if Dylan had clearly let go of the leash on this gorgeous love song somewhere down the line. Possibly, if the "covenant woman" was none other than Helena Springs, as has long been rumored, their breakup shortly before the *Saved* sessions may have colored his commitment to the song. Certainly he never got back to the white heat of the November Warfield performances, and the song was dropped from the set altogether when touring resumed in April.

The problems with *Saved* are not entirely confined to Dylan's lackluster vocals or a band wanting to go home. The sound itself has none of the textured quality of *Slow Train Coming*. In particular, whoever was responsible for miking the drums committed the sin of lifelessness. According to Rosato, this problem was resolved at some point mid-sessions.

Arthur Rosato: *"We had a problem getting the drum sound because [Keltner] was working with an engineer he'd never worked with before. I'm in the booth and I'm listening to these drums that sound like boxes, they sounded just horrible. First thing the guy did was tape all of Jim's drums. It just killed the drums. And Jim's looking at me, like 'What am I gonna do?' 'Cause he always respects what the engineer is doing. To him, they have an idea of what the producer wants and Jim's basically a session guy. I just said, 'Let's take the tape off.' So we went back and recorded some of that stuff again."*

Yet Keltner still fails to leap out of the speakers, not only performing a major disservice to perhaps Dylan's finest beatmaster, but losing the central focus of the live sound at the time. "Solid Rock" is particularly unpleasant. Paul Williams, in his "One Year Later" pamphlet, argues convincingly (and at length) that Dylan's disemboweling of "Solid Rock" was axiomatic of a general lack of attention to detail on the album as a whole:

I have problems with all the arrangements (or really lack of arrangements) . . . on Saved *but the most subtle and interesting case is that of "Solid Rock." To my ears, there were a couple of nights in San Francisco in November 1979 when Dylan and Tim Drummond and the band really found the heart and soul of "Solid Rock." The audience thought so too—people who'd never heard the song before jumped to their feet to show their enthusiasm at the end of the song . . . As near as I can figure it, Dylan and cohorts saw that the song was a crowd-pleaser and started playing it for excitement and—with the best of intentions—thereby lost touch with what it was that made the song so exciting. What they did is they sped it up. In doing so they dropped a note from that perfect bass line, so it wasn't perfect anymore, and Dylan allowed his approach to the vocal to change with the primary effect that the tension that ruled the song in such extraordinary fashion disappears and instead it becomes another rave-up. Look we're playing "Solid Rock," ha, ha. I know they were just trying to make it better, and I don't mean to be critical about it. What I'm trying to do is throw some light onto those moments when greatness comes and then goes again. Dylan has talked about "learning to do consciously what I used to do unconsciously," mostly I think in the context of songwriting. I think* Saved *demonstrates that the days have passed when divine grace would see to it that he always could capture a song in its prime by randomly running into the studio.*

Saved was no mere lapse of judgment on Dylan's part (say, like *Self Portrait*), but a highly significant fall from grace (at least as a studio artist). It ushered in a new era of indecision in the studio. Prior to *Saved,* even when he had made bad calls, there had always been a sureness to Dylan's judgments in the studio. After the sonic wasteland that was *Street-Legal,* he had managed to come up with one of his best-sounding albums to date. But Wexler was no closer to understanding Dylan than any of his latter-day producers.

If Dylan's impatience with the studio process had always been a problem, the advent of twenty-four-track studios as industry norm, and consumers' increasing insistence on modern-sounding fodder for their hi-fi, demanded a reevaluation by Dylan of his working methods if he wished to remain a commercial artist. However, the critical *and* commercial disaster that was *Saved* did not alone force his hand. Dylan was about to lose his grip on the successor to *Saved,* which, again, should have been a showcase for some of his finest worksongs. The repercussions of *Saved*—Dylan's grandest failure—would continue to reverberate through all of the mercy years.

SHOT OF LOVE

Recorded: April 2 to mid-May 1981
Released: August 12, 1981

Side 1: Shot of Love. Heart of Mine. Property of Jesus. Lenny Bruce. Watered-Down Love.
Side 2: Dead Man, Dead Man. In the Summertime. Trouble. Every Grain of Sand.

Other official cuts:

45: Let It Be Me.
45: The Groom's Still Waiting at the Altar.
Biograph: Caribbean Wind.
The Bootleg Series: Every Grain of Sand. You Changed My Life. Need a Woman. Angelina.

Producers:
1–4, 6–9 Arthur Rosato
5 Jimmy Iovine
11 "Bumps" Blackwell, Chuck Plotkin, and Bob Dylan
10, 12–13 Chuck Plotkin and Bob Dylan

Musicians:

1–13 Bob Dylan (piano)
1–13 Jim Keltner (drums)
1 Jennifer Warnes (backing vocals)
1–12 Fred Tackett (guitar)
1–12 Tim Drummond (bass)
1–13 Clydie King (second vocals)
2–12 Regina McCrery (backing vocals)
2–12 Carolyn Dennis (backing vocals)
2–12 Madelyn Quebec (backing vocals)
5–12 Steve Ripley (guitar)
5–9 Carl Pickhardt (keyboards)

5 David Mansfield (guitar)
5 Stephen Soles (guitar)
5 Bobbye Hall (percussion)
12 Benmont Tench (keyboards)
10–12 Danny Kortchman (guitar)
13 Chuck Plotkin (drums)
13 Donald "Duck" Dunn (bass)
13 Willie Smith (organ)
13 Ron Wood (guitar)
13 Ringo Starr (tom-tom)

1. RUNDOWN STUDIOS
SANTA MONICA, CALIFORNIA
SEPTEMBER 23, 1980
Every Grain of Sand [I]
Every Grain of Sand [II]

2. RUNDOWN STUDIOS
SANTA MONICA, CALIFORNIA
OCTOBER 1980
Property of Jesus
Caribbean Wind
She's Not for You
The Groom's Still Waiting at the Altar
Let's Keep It Between Us
Yonder Comes Sin

3. RUNDOWN STUDIOS
   SANTA MONICA, CALIFORNIA
   MARCH 11, 1981
Shot of Love
You Changed My Life [I]
You Changed My Life [II]

4. RUNDOWN STUDIOS
   SANTA MONICA, CALIFORNIA
   LATE MARCH 1981
instrumental jam
Heart of Mine
instrumental jam
Let's Begin
Every Grain of Sand [instrumental]
instrumental jam
Yes Sir, No Sir (Halleluiah) [instrumental]
Please Be Patient with Me [Regina Havis]
Let's Begin
No Man Righteous (No Not One) [Regina Havis]
Is It Worth It? [instrumental]

5. MISCELLANEOUS STUDIOS
   LOS ANGELES, CALIFORNIA
   LATE MARCH 1981
Every Grain of Sand
Need a Woman
Angelina
The Groom's Still Waiting at the Altar
Almost Persuaded
Tune After Almost
In the Summertime
You Can't Make It on Your Own
Rockin' Boat
Borrowed Time
I Want You to Know I Love You
Gonna Love Her Anyway [instrumental]
Wait and See

6. STUDIO 55
   LOS ANGELES, CALIFORNIA
   MARCH 31, 1981
Caribbean Wind

7. UNITED WESTERN STUDIO A
   LOS ANGELES, CALIFORNIA
   APRIL 2, 1981
Yes Sir, No Sir (Halleluiah)
Fur Slippers
Let It Be Me
Is It Worth It?
Ah Ah Ah Ah [I]
Ah Ah Ah Ah [II]

Ah Ah Ah Ah [III]
Rumored: *The King Is on the Throne*

8. MISCELLANEOUS STUDIOS
   LOS ANGELES, CALIFORNIA
   EARLY APRIL 1981
Child to Me
Wind Blowin' on the Water
All the Way Down
My Oriental Home [instrumental]
It's All Dangerous to Me [instrumental]
Borrowed Time
More to This than Meets the Eye [instrumental]
Straw Hat [instrumental]
Instrumental Calypso
Walking on Eggs [instrumental]
Well Water [instrumental]
All the Way [instrumental]

9. RUNDOWN STUDIO
   SANTA MONICA, CALIFORNIA
   APRIL 6 AND 7, 1981
Shot of Love
Caribbean Wind
Rumored: *Let's Keep It Between Us*
         She's Not for You

10. RUNDOWN STUDIO
    SANTA MONICA, CALIFORNIA
    APRIL 23, 1981
Heart of Mine [instrumental]
Trouble
Magic
Don't Ever Take Yourself Away [I]
Don't Ever Take Yourself Away [II]
You Changed My Life [I]
Shot of Love
Mystery Train
Half as Much
The Groom's Still Waiting at the Altar
Dead Man, Dead Man
You Changed My Life [II]
Rumored: *Be Careful*

11. RUNDOWN STUDIO
    SANTA MONICA, CALIFORNIA
    LATE APRIL 1981
Shot of Love
Property of Jesus
Watered Down Love

Rumored: *Ain't Gonna Go to Hell for Any-*
          body
        Blessed Is the Name
        City of Gold
        Ye Shall Be Changed
        I Will Love Him
        Yonder Comes Sir
        Stand by Faith
        Heart of Stone

12. CLOVER STUDIOS
    HOLLYWOOD, CALIFORNIA
    EARLY TO MID-MAY 1981
Need a Woman [I]
Need a Woman [II]
Angelina [I]
Angelina [II]

Heart of Mine
Property of Jesus
Lenny Bruce [I]
Lenny Bruce [II]
Watered-Down Love
Dead Man, Dead Man
In the Summertime
Trouble
Every Grain of Sand
Let It Be Me
Mystery Train
The Groom's Still Waiting at the Altar

13. CLOVER STUDIOS
    HOLLYWOOD, CALIFORNIA
    LATE MAY 1981
Heart of Mine

Dylan may not have been about to reevaluate his methodology in the studio after the *Saved* debacle, but he certainly could not be accused of failing to apply himself when it came to his next vinyl excursion. Dylan's increasing aversion to the studio throughout the 1980s (and into the '90s) is, I suspect, largely frustration at how long it takes to make an album in today's high-tech, high sheen, lo-fi marketplace. As late as 1986, Dylan was asking guitarist Ira Ingber, when getting ready to record *Knocked Out Loaded,"* "Can we do it in a week?"

For *Shot of Love,* Dylan was prepared to put in the time not only to cut a strong album of songs, but to make sure that it sounded how he wanted it to. For the first time since *Blood on the Tracks,* Dylan would coproduce one of his own albums. He also rigorously rehearsed many of the songs he wanted to record, even performing a couple of them during a brief nineteen-date tour of the northwest in the fall of 1980.

As it is, *Shot of Love* would fail on its own terms, not because of poor production (I tend to agree with Dylan that it is one of his best-sounding albums), or because it was overly concerned with one thematic preoccupation, but largely because the songs that should have been the album's core had already eluded Dylan by the time the sessions began, and their replacements were disappointingly lightweight.

Part of the problem was the Record Machine itself. In the 1960s record companies were geared up to putting out albums every six months if product was there to be had. Even within as tight a span of time as a single year—between, say, *Another Side* and *Highway 61 Revisited*—Dylan had been able (indeed, was expected) to make *Bringing It All Back Home.* In the period from 1979 to 1981 many of the words filling his head were falling to the floor because Columbia were not about to put out two Dylan albums a year, particularly two evangelical albums. When he presented CBS with a mixed, sequenced live album of the gospel shows, *Solid Rock,* they passed on it. If Dylan had gone into the studio in October 1980—as he should have—Columbia would almost certainly not have released the results, three months after *Saved* had barely blipped in *Billboard.*

As such Dylan spent the latter part of September and all of October rehearsing at Rundown, with a band on retainer, for the most uneconomical of tours, and recording some new originals for his own publishing company, Special Rider, on the Rundown eight-track. At least nine new Dylan originals were rehearsed and recorded at this juncture—more than enough for a new album if one considers the epic nature of four of these songs, "Every Grain of Sand," "The Groom's Still Waiting at the Altar," "Caribbean Wind," and "Yonder Comes Sin."

Of the four major new works rehearsed that October, it was "Caribbean Wind" that would end up, after a chequered history of rewrites, in the most dissolute form. The "Caribbean Wind" that eventually appeared on *Biograph* suffered much at the hands of its editor. A careful analysis of most Dylan rewrites suggests that he is usually a very good editor of words. It is rare for Dylan to take an image out of a song and replace it with an inferior one—even most of the rewrites made to "Idiot Wind" between New York and Minneapolis were strong, only for the Sound 80 performance to betray the song. What Dylan has been guilty of on occasions is a certain coyness in his rewrites. Bobby Neuwirth once said that Dylan, like any great artist, is naked in his art. Unfortunately, the man in him has sometimes endeavored to clothe that artist. In the case of "Caribbean Wind," Dylan gave the wordsmith an entirely new wardrobe. As Paul Williams has written:

A comparison of the two versions of "Caribbean Wind" that are available to us [the November 12, 1980, Warfield performance and the April 7, 1981, Biograph recording] suggests that the intimacy, the very personal nature of the song and the intensity of meaning it has for the singer . . . has provoked doubt about the song's success and has caused songwriter-as-editor to tinker with the song, to try to obscure or even destroy its more personal elements. Alas, he is successful. The later version, while still filled with the shadow of greatness to an intriguing and frustrating degree, has lost its focus.

In fact, Williams lacked the complete picture, failing to refer to the copyrighted October 1980 Rundown recording (the lyrics of which were certainly available to him) and not having access to a recently emerged studio version recorded between the two takes he refers to. These other recordings actually suggest that the wholesale rewrites employed on the *Biograph* version were, in part, a recognition by Dylan of his own inability to keep his hand on the song's plow long enough to craft it in the studio.

Not surprisingly, the lyrical variants between the October 1980 rehearsal and the song's solitary live performance the following month are few and far between—and invariably superior (for example, "As the days turned to minutes, and the minutes turned back into hours"). The November version is also a couple of dimensions removed from the October run-through as a performance. (Given that an eminently enjoyable mono "board" tape exists of this performance, it suggests a rare degree of ineptitude to have issued two three CD boxed sets of Dylan "rarities" and still have left this pearl in its shell.)

The shock of recognition that greeted this song when Dylan fans got to hear the audience tape of this November 12 show is hard now to convey. After two years of browbeating, "Caribbean Wind" seemed a lot like the old Dylan, disaffected with love and on the run from the End times—hence his Leadbelly rap that prefaced the song, "Some people liked the old songs, some people liked the new songs, but he didn't change, he was the same man." (Hint.)

Though Dylan seemed unhappy with the live performance, refraining from performing the song again at the remaining fall 1980 shows, Dylan knew that "Caribbean Wind" was an important song, opening up a new approach much as "Mr. Tambourine Man," "Visions of Johanna" or "Tangled Up in Blue" had in earlier times (talking to Paul Williams backstage at the Warfield, Dylan enthused about the way the song took the listener outside of time). So when it came time to begin work on what became *Shot of Love* "Caribbean Wind" was as much of a starting point as "Visions of Johanna" had been for *Blonde on Blonde*. After booking a session at Studio 55 in L.A., Dylan called in Jimmy Iovine (he was probably already looking for a potential coproducer for the album to come). The March 31 session, though, did not make either Dylan or Iovine very happy.

Arthur Rosato: *"We did 'Caribbean Wind' at Studio 55. It was hell recording that particular song. I had told Bob, 'You gotta give me that song to record. Let's do a really good job with that.' And he said, 'Let's get Jimmy Iovine.' He would call everybody he knows to come down so we would have a band of like fifteen people. When we did 'Caribbean Wind' I had the original recording that I did back at [Rundown]. I played that for all the musicians. That's a much better version because that's the first time, live. When we got over to Studio 55 all the musicians loved the song. It had that 'Rolling Stone' feel to it. So Bob finally shows up about three hours late, which was pretty much on time for him. At Santa Monica studio he was there every day—pretty much same time—he was real comfortable [there] but this was a different gig. As soon as the musicians ran through it once he goes, 'Nah, nah, nah, that's all wrong.' They could see it coming because they had all worked with him before, 'Oh, here we go.' And instead of that version he turned it into this country and western thing, like boom-chicka kinda stuff. That went on for a few hours. Meanwhile Jimmy had heard this*

other version and is going, 'What are we gonna do? Okay, we'll go with this guy,' 'cause he always wanted to work with him. Then they had these backing vocalists singing this like train whoosh and that was really bad. I don't even know how he ended up keeping it. Toward the end of the session I think Bob himself even realized it wasn't working and [said] let's go back and try the original version. At the end of the session he was asking Jimmy Iovine to go out and get the lyrics for 'White Christmas'! Jimmy didn't want anything to do with this session anymore. Bob didn't really know how to work with a producer."

If the "Caribbean Wind" recorded at Studio 55 was still recognizably "Caribbean Wind," Dylan had clearly begun to disguise its stronger religious elements (the narrator no longer talks of Jesus and "the rain") and, in a confused attempt to blur the ménage à trois element that is implicit in the song (which links it to "Visions of Johanna" and "Tangled Up in Blue"), cut some highly evocative lines.

Although a particularly dumb stop-start arrangement repeatedly applies the brakes to the song's cumulative power, Dylan still conjured up a vocal of some resilience, while some of the rewrites transcend the merely cute (the Dantesque "circle of ice" contrasts nicely with "the furnace of desire"). However, Dylan determined he would work on the song again, pushing it even further from its original form.

When it came time to return to another L.A. studio (possibly Rundown) seven days later, it was a whole new song and the furnace of desire had been reduced to its dying embers. It is hard to disagree with Williams when he says of the new lyrics, "The opening couplet is excellent. All the other substitutions (more than half the lyrics of the song) are 'fake Dylan'—clever phrases with no story to tell, no purpose behind them other than holding the space formerly occupied by a more honest or revealing phrase." (As a further insult, the version in *Lyrics* has been so badly transcribed that "Redeemed men" have become "Arabian men"—huh?—"Were we sniper bait?," actually a great line, has become "Did we snap at the bait?," and "chrome brown eyes" are now "lone brown eyes." Yeuuch!)

In fairness to Dylan, he clearly sensed the loss himself. The rewrites may well have reflected his increasing sense of detachment from the song's original sentiments. Talking about "Caribbean Wind" for the notes to *Biograph,* he displayed a surprising grasp of what had gone wrong with the song:

Sometimes you'll write something . . . very inspired, and you won't quite finish it for one reason or another. Then you'll go back and try and pick it up, and the inspiration is just gone. . . . Then it's a struggle. Frustration sets in. I think there's four different sets of lyrics to ["Caribbean Wind"], maybe I got it right. I don't know. I had to leave it . . . "

And leave it he did. Having made two attempts at "Caribbean Wind" in the first week of work on his next album, Dylan did not apparently return to the song when the *Shot of Love* sessions found a permanent home at Clover Studios during the third week of April, though the March 31st "Caribbean Wind" did make the shortlist for mixdowns, being mixed on May 18, along with "Angelina" and "Magic." (Dylan would later tell NME editor Neil Spencer that he left it off because it was "quite different to anything [else] I wrote.")

"The Groom's Still Waiting at the Altar" almost suffered a similar fate to "Caribbean Wind." Even in its salvaged, *Shot of Love* form it lacks the intensity of a couple of the performances at the Warfield the previous fall. Though it was

added to *Shot of Love* when it became part of Sony's Nice Price series—primarily because of some enthusiastic airplay as the B side to "Heart of Mine"—it had not been Dylan's intention to include the track on the album. Talking to Cameron Crowe in 1985, Dylan said that he felt he had lost the riff somewhere down the line (speeding the tapes up slightly for the single didn't help). I have to agree with Dylan. The released 45 makes for a good rant, the band self-evidently enjoyed playing the song (at the end of the unedited album take someone can be heard exclaiming, "Smokin'!") and the wordplay is delightful, but what happened to the tune?

Also one very important lyric had been rewritten by April 1981. The original chorus reflected Dylan's determination to keep pressing on—"Set my affections on things above/let nothing get in the way of that love"—seeing witchy women like Claudette as distractions he must learn to walk away from (witness the beautifully dismissive "If you see her on Fanning Street, tell her I still think she's neat"). The *Shot of Love* version's chorus focuses instead on a world on the brink—a familiar motif overstated (when Dylan first ran through the song at Rundown he kept the Fanning Street line but dispensed with "affections on things above").

If "Caribbean Wind" and "The Groom's Still Waiting at the Altar" were casualties of the six months that separate their original Rundown forms from *Shot of Love* counterparts, "Every Grain of Sand" lost none of its latent power. Apparently written on his Minnesota farm in the summer of 1980, "Every Grain," the most hymnal of Dylan songs, benefits immensely from the stately accompaniment it was given on *Shot of Love,* while Dylan's two harmonica breaks at verse ends (never duplicated in concert) betray a startling musicality for such an untutored harp player.

The demo of "Every Grain of Sand"

that appears on *The Bootleg Series* is a very different performance. Of all the demos cut at the time, it is perhaps the least satisfactory. Its inclusion on *The Bootleg Series* came as a result of a suggestion to compiler Jeff Rosen (the demo had been sent to Graham Nash, who in turn gave a copy to archivist Joel Bernstein, who felt it surpassed the *Shot of Love* version). Either I cannot hear the demo's simple beauty or it really is not very good. It reminds me of the solo outtake of "Up to Me" in that Dylan has yet to figure out how he wants to bend the words, so he sings the whole shebang in a very flat, un-Dylanlike way, disconcerting enough to initially beguile but not to endure sustained examination.

It would be interesting to know whether Rosen referred to the original eight-track tape when considering this demo for *The Bootleg Series,* or if he just pulled out the demo reel/cassette sent to Special Rider in 1980. On the original eight-track is another take of "Every Grain" and, though it still fails to scale the dizzy climes the album take inhabits, it convinces in a way the acoustic version on *The Bootleg Series* does not. By the time of day this second take was cut, Dylan's touring band had finally assembled at Rundown and just as Dylan hits, "In the fury of the moment . . . " Keltner kicks in. Soon enough bass, acoustic guitar, piano, and a Fender-Rhodes electric organ fill in the space around him (though, once again, there is no harmonica solo).

The other significant demo made in October 1980, "Yonder Comes Sin," seems to have been quickly, and definitively, discarded by Dylan. He never performed the song in concert, there is no real evidence it was ever attempted at any of the sessions in April or May 1981, and it was apparently the one song Dylan personally nixed from *The Bootleg Series.* And yet "Yonder Comes Sin" is no minor song. Taking its inspi-

ration from Ma Rainey's "Yonder Comes the Blues," the song is a powerful seven-verse catalogue of sin in all its guises. Perhaps Dylan felt it was too unequivocal given that *Shot of Love* was supposed to mark a change in emphasis (though "Property of Jesus" is hardly Dylan being mellow). He may also have been embarrassed by some of its lyrical lapses (Jeremiah preaching repentance and the critics giving him bad reviews . . . ho-hum). Whatever the case, "Yonder Comes Sin" was the one 1980 demo ("Makin' a Liar" excepted) absent from a list of songs under consideration for the *Shot of Love* sessions.

Of the other five songs demoed in October 1980, "Let's Keep It Between Us" and "City of Gold" were regulars on the fall 1980 tour. The Rundown version of "Let's Keep It Between Us," the one used for copyright purposes, formed the basis for Bonnie Raitt's 1981 recording, and uses a far stronger melody line, though it ain't the fully fermented, heady Memphis brew on offer at the fall shows. "Property of Jesus" would require a little more work (though it would lose a fine couplet in the process, in which he refers to "bragging about knowledge and experience" but admits to "lonesome ways and wasted days." "She's Not for You," apparently attempted at one of the pre-Clover sessions, was a lightweight "leave her alone" song that fits Dylan's description of the *Shot of Love* material ("something that could have been made in the 1940s or maybe the fifties") better than most. Lines about her getting a little restless now and then but knowing that ol' faithful will surely take her back again are certainly clichéd enough to suggest another "Heart of Mine." The last of the five "minor" new works apparently attempted at the fall 1980 rehearsals is listed as "Makin' a Liar" on the rehearsal sheets, though no such song was ever copyrighted or performed.

Between December 4, 1980, when Dylan and his band wrapped up their northeast tour in Portland, Oregon, and March 1981, when rehearsals resumed for an album/tour double-header, Dylan added a whole new layer of songs to these works. He also worked on some basic arrangements prior to heading for the recording studio. Two rehearsal tapes from different ends of March show Dylan working on new songs like "Shot of Love," "You Changed My Life," "Heart of Mine," "Yes Sir, No Sir (Halleluiah)," and "Is It Worth It?" Though only "Shot of Love" suggested any real caliber, the sheer number of songs Dylan had stockpiled by the end of March 1981, something like thirty new originals (excluding instrumentals), required a whole selection process before bona fide sessions could take place. Before the recording of *Shot of Love* commenced, Dylan embarked on a tour of L.A. recording locations, trying out songs *and* searching for a studio vibe.

Arthur Rosato: *"We did like a studio tour and that's where a lot of those outtakes came from. Bob decided that we should check out some studios, so we'd record in people's garage setups and do one song, then we went over to United Western (Oceanway now) and we recorded a bunch of stuff. It was more like sounds—ooh ooh—that kinda stuff, that's all United Western."*

These pre-Clover sessions lasted from the end of March until some point in early to mid-April. They included the "Caribbean Wind" session at Studio 55, at least one session at United Western Studio A (on April 2), and sessions (possibly at Rundown itself) on the sixth and seventh, during which Dylan and the band cut an early version of "Shot of Love." This "Shot of Love" was one of the few cuts from all these sessions to be under consideration when it came to mixing *Shot of Love* itself (though Dylan had already recut the song at

Rundown, with legendary rock and roll producer "Bumps" Blackwell).

This early "Shot of Love" is a terrific performance in its own right. Rather than the wailing banshees who introduce the album, this take begins with a little piano roll, a light drum fill, and Dylan belting out that first line, "Don't need no shot of heroin to kill my disease." A stark percussive feel dominates. With the band coming in on the first chorus, this is a discernibly more laid-back rendition that allows Dylan to sing, not growl, the words (I find the album take equally magnificent, just in a very different way).

The United Western session also threw up a couple of worthy recordings, including the first of a handful of covers tried at these sessions. The "Let It Be Me" recorded on April 2 highlights one more example of Dylan's utter perversity in the "what to release" department. This "Let It Be Me" may even surpass that tender highlight of *Self Portrait*. With the girl singers in bearable mode, and both Dylan and Clydie King sticking to the right notes, beset by forceful but appropriate full band backing, this version is to the cacophonous Clover take—issued as a B side to the European "Heart of Mine"—what the 1969 "Let It Be Me" was to most of its fellow self-portraits.

The other lost song from the United Western session is "Fur Slippers," which was copyrighted in 1982 and has some of the dumbest lyrics this side of country (as in all she left me were her fur slippers. Say no more). Not surprisingly, it works a whole lot better as a song than a lyric, featuring some nice picked electric guitar from, I presume, Tackett, some spirited backing vocals and handclaps from the gals. Dylan even sings the words without cracking up. Probably, with hindsight, too good for *Down in the Groove*.

I call "Fur Slippers" "the other lost

song" because the three remaining songs cut at United Western are all part of what for a long time was one of the most mysterious tapes in Dylan collectors' hands. To briefly descend into the realms of true arcania, a ninety-minute tape of outtakes emerged in the late 1980s, comprising fourteen vocal tracks and ten instrumentals. It came with no date attributed and (initially) lacked even an accurate track listing. The curious thing about this tape—which was bizarrely attributed to the *Empire Burlesque* sessions in some quarters—was that not only did none of the songs appear on other tapes (a common clue), but none of the riffs or lyrics ended up reused. That said, the tape always sounded like the standing band formulated at Rundown, and the various allusions to damnation and salvation in the lyrics tended to suggest the Rundown era. In fact, the tape had been surreptitiously acquired via the agency responsible for (belatedly) copyrighting these songs (hence the lack of recording information, though a largely reliable track-listing, based on the copyright files, finally appeared in 1989, courtesy of Jeff Friedman's discographical section in Bob Spitz's appalling Dylan biography).

At least the first four songs on this copyright tape can be accurately assigned—"Is It Worth It?," "Ah Ah Ah Ah," and "Yes Sir, No Sir (Halleluiah)" to United Western, April 2, and "Magic" to Rundown, April 23. All four were clearly being worked up into "songs" (rehearsal versions of "Is It Worth It?" and "Yes Sir, No Sir (Halleluia)" exist, while "Ah Ah Ah Ah" goes through at least three increasingly silly incarnations at United Western before Dylan gives up on it). "Magic," coming from what may have been one of the last sessions at Rundown, recently also appeared (with a slightly different mix) on a separate *Shot of Love* outtakes tape, along with "Don't Ever Take

Yourself Away" (from the same session). It seems to have been pulled to some kind of master reel at the time (along with "Trouble" and "You Changed My Life"), suggesting that it was under consideration for some purpose, though (fun as it is) it would hardly warrant inclusion on *Shot of Love*.

The remaining twenty cuts on the copyright tape are even more ill-formed than these four outtakes, something reflected in the frequently incongruous titles assigned them at the time. Though not copyrighted until much later, most of these songs appear on a contemporary list of possible songs for Clover. (The songs *not* listed are "Yes Sir, No Sir (Halleluiah)," "Child to Me," "Wind Blowin' on the Water," "Instrumental Calypso," and "Tune After Almost." There is one title on this list—"The King Is on His Throne"—that does not appear on the copyright tape.)

All twenty songs appear to derive from the (other) pre-Clover sessions Rosato referred to earlier. According to Rosato, the playful meanderings on most of these tracks were quite deliberate on Dylan's part, perhaps a semiconscious attempt to return to the improvisatory experiments of 1965. Also on the same list, and therefore presumably attempted at the pre-Clover sessions, are three other songs, "Let's Keep It Between Us," "She's Not for You," and "Be Careful."

After his tour of L.A. studios, Dylan continued recording at Rundown, seemingly without any specific plans to switch to a more orthodox studio. Clearly these Rundown sessions were no tour rehearsals. The session on the twenty-third (credited erroneously to Clover in the *Bootleg Series* booklet) was certainly intended as part of the *Shot of Love* sessions. Dylan again attempted the album's title track. One of several songs not finished that day, "Shot of Love" finds Dylan trying out new lines ("Use me and abuse me, drop me in a hole"), much as he does with "The Groom's Still Waiting at the Altar." "Heart of Mine," a somewhat hesitant "Mystery Train," and "Dead Man, Dead Man" also all fizzle out before Dylan can muster complete (or, in the case of "Heart of Mine," any) vocals.

One song that did reach a worthwhile resolution on the twenty-third was the lilting but lightweight "Don't Ever Take Yourself Away," which made it to the *Shot of Love* mixdowns. One more song in the "Heart of Mine" mould, it has far more to recommend it than the ghastly "You Changed My Life" featured on *The Bootleg Series,* also cut on the twenty-third. Dylan can be heard teaching "You Changed My Life" to the band (though the finished take is absent from the reel I referred to, along with "Trouble" and "Magic," all three are listed on the box—they had presumably been pulled to a master reel). The song itself is a sub-"What Can I Do for You" attempt to express his gratitude to the Lord. The most intriguing mystery that relates to this song is what happened to the version copyrighted in 1982. In this version the final verse has the narrator being beset on every side by trucemakers and partakers of every whim and asking the Lord to make his faith greater (evidence of a slide toward apostasy?).

After this whole series of dry runs, Dylan finally settled on Clover Studios, a convenient swing down Santa Monica Boulevard from Rundown, and the Springsteen-tested combination of producer Chuck Plotkin and engineer Toby Scott, to lay down the real thing. However, Dylan did not entirely abandon Rundown, embellishing and cleaning up some of the Rundown recordings at Clover (many of these tapes ended up in Clover tape boxes—notably the April 6th "Shot of Love"—just to confuse matters a tad).

By the time he had settled in Clover, Dylan had already short-listed the dozen

or so cuts he had in mind for *Shot of Love,* recording only a handful of outtakes (as opposed to alternate takes) at these sessions. However, at least one masterpiece still got lost in the shuffle. "Angelina" was another story of a remarkable woman unfazed by the finishing end. Though I have to agree with Dylan—that there is no obvious slot for "Angelina" on *Shot of Love,* hence its omission—the song demanded official status long before *The Bootleg Series.* The savage beauty of the lady in question is beautifully understated by the performance Dylan gives on *The Bootleg Series.* However, a more full-blooded arrangement of the song was also attempted at Clover. On the evidence of its less finished lyrics, I presume they attempted the full band version first. One interesting example of Dylan's reuse of images appears in the earlier take, "Praising the dead as she rode a donkey through the crowd, or was it a hyena?" Ironically, the full band take, inferior as it is, may well have fitted the album far better.

The other outtake to make *The Bootleg Series,* "Need a Woman," has a few good lines drawn from Dylan's myriad ways of saying please-lemme-get-my-rocks-off (this didn't stop Ry Cooder writing a bad parody of Dylan when he reworked the song for his *Slide Area* album), though "Angelina" it ain't. The only other known outtakes from Clover, "Groom" excepted, were both covers, a spirited "Mystery Train" and the decidedly disappointing "Let It Be Me."

On the evidence of the recording dates available, the Clover sessions spanned a couple of weeks (to May 11 or thereabouts), though given the relatively small number of songs *Shot of Love* was finally permed from, and the fact that Dylan persevered with cutting the songs live, the sessions may not have run day in, day out. The songs on *Shot of Love* have certainly not been done to death—indeed in the cases of "Dead

Man, Dead Man," "Watered-Down Love," and "In the Summertime," they have yet to reach optimum temperature.

"In the Summertime," in particular, suffers from a half-baked arrangement that is largely redeemed by a fine vocal and some exemplary harmonica work. (I still go back to the tape of that night at Earl's Court when Dylan first sang "In the Summertime" live should I want to hear Dylan finding the heart of this song, in particular the way he sings the line that shook me first time around, "The warning that came before the flood/that set everybody free.") As Williams rightly observes, on the album take, "the whole song is framed by harmonica," though the concluding thirty-second harmonica solo that (very, very) abruptly fades at song end (like some ham-fisted engineer just went *djonk* with the fader) should have been left to resolve itself, which it does some forty seconds further down the line, making what would have been a perfect companion to "Every Grain of Sand"'s hymnal fade.

"In the Summertime" was not the only song to have scissors taken to it. "Watered-Down Love" (originally titled "Pure Love") suffered the same fate as "Trouble In Mind," losing its last verse (the one about mistaking kindness for weakness). Presumably this was all part of pruning the album to forty-five minutes.

Aside from "Shot of Love"—if we assume for the moment that the Rundown version does indeed postdate the Clover sessions—Dylan was to make one further last-minute substitution. A rough mix of one of the trial sequences for *Shot of Love* contains an alternate "Heart of Mine," as well as the unedited "Watered-Down Love." This alternate "Heart of Mine" is a product of the same Clover sessions as the remainder of the album. It is the official "Heart of Mine" that came as an afterthought, one I personally find quite hard to listen

to. Williams loves "the looseness of the track," and usually I'm all for a little sloppiness in the studio. However, the three drummer/percussionists—Chuck Plotkin, Ringo Starr, and Jim Keltner (probably the only one who knows the actual tune)—sound like they're playing three different songs.

Since the Clover "Heart of Mine" was mixed on May 24, the official version was cut after the mixing sessions themselves, in late May. The use of a makeshift outfit on this track—first-class sessionmen like Donald "Duck" Dunn and Keltner slumming it with English booze-and-blues merchants like Ron Wood and Ringo Starr—suggests that the *Shot of Love* band had temporarily disbanded, awaiting the resumption of tour rehearsals at the beginning of June. The original "Heart of Mine" features Dylan's usual band and has a surprisingly sweet vocal (and a great double entendre, "Don't let her pour out her wine," lost by late May), perhaps the result of Dylan trying a little too hard to hit his notes. The song's bittersweet quality is enhanced by a ghostly *Blonde on Blonde* organ, presumably the work of Heartbreaker Benmont Tench, and as a musical performance has no obvious faults. Dylan, though, evidently felt that the released version fit a whole lot better between the album's strident opener and its uncompromising update of "Positively 4th Street," "Property of Jesus." Indeed, he admitted as much to the members of L.A.'s post-punk Plugz at a 1984 rehearsal.

Bob Dylan: *"It was done a bunch of different ways . . . but I chose for some reason a particularly funky version of that—and it's really scattered. It's not as good as some of the other versions, but I chose it because Ringo and Ronnie Wood played on it and we did it in, like, ten minutes."*

It had taken Dylan two months of studio work to arrive at *Shot of Love,* and though it was no masterpiece, it was a far stronger statement than *Saved*. Not surprisingly, it was also an album he wanted to champion—he told one radio interviewer he felt the same way about *Shot of Love* as he had after recording *Bringing It All Back Home*. Touring Europe in the summer and the States in the fall, Dylan did not stint from playing the new songs (though *Shot of Love*'s finest moment, "Every Grain of Sand," would not make its live debut until the final show of the year). However, *Shot of Love* would fare

even worse than *Saved* on the *Billboard* chart and when the tour wound to its end in Florida in late November, Dylan decided the time had come for a rest. When Howard Alk was found dead at Rundown itself on New Year's Day, 1982, it signaled the end of the Rundown era. For Dylan the years from 1978 to 1981, a period of tremendous rejuvenation as a songwriter, coincided with an ever-declining commerciality he had failed.

No Man Righteous —
Pressin on - guitar —
Its All over now Baby blue o
4th time Around o
shes not for you /
* picked up a couple of years
* if you could read my mind
yonder comes sin /
* willin
serve Somebody —
what can I do —
change my way —
lets keep it between us /
Groom still waiting at the Altar /
* Rainbow connection
Grain of Sand /
Carribean Wind /
Cover down —
Slow Train —
makin a liar /
Blue Blue River ?
Simple Twist o .
* Somewhere over the rainbow
In the garden —
Wake up —
Aint gonna go to hell for anybody —
* Sweet Caroline
* show me the way
* Fever
* Goin on

* Mary of the Wild Moor
* Abraham Martin and John
* Sadsongs and Waltzes
Precious Angel —
Tangled up in blue o
Blowin in the wind o
* Heatwave
* Fallin in love } Regimen
* Back stairs
Ramona o
~~Simple Twist~~
Covenant Woman —
* What about me — girls
* Going to see the king
I believe in you —
Just like a woman o
* We just Disagree
love is Vain o
Maggies Farm o
Animals —
Do right (changes #4) —
* Do it in love
Solid Rock —
In the garden —
Rolling Stone. o
Senor o
Dont think Twice o
you dont know me ?
Saved by the Grace of your love ?
I apologize ?
* This nite won't last forever

INFIDELS

Recorded: April 11 to May 8, 1983
Released: November 1, 1983

Side 1: Jokerman. Sweetheart Like You. Neighborhood Bully. License to Kill. Side 2: Man of Peace. Union Sundown. I and I. Don't Fall Apart on MeTonight.

Other official cuts:

45: Angel Flying Too Close to the Ground.
Down in the Groove: Death Is Not the End.
The Bootleg Series: Foot of Pride. Tell Me. Someone's Got a Hold of My Heart. Lord Protect My Child. Blind Willie McTell.

Producers:

1–2 Bob Dylan and Mark Knopfler
3 Bob Dylan

Musicians:

1–3 Bob Dylan (guitar/piano/harmonica/vocals)
1–2 Mick Taylor (guitar)
1–2 Mark Knopfler (guitar)
1–2 Alan Clark (keyboards)

1–2 Robbie Shakespeare (bass)
1–2 Sly Dunbar (drums)
2–3 Clydie King (backing vocals)
3 Full Force (backing vocals)

1. THE POWER STATION
   NEW YORK
   MID-APRIL 1983
Sweetheart Like You [incomplete]
Sweetheart Like You [fragment]
Sweetheart Like You [instrumental]
Sweetheart Like You [incomplete]
Sweetheart Like You [incomplete]
Sweetheart Like You [three fragments]
Sweetheart Like You

2. THE POWER STATION
   NEW YORK
   APRIL 11 TO MAY 8, 1983
Tell Me [I]
Tell Me [II]
Someone's Got a Hold of My Heart [I]

Someone's Got a Hold of My Heart [II]
Death Is Not the End*
Foot of Pride [I]
Foot of Pride [II]
Julius and Ethel
This Was My Love [I]
This Was My Love [II]
Angel Flying Too Close to the Ground*
Union Sundown
Union Sundown*
Jokerman*
Don't Fall Apart on Me Tonight*
Clean Cut Kid
Dark Groove [instrumental]
Don't Fly Unless It's Safe [instrumental]
Sweetheart Like You [I]
Sweetheart Like You [II]*

Lord Protect My Child
Blind Willie McTell [I]
Blind Willie McTell [II]
Neighborhood Bully*
License to Kill
Man of Peace
I and I*
The Green, Green Grass of Home
Rumored: *Sultans of Swing*

3. THE POWER STATION
   NEW YORK
   JUNE TO JULY 5, 1983
Death Is Not the End [overdubs]
Sweetheart Like You [overdubs]
Don't Fall Apart on Me Tonight [overdubs]
Union Sundown [overdubs]
Angel Flying Too Close to the Ground [overdubs]
Jokerman [overdubs]
I and I [overdubs]

It seems de rigeur for major rock artists to have their very own "great lost album." The Beatles have their *Get Back,* the Beach Boys have *Smile,* the Who have *Lifehouse,* the Stones have *Black Box,* Richard Thompson has the original *Shoot Out the Lights.* Some, like Neil Young, have had more than their fair share of mightabeens. In Dylan's case, it is only really in the 1980s that his great lost albums begin to stack up. Indeed I'd be hard-pressed to name an album between *Shot of Love* and *Under the Red Sky* where the choice of tracks has not been dubious at best— and I base this only on what I have had the opportunity to appraise.

Never, though, would Dylan deal such a body blow to one of his own works as he did in June 1983, when he returned to Power Station to rework an album he had spent a month recording that spring. If Dylan had released the album Mark Knopfler and he had assembled in May, I don't doubt we would still be calling him to account for the omission of "Someone's Got a Hold of My Heart" (and probably "Tell Me"), and the inclusion of "License to Kill" and "Neighborhood Bully." Yet—I broach no discussion on this point—*Infidels* would have stood as Dylan's one true masterpiece of the eighties. The *Infidels* that was so nearly released comprised nine cuts:

1. Jokerman
2. License to Kill
3. Man of Peace
4. Neighborhood Bully (end of side one)
5. Don't Fall Apart on Me Tonight
6. Blind Willie McTell
7. Sweetheart Like You
8. I and I
9. Foot of Pride

Made in the days when albums came in two parts, the second side of this *Infidels* would have had no more than a half-dozen peers in Dylan's oeuvre (and only one since *John Wesley Harding*). The balance this album achieves would have been something quite different from its released twin. Side one concerns itself wholly with the state of a world on the brink. As false prophets stalk the world, the narrator fears the countdown to Armageddon has begun. In this context even Dylan's song about a beleaguered Israel, "Neighborhood Bully," comes across as more than just the Zionist rant it has been painted as:

Bob Dylan: *"You [shouldn't] make it [so] specific . . . to what's going on today. What's going on today isn't going to last, you know? The battle of Armageddon is specifically spelled out: where it will be fought and, if you wanna get technical, when it will be fought."*

On side two Dylan begins to turn his gaze on how individuals might confront the End times. In the case of "Blind Willie McTell" its narrator has become commentator, perhaps the last commentator, on human folly. While Blind Willie McTell sings the world's eulogy, the narrator of "Foot of Pride" is covered in "the dust of a plague that has left this whole town afraid."

The other three songs deal with more familiar terrain, the narrator's "women troubles," even though the backdrop of Revelations remains. In "Sweetheart Like You," Dylan advises the subject that she should be at home, "taking care of somebody nice," not in some dive (The Lion's Den?) where you "gotta crawl across cut glass to make a deal." (There is a similar sentiment expressed in "Someone's Got a Hold of My Heart," where, in the face of a storm of biblical proportions—indeed the fall of Babylon revisited—the singer advises his love to "go inside and stay warm.") Deliberately bringing the wrath of the politically correct generation down upon himself, Dylan chooses to portray the women on *Infidels* as angels of the hearth ("how sweet she sleeps, how free must be her dreams"; "She just sits there, as the night grows still").

"I and I," the one song on this side only marginally tampered with on the released album (though Dylan still took the two electric guitars, previously panned far left/far right, and "centered" them—what is this, Bob, back to mono?), is the real jewel in this catalogue of heartaches. The problems facing the kingdoms of the world are making the narrator feel afraid, so he rises from his bed, leaving the strange woman who is lying there to dream her untroubled dreams. The penultimate verse is a masterpiece of understatement, echoing both a key element of Western folklore (the train as ——, pick your own motif) and his own holy slow train. Dylan and the band function as one preassembled unit throughout the song, Sly and Robbie instinctively knowing exactly when they should be in your face and when they should be in the next room with the door closed.

Indeed Dylan's choice of musicians on *Infidels* was inspired. Alan Clark, alter-

nating between piano and organ, did all that was required of him. Sly and Robbie as a rhythm section were designed to give the whole album "a contemporary feel" without sounding like they had used the dreaded click-track. Mark Knopfler's trademark licks, when dirtied up by Mick Taylor's blues-breaking leads, compounded the album's commerciality, yet were rooted in a sound very different from *Slow Train Coming.*

Unfortunately, this band's finest four minutes—perhaps Dylan's greatest studio recording of the eighties—the electric "Blind Willie McTell," still remains unreleased. As with the New York *Blood on the Tracks* sessions, Mr. Rosen devoted a generous chunk (twenty-five minutes, no less) of *The Bootleg Series* to the lost *Infidels* tracks. Yet, just like *Blood on the Tracks,* of the five cuts scheduled for the original album (alternates of "Jokerman," "Sweetheart Like You," and "Don't Fall Apart on Me Tonight" plus the electric "Blind Willie McTell" and "Foot of Pride"), just "Foot of Pride" ended up on *The Bootleg Series.*

Which is not to say that the likes of "Tell Me" (a previously unknown take that, for once, is more than equal to its bootlegged counterpart) or "Someone's Got a Hold of My Heart" did not warrant air. Still, I would have thought the logical starting point for a collection of outtakes would be those songs that nearly made it, the songs Dylan pulled at the last minute. And there is no finer example than the electric "Blind Willie McTell."

What I cannot figure out—and maybe Greil Marcus, who finds the electric "Blind Willie McTell" "slick and lifeless," can tell me—is what one gets from the acoustic version on *The Bootleg Series* that one cannot get from the electric take, with interest. What Dylan gained in 1965 by "going electric" was the key element of interplay other musicians could bring to a song. Listening to Dylan play solo might be quite riveting, but the listener is entirely focused on one figure center stage. There is no shock of recognition when a bass line crashes into a guitar riff, which bounces off the vocal that then . . . and so on.

The acoustic "Blind Willie McTell" is exactly the performance you would expect if someone hummed you the melody, read you the lyrics, and said it was a piano/guitar performance. If anyone else gave the same vocal performance, you might wheel out the tour de force plaque. But then, as Paul Cable put it (talking about the Gaslight version of "Moonshine Blues" of all things), "[It] is a reoccurring facet of Dylan [that] he seems to put everything he has into a song on one occasion, then you hear another version on a different tape and by comparison he chucks the whole thing away." Not that Dylan exactly throws the acoustic "Blind Willie McTell" away—it's just that the electric take explodes with surprises that in no way diminish the impact of the lyrics. From Dylan's cough on the second line as his voice strains to hit the note to the tap of (surely Dylan's) a shoe counting the band in on the second verse, the way he sings "can strut" like "in-struct," the delightful harmonica interludes, that classic way Dylan has of running the words in the first half of a line together just so he has time to bend the remainder of the line to the beat in his head (an ol' bluesman's trick)—all work together to provide a breathtaking cut. And I ain't even mentioned the way the song bu*ilds* to a crescendo like only a band can do. Sorry, Greil, you're wrong.

The other mea culpa omissions from the original *Infidels* were certainly "Jokerman" and "Foot of Pride." "Foot of Pride," which at least made *The Bootleg Series*, is a performance today's grunge-merchants would do well to take note of, being almost entirely devoid of a

tune or structure beyond a beat. Yet it is everything a Dylan performance should be. There can be few Dylan songs with a vocal more difficult to emulate (good try, Lou, but no laurel), nor more densely packed imagery. To unravel the whole thing would take years—and isn't that the way it should be?

"Jokerman" is equally elusive. Indeed, *Infidels* remains a very wordy album (in either incarnation). The differences between the original "Jokerman" and the released "Jokerman" are far subtler than, say, "Idiot Wind." Yet they shed light on Dylan's recent tendency to overwork the finished article. Although from a literary point of view, it would be hard to fault Dylan's lyrical rewrites on "Jokerman," I've never found anything wrong with the lyrics in the first place (I mean, "no storebought shirt for me on my back, one of the women must sit in the shack and sew one" is a great rhyme scheme). Likewise, in cold isolation, the new vocal Dylan overdubbed in June, after the musicians had gone home (or, in Knopfler and Clark's cases, on tour), sounds perfectly fine, particularly with that great opening line—that is, until you A–B it with the original to contrast passion with artifice, heart and soul versus control.

What happened? Well, after twenty-two years of cutting his albums live, and one month at Power Station with Shakespear, Dunbar, Clark, Knopfler, and Taylor recording every song "as is," Dylan felt dissatisfied by something he couldn't quite put his finger on:

We put the tracks down and sang most of the stuff live. Only later, when we had so much stuff . . . [did] I want to fill [the sound] up more. I've never wanted to do that with any other record . . . Did you ever listen to an Eagles record? . . . Their songs are good, but every note is predictable. You know exactly what's gonna be before it's even there. And I started to sense some of that on Infidels,

*and I didn't like it, so we decided to
redo some of the vocals.*

It wasn't just the vocals that Dylan
"decided to redo." In a savage reappraisal of the work to date, Dylan
scrapped "Foot of Pride" and "Blind
Willie McTell." Despite having seven
originals and some fourteen covers (including "This Was My Love," "The
Green, Green Grass of Home," "Sultans
of Swing," and "Angel Flying Too Close
to the Ground") to perm from, Dylan
replaced these two important works
with just one four-minute "state of the
nation" address. "Union Sundown"
somehow manages to display the same
kind of naïveté in economic matters as
Dylan had previously displayed with
Hal Lindsey's rabid religious tracts. Yet
it seems to have been a song he refused
to give up on. An early *Infidels* outtake
has Dylan singing "dummy" lyrics over
a familiar attack of two guitars and
piano. The version Special Rider copyrighted, which presumably postdates
this dummy version, has a full set of
lyrics (including an astonishing lost
verse about a man in a mask in the
White House understanding the shape
of things to come), but has only the
most rudimentary, piano-driven accompaniment, almost suggesting a publisher's demo. Dylan subsequently
combined some kind of basic track (cut
with Knopfler, Taylor, Shakespeare, and
Dunbar, and possibly Clark) with an entirely new vocal, grafted on at the June
mixing sessions.

That Dylan should waste his time on
such a piece of tosh when he had the perfect partner for "Sweetheart," "Don't
Fall Apart on Me Tonight" and "I and I"
in "Someone's Got a Hold of My Heart"
may well suggest just how perverse his
artistic judgments have become (at least
the artist responsible has more of an excuse for exercising his questionable judgment than a compiler like Jeff Rosen,
whose use of a truly lame version of

"Someone's Got a Hold of My Heart"
on *The Bootleg Series* begs ridicule).

"Someone's Got a Hold of My Heart"
provides a rare example of Dylan
reusing not just various lines but a
song's entire sensibility to create a new
song a couple of years down the line.
Although this has been a popular technique for many fine singer-songwrit-
ers—Costello, Springsteen, and Young
all spring to mind—Dylan almost never
reworks a song he has discarded. The
trash can is usually its final resting place,
bootlegs notwithstanding. Not so,
"Someone's Got a Hold of My Heart,"
from which Dylan extracted the core of
"Tight Connection to My Heart (Has
Anybody Seen My Love)" for *Empire
Burlesque*. The version of the song on
The Bootleg Series makes the debt very
plain, being almost a prototype arrangement for the latter (the live version of
"Tight Connection," performed in
1990, has even more in common with
"Someone's Got a Hold of My Heart").
However, this is Holiday Inn land for
Dylan and the band, with a vocal that
sounds no more than a guide vocal, certainly not a serious attempt to replicate
the passion of its bootlegged self (the
oft-bootlegged outtake burning with the
fever of unconsummated love).

Further evidence, were it needed, that
Dylan's perspective on his own work
went walkabouts at the end of the *Infidels* sessions (never to return?) can be
found on the one cover from these sessions to become Columbia product.
Willie Nelson's "Angel Flying Too Close
to the Ground," according to a Dylan
interviewed at the end of the June sessions, was actually under consideration
for the album. As it happens Dylan decided to hide the song away on the first
Infidels 45, although again only after a
little resculpting had taken place. This
time the "touch-ups" did not involve
Dylan's (or Clydie King's) vocals, save
for bringing them up in the mix. Some
serious tampering, though, was done to

the rhythm track, losing some great little drum rolls, while Dylan has also dubbed over his original harmonica breaks (both of them) with a couple of atonally inappropriate, not to say skewered, harp solos (the original version appears on the *Rough Cuts* bootleg CD). Dylan also fails to apply the fader early enough, allowing the song to go on a good thirty seconds beyond the point of no return.

In the post-*Infidels* world, Dylan would finally abandon his Luddite ways in the studio. Though he would still refuse to build tracks instrument by instrument, the vocal overdub became a useful way of disguising failing lung power. Ironically, Dylan's determination to cut *Infidels* live had done little to impair the songs. (A fascinating, nay unique, insight into Dylan's approach to recording can be found on a circulating tape of the *Infidels* ensemble working on "Sweetheart Like You" in the studio. On the basis of what sounds like an open-mike tape [sometimes the engineer runs a two-track "log" tape of a session using an open mike in the studio] and the two known outtakes of "Sweetheart," this was a song that, lyrically at least, took shape in the studio.)

If anything a live-in-the-studio album as strong as the original *Infidels* should have vindicated Dylan's previous working methods. Because of the superb unit he had been playing with, and the state-of-the-art twenty-four-track facilities the Power Station offered, Dylan could have easily masked any musical or vocal faux pas without restructuring the entire album. As it is, the reconfigured *Infidels* is a blurred Polaroid snapshot of an original self-portrait.

EMPIRE BURLESQUE

Recorded: July 1984 to March 1985
Released: June 8, 1985

Side 1: Tight Connection to My Heart (Has Anybody Seen My Love). Seeing the Real You at Last. I'll Remember You Clean Cut Kid. Never Gonna Be the Same Again. Side 2: Trust Yourself. Emotionally Yours. When the Night Comes Falling from the Sky. Something's Burning, Baby. Dark Eyes.

KNOCKED OUT LOADED

Recorded: July 1984 to May 1986
Released: August 8, 1986

Side 1: You Wanna Ramble. They Killed Him. Driftin' Too Far from Shore. Precious Memories. Maybe Someday. Side 2: Brownsville Girl. Got My Mind Made Up. Under Your Spell.

Other official cuts:

45: Band of the Hand (It's Helltime Man).
The Bootleg Series: When the Night Comes Falling from the Sky [I].

Producers:

1–7 Bob Dylan
8–9 Bob Dylan and Arthur Baker
10 Bob Dylan and Dave Stewart

11 Tom Petty
12–14 Bob Dylan

Musicians:

1–14 Bob Dylan (guitar/harmonica/vocals)
1 Anton Fig (drums)
1 John Paris (bass)
1–2 Ron Wood (guitar)
2 The Al Green Band
3 musicians unknown
4–5 Don Heffington (drums)
4 Carl Sealove (bass)
4, 12 Ira Ingber (guitar)

4 Vince Melamed (synthesizer)
4–5, 7, 11–14 Madelyn Quebec (second vocals)
5, 11, 13 Mike Campbell (guitar)
5, 9, 11, 13 Benmont Tench (keyboards)
5, 11, 13 Howie Epstein (bass)
5 Bob Glaub (bass)
5 Jim Keltner (drums)
6 Little Steven (guitar)

6 Roy Bittan (keyboards)
6–7, 9 Robbie Shakespeare (bass)
6–7 Sly Dunbar (drums)
7, 9 Richard Scher (synthesizer)
7, 12 Al Kooper (guitar)
7 Stuart Kimball (guitar)
7 Mick Taylor (guitar)
7 Ted Perlman (guitar)
9 Urban Blight Horns (horns)
9 Bashiri Johnson (percussion)
9, 11–14 Carolyn Dennis (backing vocals)
9, 11–14 Queen Esther Marrow (backing
   vocals)
9 Peggi Blue (backing vocals)
9 Debra Byrd (backing vocals)
9 David Watson (saxophone)
10 Dave Stewart (guitar)
10 Clem Burke (drums)
10 Patrick Seymour (keyboards)
10 John McKenzie (bass)
11, 13 Tom Petty (guitar/backing vocals)

11, 13 Stan Lynch (drums)
11 Stevie Nicks (backing vocals)
11, 13 Elisecia Wright (backing vocals)
12 Raymond Lee Pounds (drums)
12 James Jamerson Jr. (bass)
12 Vito San Flippo (bass)
12 T-Bone Burnett (guitar)
12 Jack Sherman (guitar)
12 Cesar Rosas (guitar)
12, 14 Steve Douglas (saxophone)
12, 14 Muffy Hendrix (backing vocals)
12, 14 Annette May Thomas (backing vocals)
13 Philip Lyn Jones (conga)
14 Steve Madaio (trumpet)
14 Larry Meyers (mandolin)
14 Al Perkins (steel guitar)
14 Milton Gabriel (steel drums)
14 Mike Berment (steel drums)
14 Brian Parris (steel drums)

1. DELTA SOUND STUDIOS
   NEW YORK
   MID- TO LATE JULY 1984
Go 'Way Little Boy
Who Loves You More?
Wolf [instrumental]
Groovin' at Delta [instrumental]
Clean Cut Kid [I]
Clean Cut Kid [II]*
Driftin' Too Far from Shore [I]
Driftin' Too Far from Shore [II]

2. INTERGALACTIC STUDIO
   NEW YORK
   LATE JULY 1984
Honey Wait
Mountain of Love

3. OCEANWAY STUDIOS
   LOS ANGELES, CALIFORNIA
   NOVEMBER 1984
In the Summertime [I]
In the Summertime [II]
In the Summertime [III]
In the Summertime [IV]
Freedom for the Stallion [I]
Freedom for the Stallion [II]
Freedom for the Stallion [III]
Instrumental I
Instrumental II
Instrumental III
Instrumental IV

Instrumental V
Instrumental VI

4. CHEROKEE STUDIOS
   LOS ANGELES, CALIFORNIA
   DECEMBER 1984
Something's Burning, Baby [I]
Something's Burning, Baby [II]
New Danville Girl*

5. CHEROKEE STUDIOS
   LOS ANGELES, CALIFORNIA
   JANUARY TO EARLY FEBRUARY 1985
I'll Remember You*
Emotionally Yours*
Trust Yourself*
Seeing the Real You at Last [I]
Seeing the Real You at Last [II]*
Maybe Someday [instrumental]*

6. THE POWER STATION
   NEW YORK
   FEBRUARY 19, 1985
When the Night Comes Falling from the Sky
[I]

7. THE POWER STATION
   NEW YORK
   LATE FEBRUARY 1985
When the Night Comes Falling from the Sky
[II]*

Never Gonna Be the Same Again*
Tight Connection to My Heart (Has Any-
   body Seen My Love)*
Waiting to Get Beat
The Very Thought of You
Straight A's in Love

8. THE POWER STATION
   NEW YORK
   MARCH 1985
Dark Eyes

9. THE POWER STATION, SHAKEDOWN
   SOUND AND RIGHT TRACK
   NEW YORK
   MARCH 1985
Tight Connection to My Heart (Has Any-
   body Seen My Love) [overdubs]
Seeing the Real You at Last [overdubs]
Clean Cut Kid [overdubs]
Never Gonna Be the Same Again [overdubs]
Trust Yourself [overdubs]
Emotionally Yours [overdubs]
When the Night Comes Falling from the Sky
   [overdubs]
Something's Burning, Baby [overdubs]

10. THE CHURCH STUDIOS
    CROUCH END, LONDON
    NOVEMBER 19 TO 22, 1985

Instrumental I
Instrumental II
Under Your Spell [backing track]*

11. FESTIVAL STUDIOS
    SYDNEY, AUSTRALIA
    FEBRUARY 8 AND 9, 1986
Band of the Hand (It's Helltime Man)

12. SKYLINE STUDIOS
    TOPANGA CANYON, CALIFORNIA
    LATE APRIL TO EARLY MAY 1986
Come Rain or Come Shine
You Wanna Ramble
They Killed Him*
Precious Memories*

13. SOUND CITY STUDIOS
    VAN NUYS, CALIFORNIA
    MID-MAY 1986
Got My Mind Made Up

14. SKYLINE STUDIOS
    TOPANGA CANYON, CALIFORNIA
    MID- TO LATE MAY 1986
They Killed Him [overdubs]
Under Your Spell [overdubs]
Maybe Someday [overdubs]
Driftin' Too Far from Shore [overdubs]
Brownsville Girl [overdubs]
Precious Memories [overdubs]

The years from 1984 to 1987 represent the nadir of Dylan's studio career. The albums he came up with in those years became ever more slight, nay superficial. Dylan followed 1985's *Empire Burlesque* with his first ever "non-album," *Knocked Out Loaded,* a half-and-half rerun of *Empire Burlesque* ("Brownsville Girl," "Driftin' Too Far from Shore," and "Maybe Someday")— and a preview of *Down in the Groove* ("You Wanna Ramble," "They Killed Him," and "Precious Memories"). The way that Dylan compiled *Empire Burlesque* and *Knocked Out Loaded,* the dearth of inspiration they appear to represent, and the modern sheen they share makes them two volumes with the same depressing story to tell.

Their starting point was certainly one and the same—the July 1984 Delta

Sound session(s) that produced "Clean Cut Kid" for *Empire Burlesque* and the basic track for *Knocked Out Loaded's* "Driftin' Too Far from Shore." With these sessions, Dylan reverted to a method of recording he'd abandoned back in the sixties: setting up sessions with no specific timetable for an album. In theory it was a method that should have had advantages over cutting an album in a single stint, when it is tempting to include "filler" songs rather than return at a later date with more songs. Unfortunately, this new approach was largely symptomatic of a man unsure of direction.

The Delta session(s) may not have been the first time Dylan entered the studio after his return from a month-long European tour on July 9, 1984. At some point in July, he attempted to record with Al Green's band at Intergalactic Studios in New York, though without any usable results. Working with these old-time Memphis musicians was not one of Dylan's better ideas. With no charts and no fixed arrangements, Dylan remained his usual undisciplined self. Ron Wood witnessed the chaos:

"All these guys from Memphis couldn't understand Bob's chord sequences. Every time he started off a new song, he'd start in a new key, or if we were doing the same song over and over, every time would be in a different key. Now, I can go along with that with Bob, but the band were totally confused, and one by one they left the studio."

We know of just two songs attempted at this session. "Honey Wait," the one song in general circulation, sounds like something between an old Chess outtake and Dylan's idea of a homage. According to Ron Wood, they also ran through the fifties classic "Mountain of Love" (Springsteen used to do a stompin' rendition of this song back in 1975.)

Before 1984 there are very few examples of Dylan returning to songs discarded from a previous album ("Hollis Brown" on *Times* and "Mr. Tambourine Man" on *Bringing It All Back Home* are the only two examples that spring to mind). Dylan's reappraisal of his working methods after *Infidels* also led to him reappraising songs from previous projects (*Oh Mercy* has seen all four outtakes reworked at various points, on *Under The Red Sky, The Bootleg Series,* and *Greatest Hits Vol. 3*). At the Delta Sound sessions, Dylan returned to "Clean Cut Kid," perhaps—with "Death is Not the End"—the most nondescript leftover from the *Infidels* sessions.

Of the other vocal tracks cut at Delta, "Driftin' Too Far from Shore" sounds to have the bare bones of a usable track. (Dylan would return to finish the song in May 1986 when, exhumed for *Knocked Out Loaded,* it came with new

vocal and drum tracks and a whole new set of lyrics.) "Go 'Way Little Boy" sounds like what it is, a guide demo for Lone Justice to learn the song. "Who Loves You More" might have had potential, though the hackneyed chorus sets a worrying precedent for the album to come: "Who loves you more? Who loves you true? Oh baby, you know I do."

Given the ephemeral nature of the songs recorded at Intergalactic and Delta, it strikes me as perverse—albeit typically perverse—that Dylan never attempted to record any of the three new originals he had rehearsed with his touring band at the end of May. Certainly "Enough Is Enough"—which was performed throughout the final two weeks in Europe—and a song usually called "Almost Done" (probably, in reality, the elusive "Angel of Rain"), both suggest a caliber not evident on the various New York recordings. "Almost Done"/"Angel of Rain" exists as a gorgeous fragment from the Hollywood tour rehearsals with a lyric that has entirely disappeared six days later when Dylan's work on the song occupies much of the first rehearsal in Verona (the day before a truly disastrous opening show).

The other unusual aspect of the Delta sessions—which carried over to most of the *Empire Burlesque* and *Knocked Out Loaded* sessions—was Dylan's new penchant for recording backing tracks, some of which he returned to later with a vocal/lyric. Though he had recorded the occasional instrumental over the years, recording a basic track with a view to overdubbing a vocal later had always been anathema to Dylan. Yet two instrumentals were recorded at Delta ("Wolf" and "Groovin' at Delta"), a further half-dozen at Oceanway in November, the basic track for *Knocked Out Loaded*'s "Maybe Someday" was recorded at one of the winter 1985 sessions, and a whole series of instrumental tracks were laid down at The Church, in London's Crouch End district, in November 1985 (one later forming the basis for "Under Your Spell").

Dylan also returned to recording covers at these 1984 sessions, a preamble to the schizophrenia of *Knocked Out Loaded.* A November 1984 session at Oceanway remains perhaps the weirdest session from this whole period. Aside from running through assorted meandering instrumentals, Dylan attempted just two vocal tracks, both covers, Ray Dorset's "In the Summertime"—painfully bad on every level—and Allen Toussaint's elegiac "Freedom for the Stallion." Amid all this dreck, the three versions of "Freedom for the Stallion" show the old Dylan struggling to assert himself in the studio. In particular the second take builds dramatically from a stuttering start. Though Dylan struggles to find the right tempo, once it gathers steam the old vocal fire is well in evidence. It ends with Dylan asking the engineer, "Okay, what did you think of that?" One assumes the reply, absent from the tape, was not, "A helluva lot better than the crap you've been putting down on tape so far."

Despite Dylan's ability to transform someone else's song in performance—at his best making it wholly his own for one clear moment—he invariably only turns to other artists' songs in the studio when his own pen has (temporarily) run out of ink. Thus *Self Portrait, Dylan, Knocked Out Loaded,* and *Down in the Groove,* and eventually *Good as I Been to You* and *World Gone Wrong,* have all coincided with periods lacking inspiration from the man himself. Despite the fact that *Empire Burlesque* was a wholly original market sample of Dylan's '84 and '85 output, days like the one at Oceanway seemed indicative of a wayward muse.

Of course, in a state of mind in which rock's greatest lyricist could write, "Come find me, baby remind me, of where we once begun," he was hardly about to abandon perverse song selections. In No-

vember 1984, as well as indulging in his Muzak session at Oceanway, Dylan cut a song at Cherokee that was a masterpiece of lyrical wit and invention, original in both conception *and* execution. And yet "New Danville Girl" would not appear on *Empire Burlesque.* As Dylan's most epic song in years, its inclusion on *Empire Burlesque*—along with the (correctly mixed) "Van Zandt" version of "When the Night Comes Falling from the Sky"—might have largely salvaged one of Dylan's most anodyne albums.

Paul Williams dismisses "New Danville Girl" as a failed epic. I can't for the life of me figure out what he is driving at when he says "the song doesn't have much to say." If the implication is that its story is less intricate than "Lily, Rosemary"—its most obvious kin (what with the Wild West motif and its scale of ambition)—I might give Paul the nod. As an analysis of the human condition, absolutely not. I actually find "New Danville Girl" a far more enjoyable listening experience than "Lily, Rosemary and the Jack of Hearts," even if I might begrudgingly admit that "Lily, Rosemary" is a better-written song.

The style adopted for "New Danville Girl" showed a rare glimpse of one guise Dylan had long hid from view—the storyteller. If every line raises questions that lead the listener across the flatlands of Texas and time, its conversational tone hints at the very mundanity the song's characters are seeking to transcend (in this they come closest to characters in plays of coauthor Sam Shepard like *True West* and *Cowboy Mouth*). If the song has a flaw, it is that the Dylan/narrator divide is as blurred as can be. Who else but Dylan would wryly observe of a fellow icon (Peck), "He's got a new one out, but he just don't look the same"? (A great line, lost on the 1986 rewrite.)

But what really separates "New Danville Girl" from both its famous predecessor "Lily, Rosemary" and its reincarnation (as "Brownsville Girl") is the stark simplicity of the song's performance. According to guitarist Ira Ingber, it was primarily because of drummer Don Heffington that the track manages to hold sway for its full twelve minutes: "As the drummer he played it with such dynamics that he actually created a song, because it's the same four chords that go over and over again." Certainly the way Heffington builds toward each chorus, incongruous as their placement might be (they come after verses six, ten, fourteen, seventeen—go figure), "grounds" the song. Heffington is ably supported by organist Vince Melamed, guitarist Ingber, bassist Carl Sealove and, most especially, Dylan, whose acoustic guitar is not for the first time the key musical brushstroke, save for when he takes up the harmonica after each chorus. Although "Brownsville Girl" is no disaster, it is hardly stark—the entire Queens of Rhythm wailing along at any interval, appropriate or not. Only Madelyn Quebec's understated second vocal is required to bolster Dylan's lead on the original.

The same musicians who so ably supported Dylan on "New Danville Girl" also cut Empire Burlesque's one redeemable nugget, "Something's Burning, Baby," quite possibly on the following day (although on the album, Sealove's bass lines have been replaced by Robbie Shakespeare's, presumably overdubbed at one of the mixing sessions in March 1985). This funeral march, coming after the apocalyptic "When the Night Comes Falling" on the album, finds Dylan once again overcome with the fumes of hell. It is the one song on the album for which a significant unreleased take resides with collectors. On this earlier take, even though Dylan is determined to make every word count, the entire lyric, from the first bridge on ("I can feel it in the night"), has yet to find its feet. That statically charged line about "the Mexico City Blues" is absent, as is the mysteri-

ous man "going around calling names" (at this stage it is "somebody parked in a truck in the shade"). The new set of lyrics were almost certainly grafted on at a later date, via a new vocal overdub, as Dylan gave in to the tinkering that has dominated his post-Infidels work. Vince Melamed's original wash of chords, which has a nice orchestral feel, should have been left well alone on the official "Something's Burning, Baby" (which contains one vocal "punch in" "shaking ground" instead of "outskirts of town" on the second bridge). As it is, a redundant second synthesizer makes for an extra layer of sound. Nevertheless, "Something's Burning, Baby" was one song that survived relatively unscathed from the "post-production" Arthur Baker inflicted on the album as a whole.

Before Baker could get his hands on the project, though, Dylan indulged in a further series of sessions, in both L.A. and New York. It was from these New Year sessions that four-fifths of the album would eventually come. Even the one abortive session—on February 19, 1985, at New York's Power Station, with Springsteen cohorts "Miami" Steve Van Zandt and Roy Bittan—was apparently quite productive, resulting in a half-dozen finished songs (according to whispers on the wire). However, nothing from the session was short-listed for the album, even the second epic from these sessions, "When the Night Comes Falling from the Sky."

Dylan's most self-conscious attempt to write a magnum opus in many a moon, "When the Night Comes Falling" as it appears on Empire Burlesque, with its "Watchtower" arrangement and painfully contemporary clutter (thanks, Arthur), promises far more than it delivers. But then, when I come to think about it, there is absolutely nothing that redeems the released version, even pre-Bakerized, save for the sneaking suspicion that somewhere in there is a great song struggling to escape the bonds of a crass arrangement (and an equally crass vocal).

Somehow the Van Zandt version transcends the song's similarities to "Watchtower" and a string of Dylanisms in its text (how about "it's the end of the chase and the moon is high" as an example), although some of the worst examples on the album version—like that line about "the northern border of Texas," which is beyond parody—are absent from this earlier take. For once I prefer almost all of the original lines ("I gave to you my heart like buried treasure"—listen to the cocksure delivery on this line). Yet even this take has a serious sonic fuck-up (to use the technical term) on *The Bootleg Series* take, surely the result of inexpert mixing from the original multitrack. The drums that are supposed to simultaneously kick in your door and punch in your windows at the beginning of the third verse prefers to sneak through the cellar on the official CD.

Of the thirteen songs from these sessions eventually released on *Empire Burlesque* or its successor, only the acoustic "Dark Eyes" would escape the indelicate touch of an engineer/producer. Ironically, "Dark Eyes" was the one song recorded entirely under Arthur Baker's supervision, being cut at the mixing sessions for *Empire Burlesque*. Coming after forty minutes of insistent, whomping drums and reverberating bass, any Dylan acoustic performance was gonna feel like the aural equivalent of cool water. According to Dylan, he wrote "Dark Eyes" specifically to wrap up the album—making it one in a long tradition of written-to-order album closers. Even after Dylan had written the song, the guitar part proved problematic as he repeatedly hit the wrong strings accidentally in the studio. With only three strings necessary for what is actually a rather trite melody, the other three strings were taped down, at which point Dylan finally got the song on tape.

Though no masterwork, "Dark Eyes" has some hidden charms. I just can't shake the feeling that he wrote the whole song just to get to those last two lines.

The remainder of *Empire Burlesque* was not so easily finished. After Dylan had "produced" the various sessions himself, he brought in flavor-of-the-month producer Arthur Baker to give the album a contemporary feel (forgetting Lester Bangs's wise assessment of this creed: "Producers, for the most part, serve absolutely no purpose beyond gussying up something fresh and alive on demos and running the band over and over the same ground till the whole place is a cemetery"). According to Dylan, "When it was time to put this record together I brought it all to [Baker] and he made it sound like a record." Unfortunately, what Baker did not do was make it sound like a Bob Dylan record.

Thanks to Special Rider (who used pre-Bakerized versions to copyright the songs), it is possible for fans to compile their own, untainted *Empire Burlesque* from a tape source. This dispenses with such flies in the ointment as the Urban Blight Horns, percussionist Bashiri Johnson and, on synth (as in synthetic), Richard Scher. I cannot recommend this procedure highly enough. Though a pre-Bakerized *Empire Burlesque* is still, at best, an innocuous collection of songs, at least fans do not have to file it with their New Order collection.

If Dylan's rationale for omitting "New Danville Girl" from *Empire Burlesque* was the worrying light of inspiration it might have cast on its brethren, then he seems to have seriously overestimated his ability to write songs worthy of comparison in the twelve months that followed. Though it is difficult to conceive of anything on *Empire Burlesque* (even "When the Night Comes Falling") sitting comfortably alongside Dylan and Shepard's panoramic playlet, the second side of *Knocked Out Loaded*, with the renamed "Brownsville Girl," was no less top-heavy.

Unlike *Empire Burlesque, Knocked Out Loaded* was constructed in a hurry, in Topanga Canyon in April and May 1986, slotted between two major tours with Tom Petty's Heartbreakers. In its released form it certainly smacks of "Empire Burlesque Part Two," if one overlooks the three disappointing covers that introduce the album. All three of the genuine remnants from *Empire Burlesque*—"Driftin' Too Far from Shore" from the July 1984 Delta sessions; "Brownsville Girl" from fall 1984 at Cherokee; and "Maybe Someday" from the same studio but January 1985— have the edge on the contemporary songs that found their way on to *Empire Burlesque*. Though the Queens of Rhythm have been obligingly dolloped on to each track, the absence of Baker's not so deft touch (and some clever lyrical rewrites on "Driftin'") suggests at least some thought on Dylan's part.

Knocked Out Loaded still suffers from a severe identity crisis, the result of a belated decision by Dylan to abandon most everything recorded in the first two weeks of sessions at Skyline, in late April to early May 1986 (the whole process apparently took a month, with a break mid-session). According to journalist Mikail Gilmore, who was in attendance at the crucial midway stage, Dylan "decided to put aside most of the rock and roll tracks he had been working on in Topanga . . . [instead] assembling the album from various sessions that have accrued over the last year." Gilmore strongly implies, in his *Rolling Stone* piece, that the songs cut at these early sessions, with the likes of Charlie Quintana, Al Kooper, Los Lobos, and T-Bone Burnett, were far superior to the lame covers Dylan used on *Knocked Out Loaded*. Al Kooper endorses Gilmore's assessment, commenting,

"There were some really wonderful things cut at those sessions."

Unfortunately, there is no real documentation of these sessions (the master reels reside in Dylan's possession, collected from Skyline at the end of the sessions, and no "safeties" were retained by the studio), and no rumored outtakes save for a version of Ray Charles's "Come Rain or Come Shine" that Ira Ingber was asked to arrange by Dylan. However, the impression given by a cover like Junior Parker's "You Wanna Ramble" and Gilmore's reference to twenty or so songs of "r & b, Chicago-steeped blues, rambunctious gospel, and rawtoned hillbilly forms" is that Dylan originally intended *Knocked Out Loaded* to be an album of covers, much like its successor.

Though an album of covers might suggest someone compensating for a lack of inspiration, the preferred route of three *Empire Burlesque* outtakes, three covers, and one track each from sessions in London with Dave Stewart of the Eurythmics and with the Heartbreakers in Van Nuys hardly smacks of real substance. In fact, an album that included the likes of "Red Cadillac and a Black Moustache," "Shake a Hand," "So Long, Good Luck and Goodbye," "Unchain My Heart," and "I'm Movin' On"—all covers performed with the Heartbreakers live in 1986—might have provided a more coherent collection, as well as being something Dylan might have been willing to promote. The ultimate gesture of contempt for the piece of product that was *Knocked Out Loaded* came when Dylan's forty-date summer tour of the United States resulted in exactly one song from *Knocked Out Loaded* ("Got My Mind Made Up") at just one show (San Diego, the first).

Ironically, the best new song Dylan recorded in 1986 was a one-off, "Band of the Hand," cut with the Heartbreakers one weekend in Sydney, between shows on the antipodean leg of the True Confessions tour, for a forthcoming film soundtrack. Though setting a worrying precedent for Dylan's next celluloid venture—the film itself was an abysmal example of teen gangsters railing at the injustice of it all—the title track provided was actually the best thing in the film (Dylan's ditty should really be known by its subtitle, "It's Helltime, Man"). The song was issued as a single in the United States just in time for the film to plummet out of sight. "Band of the Hand" is a refreshing hint of what *Knocked Out Loaded* might have been if Dylan had stuck to "r&b and Chicago-steeped blues." With the slimmest of melodies, it nevertheless retains the bellicose energy of the possessed, coming a lot closer to the dementia of "Foot of Pride" than the antiseptic material Dylan was set to provide for his own return to acting in *Hearts of Fire*. But then he wasn't as yet burnt out from exhaustion.

DOWN IN THE GROOVE

Recorded: August 27, 1986 to May 1987
Released: May 31, 1988

Side 1: Let's Stick Together. When Did You Leave Heaven? Sally Sue Brown. [Death Is Not the End]. [Had a Dream About You Baby]. Side 2: Ugliest Girl in the World. Silvio. Ninety Miles an Hour (Down a Dead End Street). Shenandoah. Rank Strangers to Me.

HEARTS OF FIRE

Soundtrack Album
Recorded: August 27 and 28, 1986
Released: October 20, 1987

Hearts of Fire: The Usual. Had a Dream About You Baby [V]. Night After Night.

Hearts of Fire [film]
Released: October 9, 1987

The Usual. Had a Dream About You Baby [I]. Night After Night. A Couple More Years.

Other official cuts:

Down in the Groove (Argentina): Got Love If You Want It.

Producers:
1 Beau Hills
2–6 Bob Dylan

Musicians:
1–6 Bob Dylan (guitar/harmonica/vocals)
1 Eric Clapton (guitar)
1 Ron Wood (bass/guitar)
1 Kip Winger (bass)
1 Henry Spinetti (drums)
1 Beau Hills (keyboards)
1 The New West Horns (horns) [overdubs]
2 musicians unknown

3 Dave Alvin (guitar)
3 Steve Douglas (saxophone)
4 Steve Jordan (drums)
4 Randy Jackson (bass)
4 Danny Kortchmar (guitar)
4–5 Stephen Shelton (keyboards)
2–5 Madelyn Quebec (backing vocals)
2–5 Carolyn Dennis (backing vocals)
4 Nathan East (bass)
4 Mike Baird (drums)
4 Raymond Lee Pounds
3–4 James Jameson, Jr.
4 Ross Valory

4 Bill Maxwell
4 Jerry Garcia
4 Bob Weir
4 Bret Mydland
4 Mitchell Froom
5 Larry Klein (bass)
6 Willie Green (backing vocals)
6 Bobby King (backing vocals)
6 Steve Jones (guitar)
6 Myron Grombacher (drums)
6 Paul Simonon (bass)
6 Kevin Savigar (keyboards)

1. TOWNHOUSE STUDIOS
    LONDON
    AUGUST 27 TO 28, 1986
The Usual [I]
The Usual [II]
The Usual [III]
Ride This Train
Had a Dream About You Baby [I]
Had a Dream About You Baby [II]
Had a Dream About You Baby [III]
Had a Dream About You Baby [IV]
Had a Dream About You Baby [V]
Old Five and Dimer Like Me [I]
Old Five and Dimer Like Me [II]
Old Five and Dimer Like Me [III]
Had a Dream About You Baby [VI]
Had a Dream About You Baby [VII]
To Fall in Love with You
Night After Night
A Couple More Years

2. SUNSET SOUND STUDIOS
    LOS ANGELES, CALIFORNIA
    APRIL 3, 1987
Just When I Needed You Most
Important Words

When Did You Leave Heaven?
Willie and the Hand Jive
Twist and Shout

3. SUNSET SOUND STUDIOS
    LOS ANGELES, CALIFORNIA
    APRIL 1987
Look on Yonder Wall
Rollin' and Tumblin'
Red Cadillac and a Black Moustache
Rock with Me Baby [I]
Rock with Me Baby [II]

4. SUNSET SOUND STUDIOS
    LOS ANGELES, CALIFORNIA
    APRIL 1987
Got Love If You Want It
Important Words
Let's Stick Together
Ugliest Girl in the World
Silvio
Shenandoah

5. SUNSET SOUND STUDIOS
    LOS ANGELES, CALIFORNIA
    APRIL 1987
When Did You Leave Heaven?
**Ninety Miles an Hour (Down a Dead End
    Street)***
Rank Strangers to Me

6. MISCELLANEOUS STUDIOS (POSSI-
    BLY MALIBU)
    LOS ANGELES, CALIFORNIA
    MAY 1987
Sally Sue Brown
**Ninety Miles an Hour (Down a Dead End
    Street) [overdubs]**

When he began putting *Knocked Out Loaded* together, Dylan might have thought he could conjure up enough original songs to make an album. After all, he'd done it before with barely half a dozen songs to his name. By the time he came to *Down in the Groove*, he had no such illusions. The studio techniques he had previously abhorred that "touched-up" recordings, overdubbed new instruments, and allowed new vocal tracks or "punch ins," were for the first time in full evidence. This time, though, there would be no new songs.

Dylan had already been required to pull out a couple of covers to meet obligations for a film he had agreed to star in at the end of his summer 1986 tour with the Heartbreakers. At a press conference before filming on *Hearts of Fire* began, Dylan had been asked about the six songs he had supposedly written for the film. He admitted he hadn't as yet written these songs. When the film eventually appeared it did feature five Dylan performances, but "When the Night Comes Falling" was from *Empire Burlesque,* and two execrable originals—"Night After Night" and "Had a Dream About You Baby"—were in the company of a couple of fine covers, John Hiatt's "The Usual" and Shel Silverstein's "A Couple More Years," both proof that Dylan could still be a strong interpreter of others. Three of these four new recordings came from two days in a north London studio just ten days after the press conference where he'd admitted to having no songs in reserve. ("Couple More Years" was almost certainly not recorded at Townhouse. The acoustic version that appears in the film is not on the soundtrack album—despite being the best song in the film by a fair few fathoms—and was probably a very late addition to the soundtrack itself. Dylan is never actually seen singing the song.)

Virtually everything recorded at Townhouse on August 27 and 28 smacked of a man desperate for the smallest shard of an idea. The circulating session tape lacks any alternate versions of "Night after Night" (perhaps it was cut in a single take) but there are three stabs at "The Usual," no less than seven ghastly takes of "Had a Dream About You Baby"—a serious contender for Dylan's worst song—three takes of a "cover" that did not make the film, Billy Joe Shaver's "Old Five and Dimer Like Me," and two improvised half-songs, "Ride This Train" and "To Fall in Love with You." "Old Five and Dimer" was probably intended for the slot in the film where Dylan sings "Couple More Years" to Molly in his barn (one of the versions Dylan recorded is acoustic, a pleasant but antiseptic performance).

Aside from "The Usual," which he managed to find some real passion for, Dylan was unable to pull another worthwhile performance out of his hat until the very end of the Townhouse sessions. After one last turgid attempt at "Had a Dream About You Baby," Dylan slips into one of those studio improvisations that remain a trademark. When the song first sidles onto tape, Dylan is just playing with a riff and speaking in tongues. The first "verse" is unintelligible and sounds vaguely like: "Don't deal go down, might take your ring/Like a dying eye upon the sea/In ages roll, for me from you/What paradise, what can I do." He finally hits upon a refrain, "to fall in love with you," just at the point drummer Henry Spinetti decides to become the bull in this particular china shop. But Dylan will not be dissuaded and perseveres with the idea for a full five minutes, rolling phrases around on his tongue, before giving up on the song, the session, and the soundtrack.

After the half-assed *Knocked Out Loaded* and the cockeyed *Hearts of Fire*, Dylan appears to have begun his next album with some kind of concept in mind. It had been seventeen years since his last album of covers and when sessions began at Sunset Sound at the beginning of April 1987, Dylan was sticking to his brief. According to Dave Alvin, who played on one of these early *Down in the Groove* sessions, Dylan told him that he was working on "Self Portrait Volume Two." As it happens, none of the songs cut at the session with Alvin would make the album, though, according to Alvin, it was quite a productive session:

"It lasted about thirteen hours—there was Al Kooper, James Jamerson, Jr., Stevie Wonder's drummer, Steve Douglas, some other horn players. We did everything from Elmore James's 'Look On Yonder Wall' to 'Rollin' and Tumblin'.' Then it got pretty funny—Bob was playing acoustic, and I joined him on electric, and he said, 'You know this song?' And he started singing this old Warren Smith tune ['Red Cadillac and a Black Moustache']. Then we cut Johnny Carroll's 'Rock with Me Baby'—we cut it once with the core band, and then this girl choir came in with a horn section, and they tracked it again. Instantly, it was like changing the sound from Elvis

Sun to Elvis RCA—very raw, to having this choir singing the chorus. . . . Then I saw him backstage a couple of years later, and he said, 'I'm sorry, Dave, we didn't use any of that stuff, did we? But you know it's gonna come out one of these days, on one of those box sets!'"

There is one other early *Down in the Groove* session for which documentation (in this case, aural documentation) is available. A five-song tape attributed to April 3, 1987—surely one of the first sessions—combined Dylan's preoccupation with postwar crooners with some good old rock and roll. The latter is exemplified by "Willie and the Hand Jive" and "Twist and Shout" while Dylan the crooner warms up for the tempo change with a very straight "Just When I Needed You Most," before attempting arrangements for two songs later recut for the album, "Important Words" and "When Did You Leave Heaven?" (these renditions are no more than prototypes for the versions earmarked for *Down in the Groove*).

Another album of covers was a perfectly logical step for Dylan, especially when, in his own words, he couldn't get into the isolated frame of mind required to write anymore. The central question was what kind of material he had in mind to record. On the basis of the songs cut with Dave Alvin, the two rock-and-roll covers at the April 3 session, and a first side that was (originally) laden with songs like "Let's Stick Together," "Got Love If You Want It," and "Sally Sue Brown," he seemed intent on having another go at the album he had a been working on for the first two weeks of the *Knocked Out Loaded* sessions. Based on cuts like "When Did You Leave Heaven?," "Important Words" and "Shenandoah"; repeated references to singers like Sinatra and Crosby and his wish to make an album of romantic ballads (songs like "I'm in the Mood for

Love," "It's a Sin to Tell a Lie," and so on) in interviews given at the time of *Biograph*; plus a penchant for the occasional "We Three" or "All My Tomorrows Belong to You" on the True Confessions tour, *Down in the Groove* could easily have become a schmaltzy *Self Portrait '87*.

As it is, Dylan's intent all along may have been to show the rich vein of music he listened to when growing up in Hibbing. After all, the eight covers scheduled for the original *Down in the Groove* spanned everything from the 1950s r&r/r&b "frat" of Wilbert Harrison, Clyde McPhatter, Slim Harpo, Arthur Alexander, and Gene Vincent, through those country cousins of rock and roll, The Stanley Brothers and Hank Snow, and back to a traditional favorite of migrant workers, "Shenandoah." All would have been songs he first came across in his "younger days."

Whatever his original intent, he was once again distracted from the task at hand. The album that would be released in May 1988 was, at best, a couple of fifths short of a concept. After amassing quite a number of songs and utilizing some of L.A.'s finest (musicians, that is)—including Raymond Lee Pounds, Ross Valory, Bill Maxwell, Jerry Garcia (cough), Brett Mydland, and Mitchell Froom (serious cough), all absent from the finished album—Dylan took a break in early May to visit Memphis and record with Ringo Starr, before flying up to San Francisco at the beginning of June to rehearse for a forthcoming tour with the Grateful Dead at the Club Front in Marin County. During these rehearsals, Dylan was apparently supplied with two lyrics by official Dead lyricist Robert Hunter, both in need of tunes. What "Silvio" and "Ugliest Girl in the World" were most in need of was a trash can. Yet Dylan seemed willing to change a couple of words around, transpose a couple of old riffs he had lying around and, voilà, two new Dylan/ Hunter songs.

On his return to L.A. Dylan proceeded to cut both songs with the core *Down in the Groove* musicians. If "Ugliest Girl in the World" makes "Some Girls" sound profound, "Silvio" was the album's most curious addition. I presume "Silvio" is Hunter's idea of the Dylanesque. It certainly has nearly as many fake Dylanisms as "When the Night Comes Falling" (for "going down to the valley to sing my song," try "I'll stand on the ocean until I start sinking, and I'll know my song well"), even though Dylan has been known to make it sound quite convincing in concert. Yet even these belated intrusions did not entirely tip the album off its axis.

Down in the Groove was readied for release in the fall of 1987 with an original sequence that ran:

1. Let's Stick Together
2. When Did You Leave Heaven?
3. Got Love If You Want It
4. Ninety Miles an Hour (Down a Dead End Street)
5. Sally Sue Brown (end of side one)
6. Ugliest Girl in the World
7. Silvio
8. Important Words
9. Shenandoah
10. Rank Strangers to Me

However, between approving a test pressing and promotional copies being sent out, Dylan decided the second side required a little more sonic clout and substituted John Hiatt's "The Usual" (from the *Hearts of Fire* soundtrack, complete with overdubbed horns, a somewhat discordant note) for Gene Vincent's "Important Words." "The Usual," the one worthwhile cut on the *Hearts of Fire* soundtrack album (it was actually released as a single in Europe),

even though it lacks a fifties vintage, quite complemented the various shots of rhythm and blues already gracing side one. Duly amended promotional copies were prepared and (this time) sent out, only for Dylan to be struck down with Youngitis again (a condition that manifests itself in the constant recalling of finished albums). As the most interesting vinyl anomaly since *Freewheelin'* Mk. 1, this "original" *Down in the Groove* (with "The Usual," not "Important Words") was accidentally released in Argentina, though there are no clues on the Argentinian cover or label to betray its alternate contents.

Seemingly determined to convince fans that all he could now muster was a series of stopgap releases, Dylan for the second time in a year abandoned an album that held together for one permed from trash cans. Pulling "Got Love If You Want It" *and* "The Usual," Dylan replaced them with one outtake from *Infidels,* the unredeemable "Death Is Not the End" (rather than, say, "Blind Willie McTell" or "Foot of Pride"), and his recent lowest-of-the-low "Had a Dream About You Baby" (which found its true bedfellow alongside "The Ugliest Girl in the World"). The running order, which had previously placed the bulk of the blasters on side A (the second side remaining more reflective), was tossed aside. That death knell to inspiration "Death Is Not the End" now sat squat still in the middle of side A, soaking up any energy that surrounded it.

The original *Down in the Groove*—balanced by "Important Words" and "Got Love If You Want It"—was no great artistic endeavor, but at least it was an album one could sit through, with some evidence that Dylan's vocal powers were not fading quite as fast as his songwriting skills. The *Down in the Groove* as released, coming hard on the heels of *Knocked Out Loaded,* confirmed in many an ex-fan's mind that the man had nothing left to say. Here, after all, are surely the two most disappointing albums in Dylan's entire twenty-nine album catalogue. That these albums coincided with two of Dylan's most disappointing tours (the U.S. 1986 Heartbreakers tour and the summer 1987 Dylan/Dead fiasco) made a gaping hole in popular perceptions of the man as enduring artist that he has never been quite able to bridge. Yet Dylan's final creative renaissance (to date) was not so far down the road he was now committing himself to.

TRAVELING WILBURYS VOLUME I

Recorded: April 3 to May 16, 1988
Released: October 18, 1988

Side l: Handle with Care. Dirty World. Rattled. Last Night. Not Alone Anymore. Side 2: Congratulations. Heading for the Light. Margarita. Tweeter and the Monkey Man. End of the Line.

TRAVELING WILBURYS VOLUME III

Recorded: April 1990
Released: October 23, 1990

Side l: She's My Baby. Inside Out. If You Belonged to Me. The Devil's Been Busy. Seven Deadly Sins. Poor House. Side 2: Where Were You Last Night? Cool Dry Place. New Blue Moon. You Took My Breath Away. Wilbury Twist.

Other official cuts:

45: Nobody's Child.
45: Runaway.

Producers:
1–3 Jeff Lynne and George Harrison

Musicians:

1–3 Bob Dylan (guitar/vocals/harmonica)	1–2 Roy Orbison (guitar/vocals)
1–3 Tom Petty (guitar/vocals)	1–3 Jim Keltner (drums)
1–3 George Harrison (guitar/vocals)	2–3 Ray Cooper (percussion)
1–3 Jeff Lynne (guitar/keyboards/vocals)	2–3 Jim Horn (saxophone)

1. BOB DYLAN'S GARAGE STUDIO
   MALIBU, CALIFORNIA
   EARLY APRIL 1988
Handle with Care

2. DAVE STEWART'S HOME STUDIO
   LOS ANGELES, CALIFORNIA
   MAY 7 TO 16, 1988
Dirty World [I]
Dirty World [II]
Rattled

Last Night
Not Alone Anymore
Congratulations
Heading for the Light
Margarita
Tweeter and the Monkey Man
End of the Line

3. WILBURY MOUNTAIN STUDIO
    BEL AIR, CALIFORNIA
    EARLY TO MID-APRIL 1990
She's My Baby*
Inside Out*
If You Belonged to Me*

The Devil's Been Busy*
Seven Deadly Sins*
Poor House*
Where Were You Last Night?*
Cool Dry Place
New Blue Moon [I]*
New Blue Moon [II]
You Took My Breath Away
Wilbury Twist
Like a Ship
Maxine
Runaway*
Nobody's Child

The two Traveling Wilburys albums—*Volume I* and *Volume III*—are bookends to the third, and briefest, of Dylan's great creative bursts (1962 to 1967, 1974 to 1983, and 1988 to 1990). The first volume not only revived interest in Dylan but was, for all of the quintet save Petty, their most successful venture of the 1980s. *Volume I* was the surprise hit of 1988. Its sequel, recorded a matter of weeks after Dylan completed his second album in less than a year, was the big flop of 1990.

The circumstances that resulted in the very first Wilburys session are well-documented. George Harrison needed to record a bonus track for a twelve-inch European-only 45 and was strapped for a studio he could use at short notice. Jeff Lynne, once a member of the Idle Race, who'd volunteered to produce the session, suggested Dylan's garage studio in Malibu (when Dylan closed Rundown in 1982, he had arranged for all the recording equipment to be installed in his garage). When they phoned, Dylan said, "Sure, come on over." Harrison had to pick up his guitar from Tom Petty, who decided to tag along. Orbison, who was working on an album with Lynne at the time, was also at a loose end that day.

The song Harrison wanted to record, a jaunty little ditty called "Handle with Care," had a couple of unfinished lines. Dylan and Petty obligingly offered sug-

gestions. They now had a song to record. With Jim Keltner playing the invisible Wilbury, they cut "Handle with Care" in a single day, Dylan's primary contribution being that unmistakable harmonica whine on the fade.

When Harrison presented the song to Warners, they informed him it was far too good for a B side. Realizing how enjoyable the recording of "Handle With Care" had been, Harrison suggested a more long-term collaboration—an album of songs by George Harrison, Bob Dylan, Jeff Lynne, Tom Petty, and Roy Orbison, aka the Traveling Wilburys. The quintet reconvened the first week in May 1988 to see whether they could create a whole album of affectionate pop along the lines of "Handle with Care." As Harrison later put it, "We had nine or ten days that we knew we could get Bob for . . . We said, "We'll write a tune a day and do it that way."

Three and a bit songs on *Volume I* feature a Dylan singing lead (all bear his lyrical stamp) including one major effort, "Tweeter and the Monkey Man," apparently cut in just two takes. According to Harrison, the song was the result of "Tom Petty and Bob sitting in the kitchen . . . talking about all this stuff which didn't make sense to me— Americana kind of stuff." If the obvious hook for the song was the New Jersey minioperas pioneered by Bruce Springsteen at peak powers (1973 to '78), it also had a less obvious model, Townes Van Zandt's "Pancho and Lefty," a song introduced into the Never Ending Tour (in lieu of "Tweeter and the Monkey Man"?) during the summer of 1989. Using a similar combination of rogues on the wrong side of the law, a wistful longing for the outlaw times depicted, and a comparable ballad structure, Dylan carved out a truly surreal tale as convoluted and as riddled with disguises as "Lily, Rosemary and the Jack of Hearts." Although it shared a clever arrangement and catchy production with the other nine cuts, "Tweeter and the Monkey Man" had very little in common with the immensely enjoyable fluff that made up the remainder of *Volume I.*

The quintet presumably did not expect the resultant album to go double-platinum, or that a huge demand for a sequel would arise, or that they would lose Roy Orbison, the most palatable singer on *Volume I,* in the interim. When the remaining quartet reassembled in April 1990 to record a second album, whimsically dubbed *Volume III,* holing up at a palatial Spanish-style ranch house in Bel-Air and using Dave Stewart's home studio, that fine Wilburys equilibrium was no longer intact.

The original tapes of *Volume III* come across at times like the Wilburys' equivalent of *The White Album*—each song seems to have a far more identifiable author, and the vocal duties are self-evidently less democratic. The dominant figure in proceedings first time around would be hard to identify. This time it was unquestionably Dylan, at least in the songwriting/vocal departments, something Jeff Lynne and George Harrison then attempted to mask during mixing.

Fifteen songs were the sum total from the *Volume III* sessions, two of which were covers—"Nobody's Child" and Del Shannon's "Runaway." (Both only released on singles, the former as a benefit for a Romanian children's fund set up by George Harrison's wife, the latter as

a B side to "She's My Baby.") Of the thirteen originals they cut, Dylan sang lead on six, as well as taking his share of vocal duties on a further three. Only "Maxine," sung by Harrison (but omitted from the album), "You Took My Breath Away" (ditto), "Poor House," sung by Petty, and "Cool Dry Place," sung by Lynne, passed over Dylan's dulcet tones entirely. Effectively, Dylan was vocalist on more than half the album.

Volume III as released, though, once again presented a somewhat distorted picture. In the summer of 1990, the original tapes were taken back to Henley-on-Thames by Lynne and Harrison, who attempted to make a Wilburys album out of these "Dylan and friends" tapes. One Dylan track, "Like a Ship," was dropped from the album, though it is actually one of the most Wilbury-like songs from the sessions. The essential idea (like a ship on the sea her love rolls over him) has a corny charm lacking in some of *Volume III*'s more earnest efforts. The serious ecological concerns of "Inside Out" and "The Devil's Been Busy" hardly accorded with the whimsy of *Volume I*—although they had an awful lot in common with Dylan's latest work, *Under the Red Sky* ("the man in the moon went home and the river went dry" could have been a line in either song).

One Dylan lead vocal was mysteriously transformed into a Wilburys ensemble performance. "She's My Baby"—as originally recorded—was another solo Dylan affair. The version on the album, though, replete with inappropriate overdubs by ex-Lizzy guitarist Gary Moore, has all the Wilburys singing a verse apiece over a pounding drum introduction presumably grafted at a later date. If anything showed that Lynne (and possibly Harrison) had no real idea what made *Volume I* such a massive hit, it was the new "She's My Baby," guaranteed to alienate most of the thirtysomethings who'd hummed along to the catchy "Handle with Care."

Other, subtler changes were also made at Dylan's expense. Though most of his vocals on "Where Were You Last Night?" survived, an annoying harmony vocal replaced his on the title phrase as repeated at the end of each verse. His vocal contribution to "Seven Deadly Sins" was also partially snipped at Henley. Even most of Dylan's harmonica-playing lost out to Lynne's "layering." On both "Poor House" and "Runaway," there had been a frantic harmonica sawing away on the original tapes that is inaudible on the released versions. An instrumental version of "New Blue Moon," with Dylan keeping up a breathless harmonica accompaniment throughout, also bit ferric dust.

Whether a closer approximation to the original tapes would have sold any better than the *Volume III* released is the stuff of conjecture but some of the "fix-ups," particularly on "She's My Baby," were hardly in keeping with the original Wilbury concept, "a very self-contained group . . . five Wilburys and one roadie." Also, leaving "Runaway" off the album might have made sense, but omitting Dylan's "Like a Ship" and Harrison's "Maxine" from

a thirty-six-minute CD was inexcusable.

What Dylan thought of the final album has not been documented. The original tapes—though Dylan's vocals lack some of the leathery toughness evident on *Under the Red Sky*—do contain the easy informality of *Volume I,* along with a tablespoon of sloppiness, for which we can presumably thank Dylan. Given that the Wilburys were never likely to rekindle the indefinable charm of *Volume I,* Dylan's domination of the proceedings second time around at least allowed for an authentic "old-time" feel, the Wilburys songs contrasting nicely with darker portrayals of love and a world gone wrong being released by Dylan at the time. It is hard not to conclude that much of worth was needlessly sanitized by Lynne and Harrison in their attempts to replicate the unique good-time feel of *Volume I.* If they had been paying attention to the two albums Dylan recorded between *Volume I* and *Volume III*—and Harrison had actually contributed to the much underrated *Under the Red Sky*—they would have realized the impossibility of their task given their reliance on Dylan's creative input.

OH MERCY

Recorded: March 7 to March 24, 1989
Released: September 22, 1989

Side 1: Political World. Where Teardrops Fall. Everything Is Broken. Ring Them Bells. Man in the Long Black Coat. Side 2: Most of the Time. What Good Am I? Disease of Conceit. What Was It You Wanted? Shooting Star.

Other official cuts:

The Bootleg Series: Series of Dreams.
Greatest Hits Vol. 3: Dignity.

Producer:

1–3 Daniel Lanois

Musicians:

1–3 Bob Dylan (piano/harmonica/guitar/
       organ/vocals)
1–3 Daniel Lanois (lap steel/dobro/guitar/
       omnichord)
1 Paul Synegal (guitar)
1 Larry Jolivet (bass)
1 Alton Rubin, Jr. (scrub board)
1 John Hart (sax)
1 Rockin' Dopsie (accordion)

2–3 Malcolm Burn (keyboards/bass/-
       tambourine)
2 Mason Ruffner (guitar)
2 Brian Stoltz (guitar)
2 Tony Hall (bass)
2 Cyril Neville (percussion)
2 Willie Green (drums)
2 Daryl Johnson (percussion)

1. STUDIO ON THE MOVE
    EMLAH COURT
    NEW ORLEANS, LOUISIANA
    EARLY MARCH 1989
Where Teardrops Fall

2. STUDIO ON THE MOVE
    1305 SONIAT
    NEW ORLEANS, LOUISIANA
    MARCH 7 TO MARCH 24, 1989
Political World *
"Broken Days" *
Ring Them Bells [I]
Ring Them Bells [II]
Man in the Long Black Coat
Most of the Time *

What Good Am I? *
Disease of Conceit *
What Was It You Wanted? *
Shooting Star [I]
Shooting Star [II]
Shooting Star [III]
Dignity *
Born in Time *
God Knows
Series of Dreams

3. VOCAL OVERDUBS
    STUDIO ON THE MOVE
    1305 SONIAT
    NEW ORLEANS, LOUISIANA
    APRIL 3 TO APRIL 12, 1989

Oh Mercy—perhaps the closest to a chimerical "best since Blood," post-Infidels Dylan may ever come—is one of the most un-Dylanesque albums in the man's oeuvre. Its sound, and the whole way that sound was arrived at, was not achieved by a live setup, but through careful sculpting and honing by Dylan, under the guidance of in-vogue Canadian producer Daniel Lanois. The last album of Dylan's (to date) to make major concessions to technology in the studio, Oh Mercy is the product of a way of thinking that takes as its starting point Sgt. Pepper, not John Wesley Harding.

And yet Oh Mercy did not signal a new Dylan, finally at one with the studio. Rather, it represents one final struggle with the beast before returning to more primitive preferences. Oh Mercy succeeded where Empire Burlesque, Knocked Out Loaded, and Down in the Groove failed, by bending existing technology to the songs' collective will. The swamp sounds that Lanois wrapped around Dylan's first all-original effort in four years were hardly accidental. Lanois had first been recommended to Dylan by U2's Bono, someone who obviously felt that he needed a "real" producer, and thought that Lanois might fit the bill. So while in New Orleans to play a show in September 1988, Dylan called on Lanois and heard some of the songs he had recorded with the Neville Brothers for their Yellow Moon album (two of which came from Dylan's protesty third album, "With God on Our Side" and "Hollis Brown"). Dylan had recently signed a new contract with Sony and was aware of the need to make an album that had impact. However, he was reluctant to reimmerse himself in the L.A. studio circuit that had proved so unproductive in the recent past. Witnessing the easy informality of Lanois's setup, Dylan began to conceive of a modern-sounding album that could be made without the tedious rigmarole of studio etiquette.

Bob Dylan: "[In New Orleans] you don't have to walk through secretaries, pinball machines and managers and hangers-on in the lobby, and parking lots and elevators, and arctic temperatures."

Badly in need of something to confound the doom merchants hard at work on his epitaph (unaware that it had already been included in Tarantula), Dylan was prepared to allow Lanois the sort of input not given any of his "coproducers" since Wexler, bowing to his recommendations for musicians and allowing him the benefit of the doubt when it came to crafting a unified sound.

That said, just as soon as Dylan, Lanois, and Lanois's assistant, Malcolm Burns, convened at New Orleans's Emlah Court, at the beginning of March 1989, things went awry.

Just two songs were recorded at Emlah Court before it was agreed that a relocation was in order. The track on Oh Mercy that sounds unlike anything else on the album, "Where Teardrops Fall," may well have originated at Emlah Court. The only Oh Mercy song to feature pedal steel, sax, or accordion, "Where Teardrops Fall" seemed like an unfortunate continuation of the mawkish balladry of Empire Burlesque.

Later in the sessions Dylan was to tackle the same theme with much greater insight, on the magnificent "Born in Time," before rejecting it from his final song selection. Dylan's rationale for preferring "Where Teardrops Fall" over "Born in Time" would certainly be fascinating to know, as would his reasons for releasing the utterly fake vocal he gave the latter on *Under the Red Sky* (something that seems like the complete antithesis of a previous ideal: "use the take that gets to the heart of the song and screw any technical flaws," in case you haven't been paying attention). Not only does the *Oh Mercy* "Born in Time" have a vocal to warp the most sturdy heartstring but it shares the same feel and sound as the remainder of the album. "Where Teardrops Fall" comes from an altogether different basket of crawfish.

That *Oh Mercy*'s alluringly subterranean sound was more a product of Lanois's sensibility than Dylan's seems indisputable. One listen to Lanois's own *Arcadia* should clinch the matter. After all, Lanois remains a musician in his own right (something that certainly endeared him to Dylan). With a band of willing cohorts on call—guitarists Mason Ruffner and Brian Stoltz, bassist Tony Hall, and drummer Willie Green—Lanois came complete with a whole textural environment to hang Dylan's songs on. And that sound lent itself naturally to Dylan's music at this point precisely because of the fluidity of his new song structures. A song like "Series of Dreams" self-consciously sets out to achieve a dreamlike state, separate from conventional linear time (in this sense it might almost be a modern-day "Sad Eyed Lady of the Lowlands"). Dylan obviously liked this approach. "Born in Time" shares this dare-I-say-it timeless quality; the verses, even the bridge, flowing down the same stream of consciousness, so that when Dylan sings, "Just when I knew who to thank, you

went blank," it sounds like the line just occurred to him (what looks dumb on paper finagles the ears just fine, trust me).

Dylan, once again, had achieved a breakthrough in his songwriting, one that has gone largely unrecognized. After hankering after reinterpreting Tin Pan Alley song forms on *Empire Burlesque* and *Knocked Out Loaded*, the key songs on *Oh Mercy* seek to deconstruct traditional forms. A song like "Most of the Time" uses its shallow line and verse breaks to extract multiple layers of meaning from every choice phrase—the way that "And I don't pretend" both concludes a thought ("I don't compromise and . . . ") and begins a new one ("I don't even care/if I ever see her again") being just one (particularly fine) example. On songs like "Most of the Time," "What Good Am I?," "Series of Dreams," "Political World," and "Dignity," Dylan seems to be taking a single thought, shattering it and following each shard part of the way.

On "Political World" the trick fails because the idea itself ("We live in a political world . . . ") cannot sustain the song, even though Dylan (and Lanois) worked long and hard on the track, cutting and pasting a whole series of vocal tracks to the same basic groove. Whole verses, including a splendid one about wine, women, and song (and how one can get by without the first two, but without the third one wouldn't last long), got snipped as the song was pared down (from five to three and a bit minutes), without ever achieving Essence of "Political World." If this approach didn't work on "Political World," it paid its way most of the time.

Dylan has always tended to write and rewrite in the studio, even when this has required him to cut a song again with the musicians on hand. Only when rerecording a lyrically dense song like "Jokerman," at the *Infidels* mixing sessions, did he seem to recognize the opportunity that modern multitrack recording afforded him to cut a new vocal *after* recording a usable basic track. With at least twenty-four "bands of sound" to play with, an engineer could (indeed should) always leave four or five tracks open for Dylan to overdub new vocals (affording him the chance to work on lyrics to the death, all the while stockpiling basic tracks with the musicians). Such an approach hardly qualified as innovation by 1989. It was standard working practice for a rock vocalist to lay down just a guide vocal when cutting a basic track, and then return to overdub the real thing. Dylan, though, was no ordinary singer-songwriter. With him a first vocal take might only contain 40 percent of the finished song.

A good example of this is "Shooting Star." You would have to be either atonally perverse or searching for the other 50 percent of your wits to think either of the (two) extant outtakes equal to the released version, one of Dylan's most affecting album "closers." Yet as an insight into Dylan's art and his working processes the alternates are invaluable (hence the popularity of bootlegs of studio outtakes; for a more detailed discussion see the "Aesthetics" section in *Bootleg*). Musically, "Shooting Star" is pretty much there even on the outtakes, save that it lacks even a frustratingly terse harmonica fade like the one that concludes the real McCoy. The apocalyptic middle-eight ("Listen to the engine . . .") is also intact, as is the shooting star motif. Yet the verses lack any definite resolution, being simply a series of lines in search of the evocative. Perhaps it was Dylan's original intention for the song to have the same kind of free-form feel as the preceding song, "What Was It You Wanted?" If so, he wisely decided to afford the song a more traditional framework and the album a fitting finale, albeit one that remains a most Dylanesque fusion of the apocalyptic and the wistful.

When Dylan rewrote "Shooting Star" is not known. However, it was probably one of the songs he worked on after they finished recording basic tracks for the album in late March—that is, before and/or during the series of overdub and mixing sessions that began in early April.

The basic tracks for *Oh Mercy* had been cut with Dylan's usual alacrity, in just three weeks, after Lanois relocated his Studio on the Move to 1305 Soniat. Dylan liked having the opportunity to work on songs alone, or with just Lanois and Burns on hand, without racking up studio time and/or scale. He also liked to know that he could get musicians at short notice when something more concrete came from an idea. The five track sheets from the sessions that I have been able to access certainly bear out Dylan's odd working hours:

"God Knows"—recorded between midnight and 4:18 A.M. on March 9
"Ring Them Bells"—recorded between 00:56 and 4:01 A.M., date unknown
Untitled song—recorded between 4:16 and 8:49 A.M. on March 12
"Dignity"—recorded between 8:56 A.M. and 7:43 P.M. on March 13
"Broken Days"—recorded between 7:54 and 11:56 P.M. on March 14

Based on these track sheets, Dylan does not seem to have entirely abandoned his cut and run approach. All of the basic tracks for these five songs, "Dignity" excepted, were "got down on tape" (to lapse into the parlance) in around four hours. The new, "disciplined" Dylan, though, was not about to sing a dummy vocal even when cutting a basic track. Here was one vocalist always trying to get a finished take, even if only "Man in the Long Black Coat" and "Ring Them Bells" appear to have retained their original vocals on the album. (There is an alternate "Ring Them Bells," in circulation, but it is a solo piano version, possibly an early demo—apart from anything else, it has an abnormally high level of hiss—though it is lyrically identical to the album, suggesting that this was one song he did not tinker with unduly. Possibly this is [the other] song attempted at Emlah Court.) All the remaining tracks on *Oh Mercy* appear to have had vocal tracks overdubbed, although some of the original vocals (assuming these are the vocals found on circulating *Oh Mercy* outtakes) sound only marginally inferior to their latter incarnations. (On "What Was It You Wanted?" the differences are almost imperceptible.)

What the five track sheets in question also detail is the dates when vocal overdubs were done. They suggest that there were ten days or so in early April when Dylan, Lanois, and Burns reworked the songs (some instruments were also overdubbed, although mostly in late April when Dylan was safely ensconced back in New York City). According to the available sheets, vocal overdubs were as follows:

"God Knows"—March 16 (that is one week after the original session, during the band sessions) and April 10. Two outtakes of this song circulate, one of which has some extended harmonica work. Of course, this song did not actually make *Oh Mercy*, being held over until *Under the Red Sky*. Of all the omissions this remains the most understandable, as well as that rarity, a song improved by its latter-day incarnation.

"Ring Them Bells"—"track twelve" (on the twenty-four-track) says "vocal (live)." Track eleven says "tele: Bob" (meaning Dylan's telecaster guitar presumably), as well as "end is good," and a date of April 6, suggesting that Dylan overdubbed some guitar on this date but left his original vocal intact.

Unknown song—lists a new vocal on April 12.

"Dignity"—has three vocal overdubs attributed to it, though only numbers two and three are dated, both to April 11 (presumably also the date of overdub number one). The third vocal overdub is also given the soubriquet, "woman lyrics." Hmmm. Since the take that appears on various bootlegs has the same vocal track (though fuck-all else) as the wretched husk of a song issued on *Greatest Hits Vol. 3* presumably one vocal track (or composite) got the vote way back in April 1989. "Dignity" was presumably still under serious consideration for *Oh Mercy* at this stage, given the effort implied in this many overdubs. Its omission from *Oh Mercy,* presumably to make way for the trite "Disease of Conceit," was a serious oversight, albeit one best left uncorrected if the only correction involved was the sort of musical plastering applied on *Greatest Hits Vol. 3*. (If all the reader has as a reference point is the *Greatest Hits Vol. 3* abortion he will be wholly unprepared for the delights of "Dignity"'s untainted self. Wiping the entire backing track, retaining just Dylan's 1989 vocal, which is then buried deep in the sand and glue of quasi-grunge, I might just compare with drawing a mustache, horn-rims, and thick, bushy eyebrows on the Mona Lisa and asking someone to recognize its power all the same. Even Dylan's piano, the fire in this particular engine room, has been wiped by 1994's answer to Arthur Baker, Brendan O'Brien.) On the original song, the interplay between Brian Stoltz's guitar, Dylan's piano, and Lanois's "rockabilly dobro" (as it is identified on the track sheet) gives the song a momentum all its own. "Foot of Pride" revisited it may be, but "Dignity" deserved better (as it happens, the *Unplugged* performance almost delivers the goods).

"Broken Days" is one of Dylan's "lost" songs though it ostensibly appeared on *Oh Mercy* as "Everything Is Broken." Listed cryptically on the track sheet as "Broken Days/Three of Us," this song was given a serious overhaul at the April sessions. Two new vocal tracks, both dated April 3, are also annotated "(new words)." New words, indeed. "Broken Days" was actually an apposite title for the original song, which cleverly compares/contrasts various malaises of the late twentieth-century with the fragmenting of a personal relationship(s). Though one of those songs that is "just a riff," "Broken Days" worked, in its own, thoroughly unpretentious way. But when Dylan came to rerecord not just a new vocal, but also his guitar *and* (additional) harmonica on April 3, he stripped the song of most of its romantic allusions so that it comes across as just another diatribe on "the shape of things to come"—"Political World" Part Two. Coming third in the groove to "Political World" (Part One) and the kitsch melodrama of "Where Teardrops Fall," "Everything Is Broken" gave few clues as to the creative renaissance evidenced by six of the remaining seven cuts on the album.

The other *Oh Mercy* song that has an attributed recording date is "Series of Dreams," one of the last songs to be recorded. According to *The Bootleg Series* notes, "Series of Dreams" was recorded on March 24, the penultimate session with Ruffner, Stoltz, Hall, and Green. Although there is no reason to suggest that this is not the date when the basic track was recorded, the vocal track on *The Bootleg Series* is self-evidently a composite of (at least) two separate vocal tracks, both from the April vocal overdub sessions (the one saving grace on *Greatest Hits Vol. 3* is that it has a complete "Series of Dreams" minus that infuriating fade in). The dead giveaway to an edited vocal can be found on the version of "Series of Dreams," that appeared on a 1991 Columbia "promo only" five-track *Bootleg Series* sampler. This should have been the same take as on *The Bootleg Series*, but it has two

lines that do not appear on the official track ("Suddenly the gate is thrown open/And you're left there holding the bag" in place of "And there's no exit in any direction/'Cept the one you can't see with your eyes") while deriving from the same basic track. Apart from anything else, the take on *The Bootleg Series* has just lost the rhyme at line's end—"eyes" does not rhyme with "drag" (it should actually rhyme with "flies," which is how Dylan ends the line "Where the time and the tempo drag/flies" on the "other" take). Evidently somebody screwed up somewhere down the line, probably when bouncing from one vocal track to another on the original multitrack.

Another alternate "Series of Dreams," apparently the same one that was given to the director of the promotional video, has one of these vocal tracks in its original, unsullied form. Finally, the original *Oh Mercy* outtake that came collectors' way in 1990, aside from containing an entire extra verse, has what is presumably the original live vocal over a pre-overdubbed backing track. As such, it remains the most authentic example of Dylan's original intentions.

Confused? Well, "Series of Dreams" on *The Bootleg Series,* aside from any vocal/instrumental overdubs made in April 1989, has been subjected to a couple of extraneous overdubs in January 1991. Though these '91 synths glisten away pleasantly enough, they do disguise some of the song's original sensibility which, I'd like to believe, intended to rely on only the most muted of melodic refrains to offset its strange rhythmic undercurrents and overlapping lines (reminiscent of the way Dylan and Alk used sounds in *Renaldo and Clara*—something also apparent in the "Series of Dreams" promo video, which is certainly one way into this most dense of songs).

"Series of Dreams" was apparently suggested to *Bootleg Series* compiler Jeff

Rosen by Dylan fanzine editor John Bauldie after Daniel Lanois had indicated, in an interview, that this was one song he wanted on the album but Dylan would not allow it. Rosen later admitted that if he had heard "Dignity" when compiling his boxed set he would have included that song. The omission of "Born in Time," "Dignity," and "Series of Dreams" from *Oh Mercy* only confirmed that Dylan's grasp of his own material was increasingly failing him as the eighties progressed. Including these cuts on *Oh Mercy*—and jettisoning "Political World," "Where Teardrops Fall," and "Disease of Conceit" (that doctor verse is strictly tenth-grade stuff)—would have ensured that *Oh Mercy*'s critical vogue extended beyond the "best since *Infidels*" temporality of contemporary reviews, into the domain of genuine classics.

1 KICK	**9** BOB ELECTRIC	**17** (BKg in 2nd Br. lit li. (H-Hand) (CLEAN UP) Bob Vocal (New WORDS) #1 3/4/89
2 SNARE 414	**10** Bob Tele Rtb o D. #1 6/4/89	**18** TAMBO (MB)
3 SNARE BETERU	**11** BASS FIX UP SAFTY #3	**19** BRIAN GTR COMP *
4 PERC. DARYL "GOOD THROUGHOUT"	**12** LEAD VOCAL #1 ANS- A = 395 - 1.005 +3 B = 390 - 0.995 +3	**20** (CLEAN UP) Bob Harp #1 #2 3/4/89.
5 DANS DOBRO	**13** DARYL TAKE CONSOS #2 SAFTY GOOD FILL ON INTRO - GOOD OUTRO	**21** BASS COMP *
6 BASS	**14** BRIAN SAFTY GTR. #2 SAFTY "2ND SOLO"	**22** VOCAL #2 COMP (NEW WORDS) 3/4/89
7 BRIANS GTR	**15** Bob O.D TELE ? 3/4/89	**23** VOC COMP. #1 3/4/89
8 BOBS GTR DI	**16** (Good in bridges + outro) DAN Elec/dobro 3/4/89	**24** D.L. RIFF COMP. *

UNDER THE RED SKY

Recorded: January 6 to March 1990
Released: September 11, 1990

Side 1: Wiggle Wiggle. Under the Red Sky. Unbelievable. Born in Time. T.V. Talkin' Song. Side 2: 10,000 Men. 2 × 2. God Knows. Handy Dandy. Cat's in the Well.

Other official cuts:

Most of the Time [promo CD]: Most of the Time.

Producers:
1–6 Don and David Was

Musicians:

1–6 Bob Dylan (piano/guitar/harmonica/
        vocals)
1 Jimmie Vaughan (guitar)
1 Stevie Ray Vaughan (guitar)
1–2, 4 David Lindley (slide guitar)
1 Jamie Muhoberac (organ)
1, 4 Don Was (bass)
1–2, 4 Kenny Aronoff (drums)
1 Paulinho Da Costa (percussion)
2, 4 Randy Jackson (bass)
3 NRBQ

4 Robben Ford (guitar)
4 Bruce Hornsby (piano)
4, 6 Waddy Wachtel (guitar)
4, 6 Al Kooper (keyboards)
6 Slash (guitar)
6 Dave Crosby (backing vocals)
6 George Harrison (guitar)
6 Elton John (piano)
6 David McMurray (sax)
6 Rayse Biggs (trumpet)

1. OCEANWAY STUDIOS
    LOS ANGELES, CALIFORNIA
    JANUARY 6, 1990
10,000 Men
God Knows
Handy Dandy [I]
Handy Dandy [II]
Cat's in the Well

2. CULVER CITY STUDIOS
    CULVER CITY, CALIFORNIA
    MARCH 2, 1990
Most of the Time

3. THE COMPLEX
    LOS ANGELES, CALIFORNIA
    MID-MARCH 1990
Some Enchanted Evening

4. THE COMPLEX
    LOS ANGELES, CALIFORNIA
    MID- TO LATE MARCH 1990
Wiggle Wiggle *
Under the Red Sky [II] *
Unbelievable *
Born in Time [I]
Born in Time [II]*
T.V. Talkin' Song [I]
T.V. Talkin' Song [II] *

2 × 2 [I]
2 × 2 [II] *
Shirley Temple Don't Live Here Anymore

5. VOCAL OVERDUBS
   THE RECORD PLANT AND THE
   COMPLEX
   LOS ANGELES, CALIFORNIA
   LATE MARCH TO EARLY APRIL 1990
Wiggle Wiggle
Under the Red Sky
Unbelievable [I]
Unbelievable [II]
Born in Time [I]
Born in Time [II]
T.V. Talkin' Song [overdub of I]

T.V. Talkin' Song [overdub of II]
2 × 2 [I]
2 × 2 [II]

6. INSTRUMENTAL OVERDUBS
   THE RECORD PLANT AND THE
   COMPLEX
   LOS ANGELES, CALIFORNIA
   APRIL 1990
Wiggle Wiggle
Under the Red Sky
Born in Time
2 × 2
Handy Dandy
Cat's in the Well

Under the Red Sky has quickly become the Dylan album responsible for the strongest disagreements among Mr. D's remaining fans. Even those with a sneaking fondness for *Self Portrait* or *Down in the Groove* would hardly place them in Dylan's hall of fame. *Under the Red Sky* seems to be an album that can be denigrated as his worst (all original) collection, while also being championed as one of his finest recent works. I fall into the latter camp. Though some consider it not much more than an afterthought after the resurgence hinted at by the Wilburys and affirmed by *Oh Mercy,* I believe *Under the Red Sky* to have a far greater sense of identity than its badly executed predecessor (unquestionably *Oh Mercy* could have made premium grade, but we're talking about the album as released here).

Perhaps I should qualify the above. First up, I have not been privileged enough to hear any songs that were rejected from *Under the Red Sky,* though one title referred to by Don Was—"Shirley Temple Don't Live Here Anymore"—sounds intriguing. Also there are at least two songs on the album cut short by premature fades, "Wiggle Wiggle" and "God Knows," the latter fade actually cutting into the final couplet ("God knows I'd get from here to there/If I had to walk a million miles by

candlelight"), one problematic vocal performance ("Born in Time"), and one inexcusable call (the version of "T.V. Talkin' Song," a counterfeit reflection of its earlier self). The album also lacks the nerve-tingling insight of a "Most of the Time."

That said, *Under the Red Sky* works as an album and *Oh Mercy* does not. *Oh Mercy* is a collection of songs, *Under the Red Sky* is a single edifice, every girder in its assigned place. Those who harp on about this or that weak track are not asking themselves does the album flow? Does time slide away? If, throughout the 1980s, Dylan was guilty of releasing collections of songs that lacked internal integrity—*Empire Burlesque,* though the exception, was chockful of clunkers—the songs on *Under the Red Sky* require their context.

Recorded at the tail end of a highly fertile two-year period that resulted in two all-original Dylan efforts plus two Wilburys albums, *Under the Red Sky* was cut over two sets of sessions, two and a half months apart. I say two sets of sessions, but the first "set" was actually a solitary session, at the beginning of January 1990, arranged with the primary intention of recording a new version of an *Oh Mercy* outtake, "God Knows" (the Was brothers had been given a piano demo of the song before the session). Producers Don and David Was, fresh from the slick massaging of Bonnie Raitt for public consumption, insisted on selecting the studio personnel. A lineup that included both Stevie Ray and Jimmie Vaughan, swapping guitar duties with David Lindley, plus Kenny Aranoff wacking out the beat, seemed like a combination bound to inspire Dylan.

"God Knows" had eluded Dylan in New Orleans. It proved awkward again. According to Don Was, "We rehearsed it a few times before (we recorded it but) that was one that we had difficulty with. The other ones we cut that day . . . went much smoother." The January 6 session was one of Dylan's most inspirational sessions in many a high crescent moon. Aside from a "God Knows" that, were it not for that fade in midflight, would be a masterpiece of diction and delivery the equal of anything on *Oh Mercy*, Dylan and the gang cut three more tracks for *Under the Red Sky*.

"10,000 Men," the least successful and most obtuse of the songs, seems to have been recorded entirely off-the-cuff. The lyrics' nonsensical qualities certainly elude me entirely. What sounds like the dynamo being cranked up at the beginning of the song is actually the sound of the multitrack swinging into action as (presumably) Don Was realizes Dylan is not just riffing in the studio. Dylan apparently never redid the song, nor was it subjected to any vocal overdub. (Dylan has never performed the song in concert, one of only two *Red Sky* songs still overlooked—the other being "Handy Dandy.")

The two remaining songs—at what proved to be one of Stevie Ray's final sessions—would eventually close out the album, Dylan for once making an album in reverse: side two, side one, then a new set of vocal tracks. "Handy Dandy" was to be subjected to overdubs by Al Kooper, pastiching his organ sound on "Rolling Stone" (presumably at Dylan's

instigation). An alternate "Handy Dandy" that must date from the same session contains a generous slice of slide à la mode and no organ. Assuming this is Stevie Ray cutting loose (he is entirely absent from the released version), it seems odd that Dylan would prefer the more sedate album version—dubbing on Kooper's organ to spruce it up. Dylan's wordplay on "Handy Dandy" I personally find quite delightful, although it seems to infuriate many. Unlike "10,000 Men," what seems at first glance like a series of nonsequiturs actually builds up a very precise portrait of this handy dandy, though the key to the song seems to lie in the third line, "Something in the moonlight still hounds him." As to who it is that remains moonstruck, I've heard one suggestion that the song is about Prince, though why he should be a target for such an unflattering portrait I cannot imagine. The usual third-person self-portrait seems like a better bet.

The ominous tone that envelops "Handy Dandy" does not abate when Dylan and the band close up shop with their very own American jump: "Cat's in the Well" (or the apocalypse revisited in ⅚ time). The finality with which Dylan asks for God's mercy at song's end, and the grinding halt it brings to the proceedings, makes for one of the bleakest resolutions to any Dylan album, even though it wrapped up a truly exhilarating session.

It is possible that Dylan entered the studio on January 6 without a specific project in mind. Whatever, with four songs in the can in a single day his mind presumably turned to coming up with more songs to complement these new visions. With a brief European tour around the bend he had two months before he could apply himself to the studio again. When he did, his first assignment was to rerecord one of *Oh Mercy*'s brightest flames, "Most of the Time."

Dylan had decided to cooperate in the making of a third promo video for *Oh*

Mercy ("Everything Is Broken" and "Political World" being numbers one and two), but preferred to redo the song in his latest guise (quite how this promotes *Oh Mercy* I'm not sure). Drawing on the same trio around which he envisaged sculpting the remainder of *Under the Red Sky*—Kenny Aranoff, David Lindley, and bassist Randy Jackson—Dylan rerecorded "Most of the Time," without making the slightest concession to its original, melancholic self. The thudding accompaniment and Dylan's "shot" vocals were a glorious preview of things to come for anyone already prepared to vouchsafe the man's genius, though hardly what was required to convince the average gotta-pay-okay MTV viewer that here was rock's finest lyricist and most expressive singer rolled into one.

One more session at this time proved to be a distraction from the matter at hand. The Was brothers wanted Dylan to record some of the *Red Sky* songs with NRBQ (New Rhythm and Blues Quintet), an eclectic combo of twenty years standing just passing back into vogue. Although Dylan and NRBQ apparently cut four songs together, including "Some Enchanted Evening" (presumably the old standard, not a new original), no audio document has as yet appeared of this intriguing combination.

Ultimately the remainder of *Red Sky* would derive from three sessions at The Complex in Los Angeles with Don Was and Randy Jackson alternating on bass, Aranoff the mainstay with the sticks, and various permutations of Robben Ford, Waddy Wachtel, and David Lindley on guitars. Though Dylan does not appear to have brought a surfeit of songs to these sessions, he had just about enough to flesh out a worthy successor to *Oh Mercy*. Inevitably the song that proved hardest to record was the one old song he'd resurrected, "Born in Time," which was attempted at least three times. David Was even suggested

his own little arrangement idea at one point:

"I'd had an idea . . . that there should be this stop-time thing, like in the Band's 'The Weight.' . . . And so they were about to start taking the song, and I thought, I've got to do this . . . and I describe[d] the effect I wanted. Well, with half perturbation and half acceptance, [Dylan] says, 'Yeah, well, we could try that.' It's the part where it goes, 'words have not been spoken—pause—or broken—pause—drum drum. . . .' And it was kinda gorgeous. In fact, I think it was a little too much for him . . . [we tried it three times and] I started to develop this unified field theory, that if something was too beautiful, if it looked like it was trying to please, then it was against his purposes."

Unfortunately, Was's idea only seems to have made Dylan more self-conscious about his performance, the last thing required at this juncture. Though I personally think that Dylan ended up picking the most self-conscious—and, therefore, the most unconvincing—of the three vocal takes attempted, none of the *Red Sky* versions fathoms the same depths as their *Oh Mercy* ancestor. There was nothing forced about the original performance, no sense that Dylan was trying to jam the words into their assigned slots. By the time of *Red Sky*, Dylan was up to his old tricks, burying true sentiments beneath the weight of clever phrases. If the entire first bridge has been blasted to kingdom come, the worst rewrite comes halfway through, when the self-reproach of "I took you close, I got what I deserved" has been transformed into the sappy "You won't get anything you don't deserve."

Not that "Born in Time" was the only *Red Sky* track to suffer at the hands of Dylan the editor. Having seemingly abandoned his previous cut-and-run methods forever—at least when it came to laying down vocals—the rerecording of any new vocal was now invariably accompanied by a new set of lyrics, much to the exasperation of the Was boys:

David Was: "*At the mixing session, the first song we were mixing he breaks out his papers again and says he's gonna redo the vocal. Now, if you say you're gonna redo the vocal at the mixing session, the producer starts to lose his mind! You've finished the tune by this time. Well, in fact, it happened on every song. He redid the vocal, having rewritten up to the point of the mixing stage. . . . The moment before he sings it, he's still writing.*"

Although Dylan appears to have left the January cuts well alone, "Handy Dandy" excepted, none of the songs cut at Complex seems to have been how Dylan wanted them. Of the six album tracks recorded there, two were subjected to major lyrical rewrites by the time Dylan began rerecording the vocal tracks—"2 × 2" and "Unbelievable"—and one song was almost entirely reworked, lyrically *and* musically, until it was stripped of its original power—"T.V. Talkin' Song."

The original "T.V. Talkin' Song" is one of the most disturbing songs in Dylan's post-evangelist output, though there is nothing in this deranged rant about TV dads and TV moms living under bombs that one couldn't have suspected from reading those mid-1980s interviews in which Dylan pooh-poohs all accoutrements of progress, or hearing some of the more psychotic raps at his religious shows in 1979 and 1980. Nevertheless, the closest parallel I can make to "T.V. Talkin' Song" is Lou Reed's "The Gun" (on that compelling return to form, 1982's *The Blue Mask*). As chilling an insight into psychosis as the released version of "The Gun" is, there was, in Reed's words, "a version of 'The Gun' that was even worse than the one on the album but we all agreed that it went way too far . . . it went over the line."

There were at least two earlier versions of "T.V. Talkin' Song," the second of which should have been included on *Red Sky*. Retaining, as it does, a great slapback arrangement that compliments an increasingly scary Dylan vocal, this take has the speaker at Speaker's Corner and the witness to his demise (in this version the crowd actually hangs the speaker from a lamppost) slowly merging into one, before Dylan employs the same pull-back technique used previously on "Black Diamond Bay" to distance himself at song's end. By this stage Dylan has already pulled the two most disturbing original verses, a prototype "news of the day" verse in which TV is credited with melting brains, and a whole verse about TV families and "the bomb." David Was certainly felt Dylan lost the song's thread somewhere: "I didn't think he was improving upon it after a certain point. . . . [When] it underwent the revisions at mix time, I think it lost something."

Though the original lyrics betray a singer using a[nother] voice to echo sentiments close to his own heart (evidence of a man even closer to the edge than his fans might have surmised), it is not really the original lyrics that make these earlier version(s) so compelling, but rather the tremendous momentum of the performance(s). The vocal on the released take is strictly single-gear stuff, Dylan's voice going from rough to gruff. On both outtakes, though, Dylan slips into character, crossing the preacher of "Black Cross" with Frankie Lee, against a spraypaint of lead instruments rooted to that ever-present slapback bass. If *Red Sky* has a pair of weak links, they are the two cuts that close side one. In both cases the flaws were largely rectifiable. The rewrites on "2 × 2" and "Unbelievable" did not require such drastic reconfiguration. In the case of "2 × 2," it is hardly surprising that there are at least two alternate versions of the lyrics given how close Dylan comes to the clichés of Bible school with lines like "seven by seven, they headed for heaven" (absent from both outtakes). Rhyming "thy will be done" with "one" on the better of the outtakes—thus presumably affirming a belief in the second coming—hardly suggests any greater level of insight. "Unbelievable" also alludes to the imminence of the end in its original incarnation ("that time has finally come"), along with more cryptic references to judgment and retribution (the aphorism "every dog has its day" appears for the second time in Dylan's work), without ever revealing its own bill of sale.

Unlike the other Complex songs, the original vocal on the much maligned title track is not much more than a dummy vocal, Dylan even asks—mid-take—whether they are taping this and then informs the engineer, while the band is playing out the song, "That's it." The released vocal has far more about it. Though the results of vocal overdubs on *Under the Red Sky* seem to have been far more hit-and-miss than on *Oh Mercy,* "Under the Red Sky" (the song) was one instance where its beauty only bloomed after Dylan redid his vocal and George Harrison, who accompanied Dylan to the session, laid down some tasteful, slidey sounds. "Red Sky" is a song, indeed an album, worthy of reexamination by those who did not give the man the benefit of the doubt at the time. As it is, as I write these words five years down the line, *Under the Red Sky* is threatening to become the final collection from the man's own rain-unraveled tales.

GOOD AS I BEEN TO YOU

Recorded: June to July 1992
Released: November 3, 1992

Side 1: Frankie and Albert. Jim Jones. Blackjack Davey. Canadee-I-O. Sitting on Top of the World. Little Maggie. Hard Times. Side 2: Step It Up and Go. Tomorrow Night. Arthur McBride. You're Gonna Quit Me. Diamond Joe. The Froggy Went a-Courtin'.

WORLD GONE WRONG

Recorded: May 1993
Released: October 26, 1993

Side 1: World Gone Wrong. Love Henry. Ragged and Dirty. Blood in My Eyes. Broke Down Engine. Side 2: Delia. Stack-a-Lee. The Two Soldiers. Jack A Roe. Lone Pilgrim.

Other official cuts:
Natural Born Killers: You Belong to Me.

Producers:
1 David Bromberg
2–3 Debbie Gold

Musicians:

1–3 Bob Dylan (guitar/harmonica)
1 David Bromberg (guitar/mandolin/fiddle)
1 unknown drummer
1 unknown bassist

1 unknown guitarist
1 unknown pianist
1 unknown horn section
1 unknown twenty-five-piece choir on *

1. ACME RECORDING STUDIO
   CHICAGO, ILLINOIS
   EARLY TO MID-JUNE 1992
Rise Again
Nobody's Fault But Mine [IX]
The Lady Came from Baltimore
Polly Vaughn

Casey Jones
Duncan and Brady
Catskills Serenade
World of Fools

2. DYLAN'S GARAGE STUDIO
   MALIBU, CALIFORNIA
   LATE JULY/EARLY AUGUST 1992
Frankie and Albert
Jim Jones
Blackjack Davey
Canadee-I-O
Sittin' on Top of the World
Little Maggie
Hard Times
Step It Up and Go
Tomorrow Night
Arthur McBride
You're Gonna Quit Me
Diamond Joe
Froggie Went a-Courtin'
You Belong to Me

3. DYLAN'S GARAGE STUDIO
   MALIBU, CALIFORNIA
   MAY 1993
World Gone Wrong
Love Henry
Ragged and Dirty
Blood in My Eyes
Broke Down Engine
Delia
Stack-a-Lee
Two Soldiers
Jack A Roe
Lone Pilgrim
Twenty-One Years
32.20 Blues
Hello Stranger
Goodnight My Love

After two relative commercial failures, with *Under the Red Sky* and *Traveling Wilburys Volume III,* and a disastrous year of touring in the wake of bandleader G. E. Smith's resignation, Dylan let two years pass by before he made any plans for a successor to *Red Sky.* Meantime the cast-iron torch songs had evidently stopped flowing again. When he finally mustered the energy to book two and a half weeks of sessions in Chicago early in the summer of 1992, it was to record *Self Portrait Vol. 3.* If the notorious first volume had a discernable country bias and the second volume (as in *Down in the Groove*) a strong fifties feel, this third installment shone its torch on traditional, and some not-so-traditional, balladeers.

In his famous "'Letter to Dave Glover" in July 1963, Dylan had written that he could no longer sing "Little Maggie," he "gotta sing" "Seven Curses." Well, "Seven Curses" had come and gone and here he was singing "Little Maggie" onstage in Perth at the start of another year on the never-ending road. In 1984 Dylan had been asked what prompted him to become a writer in the first place and he had replied, "I just wanted a song to sing, and there came a certain

point where I couldn't sing anything. So I had to write what I wanted to sing 'cause nobody else was writing what I wanted to sing." Returning to the "folk process," Dylan no longer felt short of "a song to sing."

From the outset of the Never Ending Tour in 1988, Dylan had peppered his acoustic sets with a grapeshot of traditional fare (e.g., "The Two Soldiers," "Trail of the Buffalo," "Eileen Aroon," "Wild Mountain Thyme," and "Wagoner's Lad.") With G. E.'s departure, Dylan temporarily abandoned his folk excavations, but by the beginning of 1992 he was once again performing one or two folk standards a night as a matter of course, songs as arcane in their pedigree as the Child ballads "The Golden Vanity" and "Barbara Allen," both highlights of later 1991 shows. In the winter of 1992, Dylan was pulling out even more obscure items (the likes of "Female Rambling Sailor" and "The Lady of Carlisle"), although his most popular staple became that well-known cry for emancipation, "Little Moses."

Yet by June 1992, when he came to record his first covers album of the 1990s—initially as an electric excursion—there is no evidence that any of these songs were even attempted at the sessions. Rather the sessions at Chicago's Acme Recording Studio, produced by Dave Bromberg, resulted in twenty-six "other" songs ("of which fifteen were eventually mixed down," according to Acme engineer Blaise Barton). This was no cursory testing of the water. Some of the twenty-six songs were recorded with a stripped-down lineup, what Barton describes as "a sort of bluegrass sound—mainly acoustic, with some fiddle and mandolin." Others benefited from horns and a full rock-and-roll quartet. On two of the tunes the band was augmented by a twenty-five-piece choir from the South Side of Chicago. Both songs in question had in fact been performed at Dylan's Warfield residency back in 1980, Blind Willie Johnson's "Nobody's Fault But Mine," and the contemporary Christian ballad "Rise Again," although there was zero possibility of Dylan hitting the same notes in 1992 as those he scaled in 1980 (hence, presumably, the choir). "Rise Again" certainly stands as an intriguing choice given the lack of ambiguity in the song's message: "Go ahead, drive nails through my hands . . ."

Doubtless some half-wit will now claim that Dylan recorded this song in 1992 because he liked the melody, and not because he was unashamedly endorsing its sentiments! Of the other songs recorded at Acme, Barton recalls six—Bromberg's own "Catskills Serenade" and "World of Fools," Tim Hardin's "The Lady From Baltimore" (which was eventually premiered in concert in 1994), American folk ballads "Duncan and Brady" (a hybrid of "Frankie and Johnny") and "Casey Jones," and the beautiful English child ballad "Polly Vaughn." These six selections suggest an attempt to represent the full gamut of "folk songs." Dylan was also evidently reverting to his old studio ways, cutting most songs live, and enjoying the chance to catch the engineer unawares.

Blaise Barton: *"You have to stay on your toes when you work with Dylan. . . . I literally sat there the whole day every day with my finger on 'record,' watching for him to start playing. The first couple of days he'd be in there looking like he wasn't doing anything, so I'd adjust a compressor or something, and then he'd just start playing."*

After the sessions, Dylan was in his usual hurry to quit town, leaving Bromberg and Barton to supervise the mixdowns. However, there was never any suggestion that he was unhappy with the results, or that the fifteen songs they mixed would not form the basis of Dylan's next album. It was just that he had a European tour booked and ready to go.

Yet when Dylan returned from one of the finer stints on the Never-Ending Tour in mid-July—having continued to ring the changes at shows, traditional ballads like "Roving Blade" and "Girl on the Green Briar Shore" vying for attention with Chuck Berry's "Around and Around"—he felt the need to intercut a couple of acoustic solo performances with the Bromberg tracks (Dylan had a perfectly serviceable garage studio in the grounds, where he had already cut two acoustic songs for use on "tribute" albums, "Pretty Boy Floyd" and "Old Man").

How many songs Dylan recorded for what became *Good as I Been to You* has been the subject of much speculation. Though stories abound of twenty outtakes or more, these surely include the fifteen songs shortlisted from the Bromberg sessions. Despite the all-around effort expended in Chicago, once Dylan came to review the Bromberg tapes (he was supposed to tinker with the Acme songs), while also cutting a couple of acoustic songs, his first folk album in nigh on thirty years quickly began to distill down to its core components: the song, acoustic guitar, voice, a lil' harmonica.

Whatever Sony's press release for *Good as I Been to You* may have claimed—that all of the songs were cut in single takes, over a couple of afternoons—this clearly wasn't so. The giveaway is the ambitious guitar work. It was never plausible adspeak that Dylan maintained this standard of playing on every track in a series of single takes, particularly after years of neglecting the instrument. In fact, with Debbie Gold—credited as production supervisor on the sleeve—lending a hand, the highly informal sessions spanned a couple of weeks. Dylan presumably had chosen Gold's help because of their long-standing friendship. It was more important for Dylan to feel comfortable than to have another "name" producer on the sleeve, getting "points."

In the end, Dylan rejected all of the Bromberg material. He dispensed with not only the Acme versions, but the songs themselves, along with every cover he'd performed in concert in the previous year (aside from the Tim Hardin and Dave Bromberg songs cut in Chicago, Dylan had also been performing some of the works of Paul Simon, John Prine, and Townes Van Zandt). None of his contemporaries were to be represented on *Good as I Been to You*. Indeed the most up to date effort on the album was a heartfelt cover of Lonnie Johnson's 1947 hit "Tomorrow Night" (written by Sam Coslow and Will Grosz, but impertinently credited as Public Domain on the CD). However, the actual recorded sources on which Dylan based his arrangements of the dozen traditional cuts were almost invariably far less ancient than the songs themselves:

"Frankie and Albert"—although Mississippi John Hurt recorded this song twice, once in 1928, once in 1963—and Dylan is presumably conversant with both recordings, as well as Leadbelly's

1939 rendition—it is the 1963 version that he has drawn from.

"Jim Jones"—definitely originates with Aussie Mick Slocum of the Original Bushwhackers and Bullockies Bush Band, who recorded this traditional ballad, with his own original tune, in 1975. It was subsequently covered by British accordionist John Kirkpatrick, from whose 1976 recording Dylan may well have acquired it.

"Blackjack Davey"—Although Dylan was performing "Gypsy Davey" as early as 1961, this version of the well-known traditional yarn of infidelity was almost certainly taken from Mike Seeger's 1988 recording (on *Fresh Oldtime String Band Music*).

"Canadee-I-O"—must surely derive from Nic Jones's version (on his marvellous 1980 collection *Penguin Eggs*).

"Sitting on Top of the World"—does originate with the legendary Mississippi Sheiks' recording, cut at their first session in February 1930.

"Little Maggie"—Given this song's bluegrass roots and Dylan's electric version at Perth in March 1992, it seems a fair bet that Dylan would have attempted this with Bromberg at the Acme sessions. As it is, Dylan did not take his arrangement from one of the two Stanley Brothers' versions (made in 1949 and 1958 respectively), despite his love of the Stanleys' work, nor the 1929 Grayson and Whitter original. Rather, it comes from Tom Paley's 1953 recording, found on the same Elektra ten-inch *Folk Songs from the Southern Appalachian Mountains* as "Jack A Roe" and "Girl from the Greenbriar Shore."

"Hard Times"—Although a late nineteenth-century favorite, from the pen of Stephen "Camptown Races" Foster, the most likely jog to Dylan's memory probably came from Emmylou Harris's rather beautiful performance on her 1991 live album.

"Step It Up and Go" was recorded twice by Brownie McGhee, once in 1940 under his own name (this version was only released in 1994). The following year, as Blind Boy Fuller No. 2, he recorded it again, as a 78 for Okeh.

"Arthur McBride" clearly derives from Paul Brady's 1976 recording (to be found on *Andy Irvine Paul Brady*).

"You're Gonna Quit Me" was actually titled "You Gonna Quit Me Blues" when originally recorded by Blind Blake in August 1927, and it is this original version that Dylan most likely drew his from.

"Diamond Joe"—Though Dylan probably learned this initially from Ramblin' Jack Elliott, he must have been conversant with Cisco Houston's original recording (on the *Hard Travellin'* album).

"The Froggy Went a-Courtin'" corresponds most closely to the version by Mike and Peggy Seeger on the 1977 *American Folk Songs for Children* set.

Though at the time of its release, *Good as I Been to You* seemed like little more than stopgap product—and despite the disparity of sources—it now stands up as the most coherent of Dylan's five albums of "covers." Though he fails to surpass definitive renditions by Lonnie Johnson, Paul Brady, or Blind Blake, or indeed the version of "Sitting on Top of the World" he cut himself thirty years earlier with Big Joe Williams and Victoria Spivey, there are some beautiful performances on *Good as I Been to You*. "Hard Times" and "Tomorrow Night" both have a world-weariness that is no longer affected, coming from a man who has been on the road too long. The trio of ballads that introduce the album also show an understanding of the "folk process" undiminished by the years when his pen was his most effective gauntlet.

That, one year later, Dylan was prepared to repeat the exercise only affirmed a pen on some kinda permanent

hold. Although this time around he was prepared to own up to his influences, in liner notes that skip from scary to scatty (quick praesis: "World Gone Wrong"— Mississippi Sheiks [24/10/31]; "Love Henry"—Tom Paley [1964]; "Ragged and Dirty"—Willie Brown [16/7/42]; "Blood in My Eyes"—Mississippi Sheiks [25/10/31]; "Broke Down Engine"— Blind Willie McTell [18/9/33]; "Delia"— Blind Willie McTell [5/11/40]; "Stack-a-Lee"—Frank Hutchinson [1927]; "Two Soldiers"—Mike Seeger [1964] via Jerry Garcia; "Jack A Roe"—Tom Paley [1953]; "Lone Pilgrim"—Doc Watson), *World Gone Wrong* continued Dylan's undisciplined rage against the dying light. However, he no longer seemed capable of applying himself for the time necessary to turn an album with moments ("Love Henry," "Blood in My Eyes," "Broke Down Engine," "Delia," and "Lone Pilgrim") into an artifact that held up all the way.

Good as I Been to You's ramshackle sound had only been arrived at after a growing dissatisfaction with more electric preoccupations. *World Gone Wrong*, on the other hand, was always conceived of as "more of the same." This time, however, Dylan stuck to his own garage setup, the album being cut in a couple of afternoons with nary an afterthought and just four outtakes (one of which, Robert Johnson's "32.20 Blues," he last attempted at the Gaslight twenty-one years earlier). If the self-conscious sloppiness that abounds in Dylan's studio work has not always been successful, *World Gone Wrong* is proof that old habits die hard.

Evidently Dylan did not live with the songs he chose for *World Gone Wrong* too long given their wholesale exclusion from the Never Ending Tour, save for exquisite performances of "Delia," "Ragged and Dirty," and "Jack A Roe" at the invite-only Supper Club shows in November 1993 and the sporadic reappearances of "The Two Soldiers." As it now stands, however world-weary the narrator of "Hard Times" or "Lone Pilgrim" may sound, I find it difficult to believe that Dylan could muster more despair than Columbia's poor executives on hearing his last two albums, all-acoustic and all covers, recorded in the man's garage—the antithesis of commercial, methinks.

SOUNDTRACKS AND TRIBUTES
(1987-1994)

Various Artists—*Folkways: A Vision Shared:* Pretty Boy Floyd.
Various Artists—*Flashback:* People Get Ready.
Various Artists—*Disney for Children:* This Old Man.
Willie Nelson—*Across the Borderline:* Heartland.
Various Artists—*The Thirtieth Anniversary Concert Celebration:* My Back Pages.
Mike Seeger—*Third Annual Farewell Reunion:* The Ballad of Hollis Brown.
Various Artists—*A Tribute to Doc Pomus:* Boogie Woogie Country Girl.
Bob Dylan—*Highway 61 Interactive CD-ROM:* Blue-Eyed Jane.

Producers:
1, 3, 7 Bob Dylan
2 Barry Goldberg
5 Don Devito
6 Andrew Bush
4, 8 Don Was

Musicians:
1–6 Bob Dylan (guitar/vocals)
2 musicians unknown
4 Willie Nelson (guitar/vocals)
4 Jim Keltner (drums)
4 Don Was (bass)
4 Reggie Young (acoustic guitar)
4 John Leventhal (guitar)
4 Mickey Raphael (harmonica)
4 Benmont Tench (keyboards)

4 Paul Franklin (pedal steel)
4 Mark Goldenberg (tremolo guitar)
4 Eric Bazilian (mandolin)
6 Mike Seeger (five-string banjo)
7 Bucky Baxter (pedal steel/mandolin)
7 John Jackson (guitar)
7 Winston Watson (drums)
7 Tony Garnier (bass)
8 musicians unknown

1. DYLAN'S GARAGE STUDIO
   MALIBU, CALIFORNIA
   SPRING 1987
   Pretty Boy Floyd

2. BELMONT HALL RECORDING
   STUDIO
   NEW BLOOMINGTON, INDIANA
   NOVEMBER 20, 1989
   People Get Ready

3. DYLAN'S GARAGE STUDIO
   MALIBU, CALIFORNIA
   JANUARY 1991
   This Old Man

4. THE POWER STATION
   NEW YORK
   OCTOBER 19, 1992
   Heartland

5. SONY STUDIOS
   NEW YORK
   NOVEMBER/DECEMBER 1992
My Back Pages [vocal overdub]

6. GRANDMA'S WAREHOUSE
   LOS ANGELES, CALIFORNIA
   MAY 19, 1993
The Ballad of Hollis Brown

7. ARDENT STUDIOS
   MEMPHIS, TENNESSEE
   MAY 9 TO 11, 1994

Boogie Woogie Country Girl
Blue-Eyed Jane
I'm Not Supposed to Care
One Night of Sin
Easy Rider (Don't Deny My Name)

6. SONY STUDIOS
   NEW YORK
   SEPTEMBER 30, 1994
   Lawdy Miss Clawdy
   Money Honey
   Any Way You Want Me (Is How I Will Be)

Good *as I Been to You* and *World Gone Wrong* were by no means the first times that Dylan had used his garage studio to create product. From 1987 onward, as Dylan began to isolate himself from the studio process, there have been several scattershot covers he has contributed to miscellaneous tributes and film soundtracks. Three of these have been solo recordings, made in his garage, 1987's "Pretty Boy Floyd," 1990's "This Old Man," and 1994's "You Belong to Me" (actually an outtake from 1992's *Good as I Been to You*).

Pleasant as these minor solo excursions are, it has been Dylan's other two recent contributions to the projects of strangers that have offered all too fleeting glimpses of some kind of vision intact. The version of "People Get Ready" he recorded with John Cougar Mellencamp's band in November 1989—for a Dennis Hopper movie entitled *Flashback*—was suitably inspired. Coming between the twin peaks of *Oh Mercy* and *Under the Red Sky*, his third attempt at Curtis Mayfield's testament of faith, cut in a single day, could happily share a carriage with its basement tape and S.I.R. 1975 predecessors. The fire of faith burns throughout Dylan's vocal performance, even when the rhythm track gets a shade too bludgeoning.

Although the Never Ending Tour and two acoustic albums of covers provide plenty of evidence that Dylan can still be

a master interpreter, by the time he cut his vocal for a new original he cowrote with Willie Nelson, a couple of days after the "30th Anniversary" bash at the Garden in October 1992, proof of any enduring mastery with words was getting a little thin on the ground. Sadly "Heartland," the song Dylan and Nelson jointly composed, was no "Tweeter and the Monkey Man." Exploring a theme already dealt with in a half-dozen songs on *Oh Mercy, Under the Red Sky,* and *Traveling Wilburys Volume III*— the betrayal of the American Dream— there was little ambiguity in its message ("There's a home place under fire tonight in the Heartland"). And yet this simple message is delivered, particularly by Dylan, with the cavernous authority of a modern-day Solomon.

"Heartland" presaged no great reawakening. Even the acoustic archeologies of 1992 and 1993 dried up in 1994. Dylan did enter the studio—actually two separate studios, one in Memphis in May, one in New York in September— but all the songs cut at these sessions— eight in all—were, once again, the work of others. Nor were any of the tracks intended for an album exclusively featuring the Bob Dylan sound. A detailed report of the two-day Memphis session at Ardent appeared in a local Memphis paper, *The Appeal*, at the time, and gives an idea of the flavor of Dylan's sessions in the city of Sun:

Bob Dylan decided he'd hang around after closing the Memphis in May Beale Street Music Festival Sunday night, so he and his band headed over to Ardent Studios Monday [the 9th] with a few dozen rolls of tape for a couple of days recording. . . . His Memphis sessions were for a couple of specific projects, both of them with a Mid-South twist. Jeff Powell engineered the sessions, which finally ended at 8 A.M. Wednesday . . . "With Dylan," Powell said, "you roll tape all the time. What we ended up with was probably five songs, and I mixed three last night." Dylan recorded "Boogie Woogie Country Girl," a 1956 hit by Big Joe Turner written by Doc Pomus, for an upcoming tribute album to Pomus. . . . Dylan also recorded "Blue Eyed Jane," a song by Jimmie Rodgers . . . the man credited as the father of modern country music. That song will be part of a Rodgers tribute CD. At first Don Was was to produce the sessions, Powell said, "Then they decided, 'Let's go in and have a good time and if we don't record anything, let's just have fun.'" Dylan produced, with Powell assisting . . . Dylan is well-known for such eccentricities as wearing a towel on his head when he wants to be treated as if he were invisible. But in the studio, Powell saw another side of Dylan. "There really wasn't any of that. He was quite lucid. He talked to me while we were mixing, made some suggestions." The third song to be finished and mixed down was Gordon Lightfoot's "I'm Not Supposed to Care." But the singer-songwriter and his band . . . got into the Memphis thing, even recording the Elvis oldie "One Night," which Dylan did in its original version, "One Night of Sin," instead of the sanitized "One Night With You." . . . [Dylan] also recorded the Southern blues classic "Easy Rider (Don't Deny My Name)," which Powell said was done in a spacy, Grateful Dead–style arrangement.

The Memphis sessions represented the first time that Dylan had used his touring band in a studio since the Heartbreakers back in 1986 (Dylan's failure to use bandleader G. E. Smith on his albums had apparently been a major source of tension between them). When he made his second studio recordings of 1994, it was not the touring band he had in tow (who it was, I know not) and if Don Was had been overlooked in Memphis, he was back behind the console as Dylan recorded three songs at his first session in a Columbia studio in nineteen years. Was, who had also supervised the Dylan/Nelson recording of "Heartland," is obviously the one producer he can still feel comfortable with in the studio.

From 1974 until his death in August 1977, Elvis Presley had recorded in an RCA studio just once, for four days in March 1975 (in 1976 two attempts were made to record at Presley's home with a mobile recording truck installed on the grounds but "the acoustics in this improvised studio presented a serious problem, and . . . compounding the technical problems was the recording method Presley insisted on, i.e., the band, the back-up singers and himself recording simultaneously"). Because of Elvis Presley's distaste for the studio, RCA was required to find increasingly inventive ways of repackaging his live shows and (overdubbed) earlier studio efforts to keep up the flow of product, while the man himself pushed his failing flesh through cabaret-style performances of familiar hits.

Dylan spent his most recent session recording tracks intimately associated with Presley. Presumably some or all of the Presley songs cut on September 30, 1994—"Lawdy Miss Clawdy," "Money Honey," and "Any Way You Want Me"—were under consideration for another of those tribute CDs that threaten to replace all new music with reinterpretations of an existing canon ("Lawdy

Miss Clawdy" never actually reaches a satisfactory resolution). Interestingly, all three selections were originally recorded by Presley in the peak year of 1956, the same year Smiley Lewis first recorded "One Night of Sin," the Presley song Dylan had cut in Memphis four months earlier.

Of the three songs cut at Sony Studios, "Any Way You Want Me (That's How I Will Be)" towers above the others. Ironically, it also appears to be the one song not cut live. After Dylan has finally despaired of "Money Honey," he says to Was, "I'll just do the ballad, y'know, and try to get that, and maybe play along with it. Let's use the track that's there. It seems to be okay. I'll try to sing to it." (The musicians had laid down a backing track at the outset of the session.) Sure enough, Dylan clangs away on rhythm guitar, hoping to find a suitable key for his voice.

When he finally finds it, the first complete take gains universal endorsement from the assembled throng in the control room, even if Dylan bemoans the lack of time left to recut the song live. A classic torch ballad like this is far more suited to Dylan's age-old vocal chords, and that rumbling resonance he can still muster, than the juvenile verve of a "Lawdy Miss Clawdy" or a "Money Honey." "Money Honey" in fact occupies most of the session, Dylan getting increasingly frustrated, at one point saying, "Maybe we should go back to the ballad." Ain't that the truth. He also provides the final word on all his session work when—after a promising start to a slightly different arrangement of "Money Honey" has broken down for the nth time—he moans, "I hate recording, man. It's just so unreal."

And yet a performance like the one Dylan pulls out for "Any Way You Want Me" once again begs the question why have his various attempts to cut an album of covers been nearly as ineffectual as his attempts to cut a live album, another field he should have made his own. If the willpower to write (and at this point it must be 90 percent perspiration) no longer resides in him, it is a greater mystery why Dylan has abandoned displaying some of his vast repertoire of other people's songs, either in concert (having covered ninety-three songs in the first five years of the NET) or at home. He has evidently abandoned what could have been a very interesting series of acoustic cover albums, reminding fans of his (and others') tangled roots.

His disenchantment with the studio is easier to understand. Although he has created some of the finest performance art of the twentieth century within its asymmetrical walls, the studio has also been a greater source of frustration (for both Dylan *and* his fans) than any other facet of the man's art. I say disenchantment with the studio, but again, I suspect, it is more a question of willpower and discipline. As he has increasingly surrounded himself with people for whom nodding is a full-time occupation, the only discipline imposed comes from within, and "disciplined" is not one epithet they're likely to put on this particular artist's tombstone. As such, the commitment required to work on an album of original songs, to bend and twist them to his peculiar vision, in a modern studio, with a band of unfamiliar musicians, is such that only a truly exceptional collection of new songs— like the ones he extracted for *Blood on the Tracks, Infidels,* and *Oh Mercy*—is likely to drive his weary bones into those narrow confines once more, cursory flirtations with tributes and soundtracks notwithstanding.

APPENDIX I: DYLAN BOOTLEG CDS FEATURING STUDIO MATERIAL

Here are details of the various bootleg CDs currently available that contain material discussed in this book, all of which should be obtainable with a little perseverance. Each CD has a star-rating from one (avoid at all costs) to five stars (essential), plus relevant track details.

ACOUSTIC TROUBADOUR ★★★★
Vigotone VT-CD 09
Lily, Rosemary and the Jack of Hearts—If You See Her, Say Hello
SOURCE: *Blood on the Tracks* outtakes

AFTER THE CRASH VOL. 1 ★★★★
Big Pink BP 001
Million Dollar Bash—Yea! Heavy and a Bottle of Bread—Please, Mrs. Henry—Crash on the Levee (Down in the Flood) (two takes)—Lo and Behold! (two takes)—Tiny Montgomery—This Wheel's on Fire—You Ain't Going Nowhere—I Shall Be Released—Too Much of Nothing—instrumental—Santa Fe—Silent Weekend—Too Much of Nothing—Sign on the Cross
SOURCE: *The Basement Tapes*
NOTE: Though an inferior source to *The Genuine Basement Tapes Vol. 3*, this version is in stereo.

AFTER THE CRASH VOL. 2 ★★
Big Pink BP 002
You Ain't Going Nowhere—Bourbon Street—All American Boy—Wild Wood Flower—See That My Grave Is Kept Clean—Comin' Round the Mountain—Flight of the Bumble Bee—Confidential to Me—I'm a Fool for You—Next Time on the Highway—The Big Flood—Don't Know Why They Kick My Dog—See You Later, Allen Ginsberg—The Spanish Song (two takes)—I'm Your Teenage Prayer—I'm in the Mood for Love—Belchezaar (two takes)—Bring It on Home—King of France
SOURCE: *The Basement Tapes*
NOTE: An inferior version of *The Genuine Basement Tapes Vol. 4*.

BOB DYLAN MEETS GEORGE HARRISON AND JOHNNY CASH ★
Living Legend LLRCD 081
Song to Woody—Mama, You Bin on My Mind—Don't Think Twice, It's All Right—Yesterday—Just Like Tom Thumb's Blues—Da Doo Ron Ron—One Too Many Mornings—One Too Many Mornings—Good Ol' Mountain Dew—I Still Miss Someone—Careless Love—Matchbox—Big River—That's All Right, Mama—I Walk the Line—You Are My Sunshine
SOURCES: *Nashville Skyline* and *New Morning* outtakes
NOTE: A copy of a vinyl bootleg.

THE BOOTLEG ★★★★
Wanted Man Music WMM 022
You're No Good—Talkin' New York—In My Time of Dyin'—Man of Constant Sorrow—Fixin' to Die—Pretty Peggy-O—Highway 51 Blues—Gospel Plow—Baby, Let Me Follow You Down—House of the Rising Sun—Freight Train Blues—Song to Woody—See That My Grave Is Kept Clean—House Carpenter—He Was a Friend of Mine—Hard Times in New York Town—Man on the Street—Talkin' Bear Mountain Picnic Massacre Blues—Standing on the Highway—Poor Boy Blues—Ballad for a Friend—Ramblin' Gamblin' Willie—Milk Cow Blues—Wichita Blues
SOURCES: *Bob Dylan* outtakes and Leeds Music Demos
NOTES: The first thirteen tracks are taken from a mono copy of the first album.

CLEAN CUTS (HENRY PORTER'S 115TH DREAM) ★
Sick Cat GRAB 003
Go 'Way Little Boy—Driftin' Too Far from Shore—Who Loves You More?—New

Danville Girl—Something's Burning, Baby—Tight Connection to My Heart (Has Anybody Seen My Love)—Clean Cut Kid—I'll Remember You—Seeing the Real You at Last—Trust Yourself—Emotionally Yours—When the Night Comes Falling from the Sky—Waiting to Get Beat—Straight A's in Love—The Very Thought of You—Never Gonna Be the Same Again
SOURCE: *Empire Burlesque* outtakes
NOTE: This CD plays way too fast.

THE DEEDS OF MERCY ★★★★
The Razor's Edge RAZ-002
Shooting Star—God Knows (two takes)—What Good Am I?—Most of the Time—Everything Is Broken—Political World—Born in Time—Dignity—Shooting Star—Disease of Conceit—Ring Them Bells—Most of the Time—What Was It You Wanted?—Series of Dreams (three takes)
SOURCE: *Oh Mercy* outtakes

DIGNITY ★★★★
A Couple More Years—Dignity—Coming from the Heart—Watered-Down Love—Keep It with Mine—Dirty World—You Ain't Going Nowhere—(I Heard That) Lonesome Whistle—Trouble in Mind—Got Love If You Want It
SOURCE: Miscellaneous outtakes from 1962 to 1989

DR. ZIMMERMAN'S ORIGINAL OLD TIME HOOTENANY ★★
Archive AP 89003
Dink's Song—In the Evening—Long John
SOURCE: Minneapolis Hotel Tape

DOWN IN THE FLOOD ★★
Archivio ARC 005
Jokerman—License to Kill—Man of Peace—Neighborhood Bully—Don't Fall Apart on Me Tonight—Blind Willie McTell—Sweetheart Like You—I and I—Foot of Pride
SOURCE: *Infidels* outtakes
NOTE: A straight copy of a famous vinyl bootleg.

THE DYLAN/CASH SESSIONS ★★★★★
Spank SP 106
One Too Many Mornings—Good Ol' Mountain Dew—I Still Miss Someone—Careless Love—Matchbox—That's All Right, Mama—Big River—Girl from the North Country—I Walk the Line—You Are My Sunshine—Ring of Fire—Guess Things Happen That Way—Just a Closer Walk with Thee—Blue Yodel No. 4—Blue Yodel No. 5—Nashville Skyline Rag*—I Threw It All Away*—Peggy Day*—Country Pie*—Tonight I'll Be Staying Here with You*
SOURCE: *Nashville Skyline* outtakes. Asterisked tracks from quadrophonic copy of *Nashville Skyline*.

THE DYLAN'S ROOTS ★★★
Skeleton SKCD 1001
San Francisco Bay Blues—Jesus Met a Woman at the Well—Gypsy Davy—Pastures of Plenty—Trail of the Buffalo—Jesse James—Car, Car—Southern Cannonball—Bring Me Back My Blue-Eyed Boy—Remember Me
SOURCE: The Gleasons, East Orange, N.J., February 1961

THE FREEWHEELIN' OUTTAKES ★★★★★
Vigotone VIGO 115
Baby, Please Don't Go—Corrina, Corrina—The Death of Emmett Till—Mixed Up Confusion—Lonesome Whistle—Talkin' John Birch Paranoid Blues—Milk Cow Blues—That's All Right, Mama—Rocks and Gravel—Going to New Orleans—Let Me Die in My Footsteps—The Ballad of Hollis Brown—Wichita Blues—Sally Gal—Whatcha Gonna Do?—Mixed Up Confusion—Rocks and Gravel—That's All Right, Mama—Mixed Up Confusion—Corrina, Corrina—Milk Cow Blues—Wichita Blues—Whatcha Gonna Do?—Babe, I'm in the Mood for You—Sally Gal
SOURCE: *Freewheelin'* outtakes

A FRIEND TO THE MARTYR (OUTFIDELS) ★★★
Silver Rarities SIRA 44
Jokerman—Don't Fall Apart on Me Tonight—I and I—Clean Cut Kid—Julius and Ethel—Death Is Not the End—Foot of Pride—Sweetheart Like You—I and I—Someone's Got a Hold of My Heart—Union Sundown—Tell Me—Blind Willie McTell—This Was My Love
SOURCE: *Infidels* outtakes

NOTE: Certain digital flaws impair an otherwise worthwhile CD. The two "I and I"s are alternate mixes.

THE GENUINE BASEMENT TAPES VOL. 1 ★★★★★
BD-200-2

All You Have to Do Is Dream—I Can't Make It Alone—Down on Me—Bonnie Ship the Diamond—One Man's Loss—Baby, Ain't That Fine—Rock Salt and Nails—A Fool Such as I—(Be Careful of the) Stones That You Throw—The Hills of Mexico—It's Alright, Ma (I'm Only Bleeding)—One Single River—Try Me, Little Girl—One for the Road—I Don't Hurt Anymore—People Get Ready—Lock Your Door—Baby, Won't You Be My Baby—Don't You Try Me Now—All You Have to Do Is Dream—Young But Daily Growin'
SOURCE: *The Basement Tapes*

THE GENUINE BASEMENT TAPES VOL. 2 ★★★★★
BD-200-3

Odds and Ends—Nothing Was Delivered—Odds and Ends—Get Your Rocks Off—Clothes Line Saga—Apple Suckling Tree (two takes)—Goin' to Acapulco—Gonna Get You Now—Tears of Rage (three takes)—The Mighty Quinn (Quinn the Eskimo) (two takes)—Open the Door, Homer (three takes)—Nothing Was Delivered (two takes)—I'm Not There—Don't Ya Tell Henry—Too Much of Nothing
SOURCE: *The Basement Tapes*

THE GENUINE BASEMENT TAPES VOL. 3 ★★★
BD-SC-1900

Million Dollar Bash—Yea! Heavy and a Bottle of Bread—Please, Mrs. Henry—Crash on the Levee (Down in the Flood) (two takes)—Lo and Behold! (two takes)—Tiny Montgomery—This Wheel's on Fire—You Ain't Going Nowhere—I Shall Be Released—Too Much of Nothing—instrumental—Santa Fe—Silent Weekend—Too Much of Nothing—Sign on the Cross
SOURCE: *The Basement Tapes*
NOTE: This volume was accidentally manufactured in mono and is consequently inferior to the other volumes in an otherwise exemplary series.

THE GENUINE BASEMENT TAPES VOL. 4 ★★★★★
BD-SC-80-07

You Ain't Going Nowhere—Bourbon Street—All American Boy—Wild Wood Flower—See That My Grave Is Kept Clean—Comin' Round the Mountain—Flight of the Bumble Bee—Confidential to Me—I'm a Fool for You—Next Time on the Highway—The Big Flood—Don't Know Why They Kick My Dog—See You Later, Allen Ginsberg—The Spanish Song (two takes)—I'm Your Teenage Prayer—I'm in the Mood for Love—Belchazaar (two takes)—Bring it on Home—King of France
SOURCE: *The Basement Tapes*

THE GENUINE BASEMENT TAPES VOL. 5 ★★★★★
BD-SC-80-06

Four Strong Winds—The French Girl (two takes)—Joshua Gone Barbados—I Forgot to Remember to Forget Her—You Win Again—Still in Town, Still Around—Waltzing with Sin—Big River—Folsom Prison Blues—Bells of Rhymney—Nine Hundred Miles—No Shoes on My Feet—Spanish Is the Loving Tongue—On a Rainy Afternoon—I Can't Come in with a Broken Heart—Under Control—Ol' Roison the Beau—I'm Guilty of Loving You—Johnny Todd—Cool Water—Banks of the Royal Canal—Po' Lazarus
SOURCE: *The Basement Tapes*

THE GENUINE BASEMENT TAPES I–II ★★
Images IM 03/04

NOTES: Packaged in a fold-out cardboard sleeve with a central metal base. The discs fit on top of each other. These are copies of the originals.
SOURCE: *The Basement Tapes*

THE GENUINE BOOTLEG SERIES (3 CDS) ★★★★★

Black Cross—I Was Young When I Left Home—Ballad for a Friend—Hero Blues—Whatcha Gonna Do?—Tomorrow Is a Long Time—Milk Cow Blues—Rocks and Gravel—Farewell—Baby, Let Me Follow You Down—That's All Right, Mama/Sally Free and Easy—New Orleans Rag—You Don't Have to Do That—Can You Please Crawl Out Your Window?—Desolation Row—Visions

of Johanna—She's Your Lover Now—The Painting by Van Gogh—What Kind of Friend Is This?—Sign on the Cross—All American Boy—Nothing Was Delivered—I Threw It All Away—Honey, Just Allow Me One More Chance—Working on a Guru—Goodbye Holly—Rock Me Mama—Nobody 'Cept You—Idiot Wind—Hurricane—Stop Now—Trouble in Mind—Yonder Comes Sin—Caribbean Wind—Don't Ever Take Yourself Away—Sweetheart Like You—Someone's Got a Hold of My Heart—Tell Me—Jokerman—Blind Willie McTell—New Danville Girl—Important Words—Dignity—Like a Ship—Series of Dreams
SOURCE: Miscellaneous outtakes from 1961 to 1990

HAVE MERCY ★★
Diamonds in Your Ear DIYE 28
What Was It You Wanted?—Series of Dreams—God Knows—What Good Am I?—Most of the Time—Everything Is Broken—Political World—Born in Time—Dignity—Shooting Star—Disease of Conceit—Got Love If You Want It—Important Words—Most of the Time—Hurricane*
SOURCES: *Oh Mercy, Down in the Groove,* and *Desire* outtakes
NOTE: The *Oh Mercy* outtakes have serious wow and flutter problems.

HIGHWAY 61 REVISITED/BLONDE ON BLONDE—THE MONO MIXES (2 CDS) ★★★
The Gold Standard BN–339/HM–313
Like a Rolling Stone—Tombstone Blues—It Takes a Lot to Laugh, It Takes a Train to Cry—From a Buick 6—Ballad of a Thin Man—Queen Jane Approximately—Highway 61 Revisited—Just Like Tom Thumb's Blues—Desolation Row—Positively 4th Street—Can You Please Crawl Out Your Window?—Rainy Day Women #s 12 & 35—Pledging My Time—Visions of Johanna—One of Us Must Know (Sooner or Later)—I Want You—Stuck Inside of Mobile with the Memphis Blues Again—Leopard Skin Pillbox Hat—Just Like a Woman—Most Likely You Go Your Way and I'll Go Mine—Temporary Like Achilles—Absolutely Sweet Marie—4th Time Around—Obviously 5 Believers—Sad Eyed Lady of the Lowlands
NOTES: Tracks taken from official mono al-

bums. The H61R disc plays *Blonde on Blonde* and vice-versa. The index mark for "Positively 4th Street" is twenty seconds early.

HIGHWAY 61 REVISITED AGAIN ★★★★★
92-BD-09-04
Can You Please Crawl Out Your Window?—Sitting on a Barbed Wire Fence—Like a Rolling Stone—Ballad of a Thin Man—Just Like Tom Thumb's Blues—Highway 61 Revisited—Positively 4th Street—It Takes a Lot to Laugh, It Takes a Train to Cry—Tombstone Blues—Can You Please Crawl Out Your Window?—Desolation Row—Queen Jane Approximately—From a Buick 6
SOURCE: *Highway 61 Revisited* outtakes

HIGHWAY 61 REVISITED AGAIN ★★★
Chapter One CO 25201
NOTES: Copy of above disc.

IMPORTANT WORDS ★★★
Wanted Man Music WMM 014
You Left Just When I Needed You Most—Important Words—When Did You Leave Heaven?—Willie and the Hand Jive—Twist and Shout—In the Summertime (three takes)—Freedom for the Stallion (three takes)—seven instrumentals—In the Summertime
SOURCES: *Empire Burlesque* and *Down in the Groove* outtakes

LIVE WITH THE BAND, AL KOOPER AND MIKE BLOOMFIELD ★★
Document DR 015CD
Midnight Train—Can You Please Crawl Out Your Window?—I Wanna Be Your Lover—Number One—Visions of Johanna—She's Your Lover Now—Jet Pilot—If You Gotta Go, Go Now
SOURCES: *Blonde on Blonde* and *Bringing It All Back Home* outtakes

THE LONESOME SPARROW SINGS ★★★★
Black Nite Crash BNC-003
You Don't Have to Do That—It's All Over Now, Baby Blue—If You Gotta Go, Go Now—She Belongs to Me—Love Minus Zero/No Limit—Miami convention mes-

sage—If You Gotta Go, Go Now—Sitting on a Barbed Wire Fence—Can You Please Crawl Out Your Window? (two takes)—From a Buick 6—Desolation Row—Can You Please Crawl Out Your Window?—I Wanna Be Your Lover—Jet Pilot—Visions of Johanna—Midnight Train—Visions of Johanna—She's Your Lover Now
SOURCE: *Bringing It All Back Home, Highway 61 Revisited,* and *Blonde on Blonde* outtakes

THE MINNESOTA TAPES (3 CDS)
★★★★
Wanted Man Music WMM 033/034/035
Ramblin' Round—Death Don't Have No Mercy—It's Hard to Be Blind—This Train—harmonica solo—Talkin' Fish Blues—Pastures of Plenty—Railroad Bill—Will the Circle Be Unbroken?—Man of Constant Sorrow—Pretty Polly—Railroad Boy—James Alley Blues—Why'd You Cut My Hair—This Land Is Your Land—Two Trains Runnin'—Wild Mountain Thyme—Howdido—Car, Car—Don't You Push Me Down—Come See—I Want It Now—San Francisco Bay Blues—Young But Daily Growin'—Devilish Mary—Candy Man—Baby, Please Don't Go—Hard Times in New York Town—Stealin'—Po' Lazarus—I Ain't Got No Home—It's Hard to Be Blind—Dink's Song—Man of Constant Sorrow—East Orange, New Jersey—Poor Omie—Wade in the Water—I Was Young When I Left Home—In the Evening—Baby, Let Me Follow You Down—Sally Gal—Gospel Plow—Long John—Cocaine—VD Blues—VD Waltz—VD City—VD Gunner's Blues—See That My Grave Is Kept Clean—Ramblin' Round—Black Cross
SOURCES: Minneapolis Party Tape and Minneapolis Hotel Tape

MORE MUSIC FROM BIG PINK ★
Early Years 02-CD-3319
All You Have to Do Is Dream—I Can't Make It Alone—Bonnie Ship the Diamond—Young But Daily Growin'—One Man's Loss—The Hills of Mexico—One for the Road—One Single River—Try Me, Little Girl—I Don't Hurt Anymore—People Get Ready—Baby, Ain't That Fine—A Night Without Sleep—A Fool Such as I—Gonna Get You Now—(Be Careful of the) Stones That You Throw

SOURCE: *The Basement Tapes*
NOTE: Copied from bootleg vinyl.

MOVING VIOLATION ★★★
Toasted CONDOR 1966
I'll Be Your Baby Tonight—The Times They Are a-Changin'—If You See Her, Say Hello—I Don't Believe You—Tomorrow Is a Long Time—You're a Big Girl Now—Simple Twist of Fate—If You See Her, Say Hello—I Don't Believe You—We'd Better Talk This Over—Coming from the Heart—I Threw It All Away—Maggie's Farm—Repossession Blues—Girl from the North Country—Knockin' on Heaven's Door—It's Alright, Ma (I'm Only Bleeding)
SOURCE: Rundown Studios, Santa Monica, 1978

THE NEVER ENDING TOUR ★
Deep MIK 012/013
The Usual (three takes)—Ride This Train—Had a Dream About You Baby (five takes)—Old Five and Dimer Like Me (three takes)—Had a Dream About You Baby (two takes)—To Fall in Love with You
SOURCE: *Hearts of Fire* outtakes

ODDS AND ENDS (UNSURPASSED MAESTRO VOL. 1) ★★★
Sick Cat 006
Whatcha Gonna Do?—Sally Gal—Suzy (The Cough Song)—You Don't Have to Do That—Jet Pilot—Working on a Guru—Let Me See—Lily, Rosemary and the Jack of Hearts—Nuggets of Rain—Hurricane—Yonder Comes Sin—Mystery Train—Watered-Down Love—Honey Wait—That's All Right, Mama
SOURCE: Miscellaneous outtakes from 1962 to 1981

OH MERCY OUTTAKES ★
Wanted Man Music WMM 042
Shooting Star—God Knows (two takes)—What Good Am I?—Most of the Time—Everything Is Broken—Political World—Born in Time—Dignity—Shooting Star—Disease of Conceit—Ring Them Bells (two takes)—Most of the Time—Series of Dreams—What Was It You Wanted?—Series of Dreams
SOURCE: *Oh Mercy* outtakes
NOTE: Contains digital noise throughout. Avoid.

OUTSIDE THE EMPIRE ★★★
Wanted Man Music WMM 060

New Danville Girl—Tight Connection to My Heart (Has Anybody Seen My Love)—Clean Cut Kid—I'll Remember You—Seeing the Real You at Last—Something's Burning, Baby—Trust Yourself—Emotionally Yours—When the Night Comes Falling from the Sky—Never Gonna Be the Same Again—Waiting to Get Beat—Straight A's in Love—The Very Thought of You—Driftin' Too Far from Shore—Who Loves You More?—Go 'Way Little Boy

SOURCE: *Empire Burlesque* outtakes

PECOS BLUES ★★★★★
Spank SP 107

Billy (two takes)—Billy (instrumental)—Turkey—Billy Surrenders—And He's Killed Me Too—Goodbye Holly—Pecos Blues (two takes)—Billy—Knockin' on Heaven's Door—Sweet Amarillo—Knockin' on Heaven's Door (two takes)—Final Theme (two takes)—Rock Me Mama (two takes)—Billy (two takes)—instrumental (two takes)—Final Theme (two takes)

SOURCE: *Pat Garrett & Billy the Kid* outtakes

POSSUM BELLY OVERALLS ★★★★
The Gold Standard NASH 105

Ghost Riders in the Sky—Cupid—All You Have to Do Is Dream—Gates of Eden—I Threw It All Away—I Don't Believe You—Matchbox—True Love, Your Love—Wonder When My Swamp's Gonna Catch on Fire—I'm a-Goin' Fishin'—Honey, Just Allow Me One More Chance—Rainy Day Women #s 12 & 35—Song to Woody—Mama, You Bin on My Mind—Don't Think Twice, It's All Right—Yesterday—Just Like Tom Thumb's Blues—Da Doo Ron Ron—One Too Many Mornings—Folsom Prison Blues*—Ring of Fire*

SOURCES: *New Morning* and *Self Portrait* outtakes

ROUGH CUTS (2 CDS) ★★★★★
The Gold Standard SRE-½

Sweetheart Like You—Someone's Got a Hold of My Heart—Lord Protect My Child—Angel Flying Too Close to the Ground—Foot of Pride—Tell Me—I and I—Union Sundown—Julius and Ethel—Jokerman—License to Kill—Man of Peace—Don't Fall Apart on Me Tonight—Neighborhood Bully—Blind Willie McTell—This Was My Love (two takes)—Angel Flying Too Close to the Ground—Dark Groove—Don't Fly Unless It's Safe—Clean Cut Kid—Death Is Not the End—Sweetheart Like You—Union Sundown—Sweetheart Like You (rehearsals)

SOURCE: *Infidels* outtakes

ROUGH CUTS ★★★★★
Black Nite Crash BNC-001/002

NOTE: Copy of above discs.

THE SESSION ★
Black Panther BPCD 022

Medicine Sunday—Can You Please Crawl Out Your Window?—I Wanna Be Your Lover—Number One—Visions of Johanna—She's Your Lover Now—Jet Pilot—If You Gotta Go, Go Now

SOURCES: *Blonde on Blonde* and *Bringing It All Back Home* outtakes

SEVEN YEARS OF BAD LUCK ★★★★
Spank SP 102

Hero Blues—Whatcha Gonna Do?—Oxford Town—I Shall Be Free (five takes)—Hero Blues—You Don't Have to Do That—Positively Van Gogh (two takes)—Just Like a Woman—Gates of Eden—I Threw It All Away—I Don't Believe You—Telephone Wire—Honey, Just Allow Me One More Chance

SOURCES: Denver Hotel Tape, *Freewheelin'* and *New Morning* outtakes

STRIP TEASE ★★★
Toasted CONDOR 1965

It Takes a Lot to Laugh, It Takes a Train to Cry—She Belongs to Me—Sitting on a Barbed Wire Fence—Love Minus Zero/No Limit—If You Gotta Go, Go Now—On the Road Again—It's All Over Now, Baby Blue—Suzy (The Cough Song)—I'll Keep It with Mine—California—New Orleans Rag—East Laredo Blues—That's All Right, Mama—Lay Down Your Weary Tune—Eternal Circle—Percy's Song—I Was Young When I Left Home—In the Evening—Long John

SOURCES: Miscellaneous outtakes from 1961 to 1965

THIN WILD MERCURY MUSIC
★★★★
Spank SP 105
If You Gotta Go, Go Now—She Belongs to Me—Visions of Johanna—From a Buick 6—It's All Over Now, Baby Blue—Medicine Sunday—I Wanna Be Your Lover—I'll Keep It with Mine—Love Minus Zero/No Limit—Can You Please Crawl Out Your Window?—Number One—She's Your Lover Now—Jet Pilot—Can You Please Crawl Out Your Window?—Visions of Johanna—She's Your Lover Now—Miami convention message—If You Gotta Go, Go Now
SOURCE: *Bringing It All Back Home, Highway 61 Revisited,* and *Blonde on Blonde* outtakes

THROUGH A BULLET OF LIGHT
(2 CDS) ★★★★
GOLOM 774554
Long Ago, Far Away—Long Time Gone—Ain't Gonna Grieve—Blowin' in the Wind—Farewell—Bob Dylan's Blues—Seven Curses—Paths of Victory—All Over You—When the Ship Comes In—The Times They Are a-Changin'—John Brown—Talkin' John Birch Paranoid Blues—I Shall Be Free—Hero Blues—Tomorrow Is a Long Time—Only a Hobo—Whatcha Gonna Do?—Gypsy Lou—Baby, Let Me Follow You Down—A Hard Rain's a-Gonna Fall—Don't Think Twice, It's All Right—Oxford Town—Masters of War—Walkin' Down the Line—The Death of Emmett Till—Bob Dylan's Dream—Quit Your Lowdown Ways—Babe, I'm in the Mood for You—The Ballad of Hollis Brown—Girl from the North Country—Boots of Spanish Leather—Let Me Die in My Footsteps—Bound to Lose—I'd Hate to Be You on That Dreadful Day—Percy's Song—Guess I'm Doin' Fine—Eternal Circle—Mama, You Bin on My Mind—Mr. Tambourine Man—I'll Keep It with Mine
SOURCES: *The Witmark Demos* and *The Times They Are a-Changin'* outtakes

TWELVE CURSES ★
Early Years 02–CD-3337
Only a Hobo—Moonshine Blues—Mama, You Bin on My Mind—Eternal Circle—Percy's Song—Seven Curses—Lay Down Your Weary Tune—Percy's Song—Suzy (The

Cough Song)—Eternal Circle—Walls Of Redwing
SOURCE: *The Times They Are a-Changin'* outtakes
NOTE: Copied from a vinyl bootleg.

VASTLY ORIGINAL WORK FROM A PLACE NO ONE'S EVER BEEN BEFORE ★
300242
Idiot Wind—Lily, Rosemary and the Jack of Hearts—If You See Her, Say Hello—You're a Big Girl Now—Tangled Up in Blue—Hurricane*
SOURCES: *Blood on the Tracks* and *Desire* outtakes.
NOTE: Copied from vinyl bootlegs.

THE WITMARK DEMOS (2 CDS) ★★
Off Beat XXCD 14
Babe, I'm in the Mood for You—Quit Your Lowdown Ways—Long Time Gone—Long Ago, Far Away—Ain't Gonna Grieve—Seven Curses—Let Me Die in My Footsteps—Bob Dylan's Blues—Talkin' John Birch Paranoid Blues—The Death of Emmett Till—Hero Blues—Only a Hobo—All Over You—Bound to Lose—Baby, Let Me Follow You Down—A Hard Rain's a-Gonna Fall—Don't Think Twice, It's All Right—Oxford Town—Masters of War—Girl from the North Country—I Shall Be Free—Tomorrow Is a Long Time—Boots of Spanish Leather—Bob Dylan's Dream—Farewell—Guess I'm Doin' Fine—John Brown—Whatcha Gonna Do?—Gypsy Lou—Paths of Victory—Walkin' Down the Line—The Ballad of Hollis Brown—I'd Hate to Be You on That Dreadful Day—Blowin' in the Wind—When the Ship Comes In—The Times They Are a-Changin'—Mama, You Bin on My Mind—Mr. Tambourine Man—I'll Keep It with Mine
SOURCE: *The Witmark Demos*
NOTE: Copied from the vinyl boxed set.

THE WITMARK YEARS (2 CDS)
★★★★
Capricorn
Blowin' in the Wind—Long Ago, Far Away—Tomorrow Is a Long Time—The Ballad of Hollis Brown—The Death of Emmett Till—A Hard Rain's a-Gonna Fall—Let Me Die in My Footsteps—Quit Your Lowdown Ways—Babe, I'm in the Mood for You—Long Time

Gone—Don't Think Twice, It's All Right—
Oxford Town—Masters of War—Walkin'
Down the Line—Talkin' John Birch Paranoid
Blues—All Over You—Bound to Lose—I'd
Hate to Be You on That Dreadful Day—I
Shall Be Free—Bob Dylan's Dream—Bob
Dylan's Blues—Boots of Spanish Leather—
Girl from the North Country—Seven
Curses—Hero Blues—Gypsy Lou—Whatcha
Gonna Do?—Ain't Gonna Grieve—Only a
Hobo—John Brown—When the Ship Comes
In—The Times They Are a-Changin'—Paths
of Victory—Farewell—Baby, Let Me Follow
You Down—Guess I'm Doin' Fine—Mr.
Tambourine Man—Mama, You Bin on My
Mind—I'll Keep It with Mine—Eternal Cir-
cle—Paths of Victory
SOURCE: *The Witmark Demos*
NOTE: A commendable attempt to put this
material in chronological order using the
same basic source tape as *Through a Bullet of
Light.*

VOLUME TWO ★
Beta CDWA 431
Walk Away—Last Night—Congratulations—
Rattled—Heading for the Light—End of the
Line—Handle with Care—Dirty World—End
of the Line*—Handle with Care*
SOURCE: *Traveling Wilburys Volume One*
outtakes

VOLUME TWO ★
Goblin CD 3003
Nobody's Child—Handle with Care—Runaway—Last Night—Congratulations—Dirty
World—Rattled—End of the Line—Heading
for the Light
SOURCE: *Traveling Wilburys Volume One*
outtakes

VOLUME FOUR ★★★
In the Groove AWCD 21
Wilbury Twist—Seven Deadly Sins—New
Blue Moon—Cool Dry Place—Runaway—
Maxine—Inside Out—Where Were You Last
Night?—You Took My Breath Away—If You
Belonged to Me—Poor House—She's My
Baby—The Devil's Been Busy—Like a Ship
SOURCE: *Traveling Wilburys Volume Three*
outtakes

VOLUME FOUR AND A HALF ★★
Adam VIII CD 49-021
Maxine—Like a Ship—Runaway—She's My
Baby—Inside Out—If You Belonged to Me—
The Devil's Been Busy—Seven Deadly Sins—
Poor House—Where Were You Last
Night?—Cool Dry Place—New Blue Moon—
You Took My Breath Away—Wilbury Twist
SOURCE: *Traveling Wilburys Volume Three*
outtakes

APPENDIX II
SOME WORKING TITLES

Like many musicians, Dylan's working titles for songs sometimes bear little resemblance to their published form. Particularly in the electric years of 1965–66, the title a song was given at a session rarely corresponded with its future nomenclature. Below is a provisional list of some working titles listed on studio boxes. In several instances (e.g., "Broken Days," "New Danville Girl") the change in title also resulted in major lyrical rewrites.

A Long Haired Mule and a Porcupine—Rainy Day Women #s 12 & 35

Alcatraz to the Fifth Power—Farewell Angelina

All for the Sake of Thee—House Carpenter

Answer to Ode—Clothes Line Saga

Bank Account Blues—I'll Keep It with Mine

Bending Down on My Stomach Looking West—You Don't Have to Do That

Black Dalli Rue—Positively 4th Street

Black Dog Blues—Obviously 5 Believers

Bob Dylan's Restless Epitaph—Restless Farewell

Broken Days—Everything Is Broken

Brownsville Girl—New Danville Girl

Early in the Morning—Call Letter Blues

Freeze Out—Visions of Johanna

Gamblin' Willie's Dead Man's Hand—Ramblin' Gamblin' Willie

Juarez—Just Like Tom Thumb's Blues

Just a Little Glass of Water—She's Your Lover Now

Lonesome Would Mean Nothing to Me—Tomorrow Is a Long Time

Lost Time Is Not Found Again—Odds and Ends

Love Copy—Abandoned Love

Lunatic Princess—From a Buick 6

Over the Cliff—Sitting on a Barbed Wire Fence

Phantom Engineer—It Takes a Lot to Laugh, It Takes a Train to Cry

Pilot Eyes—Jet Pilot

Pure Love—Watered-Down Love

Sing Tattle O'Day—Little Brown Dog

Solid Road—Rocks and Gravel

This Evening So Soon—Tell Ol' Bill

What You Can Do for Your Wigwam—Pledging My Time

Worse Than Money—She Belongs to Me

APPENDIX III
INDEX OF DYLAN COMPOSITIONS

All asterisked songs are uncopyrighted and cannot be authenticated as Dylan compositions, but are presumed from external evidence to be his. Joint compositions are duly credited.

APPENDIX IV
INDEX OF COVERS RECORDED BY
DYLAN

APPENDIX V
DESIRE SESSION CHARTS

Studio data (or track) sheets are used by studio engineers to indicate who is playing on each recorded track. Such information is usually written prior to the recorded take(s), along with the song title and CO number. Such sheets provide the most accurate information as to what songs were recorded and who played on them at any given session.

Every engineer has his own shorthand for which instruments are recorded on each track in a multitrack studio. Some of these are very obvious, others less so. On the *Desire* sessions the abbreviations are as follows:

BD—Bass Direct
SN—Snare Drum
HH—High Hat
GROUP—Girl Singers (14th only)
DR L—Drums Left
DR R—Drums Right
GIT 1—Guitar 1
GITR—Guitar 2
HARM—Harmonica
ORG—Organ
V—Vocal (Dylan's)

BOB'S GIT—Dylan's Guitar (Acoustic)
ACC GIT—Acoustic Guitar
EL GIT—Electric Guitar
TPT—Trumpet
TAMB—Tambourine
HARMONY VOICE—Emmylou Harris's vocal
BOB V—Vocal (Dylan's)
DNU—Do not use
PERC—Percussion

16 TRACK IDENTIFICATION CHART
CBS RECORDS

TITLE: BOB DYLAN — RITA MAE

SESSION: | JOB NO: 20774 | PRODUCER: D. KITE | ENGINEER: D... S.K / L.J | DATE: 7/14/7-

NO.	CO. NO.	1	2	3	4	5	6	7	8
1		B.D.	SN HH	GROUP	DR L	DR R	BASS	GIT 1	GITR
		9	10	11	12	13	14	15	16
		HARM	ORG	V	MANDOLIN	VOCALS GIT	PIANO	VIOLIN	ACCORDIAN

NO.	CO. NO.	1	2	3	4	5	6	7	8
2			SN	RF HHAT	DR L	DR RF	BASS	7	8
		9	10 (B.B GTN NGTO-TK 2)	11 V	12 MANDOLIN	13 BNJ GIT	14 GROUP	15 VIOLIN	16 ACCORDIAN

NO.	CO. NO.	1	2	3	4	5	6	7	8
3		1	2	3	4	5	6	7	8
		9	10	11	12	13	14	15	16

CR 1721

16 TRACK IDENTIFICATION CHART

CBS RECORDS: **Bob Dylan** SESSION: JOB NO. **120820** PRODUCER **De Vito** ENGINEER **D.M.–LW** DATE **7/28/75 MON**

TITLE: Money Blues. 121707 — DOLBY

NO.	CC. NO. 1	2	3	4	5	6	7	8
1	BD	SN	R Dr.	R Dr.	Bass	Acc Git	Acc Git	EL Git Eric
CO. NO.	9 VINNIE Mandol.	10 Accordion.	11 Tpt. Harmonica.	12 Tpt. Violin Organ	13 Organ Violin Harmony Tambourine	14 Harmony Voice	15 BoB V	16 BoB Git.

TITLE: 121708 Valley — DOLBY

NO.	CO. NO. 1	2	3	4	5	6	7	8
2	BD	SN	L R	Drums L R	Bass	Acc Git	Acc Git	EL Git Eric
CO. NO.	9 VINNIE Mandolin	10 Accordion.	11 Harmonica	12 Tpt	13 Organ Violin Tamb.	14 Harmony Voice	15 BoB V	16 BoB Git

TITLE: O'Sister. CC 12170 — DOLBY

NO.	CO. NO. 1	2	3	4	5	6	7	8
3	BD	SN	L R	Drums L R	Bass	Acc Git	Acc Git	EL Git Eric
CO. NO.	9 VINNIE Mandolin	10 Accordion	11 Harmonica	12 Tpt.	13 Organ Violin Tamb.	14 Harmony Voice.	15 BoB V	16 BoB Git

CR 1721

16 TRACK IDENTIFICATION CHART
CBS RECORDS BOB DYLAN

SESSION | JOB NO. 120870 | PRODUCER DE VITO | ENGINEER DM. LW | DATE 7/28/75

MCU DOLBY

NO.	CC. NO.	TITLE							
1	1	2	3	4	5	6	7	8	
				Blue Cup of Coffee DNU	BASS.	Acc G.T.	Acc G.T.	E.L. G.T. STRG	
	9	10	11	12	13	14	15	16	
	VINNIE MANDOLIN.	ACCORDION.	Harmonica	Trumpet	VIOLIN	Harmony.	Bob V	Bob G.T.	
2	CO. NO.	TITLE							
	1	2	3	4	5	6	7	8	
					Mullin	Harmony	Bob	Bob G.T.	
	9	10	11	12	13	14	15	16	
3	CO. NO.	TITLE		Cat Fish (Check out)			MC BIGBAND		
	1	2	3	4	5	6	7	8	
	BD	SN	L Dr	R Dr	BASS			Eric.	
	9	10	11	12	13	14	15	16	
	VINNIE Mandolin GIT. Fiddle,	Acc sax Harmonica			Vital Piano.	Harmony	Bob	Bob El G.T.	

CBS RECORDS BOB DYLAN

| | TITLE | SESSION | JOB NO. 120870 | PRODUCER DE VITO | ENGINEER DON MEEHAN / LW | DATE 7/28/75 |

CATFISH · TK 1 2 9:25 16. INC. DOLBY

CR 1721

16 TRACK IDENTIFICATION CHART
CBS RECORDS BOB DYLAN

SESSION _____   JOB NO. 120870   PRODUCER DeVito   ENGINEER John LW   DATE (MASTER) 7/28/75

No. 1 — TITLE: DURANGO

CC. NO.							
1 BD	2 SN	3 L DR	4 R DR	5 BASS	6 ACC GIT OVU	7 ACC GIT OVU	8 EL GIT ERIC
9 VINNIE MANDOLIN	10 ACCORDION	11 HARMONICA OVU	12 trumpet	13 VIOLIN	14 HARMONY VOICE	15 BOB V	16 BOB GIT

No. 2 — CO. NO.   TITLE: _____

1	2	3	4	5	6	7	8
9	10	11	12	13	14	15	16

No. 3 — CO. NO.   TITLE: _____

1	2	3	4	5	6	7	8
9	10	11	12	13	14	15	16

TRACK IDENTIFICATION CHART
CBS RECORDS · Bob Dylan

TITLE: HURRICANE   SESSION   JOB NO. 120876   PRODUCER: Devito   ENGINEER: Don LW.   DATE: 7/29/75

CO. NO.	1	2	3	4	5	6	7	8
1	BD	SN	Dr	Dr	BASS	Harmony voice	2 El Gits	Eric El Git
	9	10	11	12	13	14	15	16
	Interprint Accordion	for Hurricane	Harmonica	Horns tpt + sax	Guitar	Congas	B+B V.	B+B Git
2	1	2	3	4	5	6	7	8
	B.D.	NS	Dr	Dr	BASS	Emmy Harmony		Hugh Git Git
	9	10	11	12	13	14	15	16
	VINNIE		Harm.	Horns.	Piano	Congas	B+B V	B+B Git
3	1	2	3	4	5	6	7	8
	9	10	11	12	13	14	15	16

CR 1721

16 TRACK IDENTIFICATION CHART
CBS RECORDS Bob Dylan

SESSION · JOB NO. 12687Y · PRODUCER Don De · ENGINEER Don Mer · DATE 7/29/75

Title: BLACK DIAMOND BAY

WITHOUT VINNIE SUGITO 45F MIC — DOLBY

NO.	CO. NO.	1	2	3	4	5	6	7	8
1	12171Z	BD	5	Dr L	Dr R	BASS	Harmony	THMB	Harm.
			VIOLIN	HARMONICA	HORNS	PIANO org.	Guitar	BoB	BoB
		VINNIE	10	11	12	13	14	15	16

Title: Money Blues. 1

NO.	CO. NO.	1	2	3	4	5	6	7	8
2		BD	SN	Dr L	Dr R	BASS	HARMONY	THMB	Hutt
		VINNIE		HARMONICA	HORNS	PIANO	CONGA	BoBV	BiG GUIT.
		9	10	11	12	13	14	15	16

Title: OH SISTER — 1 TKS

NO.	CO. NO.	1	2	3	4	5	6	7	8
3		BD	SN	Dr L	Dr R	BASS	Harmony overdub.		
		VIOLIN				Harmony SS 7/30/75	Harmony NY SS 7/30/75 #1	BoB	BoB GUIT
		9	10	11	12	13	14	15	16

CR 1721

TRACK IDENTIFICATION CHART

CBS RECORDS Bob Dylan | TITLE CATFISH | SESSION | JOB NO. 13687Y | PRODUCER Devito | ENGINEER Damone LW | DATE 7/29/75

NO.	CO.NO.	1	2	3	4	5	6	7	8	9	10	11	12	13	14	15	16
1	CATFISH	BD	Snare	Dr L	Dr R	Bass	Harmony voice				Violin					Bob V	Bob El Git
2	MOSAMBIQUE	BD	Snare	Dr L	Dr R	Bass	Harmony vox	Tamb	DN V Tbe	Vinnie El Git		Harmonica	Horns	Piano	Conga	Bob V	Bob Git
3	CATFISH #2	BD / BDD Snare	Snare Guitar	Dr L	Dr R	Bass	Harmony voice	Tamp		Vinnie El Git	Violin	Harmonica	Horns	Piano	Quacca	Bob V	Bob Git

CR 1721

10 TRACK IDENTIFICATION CHART SHEET!
CBS RECORDS - Bob Dylan.
SESSION
JOB NO 08883
PRODUCER B. Vito
ENGINEER Don LW
DATE 7/30/75

NO.	CC. NO.							
	① DNU	TITLE Golden Loom	TK 1,2)	TK 2 Comp A-on 7	On LG		DOLBY	
	1	2	3	4	5	6	7	8
					Bass	(Harmony voc. Hom during verse cum	Cover Pno.	Covert
	9	10	11	12	13	14	15	16
		Violin			Piano		Bob voc	Bob git
	②Harmso.NO. VERSE 3	TITLE 4,104	Git Sister			+K 1(1c)	(TK 2 (2a)) TK3	NOTICE MIDDLE
	BD Verse 2 ForeR	2 Dr R	3 Dr L	4 Dr R	5 Bass	6 Harm voc	7 Perc. frank gr End off	8
	9	10 Violin	11	12 Git most of 950	13 Piano	14	15 Bob voc	16 Bob git
	③co.No. BostRidge BD BD MnO	TITLE One have Cup of Coffee #2 ① Splice Final Tight Top !!						
	1 BD	2 Dr.	3 Dr L	4 Dr R	5 Bass	6 Harmony vii.	7 Perc	8
	9	10 Violin	11	12	13 TBE.	14	15 Bob voc	16 Bob git

10 TRACK IDENTIFICATION CHART
CBS RECORDS

SESSION | JOB NO. 0883 | PRODUCER Smith | ENGINEER John LW | DATE 7/30/7

NO.	CO. NO.	TITLE	3	4	5	6	7	8
1	1 BO	2 Snare Dir	Dr L	Dr R	Bass	Harmony Voc.	Bell Perc. (bell)	8
	9	10 VIOLIN	11	12	13	14	15 Bob Voc.	16 Bob Git.
2	1 BO	2 Snare Dir	3 Dr L	4 Dr R	5 BASS	6 Harmony Voc.	7 Perc. Conga	8
	9	10 VIOLIN	11	12	13	14	15 Bob Voc.	16 Bob Git.
3	1 BO	2 Snare Dr.	3 Dr L	4 Dr R	5 BASS	6 Harm. Voc.	7 Perc. Conga	8
	9 Snare	10 VIOLIN	11	12	13	14	15 Bob Voc.	16 Bob Git.

CR 1721

IO TRACK IDENTIFICATION CHART
CBS RECORDS

TITLE: Bob Dylan

SESSION: JOB NO. 120883 PRODUCER: Devito ENGINEER: Don LW DATE: 7/30/75

NO.	1	2	3	4	5	6	7	8
TITLE	Ices			Patch 1 + 2				
	BO	Snare R	Drl	Orr R	Bkss	Harm Voc	Perc Bells	
	9	10	11	12	13	14	15	16
		Violin					Bob Voc	Bob Git

"Willie Aston and crashed it out"

NO.	1	2	3	4	5	6	7	8
TITLE	Mustambique			Tk3 Tk4	#5	Out by 3:18		
	DD	Snare	Dr L	Dr R	Bass	Harm Voc	Perc Light Bells	
	9	10	11	12	13	14	15	16
		Violin	Fade - Start Abt 2:35				Bob Voc	Bob Git

NO.	1	2	3	4	5	6	7	8
TITLE								
	1	2	3	4	5	6	7	8
	9	10	11	12	13	14	15	16

16 TRACK IDENTIFICATION CHART
CBS RECORDS

TITLE: Bob Dylan
SESSION
JOB NO. 130883
PRODUCER: DeVito
ENGINEER: Ph. LW DATE 7/30/75

NO.	CC. NO.	1	2	3	4	5	6	7	8
	TITLE: ONE MORE CUP OF COFFEE	BP	Dr. Snare	Dr. L	Dr. R	BASS	HARMONY VOC	Pete CONGA ON TK!	16 BiB GiT

| | | 9 | 10 | 11 | 12 | 13 | 14 | 15 | 16 |
| | | BoB | VIOLIN | Accordian | GiT. VINNIE | 13 | 14 | BiB VOC. | 8 |

| NO. 2 | CC. NO. TITLE: ISIS FROM TK1 | BP | Dr Snare | Dr L | Dr R | BASS | HARM VOC | C CONGA | 8 |
| | | 1 | 2 | 3 | 4 | 5 | 6 | 7 | |

| | | VIOLIN | | 11 | 12 | 13 | 14 | 15 | 16 |
| | | 9 | 10 | | | | | BoB VOC | BoB GiT |

| NO. 3 | CC. NO. TITLE: | 1 | 2 | 3 | 4 | 5 | 6 | 7 | 8 |
| | | 9 | 10 | 11 | 12 | 13 | 14 | 15 | 16 |

CR 1721

10 TRACK IDENTIFICATION CHART
CBS RECORDS

SESSION | JOB NO. | PRODUCER Devito | ENGINEER DSM LW | DATE 7/31/75

BOB DYLAN ABANDONED Before/ Abandoned

1

1	2	3	4	5	6	7	8
BD	SN	DR L	DR R	BASS	Harm in Ind.	CONGA L	12 GIT (ADD-41) ON TR 13) CONGA R
9	10	11	12	13	14	15	16
	VIOLIN		ACC.GIT.			Voc. BOB	BOB's GIT.

TITLE Love Crazy tk 1 2 1 Harm 2 Harm

2

TITLE Sarah pt 1 tk 5 S-29 BUILD FIDDLE each tke

1	2	3	4	5	6	7	8
BD	SN	DR L	DR R	BASS			TBE
9	10	11	12	13	14	15	16
	VIOLIN					Voc BOB	BOB's GIT

3

TITLE Isis FROG BEFORE HARM GIT/FILL - RE-EMERGE TK 7 GUITAR TK 2 PIANO ON 2 G

CUT ER DOWN OT HALF;

1	2	3	4	5	6	7	8
BD	SN	DR L	DR R	BASS		TAMB.	
9	10	11	12	13	14	15	16
	VIOLIN		TBE ONLY	PIANO- BOB.		Voc. BOB.	GIT. BOB BAND TBE

16 TRACK IDENTIFICATION CHART
CBS RECORDS

CR 1721